D0060825

THE TRANSFORMATION OF THE GULF

Politics, economics and the global order

Edited by David Held and Kristian Ulrichsen

Routledge
Taylor & Francis Group

LONDON AND NEW YORK

First published 2012
by Routledge
2 Park Square, Milton Park, Abingdon, Oxon, OX14 4RN

Simultaneously published in the USA and Canada
by Routledge
711 Third Avenue, New York, NY 10017

Routledge is an imprint of the Taylor & Francis Group, an Informa business

British Library Cataloguing in Publication Data
A catalogue record for this book is available from the British Library

Library in Congress Cataloging-in-Publication Data
The transformation of the Gulf: politics, economics, and the global
order/edited by David Held and Kristian Ulrichsen.
p.cm.
Includes bibliographical references and index.

1. Gulf Cooperation Council. 2. Globalization–Persian Gulf States.
3. Persian Gulf States–Politics and government–21st century. 4. Persian
Gulf States–Economic conditions–21st century. I. Held, David II.
Ulrichsen, Kristian.
DS201.2.T73 2011
341.24'77–dc22   2011000595

ISBN: 978-0-415-57451-8 (hbk)
ISBN: 978-0-415-57452-5 (pbk)
ISBN: 978-0-203-81321-8 (ebk)

Typeset in Bembo by PDQ Typesetting Ltd.

MIX
Paper from
responsible sources
FSC
www.fsc.org   FSC® C004839   Printed and bound in Great Britain by the MPG Books Group

CONTENTS

Plate section can be found between pages 40 and 41

FIGURES

TABLES

ABBREVIATIONS

AAOIFI	Accounting and Auditing Organization for Islamic Financial Institutions
ADFD	Abu Dhabi Fund for Development
ADIA	Abu Dhabi Investment Authority
ADNOC	Abu Dhabi National Oil Company
AFESD	Arab Fund for Economic and Social Development
AGFUND	Arab Gulf Fund for United Nations Development
AGS	Arab Gulf States
AHDR	Arab Human Development Report
AMF	Arab Monetary Fund
AWDS	Arab Women's Development Society
BADEA	Arab Bank for Economic Development in Africa
BM	Ballistic Missile
BMD	Ballistic Missile Defence
BTI	Bertelsmann Transformation Index
CBB	Central Bank of Bahrain
CCS	Carbon Capture and Sequestration
CEDAW	Committee on the Elimination of Discrimination against Women
CIRS	Center for International and Regional Studies
CITC	Communications and Information Technology Commission (Saudi Arabia)
CMA	Capital Market Authority
CML	Capital Market Law (Saudi Arabia)
CNPC	China National Petroleum Company
CSS	Cultural and Social Society (Kuwait)

DAC	Development Assistance Committee
DFSA	Dubai Financial Services Authority
DIFC	Dubai International Financial Centre
DIFX	Dubai International Financial Exchange
DPA	Dayton Peace Agreement
ESCA	Emirates Securities and Commodities Authority
EU	European Union
FDI	Foreign Direct Investment
FNC	Federal National Council (UAE)
FOI	Freedom of Investment
FSA	Financial Services Authority (United Kingdom)
FTA	Free Trade Agreement
FTS	Financial Tracking Service
GAO	General Accountability Office (Washington, DC)
GAPP	Generally Accepted Principles and Practices
GASCO	Abu Dhabi Gas Industries
GCC	Gulf Cooperation Council
GDP	Gross Domestic Product
GHG	Greenhouse Gas
GONGO	Government-Organized Non-Governmental Organization
GRF	General Reserve Fund (Kuwait)
GSM	Global System for Mobile Communications
GTL	Gas to Liquid Fuels
HIPC	Highly Indebted Poor Country
HPAD	Hydrogen Power Abu Dhabi
IAEA	International Atomic Energy Agency
ICG	International Crisis Group
ICT	Information and Communications Technology
IEA	International Energy Agency
IFI	International Financial Institution
IFRS	International Financial Reporting Standards
IFSB	Islamic Financial Services Board
IIFM	International Islamic Financial Market
IISS	International Institute for Strategic Studies
IMF	International Monetary Fund
IOSCO	International Organization of Securities Commissions
IPCC	Intergovernmental Panel on Climate Change
IPIC	International Petroleum Investment Company (Abu Dhabi)
IRA	Independent Regulatory Agency
IRENA	International Renewable Energy Agency
ISC	International Securities Consultancy
IsDB	Islamic Development Bank
ISN	International Relations and Security Network
IWG	International Working Group

JODCO	Japanese Oil Development Company
KACST	King Abdulaziz City for Science and Technology
KAUST	King Abdullah University of Science and Technology
KCIC	Kuwait–China Investment Company
KEPCO	Korea Electric Power Corporation
KFAED	Kuwait Fund for Arab Economic Development
KFH	Kuwait Finance House
KIA	Kuwait Investment Authority
KSA	Kingdom of Saudi Arabia
KSE	Kuwait Stock Exchange
LDC	Least-Developed Country
LEED	Leadership in Energy and Environmental Design
LIC	Low-Income Country
LNG	Liquefied Natural Gas
MAN	Movement of Arab Nationalists
MENA	Middle East and North Africa
MICE	Meetings, Incentives, Conferences, Exhibitions
NDI	National Democratic Institute
NGO	Non-Governmental Organisation
OAU	Organization of African Unity
ODA	Official Development Assistance
OECD	Organization for Economic Cooperation and Development
OFID	OPEC Fund for International Development
OPEC	Organization of Petroleum Exporting Countries
OWA	Oman Women s Association
PIFSS	Public Institute for Social Security
PLO	Palestine Liberation Organisation
POGAR	Programme on Governance in the Arab Region
PTT	Post, Telegraph and Telecommunications (Ministry of, Saudi Arabia)
QFC	Qatar Financial Centre
QFCRA	Qatar Financial Centre Regulatory Authority
QIA	Qatar Investment Authority
REDF	Real Estate Development Fund (Saudi Arabia)
RFFG	Reserve Fund for Future Generations (Kuwait)
ROA	Return on Assets
SABIC	Saudi Basic Industries Corporation
SAMA	Saudi Arabian Monetary Agency
SDR	Special Drawing Rights
SEC	Securities and Exchange Commission (United States)
SFD	Saudi Fund for Development
SSM	Surface-to-Surface Missile
SWF	Sovereign Wealth Fund
TRA	Telecommunications Regulatory Authority

UAE	United Arab Emirates
UNDP	United Nations Development Programme
UNESCWA	United Nations Economic and Social Commission for West Asia
UNOCHA	United Nations Office for the Coordination of Humanitarian Affairs
UNRWA	United Nations Relief and Works Agency
WANA	West Asia–North Africa
WCSS	Women's Cultural and Social Society (Kuwait)
WMD	Weapons of Mass Destruction
WTO	World Trade Organization

NOTES ON CONTRIBUTORS

Abdulkhaleq Abdulla is Professor of Political Science at Emirates University and the lead author of the 2008 Arab Knowledge Report. He holds a PhD in Political Science from Georgetown University and an MA from the American University in Washington, DC. He was a Fulbright Scholar and a visiting professor at the Center for Contemporary Arab Studies, Georgetown University. Professor Abdulla is the author of several books and more than 30 articles. His recent books include *The Gulf Regional System* and *Narrative of Politics*, both published in 2006.

Gawdat Bahgat is Professor at the Near East South Asia Center for Strategic Studies, National Defense University, Washington, DC. His areas of expertise include energy security, counter-terrorism, weapons of mass destruction, international political economy, the Middle East, the Caspian Sea/Central Asia and American foreign policy. Professor Bahgat is the author of seven books and about 200 scholarly articles. His work has been translated into several foreign languages. Professor Bahgat has also been invited to and presented papers at conferences in Australia, Europe and the Middle East.

Sultan Barakat is Professor of Politics and Director of the Post-war Reconstruction and Development Unit (PRDU) at the University of York. His research, which is frequently conducted on behalf of major international organisations, attempts to bridge the divide between theory and practice in order to strengthen assistance to conflict-affected contexts. He is the editor of *Reconstructing Post-Saddam Iraq* (2007) and *After the Conflict: Reconstruction and Development in the Aftermath of War*, 2nd edition (2010).

John Chalcraft is a Reader in the History and Politics of Empire/Imperialism at the London School of Economics and Political Science (LSE). Previous posts include a Lectureship at the University of Edinburgh and a Research Fellowship at Gonville and Caius College, Cambridge. His research focuses on history from below in the Middle East. He is the author of *The Striking Cabbies of Cairo and Other Stories: Crafts and Guilds in Egypt, 1863–1914* (State University of New York Press, 2004) and *The Invisible Cage: Syrian Migrant Workers in Lebanon* (Stanford University Press, 2009).

Christopher M. Davidson is a Reader in Middle East Politics and Deputy Head in the School of Government and International Affairs, Durham University. He was formerly Assistant Professor at Zayed University in the United Arab Emirates and Visiting Associate Professor at Kyoto University in Japan. He is the author of four single-authored books, including *Dubai: The Vulnerability of Success, Abu Dhabi: Oil and Beyond* and most recently *The Persian Gulf and Pacific Asia: From Indifference to Interdependence* (all with Columbia University Press). In addition, he has authored several peer-reviewed journal articles on the politics and political economy of the Gulf, published in *Middle East Policy, Middle Eastern Studies, Asian Affairs* and the *British Journal of Middle Eastern Studies*.

Anoushiravan Ehteshami is a Professor and Dean of Internationalisation and also Professor of International Relations in the School of Government and International Affairs, Durham University. He was the founding Head of the School of Government and International Affairs at Durham University (2004–9) and is Director of the ESRC-funded Durham–Edinburgh–Manchester Universities' £5.2 million Centre for the Advanced Study of the Arab World (CASAW).

Laura El-Katiri is a Junior Research Fellow at the Oxford Institute for Energy Studies and writes for the Institute's oil and gas programmes. Her work focuses on Middle Eastern energy-related issues, particularly of the GCC states, including oil and natural gas in the GCC states, the political economy of resource wealth and GCC economic development. She holds a BA in Arabic and Economics from the University of Exeter and an MPhil in Modern Middle Eastern Studies from the University of Oxford.

Bassam Fattouh is the Director of the Oil and Middle East Programme at the Oxford Institute for Energy Studies, a Research Fellow at St Antony's College, Oxford University and Professor of Management and Finance at the School of Oriental and African Studies. He has published a variety of articles on the international oil pricing system, OPEC pricing power and the dynamics of oil prices, his articles appear in *Energy Economics, The Energy Journal* and *Energy Policy*. Recently, Dr Fattouh served as a member of an independent expert group established to provide recommendations to the 12th International Energy

Forum (IEF) Ministerial Meeting in Cancún (29–31 March 2010) for strengthening the architecture of the producer–consumer dialogue through the IEF and reducing energy market volatility. Dr Fattouh has also published in non-energy related areas, his papers having appeared in the *Journal of Development Economics*, the *Oxford Review of Economic Policy*, *Economic Inquiry*, *Empirical Economics*, the *Journal of Financial Intermediation*, *Economics Letters* and *Macroeconomic Dynamics*, as well as in other journals and books.

David Held is the Graham Wallas Chair in Political Science at the London School of Economics and Political Science (LSE). Among his most recent publications are *Cosmopolitanism: Ideals and Realities* (2010), *Globalisation/Anti-Globalisation* (2007), *Models of Democracy* (2006), *Global Covenant* (2004), *Global Transformations: Politics, Economics and Culture* (1999) and *Democracy and the Global Order: From the Modern State to Cosmopolitan Governance* (1995). His main research interests include the study of globalisation, changing forms of democracy and the prospects of regional and global governance. He is a Director of Polity Press, which he co-founded in 1984, and General Editor of *Global Policy*.

Steffen Hertog is a Lecturer in Comparative Politics at the London School of Economics and Political Science (LSE). He was previously Kuwait Professor at the Chaire Moyen Orient at Sciences Po-Paris. His research interests include Gulf politics, Middle East political economy, political violence and radicalisation, and he has published in journals such as *World Politics*, the *Review of International Political Economy*, *Comparative Studies in Society and History*, *Business History*, *Archives Européennes de Sociologie* and the *International Journal of Middle East Studies*. His book about Saudi state-building, *Princes, Brokers and Bureaucrats: Oil and State in Saudi Arabia*, was published by Cornell University Press in 2010.

Miklós Koren is an Assistant Professor in the Department of Economics of Central European University, a research fellow at IEHAS and a research affiliate of CEPR. His research interests are in international trade and economic growth. His current research focuses on the firm-level effects of imported inputs and imported machinery, and the diversification of macro-economic volatility through trade. Miklós received his PhD from Harvard University in 2005. He has worked at the Federal Reserve Bank of New York and was the 2007 Peter Kenen Fellow at Princeton University.

Wanda Krause is currently teaching politics at the School of Oriental and African Studies (SOAS), UK. She has a doctorate in Politics from the University of Exeter, UK. Her research dealt with civil society development, gender politics and Islamism in the Arab states. Her background studies, which she conducted in Canada, Germany, Egypt and the UAE, include international relations, linguistics, social psychology and Arabic studies. Dr Krause's most recent book is *Women in Civil Society: The State, Islamism and Networks in the UAE*

(Palgrave Macmillan, 2008). Her forthcoming book to be released in 2011 is titled *Civil Society and Women Activists in the Middle East* (published by I.B. Tauris).

Giacomo Luciani is the Director of the Gulf Research Center Foundation in Geneva. He is a Global Scholar of Princeton University and teaches at the Graduate Institute of International and Development Studies in Geneva and at Sciences-Po in Paris. His research interests cover the politics and economics of the international oil and gas industry and the political economy of the Arab oil exporting countries. He has published extensively, notably on rentier states, political participation, and the role and limits of the national bourgeoisie in oil exporting countries.

Neil Partrick is a Middle East consultant (http://partrickmideast.org). He is presently conducting research for an LSE Kuwait Programme paper on the GCC, and is working on separate analyses of Saudi Arabia's domestic politics and its foreign policy. Until mid-2009 Dr Partrick was an Assistant Professor of Political Science at the American University of Sharjah in the UAE, at which time he authored another LSE Kuwait Gulf programme paper, *Nationalism in the Gulf States*. Neil Partrick was formerly a senior analyst at the Economist Intelligence Unit, Head of the Middle East Programme at the Royal United Services Institute (RUSI) in Whitehall, London, and an editor/analyst at the Palestinian research centre in Jerusalem, Panorama.

Greg Power is a parliamentary specialist and Director of Global Partners, a social-purpose company working on projects to support democratic politics. He has worked on the development of legislative institutions and political parties in the Middle East, Africa and the Balkans, including work in Oman, Bahrain, Kuwait and Iraq. He has published many articles and papers on parliamentary development, the most recent being: *Handbook on Parliamentary Ethics and Conduct for Parliamentarians* (Global Organisation of Parliamentarians Against Corruption, 2010) and *The Politics of Parliamentary Strengthening: Understanding Incentives and Institutional Behaviour in Parliamentary Support* (WFD/Global Partners, 2011). Between 2001 and 2005 he was special adviser to Rt Hon Robin Cook MP and Rt Hon Peter Hain MP, working with both Leaders of the House of Commons on parliamentary reform and wider issues of democratic renewal. Prior to this he was Director of the Parliament and Government Programme at the Hansard Society. He is a Senior Visiting Fellow at the LSE's Centre for Global Governance.

Paul Segal is a Lecturer in Economics at the University of Sussex and Visiting Senior Research Fellow at the Oxford Institute for Energy Studies. He works on growth and the distribution of income in resource-rich countries, energy economics, and global inequality and poverty. He has been a consultant economist at the United Nations Development Programme in New York and a Research Fellow at Harvard University.

Silvana Tenreyro is Reader in Economics at the London School of Economics and Political Science (LSE), Research Director of the Macroeconomics Programme at the International Growth Centre, Research Associate at the Center for Economic Performance (CEP) and Research Fellow at the Center of Economic Research (CEPR). She acts as Associate Editor for the *Review of Economic Studies*, the *Journal of the European Economic Association*, the *Economic Journal* and *Economica*, and as an Editorial Panel Member for *Economic Policy*. She has been elected member of the Council of the European Economic Association (EEA) and chairs the Committee on Women in Economics of the EEA; she also acts as an *ex officio* member of the Royal Economic Society Women's Committee. Prior to joining the LSE she worked at the Federal Reserve Bank of Boston. Dr Tenreyro obtained her PhD and Masters in Economics from Harvard University. Her work has been published in top academic journals, including the *American Economic Review* and the *Quarterly Journal of Economics*.

Mark Thatcher is Professor in Comparative and International Politics, Department of Government, London School of Economics and Political Science (LSE). He has taught in Paris, Oxford and London and been a fellow at the European University Institute, Florence. His research is in the field of comparative regulation and public policy. It focuses on the design and creation of regulatory institutions and the effects of those institutions on the relationships between politics and markets. Recent publications include *Internationalisation and Economic Institutions: Comparing European Experiences* (Oxford University Press, 2007 and paperback, 2009) which won the 2008 Charles Levine Prize; 'Regulatory agencies, the state and markets: a Franco-British comparison', *Journal of European Public Policy*, 14(7), October 2007; 'Varieties of capitalism in an internationalized world', *Comparative Political Studies*, 37(7), September 2004; and *Governing Markets in Gulf States* (Working Paper for the Kuwait Programme on Development, Governance and Globalisation in the Gulf States, 2009).

Kristian Ulrichsen is Deputy Director of the Kuwait Programme on Development, Governance and Globalisation in the Gulf States and a Research Fellow at the London School of Economics. He was formerly a senior analyst at the Gulf Centre for Strategic Studies in London and holds a PhD from the University of Cambridge. His research focuses on the history of Iraq and on political and security transitions in the Gulf States. He is the author of *The Logistics and Politics of the British Campaigns in the Middle East, 1914–1922* (Palgrave Macmillan, 2011) and *Insecure Gulf: The End of Certainty and the Transition to the Post-Oil Era* (Hurst, 2011).

Rodney Wilson is a Professor and Director of the Islamic Finance Programme at Durham University. He chairs the academic committee of the Institute of Islamic Banking and Insurance in London and is consultant to the Islamic Financial Services Board with respect to its Shariah Governance Guidelines. He has written numerous books on Islamic finance for leading international publishers including Edinburgh and Columbia University Presses and Brill, and has recently published articles on Islam and capitalism, *sukuk* securities, Shariah-compliant private equity finance and Islamic finance in the GCC. During the early part of 2009 he was a Visiting Professor at the Qatar Foundation's Faculty of Islamic Studies in Doha.

Steven Wright specialises in the politics and international relations of the Arabian Gulf, United States foreign policy and international security. He is currently an Acting Head of Department and an Assistant Professor in International Affairs at Qatar University. He is also currently the Assistant Editor of the *Journal of Arabian Studies* and is an Honorary Research Fellow of the Institute for Arab and Islamic Studies, Exeter University. Dr Wright was educated at the University of London where he received a degree in social and political science, and also at Durham University where he obtained an MA and a PhD in international relations. He has held visiting research fellowships at the Centre for Global Governance, London School of Economics and Political Science (LSE), and also at Durham University where he was the Sir William Luce Research Fellow.

Steven A. Zyck is an Associate of the Post-war Reconstruction and Development Unit at the University of York. With a primary research focus upon the security development nexus, he has examined topics such as aid financing, the demobilisation of armed groups and the political legitimacy and economic growth in, most notably, the Middle East and Central and South Asia.

PREFACE

This book addresses the political and economic transformations underway in the six states of the Gulf Cooperation Council (GCC) and their repositioning within the global order. The chapters focus on issues of political development and economic diversification, evolving frameworks of governance, changing security structures and the impact of globalisation in these rapidly evolving polities. The book represents the outcome of the first three years' research of the Kuwait Programme on Development, Governance and Globalisation in the Gulf States. This is a ten-year multidisciplinary global programme funded by the Kuwait Foundation for the Advancement of Sciences and based at the London School of Economics.

The present volume is the first step in a wide-ranging research agenda focusing on the dynamic interaction of the Gulf states with globalising processes. The Kuwait Programme continues to commission research into the reformulation of socio-political and economic structures in the GCC states and to investigate how developments and trends in the Gulf themselves shape the outcomes of globalisation. In addition, the Kuwait Programme supports academic researchers and PhD students at the London School of Economics and Political Science and an academic network between the LSE and research institutions and universities in the Gulf states. It hosts a regular seminar series and occasional public lectures in London and major biennial international conferences in Kuwait.

The editors wish to acknowledge their debt to the Kuwait Foundation for the Advancement of Sciences for their valuable advice, financial support and logistical assistance. Particular thanks go to Professor Ali Al-Shamlan, Director-General of KFAS, his successor, Dr Adnan Shihab-Eldin, the KFAS Board, and Khalid Al-Muhailan and the Office of International Programmes. We also extend our thanks to the LSE, and LSE Global Governance in particular, for their infrastructural support and to Victor Dahdaleh for his encouragement and contribution.

We are grateful to Patricia Morris for preparing the charts, maps and diagrams that illustrate the Introduction to the volume and to Joe Whiting and Suzanne Richardson at Routledge for their editorial assistance and backing. At LSE, we wish to thank Eva-Maria Nag, Harriet Carter and Dominika Spyratou for their help and support throughout this project. Ian Sinclair has been an administrator of genius without whom the Kuwait Programme would be infinitely poorer, and we are indebted to him for his extraordinary input and unfailing patience and good humour.

D.H.
K.U.

EDITORS' INTRODUCTION

The transformation of the Gulf

David Held and Kristian Ulrichsen

This book examines the transformations sweeping the six member-states of the Gulf Cooperation Council (GCC). It adopts a multidisciplinary approach to study the processes of change and their political, economic and social impact. A combination of internal and external dynamics are reformulating the Gulf states' institutional and governing structures and repositioning them in the global order. Domestic and global forces are interacting, shifting power relations and injecting new drivers into economic and foreign policy-making. The result is a region in flux as traditional structures and concepts of governance coexist uneasily alongside newer obligations and demands for reform. This became clear during the series of Arab uprisings that began to sweep through the Middle East in 2011. Simultaneously, the Gulf states are becoming active global players.

The symbiosis between profound domestic change and global realignments provides the backdrop for the chapters of this book. They explore how the GCC states are channelling and incorporating powerful new forces, and the implications of this for development, governance and governing structures, as well as for shifting geo-political and geo-economic relations. They assess the major trajectories of change that are leading to new forms of political economy and societal organisation in the Gulf monarchies as they enter what has been labelled a 'post-traditional' phase (Peterson 2005: 2). Crucially, the authors examine the political and economic transformations as well as the social and cultural changes in this complex and vital world region. Together, they provide a valuable account of the recent emergence of the GCC states as distinctive and powerful actors on the regional and global stage, as well as the challenges and obstacles to reform that lie ahead.

Through a mixture of comparative and country-specific studies and a selection of cross-cutting themes, a rich portrait emerges of great change in the Gulf states and in their relationships with the rest of the world. The narrative fits into a broader story of the rebalancing of the global order and contextualises the repositioning of the Gulf between West and East. This opens up alternative models of economic and political development and pathways of engagement with global governance structures and international institutions. New and emerging linkages hold significant consequences for issues as diverse as the direction of trade and financial flows and foreign direct investment, the evolution of multilateral decision-making and regional security structures, and the reframing of global governance at a time of systemic changes to the post-1945 architecture.

The Gulf states' hydrocarbon reserves and financial resources constitute the pivot around which this global reordering is taking place. The GCC has developed as the centre of geo-economic gravity in West Asia, while thickening commercial ties with South and East Asia are injecting a new dynamic into its engagement with the international system. Although the external guarantees provided by the United States remain the linchpin of the GCC states' security, the growing internationalisation of the Gulf reflects the diversification of its geo-political interests and choice of strategic partnerships. Particularly in Qatar and the United Arab Emirates, and (to a lesser extent) Saudi Arabia, there are developing innovative foreign policies underpinned by an ambition to utilise domestic resources to project a global reach. These shifting interests are realigning the intra-regional and international relations of the Gulf in subtle yet important ways.

The Gulf in historical context

The Gulf has been a commercial and strategic asset to outside powers for many centuries, and its linkages with the wider world extend back into late antiquity and the pre-Islamic period. It is pivotally positioned astride the major trade routes between India and Europe and a dense network of transoceanic linkages connect it to the broader Indian Ocean world. Local shipbuilders and sailors constructed and navigated the *dhows* and *booms* that sailed each season from the Gulf to the Indian subcontinent and along the coastline of East Africa. They exchanged cargoes of Arabian ponies, dates and pearls for goods such as rice, timber and cotton as intricate patterns of intra- and inter-regional trade developed. Powerful processes of migration and acculturation augmented these maritime flows and gave them a particularly human dimension (Potter 2009:10–11). These multifaceted patterns of exchange and settlement formed a web of interconnections that tied the trade and peoples of the region into broader, overlapping communities, such as that between the Sultanates of Oman and Zanzibar. They also left a distinctive legacy in the form of a cultural sphere of influence that shaped, in part, a cosmopolitan identity and an externally focused trading mentality throughout the Indian Ocean region (Metcalf 2007: 9).

This intermixing of peoples and cultures influenced the development of states and societies in the Gulf. Involvement in maritime trade fostered an outward-oriented mentality among the nascent sheikhdoms on the Arabian (and Persian) coastline of the Gulf. Kuwait and Dubai developed into regional entrepôts that serviced the trade of the northern and southern Gulf respectively, while Kuwait and Bahrain also became world centres of the pearling trade. This activity dominated traditional industry in the Gulf until it collapsed in the 1930s following the introduction of Japanese cultured pearls and the onset of the Great Depression. Local coalitions of ruling and influential merchant families governed their polities through pragmatic political-economic alliances that laid the foundation for the policies of the oil era (Crystal 1990: 4). A cycle of external penetration and local accommodation developed as local sheikhs sought to maximise their own autonomy and prestige within the parameters available to them by playing on local and regional events and great power rivalries to their advantage (Anscombe 1997: 172).

Accordingly, the Gulf region has neither been peripheral to world history nor defined solely by its possession of some of the largest oil reserves in the world. During the nineteenth century, it functioned as a crucible of dynamic interaction between internal (tribal) and external influences. These shaped the development of the coastal sheikhdoms into proto-state entities and their incorporation into quasi-formal British-Indian protectorates (see Plate 1). Oman and Saudi Arabia escaped formal penetration but fell into the informal political and security orbit of the United Kingdom and (after 1945) of the United States. Oil was discovered in significant quantities in the 1930s and 1940s and provided the revenues that eased the transition from colonial dependency to eventual statehood (Said Zahlan 1998: 24). Together with the external security guarantee against their more powerful and expansionist neighbours Iraq and Iran, oil revenues facilitated the political survival and the persistence of the traditional monarchical systems on the Arabian Peninsula (Kostiner 2000: 186) (see Plate 2).

European Great Power rivalries and competition for influence in the late-nineteenth and early-twentieth centuries dramatise the enduring geo-strategic value of the Gulf. They also provide a pattern of continuity in the region's myriad interactions with outside powers and peoples. British considerations of imperial security and the route to India gradually gave way to American-led concerns for energy security. Yet the underlying strategic and commercial interests that motivated successive waves of Portuguese, Dutch, Ottoman, British and latterly US intervention represent a constancy throughout the modern history of the region. Successive foreign incursions powerfully impacted the socio-political development of ruling structures in the formative years of proto-state formation before the discovery and extraction of oil (Anderson 1991: 9).

The development of the Gulf states since 1945

The domestic setting

Revenues from the extraction and export of oil transformed the socio-economic structures and patterns of development in the Gulf states. On the domestic level, rents accruing from the export of oil enabled the sheikhdoms to evolve from little more than city-states dominated by local coalitions between ruling families and the merchant elites to modernising centralised states. Oil began to be exported in commercial quantities in the late-1940s and production rose rapidly in the 1950s and 1960s. This coincided with the formative passage to independence of Kuwait (1961) and the United Arab Emirates (UAE), Bahrain and Qatar (1971) and the early processes of modern state formation in Oman and Saudi Arabia (Bromley 1994: 120). Oil rents transformed the political economy of the Gulf states, shaped the nature of state–society relations and determined their subsequent development (see Plate 3). Moreover, the impact of oil rents became intertwined with emerging state structures and gave rise to pronounced socio-economic peculiarities (Luciani 1990: 69).

The accrual of oil revenues accelerated sharply in the years that followed the oil price boom in 1973. They provided the growing state structures with the financial wherewithal to reformulate traditional tribal structures into modern forms of governance. Redistributive mechanisms of socio-political control emerged within a highly stratified economic framework encompassing nests of rentiers flowing downward from the state at its apex. New bureaucratic structures integrated existing (merchant) and new (middle-class) groupings into emergent polities as ruling families co-opted support and acquired legitimacy through the spread of wealth to their citizenry. Moreover, the influx of oil rents enabled the monarchies to manage the scale and rapidity of their socio-economic transformation in the 1960s and 1970s with minimal social upheaval. Chapter 8 by Laura El-Katiri, Bassam Fattouh and Paul Segal examines the evolution of the welfare state in Kuwait as a case study of the mechanisms through which oil wealth became translated into economic and social development. The socialisation of national identities also grafted a human dimension onto these processes of state construction through a process of state-led invention in national traditions, although Neil Partrick's chapter also highlights the fluidity and contested nature of identities within the GCC states as a whole (Chapter 2).

The advent of seemingly limitless resources spread over small indigenous populations in the 1970s stitched networks of patronage and vested interests firmly into the fabric of Gulf societies. Unique patterns of employment based on dual labour markets for citizens and predominantly migrant-labour expatriates entrenched these interests as public sector employment became another means of wealth redistribution to citizens while lower-paid foreign labourers populated the private sector (Teitelbaum 2009: 60) (see Figure 0.1). The primary twenty-first-century challenge for Gulf policy-makers is one of reformulating mechanisms that developed during a period of seemingly limitless resources and comparatively small populations. High demographic growth and the legacy of perverse economic incentives alongside notions of citizen entitlement pose systemic challenges to the maintenance of the social contract as laid down during the transition into the oil era. They also complicate strategies to tackle high rates of local unemployment and inculcate a productive culture necessary for meaningful economic diversification and moves toward post-rentier structures of governance. Escalating protests in Bahrain, Oman and parts of the Eastern Province of Saudi Arabia in early 2011 highlighted and reflected the urgency and scale of the socio-economic grievances that built up during this period of intense capital accumulation.

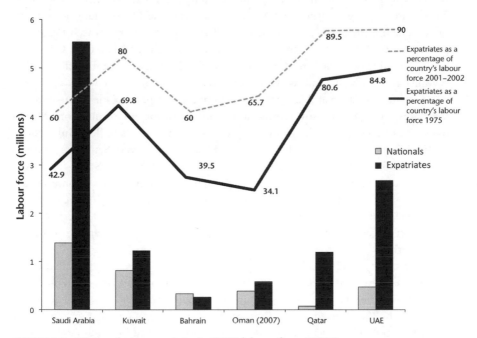

FIGURE 0.1   Nationals vs expatriates in GCC labour force (2009)

Source: World Bank Statistics.

The international setting

Oil exports integrated the Gulf states firmly into the international economic system as Gulf oil became a motor of Western economic growth in the postwar era. Securing stable access to regional supplies and the Western guarantees of security that underpinned this became the pillars that structured the international relations of the Gulf after 1945. Mutual economic interdependencies bound the oil-producing Gulf states into the world economy and predated the acceleration of economic globalisation in the 1970s and global interconnections in the 1990s (Ehteshami 2007: 110). Gulf oil supplied 51 per cent of British requirements in 1971 while Saudi Arabia and the United States enjoyed a similarly symbiotic relationship. The overlapping value of oil and concern for

Gulf security culminated in the 1980 Carter Doctrine warning that 'any attempt by an outside force to gain control of the Persian Gulf region will be regarded as an assault on the vital interests of the United States of America' (quoted in Ulrichsen 2011: 15).

The Carter Doctrine reflected and anticipated the turbulent cross-currents of conflict that marked the period of state-building and consolidation. Inter-state wars, intra-societal unrest and an ongoing struggle for regional hegemony all played a formative role in shaping the contemporary state system in the Gulf. Three inter-state wars (the 1980–88 Iran–Iraq war, the 1990–1 Iraqi occupation of Kuwait and the 2003 US-led invasion of Iraq) redrew the balance of regional power and unleashed powerful forces of dissent and change. The Gulf Cooperation Council was formed in May 1981 as a defensive bulwark against the Iranian revolution in 1979 and subsequent Iraqi invasion. Yet it was neither a political nor a military alliance and lacked an integrative supra-national decision-making mechanism for pooling sovereignty akin to the European Commission. Moreover, it suffered from lingering suspicions among the smaller Gulf states, particularly Qatar but latterly also the UAE, of perceived Saudi hegemonic designs in the Arabian Peninsula (Nonneman 2005: 145). The Saudi-led intervention to restore order in Bahrain in March 2011 demonstrated some of the motivations (but also tensions) driving policy-making at the GCC level. Nevertheless, the fact of its survival over three turbulent decades sets it apart from every previous attempt to create a durable inter-state organisation in the Arab world.

Neither the GCC nor the individual states' high levels of military expenditure proved sufficient to prevent the Iraqi occupation of Kuwait in August 1990. The invasion had momentous consequences for internal and external developments in the Gulf. It led to an unprecedented level of external intervention as more than 600,000 American and coalition troops arrived in Saudi Arabia prior to the launching of Operation Desert Storm in January 1991. The retention thereafter of American forces on Saudi territory to protect the Kingdom enraged and radicalised Islamist militants led by Osama bin Laden who subsequently formed the nucleus of al-Qaeda (Halliday 2005: 150). The rise of this aggressive, transnational and non-state actor was a momentous, albeit unintended, consequence of the 1991 Gulf War. It was symbiotically interlinked with the other legacy of the war, namely a sustained and visible American military presence in the Gulf. Together, they linked old problems in new ways by intertwining internal and external developments as each fed off the other in a globalising environment (see Figure 0.2).

Internal challenges and societal dissent were far from new phenomena in the Arabian Peninsula. During the 1950s and 1960s, Egyptian, Palestinian and Syrian educators acted as lightning-rods for the dissemination of Arab nationalist and (later) Islamist ideals (Fandy 2007: 77). Oil-field workers organised class-based struggles, particularly in the Eastern Province of Saudi Arabia and Bahrain in the same period, before labour relations were suppressed and brought

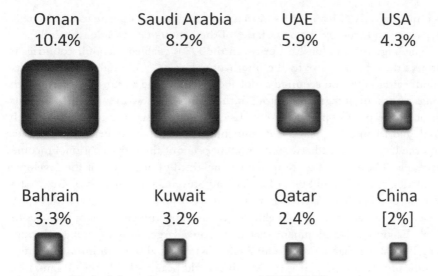

Oman	Saudi Arabia	UAE	USA
10.4%	8.2%	5.9%	4.3%

Bahrain	Kuwait	Qatar	China
3.3%	3.2%	2.4%	[2%]

FIGURE 0.2   Yearly defence spending as per cent of GDP (2008)

Source: The Stockholm International Peace Research Institute (SIPRI) http://milexdata.sipri.org/.

Notes
1. [ ] = SIPRI estimate
2. Figures for Bahrain do not include extra budgetary spending on defence procurement.
3. Figures for Oman (2007) are for current expenditure on defence and national security and are for current spending only (i.e. exclude capital spending).
4. Figures for Qatar (2007) and Saudi Arabia are for defence and security. Figures for Saudi Arabia are for the adopted budget, rather than actual expenditure.
5. Military expenditure of the United Arab Emirates is uncertain and lacking in transparency. The only available source of data is from IMF Staff Country Reports and IMF Government Finance Statistics. The Country Reports include two lines relating to military expenditure: The 'Goods and Services' expenditure of the Defence and Interior Ministries (which does not include military wages, salaries and pensions), and 'Abu Dhabi Federal Services', which the report says are 'mainly' defence and security expenditures. The Government Finance Statistics give only the Goods and Services figures. The SIPRI figures are estimated as 80% of the 'Abu Dhabi Federal Services' item, plus 100% of the 'Goods and services' figures. The latter item is estimated for 2006–07 assuming a constant real value.
6. The figures for China are for estimated total military expenditure, including estimates for items not included in the official defence budget. The estimates for the years 1999–2009 are based on publicly available figures for official military expenditure and for certain other items, and estimates for other items where there is no publicly available data. These estimates are based on the percentage change in official military expenditure and on the assumption of a gradual decrease in the commercial earnings of the People's Liberation Army (PLA).

under close state supervision (Vitalis 2009: 150). Sustained episodes of internal contestation occurred in Oman (1965–75), Saudi Arabia (1979) and Bahrain (1994–9), motivated by socio-economic unrest stemming from marked inequalities in development and selective modernisation. These created visible divisions between 'haves' and 'have-nots,' and sharpened and widened existing fissures within Gulf polities. Nevertheless, the challenge posed by al-Qaeda in the 1990s was qualitatively different in its capacity to mobilise and operate transnationally, bypassing and eroding the boundaries of the nation-state (Kaldor 2007: 32).

The huge rise in global oil prices in the 1970s enabled the Gulf countries to project their influence onto the international arena. Although this accelerated rapidly after 2000 and acquired a global dimension, the region has a particularly long record of integration into South–South frameworks. This took place through the provision of generous developmental assistance to predominantly Arab and Islamic recipients. Aid contributions in Saudi Arabia, Kuwait, Qatar and the UAE averaged between 6 and 8 per cent of their gross national incomes between 1974 and 1979 as compared to one-third of one per cent for developed countries, as detailed in Sultan Barakat and Steven Zyck's analysis of Gulf states' assistance to conflict-affected environments (Chapter 15). Shortly after independence, Kuwait and the UAE established formal governmental donor agencies for Arab Economic Development that distributed large sums of money through largely bilateral channels. In Saudi Arabia, King Faisal built an infrastructure of Islamic organisations, such as the Muslim World League (1962), the Organisation for the Islamic Conference (1972) and the International Islamic Relief Organisation (1975). These enhanced Saudi status in the wider Islamic world-community but also promoted a conservative and sometimes militant brand of Islam whose influence spread far beyond the borders of the Kingdom (Al-Rasheed 2008: 101).

The Gulf in the global age

Accelerating processes of globalisation in the 1990s and 2000s gave rise to new forms of political economy and enmeshment in multiple layers of global governance. Gulf communities became connected to leading conduits of 'global politics' with the aim of addressing a broad range of global challenges (Held and McGrew 2002: 5). New globalising flows of capital and labour, shifts in geo-economic strength and changing patterns of trade began to rebalance power relations across the world. All of the GCC states, culminating in Saudi Arabia in 2005, acceded to the World Trade Organisation and began to attract significantly greater flows of foreign direct investment. In addition, they promoted themselves as financial hubs for the wider West Asian and North African region. A combination of the Gulf states' oil reserves and capital accumulation during the 2002–8 oil price boom positioned them as a strategic and commercial pivot around which shifts in the global balance of power were taking place (see Plates 4 and 5). Thickening economic linkages with Russia, China, India, and South and East Asian nations shifted the orientation of the GCC states eastward. Although political and security ties with the United States and Western Europe remained intact, an internationalisation of the Gulf occurred through deepening energy interdependencies and changes in the direction of non-oil trade flows in petrochemicals, plastics and aluminium with Asian partners.

These macro-trends determined the contextual parameters for the Gulf states' new global profile. They converged with policy decisions on how to deploy the substantial revenues that accrued after oil prices began to rise in 2002, and with the appearance of systemic flaws in the Western-led 'Washington consensus' of economic development (Held and Mepham 2007: 207). Cumulatively, these developments enhanced the international profile and repositioning of the GCC states within an international system in flux following the 2007–9 global economic crisis (see Figures 0.3 and 0.4). During this period, the Gulf states leveraged their financial influence in international debates about the reshaping of the institutional architecture of global governance. Gulf-based sovereign wealth funds played a visible role in recapitalising Western financial institutions such as Merrill Lynch, Citigroup and Barclays Bank during the initial stages of the global financial crisis. They also acquired high-profile stakes in iconic global brands such as Harrods, Ferrari and Porsche. Meanwhile, Abu Dhabi and Qatar began to carve out specialist niches to become world leaders in specific fields, such as renewable energy research and diplomacy mediation respectively. These developments reflected an acknowledgement of, and confidence in, their new-found projection of global influence.

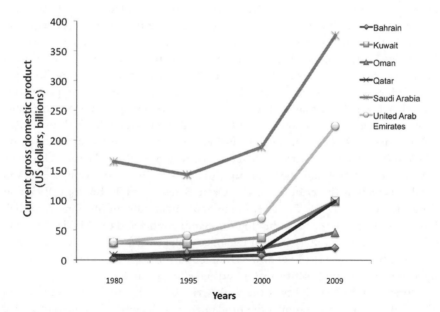

FIGURE 0.3 GDP in GCC countries (1980–2009)

Source: IMF World Economic Forum Outlook Database October 2010.

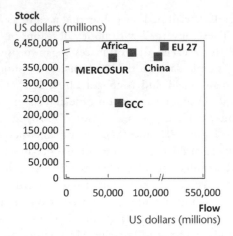

FIGURE 0.4 Major FDI indicators to/from GCC (2008)

Source: UN Conference on Trade and Development.
http://www.unctad.org/Templates/Page.asp?intitemID=1923&lang=1 and http://stats.unctad.org/FDI/TableViewer/tableView.aspx

Gulf acquisitions of landmark Western corporations represent the most high-profile dimension of the broader transformation of global power relations underway. This shift contains many elements ranging from greater participation in international organisations and global governance to the creation of world-leading niche developments in the region. GCC states are leading a revolution in higher education in the Middle East and North Africa and creating hubs for knowledge agglomeration designed to ease the transition toward productive economic bases. More than 100 colleges and universities opened in Saudi Arabia alone between 2003 and 2009 while Qatar and the UAE established more than 40 branches of Western universities during the same period (Romani 2009: 4). These included tie-ups with world-class institutions such as Harvard University's Dubai Initiative and the launching of NYU's liberal arts campus in Abu Dhabi, as well as the creation of the Qatar Science and Technology Park and Education City in Doha. The opening in September 2009 of the King Abdullah University of Science and Technology in Saudi Arabia and the Masdar Institute of Science and Technology in Abu Dhabi complemented strategies of buying in expertise by creating richly endowed indigenous institutions intended to develop into world-leading platforms for cutting-edge research.

Other flows add weight to the Gulf's rise as a regional heavyweight and global player. A case in point is the fundamental reshaping of the map of global aviation power. Etihad, Emirates and Qatar Airways have developed into global 'super-connectors' capable of linking any two points in the world with one stopover in the Gulf. These airlines reflected and reinforced the realignment of inter-regional trade and exchange in their choice of new routes, as Qatar Airways began direct flights to Sao Paolo and, alongside Emirates and Etihad, launched competing routes to Tokyo in 2010. Enormous, new state-of-the-art airport facilities are being developed to meet the requirements of handling the super-generation of long-range aircraft such as the Airbus A380, with 90 on order by Emirates alone (*Economist*, 2010). Not to be outdone, Etihad made headlines around the world in 2008 with the largest single aircraft order in aviation history for 100 aircraft along with options for a further 105, at a potential cost of $43 billion. Its chief executive explained the benefits Etihad derives from operating within the political economy of Abu Dhabi, and as a latecomer relative to established European 'legacy' carriers:

> I don't have to tackle the union issues of these other carriers... When it comes to other carriers, we are both similar service airlines, but they are bound by agreements, employment agreements, 15, 20, 30, or 40 years old that are very hard to renegotiate. They are bound by infrastructure – facilities and bases that were right for them 30 years ago or even 20 years ago, but aren't today. I am fortunate that I have a clean sheet of paper.
>
> (*The Gulf*, 2010)

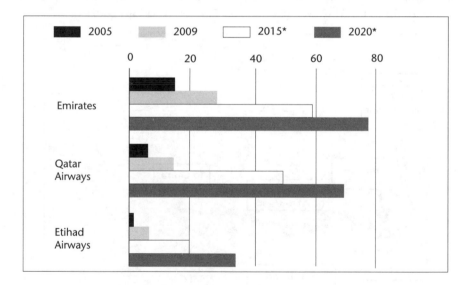

FIGURE 0.5   Passengers carried by airline (million)

Source: Air Transport.   *Forecast

These comments encapsulate the commercial advantages to local operators of working without the constraints imposed by organised labour on European and North American competitors, and by the less stringent social welfare requirements that impart a certain advantage over Western rivals.

Nevertheless, and as hinted above in the reference to the lack of worker rights, the transition into the global arena was far from seamless (see Figures 0.6

and 0.7). The rise and global reach of al-Qaeda was a symptom of the dark underside of new patterns of state building and of global interconnectedness. The terrorist attacks on 9/11 highlighted the myriad linkages between globalisation and security as al-Qaeda exploited transnational flows of finance and people and utilised new technologies of communication to plan and carry them out. The realisation that 17 of the 19 hijackers were nationals of GCC states (15 from Saudi Arabia and two from the UAE) provided a sobering demonstration of these states' vulnerabilities to opposition toward their rulers' political and security alliances with the United States. Saudi Arabia, Dubai and other Gulf states also played an active (if unwitting) role as hubs for the illicit networks that underpinned the financing of terrorist networks within the GCC and elsewhere. Both the final report of the 9/11 Commission and an independent task force set up by the Council on Foreign Relations in 2002 addressed Saudi Arabia's alleged role in terrorist financing, although neither uncovered any evidence that the Saudi government as an institution was itself involved. Nonetheless, the Council on Foreign Relations report was particularly critical of Saudi-based support for international terrorist organisations, and concluded bluntly that 'for years, individuals and charities based in Saudi Arabia have been the most important source of funds for Al Qaeda' (Council on Foreign Relations 2002: 1).

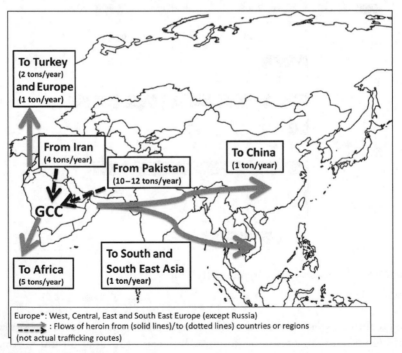

FIGURE 0.6 Heroin flows to and from GCC (2002–2009)

Source: UN Afghan Opium Report (2009) 'Addiction Crime and Insurgency: The transnational threat of Afghan opium'.

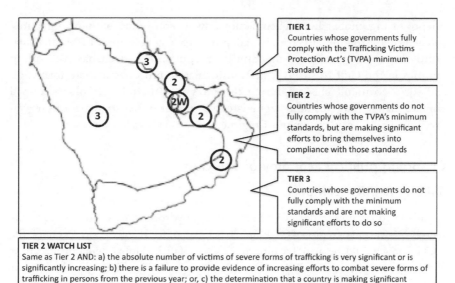

TIER 1
Countries whose governments fully comply with the Trafficking Victims Protection Act's (TVPA) minimum standards

TIER 2
Countries whose governments do not fully comply with the TVPA's minimum standards, but are making significant efforts to bring themselves into compliance with those standards

TIER 3
Countries whose governments do not fully comply with the minimum standards and are not making significant efforts to do so

TIER 2 WATCH LIST
Same as Tier 2 AND: a) the absolute number of victims of severe forms of trafficking is very significant or is significantly increasing; b) there is a failure to provide evidence of increasing efforts to combat severe forms of trafficking in persons from the previous year; or, c) the determination that a country is making significant efforts to bring themselves into compliance with minimum standards was based on commitments by the country to take additional future steps over the next year

FIGURE 0.7   US State Department 'Trafficking in Persons Report', 2010

Source: US State Department (2010) 'Trafficking in Persons Report'.

The Gulf states' emergence as global actors thus represents a moment of great importance in both its positive and negative aspects. It reflects a new-found determination to engage proactively in reformulating international regulatory structures in order to maximise their own interests and objectives. This projection of a greater voice is indicative of their increased confidence in the international arena and part of the realignment of the Global South aimed at reworking the architecture of global governance as it emerges from the 2007–9 crisis. These contours have already started to reshape debates over the restructuring of global financial institutions such as the International Monetary Fund, driven by Saudi Arabia's membership of the G20. Elsewhere, Abu Dhabi's successful bid to host the headquarters of the newly established International Renewable Energy Agency (IRENA) in 2009 marked the first instance of an international organisation basing itself in the Middle East. Qatar's hosting of the Gas Exporting Countries Forum is another instance of Gulf states' prominent enmeshment in new frameworks of energy governance.

The international politics of climate change provide an example of the GCC states engaging globally in order to minimise any potential threat to their domestic interests. With the notable exception of Oman, the GCC countries developed a reputation for obstructionist tactics at successive rounds of negotiations, focusing on the economic implications of climate change rather than its direct environmental impacts (Depledge 2008: 20). This was driven by policymakers' acute awareness that proposals to reduce carbon emissions and global dependence on oil represented a serious threat to the political economy of the oil-producing monarchies. Their actions were consistent with ruling elites' pursuance of regime survival by adapting to changes in the international political economy around them. Similar pragmatism had enabled the ruling families in the Gulf to survive the transformative processes of state formation and socio-economic changes during the entry into the oil era. Policies toward climate change thus constitute an updated version of earlier strategies of survival predicated on a keen awareness of regime interests and state objectives.

Changing political economy of the Gulf

Shifting political contours

As oil-based economies heavily reliant on the hydrocarbons sector for approximately 50 per cent of regional GDP and 80 per cent of fiscal and export revenues, the GCC states would be acutely impacted by any fall in global demand for oil or changing energy mix in a climate-aware environment. This highlights the manner in which global issues intertwine with considerations of domestic stability and continuity in the Gulf. This notwithstanding, during the course of the twenty-first century the political economy of the Gulf states is likely to shift decisively toward post-rentier structures of governance. Although rates of resource depletion vary widely and are decades away in Kuwait, Saudi Arabia, Qatar and Abu Dhabi, existing oil reserves are projected to run out in Bahrain and Oman within twenty years. Moreover, changing demographic patterns are straining the redistributive mechanisms set up in the 1970s, as well as a labour market that is neither aligned with, nor capable of, absorbing a large citizen workforce. Underlying these developments is awareness by policy-makers of the urgency of moving beyond a culture of citizen entitlement and embedding notions of productivity and value creation in strategies of economic diversification.

This involves difficult political choices in stripping away layers of vested interests and reformulating the basis of legitimacy among successive generations lacking experience of pre-oil hardships and taking for granted the redistribution of wealth and public goods (Dresch and Piscatori 2004: 34). The centrality of oil rents in constructing and maintaining the social contract binding state and society in the Gulf states magnifies the domestic challenges that lie ahead. States in transition are vulnerable to contestation and erosion of regime legitimacy. This threat is magnified in rentier polities if mechanisms for co-opting political support and popular acquiescence begin to break down. Developments in neighbouring Yemen demonstrate how the process of managing depleting oil reserves can become contested and violent (Hill 2010: 108). While the GCC states undoubtedly have greater material resources to cushion the transition toward post-oil structures of governance, their dependence on oil has both been longer-lasting and more deeply embedded into their domestic political economy. The crisis of governance in Yemen thus confronts Gulf states' policy-makers with a warning of the complexities that lie ahead in reforming socio-economic ties and renewing the bases of political legitimacy and regime authority.

In the late-1990s and early-2000s all six GCC states embarked on processes of significant political change consonant with local socio-political and cultural norms, as described by Abdulkhaleq Abdulla (Chapter 5). These aimed to introduce a measure of political pluralism and a participatory dimension, and renew the legitimacy of ruling elites while co-opting oppositional groups in a carefully managed top-down process of incremental change (Ehteshami and Wright 2007: 915) (see Figure 0.9). Greg Power's contribution to this book also draws out the different speeds with which these institutional developments occurred, in addition to the diverse obstacles encountered by each (Chapter 1). However, the initial reforms did not lead to substantive changes in the pattern or distribution of power within Gulf polities. Instead, they resulted in a stalled 'halfway house' that resulted either in a flawed process of reform (in Kuwait and Bahrain) or did not translate early promise into significant progress (in Qatar, Saudi Arabia and the United Arab Emirates) (Ottaway 2005: 6) (see Plate 6).

This incomplete outcome leaves largely untouched the domestic balance of power, which remains vested in ruling families and their neo-patrimonial networks of political−economic control. Reforms have been introduced in a careful, state-led process of change that is described both in Wanda Krause's chapter on the position of women (see Figure 0.8) in government-supported organisations and their role in assisting state objectives and shaping development (Chapter 4), and in John Chalcraft's examination of labour migration as an element in the construction and consolidation of political order (Chapter 3).

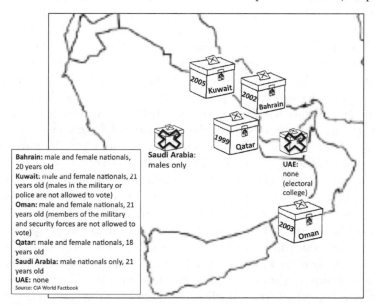

Bahrain: male and female nationals, 20 years old
Kuwait: male and female nationals, 21 years old (males in the military or police are not allowed to vote)
Oman: male and female nationals, 21 years old (members of the military and security forces are not allowed to vote)
Qatar: male and female nationals, 18 years old
Saudi Arabia: male nationals only, 21 years old
UAE: none
Source: CIA World Factbook

Saudi Arabia: males only

UAE: none (electoral college)

FIGURE 0.8 Granting universal suffrage in the Gulf

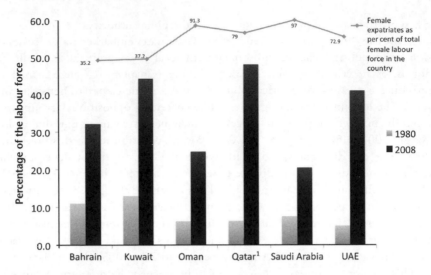

FIGURE 0.9   GCC female labour force (+15 years old)

Sources: The World Bank Labour Force Statistics Data. International Labour Organisation.
The female expatriate labourers as a percentage of total female labour force percentages were calculated from data from the International Labour Organization (2001) 'Gender and Migration in Arab States: The Case of Domestic Workers'. Saudi Arabia's percentage (2010) is from http://www.cdsi.gov.sa/ 1.
Source: Qatar Information Exchange.

Similar state-sanctioned discourse on values such as human rights also accompanied this partial opening of political space, albeit in a carefully controlled intersection of local contexts and global trends. Human rights advocacy has entered the political and public arena and in December 2008 human rights organisations throughout the Gulf states actively marked the 60th anniversary of the Universal Declaration of Human Rights with a range of activities and public diplomacy outreach designed to spread awareness of the concept. These measures notwithstanding, the GCC states continue to delay the actual implementation of human rights instruments such as the International Covenant on Civil and Political Rights (ratified by Kuwait and Bahrain only) and the International Covenant on Economic, Social and Cultural Rights (ratified by Kuwait alone). The situation is complicated by the demographic imbalances stemming from the presence of migrant labour groups with few civil or political rights that form the majority in Kuwait, Qatar and the UAE, and substantial minorities in Bahrain, Oman and Saudi Arabia. In this context, the issue of what sort of rights, and for whom, becomes tied to issues of national identity, class relations and broader hierarchies of power and control (cf. Ulrichsen 2011b). In the face of intensifying transnational and sub-state flows of ideas, people and information, the success or otherwise of state-led efforts to control the processes of reform will play a critical role in determining whether the transition toward a post-oil political economy is consensual and incremental or contested and possibly violent.

Changing economies in the Gulf

The question of the nature and extent of political reform ties into the themes explored in the second section of this book, which examine the economic transitions undertaken during the past decade and the evolution of economic structures in the GCC states. During the second oil boom (2002–8) the GCC states accumulated an estimated $2.4 trillion in oil revenues, with an estimated $1.5 trillion ending up in regional sovereign wealth funds (Seznec 2008: 97). The size of this capital accumulation, although frequently overstated in Western accounts, nevertheless enhanced the Gulf states' global reach. The chapters by Rodney Wilson on Islamic finance (Chapter 7) and Gawdat Bahgat on sovereign wealth funds (Chapter 10) each examine different aspects of the Gulf's engagement with the international financial system and assess their implications for governance regionally and internationally. The global economic and financial crisis visibly demonstrated the linkages that bound Gulf economies inextricably to broader processes, and also made clear their stake in shaping the response and recovery measures. Gulf reactions were responsible and measured, as Gulf-based sovereign investment played an important role in recapitalising faltering Western financial institutions and Saudi Arabia won international praise for its role in stabilising world oil markets.

Gulf states' utilisation of the second oil windfall provided a further sign of maturation in economic policy-making. Compared with the first oil boom (1973–82) the Gulf states followed more responsible fiscal policies that diverted oil revenues into economic diversification strategies. The chapter by Miklós Koren and Silvana Tenreyro describes how these plans reduced economic volatility and over-reliance on sector-specific income (Chapter 9). This was matched by greater emphasis on constructing regulatory structures (of varying degrees of independence) designed to manage the governance of markets in the Gulf states, as is clear in Mark Thatcher's contribution (Chapter 6) dealing with the telecommunications and financial sectors (see Figure 0.12). These chapters add great analytical depth to recent research focusing on the rise of a growing Gulf economic elite that operates with increasing autonomy from the state and has been important in driving socio-economic growth in these changing polities (Aarts and Nonneman 2005: 180–1). Narrowing down the focus to energy and sustainability policies, the chapter by Steffen Hertog and Giacomo Luciani identifies a marked preference for project-based technocratic enclaves as being more likely to be successful than broader regulatory strategies in shifting consumer and business behaviour (Chapter 11).

All of the chapters in this section focus on aspects of the current and future role of hydrocarbons in GCC economies. They paint a picture of an economic transition in flux (see Figure 0.10 and Table 0.2) as new processes of institutionalisation come up against nests of patronage-based and personalised networks. This became evident in the corporate crises that shook Dubai and Saudi Arabia in 2009, exposing the fragility of the governance of markets in the GCC. They exposed, in particular, critical shortcomings in transparency, uneven access to information, inconsistent standards of regulation and the continuing vulnerability of economic governance to opaque and overlapping private and familial linkages. Moreover, initial reactions to popular demands for reform in the 2011 'Arab Spring' only complicated longer-term strategies of economic transition.

TABLE 0.1 Telecommunications Infrastructure Index and its components

	Estimated Internet users per 100 inhabitants	Mobile subscribers per 100 inhabitants	Personal computers per 100 inhabitants	Total fixed broadband per 100 inhabitants
Bahrain	51.95	180.51	74.58	16.12
Kuwait	31.57	97.28	22.22	0.93
Oman	16.84	115.58	16.88	1.15
Qatar	34.04	131.39	15.69	8.07
Saudi Arabia	30.55	142.85	68.25	4.16
UAE	65.15	208.65	33.08	11.79

Source: United Nations E-Government Survey 2010.

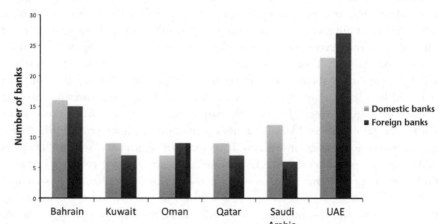

FIGURE 0.10 Commercial banks in GCC countries[1]: domestic and foreign[2] (2008)

Source: GCC Central Banks and Al-Hassan, Abdullah, May Khamis, and Nada Oulidi (2010) 'The GCC Banking Sector: Topography and Analysis'. IMF Working Paper, International Monetary Fund.

Notes
1. There are heavy entry barriers and licensing restrictions for foreign banks, including GCC banks, in all the GCC contries except Bahrain. Foreign ownership is restricted to 35 per cent in Oman, 49 per cent in Kuwait and Qatar, 40 per cent in Saudi for non-GCC nationals and 60 per cent for GCC nationals and 40 per cent in UAE.
2. 'Domestic banks' refers to banks that are majority owned by domestic shareholders. 'Foreign banks' are banks that a majority-owned by foreign shareholders.

TABLE 0.2 GCC: mergers and acquisitions (2007) (in millions of US dollars)

Acquiror/ target country	Bahrain	Kuwait	Oman	Qatar	Saudi Arabia	UAE	Inter- GCC investment
Bahrain[1]		395.8	155.5	200.8	0.0	0.1	752.2
Kuwait	422.0		18.3	21.8	12,536.6	86.7	13,085.4
Oman	0.0	0.0		199.6	0.0	0.0	199.6
Qatar	5.8	4,249.2	322.7		0.0	820.7	5,398.5
Saudi Arabia	0.0	957.2	451.3	0.0		3,364.2	4772.8
UAE	1,141.9	118.4	427.6	0.0	485.9		2,173.8
Total GCC	1,569.8	5,720.7	1,375.5	422.2	13,022.5	4,271.8	26,382.4

Source: Espinoza, Raphael, Ananthakrishnan Prasad and Oral Williams (2010) Regional Financial Integration in the GCC: IMF Working Paper, International Monetary Fund.

Note
1. Retail banks only. In addition Bahrain has a wholesale banking system with assets of $450 billion of which $50 billion are domestic assets.

This occurred as regimes preemptively announced public sector pay and benefit increases and additional job creation in government ministries. These short-term policy decisions exacerbate the challenges of reformulating dual and imbalanced labour markets, streamlining and incentivising national workforces and strengthening private sector development. How these diverging trajectories play off each other will be critical to determining whether a paradigm shift in economic relationships is likely to occur. This, in turn, will either complement or hold back the ambitious strategies of economic diversification and development currently underway in each GCC state. With the transition to post-oil economies drawing close in Bahrain and Oman, untangling state–business relations represents the central issue framing the possible reformulation of state–society relations and mechanisms of interaction in these redistributive polities.

Geo-political and geo-economic realignments

Profound shifts in the locus of global geo-political and geo-economic power are rebalancing East–West ties, as the rise of economic superpowers in the Pacific and South Asia contrasts with the relative decline in economic share of established markets in Europe and North America (see Figures 0.11 and 0.12). The energy-intensive processes of industrialisation underway in China and India are particularly salient to the emergence of more complex inter-linkages with the GCC states. Christopher M. Davidson's chapter explores the thickening linkages between Pacific Asia and the Gulf which, while based firmly on energy security requirements, are diversifying into petrochemicals, sovereign wealth investments and the provision of labour (Chapter 16). Kristian Ulrichsen's

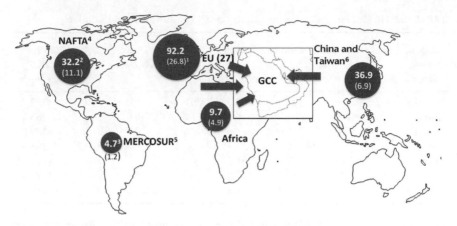

FIGURE 0.11   GCC imports in billions of US dollars (2008)

Source: Data from ITC calculations based on COMTRADE statistics.

Notes
1. All numbers in brackets are GCC exports in US dollars (billions) from 2001, except Africa's bracketed data is from 2006, not 2001. EU in 2001 is EU-15.
2. 2009 figures.
3. 2009 figures.
4. North American Free Trade Agreement.
5. Mercado Común del Sur (Common Market of the South).
6. Includes China, Taiwan/Chinese Taipei, Hong Kong, Macao.

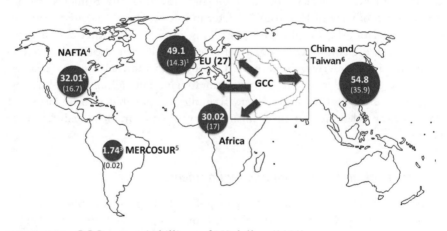

FIGURE 0.12   GCC exports in billions of US dollars (2008)

Source: Data from ITC calculations based on COMTRADE statistics.

Notes
1. All numbers in brackets are GCC exports in US dollars (billions) from 2001, except Africa's bracketed data is from 2006, not 2001. EU in 2001 is EU-15.
2. 2009 figures.
3. 2009 figures.
4. North American Free Trade Agreement.
5. Mercado Común del Sur (Common Market of the South).
6. Includes China, Taiwan/Chinese Taipei, Hong Kong, Macao.

chapter on Gulf security emphasises another emerging linkage between the Gulf and South and South-East Asia, namely a new 'oil-for-food' nexus between the ASEAN (Association of South-East Asian Nations) and GCC states (Chapter 13). This matches the former's energy security requirements to the latter's search for access to agricultural land in an attempt to attain food security and alleviate domestic water scarcities.

Burgeoning Gulf–Asia ties are primarily based on bilateral linkages and negotiations over free trade agreements. These hold significant implications for regional integration and global governing structures. The GCC as a collective entity signed its first Free Trade Agreement (FTA) with Singapore in 2008 and is in negotiations with the European Union, Japan, South Korea, India, Pakistan, China and New Zealand. Negotiations with the EU have been ongoing since 1990 and appeared to reach a standstill in 2009, despite periodic declarations from both sides of a revival. They contrast sharply with the progress made by the GCC in free trade negotiations with its Asian partners. These diverging pathways demonstrate the shifting nexus of political and economic linkages that are repositioning the Gulf in the international system. Trade-focused agreements with Asian powers offer the GCC states a plausible range of alternative partnerships to the more politically interventionist EU and United States. Particularly in the case of China, its pragmatic foreign policy and emphasis on non-intervention and state sovereignty is especially attractive to Saudi Arabia and the other Gulf states. This has significant potential ramifications for the future of normative concepts of global governance as blocs of developing nations coalesce in a loose and informal counterweight to Western-led discourse on notions of multilateral governance and what constitutes a global norm.

Anoushiravan Ehteshami and Steven Wright complement the chapters on the internationalisation of the Gulf by describing the realignment of regional power and influence. Ehteshami explores the significance of this shift away from Egypt and Iraq as traditional poles of gravity toward the GCC as the centre of strategic influence, security trends and international relations in the Middle East (Chapter 12). Meanwhile Wright focuses on the drivers of foreign policy in the GCC and the emergence of a distinctive approach in Qatar that has earned it international acclaim as a diplomatic mediator (Chapter 14). Although the challenge from increasingly non-state actors and destabilising flows remains, the GCC states have taken innovative steps to identify and adapt to their volatile and dynamic regional environment. Accommodating the rise of China and India's re-emergence as regional actors risks opening a gap between the Gulf states' political and security ties with the United States and its eastward economic and energy focus. This offers both an opportunity to create a more inclusive and sustainable regional security architecture and a challenge, should access to resources become sharpened and a potential zone of contestation arise in a future energy-hungry world.

Cross-cutting themes

This volume makes an original and substantive contribution to the literature on globalisation and the evolving political economy of the Gulf states. A number of cross-cutting themes and perspectives emerge. One is the multifaceted and dynamic participation of the GCC states within the processes of global change (cf. Held et al. 1999). The Gulf states have acquired greater confidence and leverage in reshaping the structural architecture of global frameworks in the aftermath of the economic and financial crisis. Their emergence as visible global actors injects a new dynamic into normative and policy-based debates on methods of global engagement amid proliferating coalitions of developing countries with broadly similar state-centric approaches. Somewhat ironically, Western policy responses in 2008–9 to the financial crisis bore considerable resemblance to the 'state-sponsored capitalism' models that have long been followed in the Gulf (and East Asian) states. These highlighted the continuing relevance of the state in the contemporary international system and suggest that global realignments may strengthen still further the durability of the state system.

An advantage of this book is that it provides material for a new theoretical perspective on the interaction between globalisation and the Gulf. Much of the book's added value lies in the analysis of the region as a barometer of globalisation and cockpit of transformative shifts in standards and patterns of living within a compressed time-period. While many changes to Gulf societies have been impressive, they have nevertheless largely left untouched the deeper structural political and economic methods of organisation. This modifies some significant generalisations in the social sciences that link globalisation to the weakening or hollowing out of states (cf. Ohmae 1995; Albrow 1996; Greider 1997; Gray 1998; Held and McGrew 2007). By contrast, older mechanisms of wealth redistribution have remained intact as regimes adapted pragmatically to the new opportunities to maximise their leverage and embed themselves at the core of a globalising international community.

The Gulf states' embrace of economic globalisation and resistance to its socio-political and cultural dimensions marks a further area of alignment with other emerging powers, notably China and India. All display an underlying scepticism of global governance as an intrusion into their sovereign leadership and prefer to view it through the prism of state-led cooperation in the governance of globalisation through inter-state cooperation. This neither diminishes the complexity of 'global' issues nor lessens the urgency of developing mechanisms for addressing them. The rapid internationalisation of the financial and economic crisis underscored the intensity and extensity of global interconnections and the necessity for coordinated and collaborative responses. Nevertheless, the fractious proceedings of the 2009 United Nations Climate Change Conference in Copenhagen demonstrated how local and global discussions may differ radically in their assessment of the issue at hand.

In addition, the broadening and deepening of bilateral and multilateral ties between the Gulf states and African and Asian partners, in particular, offers alternative models of economic and political development and pathways of global enmeshment. Policy-makers in the GCC frequently cite the developmental state paradigm followed by East Asian countries, and particularly Singapore, as an inspirational model for their own development planners (Hvidt 2009: 399). The combination of state guidance with private initiative in opening up economies while maintaining politically authoritarian structures runs counter to much academic discourse linking economic and political liberalisation. The example of China, India and the 'East Asian Tigers' also provides instances of states managing their global enmeshment largely on their own terms and using their economic strength as leverage in the international arena. An emerging 'Gulf consensus' concentrates on maximising the practical benefits from shaping the governance of globalisation rather than any normative affiliation to, or participation in, debates about concepts of globalisation or global governance.

Consequently, the Gulf states find themselves caught within overlapping and potentially conflicting pathways of development. The rise of complex transnational issues and the failings of the Washington consensus has exposed the unsuitability of existing frameworks of global organisation and redirected attention to possible alternatives. By virtue of their hydrocarbon and financial reserves, and geographical location, the GCC states are centrally positioned to act as a pivot around which the rebalancing of the global order is taking place. This notwithstanding, internal debates within the Gulf states on methods of socio-political organisation and the juxtaposition of rapid change with deeper entrenched networks of patronage remain to be resolved, and could threaten social cohesion in the future. Burgeoning debates over the perceived erosion of identity among Gulf nationals suggest how states and societies in transition can become vulnerable to contestation should domestic consensus over the pace and direction of change begin to break down. The interaction of global processes with internal dynamics of change and resistance in the Gulf states thus injects new dynamics into debates on the loci of local and global transformations and the manner in which each plays off the other.

The chapters in this book make a distinctive addition to the study of the contemporary Gulf states. Their strength is that the contributing authors examine the interaction between domestic and external dynamics influencing the transformation of these polities in a global era. They differ from earlier approaches that sought to explain the transformative impact of oil wealth through the theoretical prisms of modernisation, core–periphery dependency or rentier economics. Rather, this book situates the Gulf states firmly within their global twenty-first-century context. It captures the dynamic meeting-points of local and global values and norms, and explores the processes of engagement and the outcomes that result. The picture of the Gulf that emerges is intensely significant as an indicator of the changing global order and the means by which local political and economic structures meet, adapt and refract globalising processes and flows.

Bibliography

Aarts, P. and Nonneman, G. (eds) (2005) *Saudi Arabia in the Balance: Political Economy, Society, Foreign Affairs*. London: Hurst.

Albrow, M. (1996) *The Global Age: State and Society Beyond Modernity*. Cambridge: Polity Press.

Al-Rasheed, M. (ed.) (2008) *Kingdom Without Borders: Saudi Arabia's Political, Religious and Media Frontiers*. London: Hurst.

Anderson, L. (1991) 'Absolutism and the resilience of monarchy in the Middle East', *Political Science Quarterly*, 106(1): 1–15.

Anscombe, F. (1997) *The Ottoman Gulf: The Creation of Kuwait, Saudi Arabia and Qatar*. New York: Columbia University Press.

Bromley, S. (1994) *Rethinking Middle East Politics: State Formation and Development*. Cambridge: Polity Press.

Crystal, J. (1990) *Oil and Politics in the Gulf: Rulers and Merchants in Kuwait and Qatar*. Cambridge: Cambridge University Press.

Depledge, J. (2008) 'Striving for no: Saudi Arabia in the climate change regime', *Global Environmental Politics*, 8(4): 9–35.

Dresch, P. and Piscatori, J. (eds) (2004) *Globalization and Identity in the Arab States of the Gulf*. London: I.B. Tauris.

Economist, The (2010) 'Aviation in the Gulf: rulers of the New Silk Road', 3–9 June.

Ehteshami, A. (2007) *Globalization and Geopolitics in the Middle East: Old Games, New Rules*. London: Routledge.

Ehteshami, A. and Wright, S. (2007) 'Political change in the Arab oil monarchies: from liberalization to enfranchisement', *International Affairs*, 79(1): 53–75.

Fandy, M. (2007) 'Enriched Islam: the Muslim crisis of education', *Survival*, 49(3): 77–98.

Gray, J. (1998) *False Dawn: The Delusions of Global Capitalism*. London: Granta Books.

Greenberg, M., Wechsler, W. and Wolowsky, L. (2002) *Terrorist Financing. Report of an Independent Task Force Sponsored by the Council on Foreign Relations*. New York: Council on Foreign Relations.

Greider, W. (1997) *One World, Ready or Not: The Manic Logic of Global Capitalism*. New York: Simon & Schuster.

Halliday, F. (2005) *The Middle East in International Relations: Power, Politics and Ideology*. Cambridge: Cambridge University Press.

Held, D. and McGrew, A. (2002) 'Introduction', in D. Held and A. McGrew (eds), *Governing Globalization: Power, Autonomy and Global Governance*. Cambridge: Polity Press.

Held, D. and McGrew, A. (2007) *Globalization/Anti-Globalization: Beyond the Great Divide*, 2nd edn. Cambridge: Polity Press.

Held, D. and Mepham, D. (eds) (2007) *Progressive Foreign Policy: New Directions for the UK*. Cambridge: Polity Press.

Held, D., McGrew, A., Goldblatt, D. and Perraton, J. (1999) *Global Transformations*. Cambridge: Polity Press.

Hill, G. (2010) 'What is happening in Yemen?', *Survival*, 52(2): 105–16.

Hvidt, M. (2009) 'The Dubai model: an outline of key development-process elements in

Dubai', *International Journal of Middle East Studies*, 41(3): 397–418.

Kaldor, M. (2007) *New and Old Wars: Organized Violence in a Global Era*. Stanford, CA: Stanford University Press.

Kostiner, J. (ed.) (2000) *Middle East Monarchies: The Challenge of Modernity*. London: Lynne Rienner.

Luciani, G. (1990) *The Arab State*. London: Routledge.

Metcalf, T. (2007) *Imperial Connections: India in the Indian Ocean Arena*. Berkeley, CA: University of California Press.

Nonneman, G. (ed.) (2005) *Analyzing Middle Eastern Foreign Policies*. London: Routledge.

Ohmae, K. (1995) *The End of the Nation State: The Rise of Regional Economies*. New York: Free Press.

Ottaway, M. (2005) *Evaluating Middle East Reform: How Do We Know When It Is Significant?* Carnegie Endowment for International Peace, Paper 56.

Peterson, J.E. (2005) *The Emergence of Post-Traditional Oman*, Durham Middle East Paper No.5, Sir William Luce Publication Series, University of Durham.

Potter, L. (ed.) (2009) *The Persian Gulf in History*. New York: Palgrave Macmillan.

Romani, V. (2009) *The Politics of Higher Education in the Middle East: Problems and Prospects*, Middle East Brief No. 36, Brandeis University.

Said Zahlan, R. (1998) *The Making of the Modern Gulf States*. Reading: Ithaca Press.

Seznec, J.-F. (2008) 'The Gulf sovereign wealth funds: myths and reality', *Middle East Policy*, 15(2): 97–110.

Teitelbaum, J. (ed.) (2009) *Political Liberalization in the Persian Gulf*. London: Hurst.

The Gulf (2010) 'Special report: Etihad Airways: staying on course', May issue.

Ulrichsen, K. (2011a) *Insecure Gulf: The End of Certainty and the Transition to the Post-Oil Era*. London: Hurst.

Ulrichsen, K. (2011b) 'Rebalancing global governance: Gulf States perspectives on the governance of globalisation', *Global Policy*, 2(1).

Vitalis, R. (2009) *America's Kingdom: Mythmaking on the Saudi Oil Frontier*. London: Verso.

PART 1

The domestic context:

Changing dimensions of political and social structures

1

THE DIFFICULT DEVELOPMENT OF PARLIAMENTARY POLITICS IN THE GULF

Parliaments and the process of managed reform in Kuwait, Bahrain and Oman

Greg Power

This chapter looks at the dynamics of political liberalisation in Kuwait, Bahrain and Oman in recent decades, focusing specifically on the evolution of their parliaments[1] as the most prominent institutions of representative democracy. Although the countries have similarities by dint of their geographical proximity, religion, economic reliance on oil and monarchical structure, the recent history of their parliaments emphasise their distinctiveness and the differential impact of social, economic and political factors on the process of gradual liberalisation in each.

At one end, Kuwait's parliament is the loudest and liveliest in the region, having sat since 1963 (albeit with unconstitutional dissolutions in 1976 and 1986) and which in recent years has increasingly challenged the Emir and the government. In Bahrain, a short-lived parliament existed for around two years in the mid-1970s and was resuscitated by the new King in 2002, partly as a means to ease sectarian tension. However, the fact that the new parliament turned out to be a pale imitation of its predecessor has been a source of continuing grievance around which much subsequent political turmoil has revolved. By contrast, the evolution of Oman's parliament has been slow, even by the standards of the Gulf. The country, which was the last in the GCC to adopt a constitution in 1996, held its first popular elections in 2003, but to a body which lacked legislative power and whose influence was confined almost entirely to economic development.

Three themes underpin the chapter's analysis of each country's political trajectory and dynamics of change. First, the process should not be understood as one of democratisation so much as one of gradual political liberalisation, whose pace and content is determined by the ruling autocracy. It is an exercise in top-down, managed reform characterised by 'guided pluralism, controlled elections and selective repression' (Brumberg 2002: 56). Liberalising autocracies are thus

> liberal in the sense that their leaders not only tolerate but promote a measure of political openness ... but they are autocratic in that their rulers always retain the upper hand ... with their ultimate reliance on the supreme authority of the monarch or president, liberalised autocracies provide a kind of virtual democracy.
>
> *(Brumberg 2003: 3)*

Political participation is thus only possible within distinct limits set by the regime. However, there are numerous pitfalls in this form of controlled liberalisation. The 'King's Dilemma', as originally set out by Huntington in 1963, is that reforms from the top often increase demands for more radical change from the bottom. The monarchical elites in the Gulf are thus walking a tightrope, for while

> they are uniformly seeking to maintain their position of power for the long-term, the dilemma they are grappling with is how to balance undertaking reform to increase their own legitimacy against allowing the pendulum of power to swing ... which could ultimately see a tangible challenge to their position.
>
> *(Ehteshami and Wright 2007: 916)*

The second theme is that political liberalisation in the Gulf is fundamentally shaped by the fact that they are rentier states. The quadrupling of oil prices during the 1970s changed the dynamic in these countries, bringing huge wealth but meaning that the economy is ultimately dependent on the expenditure of the state as the principal recipient of oil rents. This has several implications for politics. In the first place, it weakens demands for political representation – where the state does not need to rely on the income of citizens or the private sector for its tax revenues, it will feel less of an obligation to give them influence over policy or spending decisions. In short, 'no taxation, no representation'. In addition, the middle classes, who would be expected to articulate these demands most forcefully, were effectively bought off in most of the Gulf countries. The merchant classes traded political power for economic wealth, or as John Waterbury puts it

> the tacit understanding has been that the bourgeoisie would renounce any overt political role and that it would follow the broad economic directives of the state, in exchange for which it would be allowed to make significant profits. The state would keep labour docile through a combination of welfare benefits and political repression.
>
> *(Waterbury 1994: 27)*

The state continues to provide the financial support to almost all of its citizens, either through direct employment in a hugely bloated public sector or by other benefits and disbursements. The political system, and the parliament within it, will therefore reflect those dynamics. Ultimately, as Larry Diamond suggests, 'oil distorts the state, the market, the class structure and the entire incentive structure' (Diamond, 2010: 98).

However, the third theme is that the legitimacy of the Gulf rulers, which has predominantly relied on oil rent, is looking increasingly shaky. The rulers themselves recognise that the rentier model is not a viable long-term strategy. As oil production declines, income falls and weakens the capacity of the state to provide for its citizens. This in turn threatens to undermine the social compact on which the current political settlement between the state, the private sector and its citizens is built.

The decline of natural resources is exacerbated by the Gulf's rapid population growth, meaning that the burden on the state to provide education, welfare and employment is steadily expanding. The UNDP's Arab Human Development Report in 2009 suggested that the Arab region as a whole needed to create around 50 million new jobs by 2020 to absorb their young population into the workforce. As a result all the Gulf states, to one extent or another, are seeking to diversify their economies and liberalise their markets. As Jill Crystal has pointed out: 'Economic liberalisation has been driven largely by the governments' fear that growing youth unemployment will metastasise into political dissent if jobs are not found, and by the hope that the private sector can postpone that day' (Crystal 2009: 43).

This is more pressing in some countries such as Oman and Bahrain which have far fewer resources, but even in Kuwait the government is initiating attempts to reform its economy. Often these demands are reinforced by voices in civil society (Ottoway and Hamzawy, 2009: 105–7) creating popular demands for greater transparency, accountability and representation – trends fed by globalisation and communication technologies which provide citizens with unprecedented access to information and political opinion (Teitelbaum 2009: 15–7). Such changes though go to the heart of a political legitimacy based on state provision. The original introduction of parliaments in Kuwait, Bahrain and Oman was in part to enhance the legitimacy of those regimes. Their evolution since, and the prospects for further development in the face of these emergent trends, illustrate the challenges of political liberalisation and the difficulties that need to be addressed.

Kuwait

Kuwait has the longest experience of participatory politics in the Gulf. Following independence in 1961, a constituent assembly was elected to develop the country's constitution which was enacted in 1962. The document falls some way short of creating a constitutional democracy, but by the standards of the Gulf it is an exceptional document, placing distinct limits on the power of the Emir and, significantly, stating that sovereignty resides in the Kuwaiti people – rather than the ruler - who elect their representatives to the National Assembly in regular and free elections.

The parliament's powers reflect this constitutional desire for checks and balances. In the first place, although 50 representatives are directly elected, the Emir can appoint up to 15 additional members who sit in parliament as ministers, giving the government an immediate 15-person advantage. Parliament has significant powers, but they are essentially negative ones: it has the power to block but little power to create. For example, the Emir nominates ministers to Cabinet, but parliament has the power to remove ministers (including the prime minister) and delay government legislation. It cannot appoint ministers or initiate laws. If parliament wins a vote of no confidence in the Prime Minister, the Emir then either has to appoint an alternative whom parliament can work with or dissolve parliament and hold fresh elections. The distribution of power between the Emir and the parliament in the constitution effectively means that each side can cancel the other out, and the system has frequently been characterised as stalemate and gridlock.

It is in this context that the ruling Al-Sabah family's style of 'managed reform' needs to be understood. Since 1963 the political system has been characterised by exactly these sorts of tussles, with the advantage see-sawing between the two, as parliament and the ruling family have sought to establish the boundaries of the other side's power. On two occasions, in 1976 and 1986, these tensions reached the point where the ruling Al-Sabah family suspended the constitution and dissolved parliament. Both times it was claimed that parliament was delaying legislation and hindering the proper functioning of government. On the first occasion the dissolution lasted until 1981, the second until 1992. However, the evolution of the parliament since 1992, and especially 2006, has presented fundamental challenges to the Al-Sabahs' control of Kuwaiti politics.

Managed reform as 'divide and rule'

The Al-Sabah family has run Kuwaiti politics since the eighteenth century, principally because it was at the head of an alliance with the trading merchants who dominated the economy before the discovery of oil. The shift to the rentier state also restructured political life. During the 1950s and 1960s the merchant families effectively gave up their right to influence policy in return for substantial government disbursements and a tacit promise that the Sabahs would not interfere in business (Crystal 1989: 431). This then left the ruling family to adopt a strategy of divide and rule for the second half of the twentieth century. At various points, in order to dilute what they regarded as potential opposition in parliament, the Al-Sabahs quietly encouraged other groups, including Sunni Islamists, Bedouin and Shia groups to organise and become politically active. In addition, the family sought to buy the support of certain politicians, generally known as 'service deputies' whose support for government policy is given in return for the state funding for their constituencies. And, when that was not enough, the electorate was expanded to include new groups of voters, such as newly urbanised Bedouin (Brown, 2007).

This fracturing of the political system is reinforced by the absence of political parties. In common with other Gulf states, political parties are banned by law and thus candidates cannot campaign as a party slate during elections. This does not stop blocs of like-minded candidates cooperating, and they have done so since the 1960s. But once elected, parliamentary groups form around fairly obvious political divisions, forming de facto political parties, which since 1992 have broadly formed into four groups – a Sunni Islamist bloc, a Shia Islamist bloc, secular liberals and 'independents' who generally support the government. However, the ban on parties means that voters elect individuals, giving an impetus to independent, local and tribal candidates, and these blocs tend to lack the level of party discipline and cohesion that characterises parties in longer-standing political systems.

While the Al-Sabahs' style of 'managed reform' succeeded in fragmenting the opposition for long periods, it also increased the number of opposition groups represented in parliament and could not prevent the growth in their support. Significantly the Islamist groups gained representation for the first time in 1992 and have featured prominently ever since. Overall, opposition groups polled strongly in elections in 1992 and 1996, and formed the majority of MPs in the parliaments elected in 1999 and 2003. Yet their effectiveness as an opposition to government has been sporadic. They have tested government ministers and blocked its measures, but the level of fragmentation within the parliament means that they have rarely worked in a concerted fashion. Opposition seems to rely on guerrilla raids on government measures rather than presenting a coherent alternative to government policy.

Post-2006: Kuwaiti politics in crisis?

However, 2006 appeared to mark a distinct shift in the relationship between parliament and government and prompted a new period of political instability. First, in January of that year, the long-reigning Emir Jaber died, prompting a crisis of succession as the designated heir to the throne, Sheikh Saad al-Abdullah, was incapacitated by illness and dementia. This raised concerns both within sections of the ruling family and parliament, heightened by the fact that the constitution states a ruling Emir can only be deposed with parliamentary approval. As parliament was in the process of removing Emir Saad, the ruling family had little option but to submit a letter of abdication and install Sheikh Sabah al-Ahmed.

The acceptance of parliament's role in the succession issue dealt a significant blow to Al-Sabah prestige (Herb 2009b: 143) but it also appeared to galvanise the opposition political blocs, who then inflicted a significant defeat over the government's electoral law. The blocs used government plans for minor redistricting to amend the law and overhaul the electoral system. The opposition sought to reduce the number of constituencies from 25 to five, so that rather than each constituency electing two representatives, they would instead elect ten. The disparate opposition groups coalesced around the argument that the government's proposals effectively gerrymandered the vote in the government's favour and bred vote-buying. The additional attempt to question the Prime Minister for the first time, in the form of a parliamentary interpellation, saw the Emir respond by dissolving the parliament and calling new elections for June 2006. At the resulting vote, the opposition won convincingly, taking more than two-thirds of the seats in parliament, around half of them Islamists.

The immediate effect was the government's acceptance of the new electoral law, but it marked the start of three years of political instability in Kuwait. In the spring of 2007 two members of the ruling family resigned following parliamentary interpellations, and in 2008 the differences between government and opposition became insurmountable as the parliament attempted to implement pay rises for state employees. The Emir again dissolved parliament and elections were held in May 2008, where the opposition groups increased their representation to 36 seats in the 50-member Assembly. Tensions rose again at the end of 2008 when the parliament again attempted to interpellate the Prime Minister, continuing until March 2009 when the Cabinet resigned and the Emir again dissolved parliament.

The subsequent elections in May 2009 were notable for three things: the relatively low turnout at 55 per cent, the election of four women MPs for the first time and a significant increase in government-supporting MPs, mainly at the expense of the Sunni Islamists. However, the political stalemate seemed set to continue. By the end of 2009, there was widespread fear that the Emir would resort to the unconstitutional dissolution of parliament, as had occurred in 1976 and 1986, when parliament again attempted to interpellate the Prime Minister and three other ministers,.

In the event, the government acceded to parliament's request, putting all four ministers before parliament for grilling, including – for the first time – the Prime Minister. Parliament, in turn, provided votes of confidence for all four, thus averting a new constitutional crisis. The significance of these events will only be determined in the years to come, but it suggests that parliament has established an important constitutional principle, further extending its right of inquiry, which it will be difficult for future Prime Ministers to avoid.

Political liberalisation v. economic reform in an 'extreme rentier' state

At the end of 2010 it appeared that Kuwait's parliament and ruling family had established a form of political stability, if resting on an uneasy and uncertain relationship. The dynamics of the parliaments preceding it were characterised by a fractious set of opposition parties, who could frustrate government, but not present alternatives. That fragmentation is, however, largely a result of the Al-Sabahs' own approach to political reform. They sought to divide opponents, but then found it difficult to manage the disparate opposition, especially on the rare occasions when they were able to work together, such as over the electoral law.

Perhaps more significantly, the content of political debate has been dominated almost entirely by the power struggle between parliament and government. Parliamentary politics has been absorbed by key issues of political reform, and this has been at the expense of other policy issues, most significantly, economic reform. The parliament is regarded as the main reason why Kuwait has failed to liberalise its economy and promote private sector development to the same degree as its neighbours in the Gulf (Herb 2009a: 377–81; Salem, 2006: 10); instead, its impact has been to 'paralyse government decision-making, suspend vital projects and forestall economic progress'.[2]

However, the role of the parliament may simply reflect the nature of the social compact in what Michael Herb has described as the 'extreme rentier state' (Herb, 2009b). Oil makes up 94 per cent of state revenues in Kuwait,[3] and 90 per cent of its employees work for the state. In these circumstances, citizens' expectations of the state are exceptionally high, but there is relatively little concern for the private sector, with few 'threads of mutual interest that usually tie together capital and wage labour' (Herb 2009a: 381). In turn, parliament itself has developed a web of self-reinforcing vested interests which seek to protect parliamentary representatives and the people who vote for them. As Herb puts it, 'Kuwait's parliament does what it is designed to do: it represents citizens, most of whom work for the state' (Herb 2009a: 384). This reflects why the parliament and government came to blows over the issue of state pensions in 2008 and resulted in the dissolution of parliament that year, and why in January 2010 the parliament sought to force government to buy and reschedule all $23.3 billion of consumer loans incurred by citizens, in a move understandably rejected by the government.

In short, the dynamics of parliamentary politics reflect the tussle over power between the parliament and the ruling family, and the particular form of social compact that underpins Kuwait's rentier state. It may be that Kuwait's oil reserves and production capacity mean that it can continue to afford its citizens' expectations for longer than its neighbours and defer economic reform. However, the parliament's approval in January 2010 of a bill designed to liberalise Kuwait's economy under the four-year development plan and strategic 'Vision Kuwait 2030' was the first of its kind and followed shortly after the four confidence motions in the government ministers. Whether this suggests a period of respite, which will focus less on the balance of power and more on the content of policy, is unclear. However, it is likely that the future development of Kuwaiti politics will continue to be characterised by a bumpy testing of boundaries between the powers of the elected representatives and those of the Al-Sabah ruling family.

Bahrain

In contrast with Kuwait, Bahrain has marginal oil supplies, occasionally high unemployment and is relatively poor by Gulf standards. As such, economic liberalisation is a less contentious issue and Bahrain first embarked on diversifying its economy at the end of the 1970s. However, over that period it has been far more politically turbulent, with tensions between the Shia population, who make up around 70 per cent of Bahrain's citizens, and the Sunni regime represented by the Al-Khalifa ruling family, spilling out into periods of civil unrest and subsequent state repression. The Bahraini parliament has played an important symbolic role in those events. Its first, brief lifespan from 1973 to 1975 was followed by unconstitutional dissolution until 2002 when it was reinstated by the new Emir, partly as a way of defusing civil unrest but with far less influence or power than its predecessor. Since then battles over the position of the parliament have become a focus for opposition groups demanding greater representation and accountability, while its election periods appear to be providing a predictable cycle of increased state harassment and victimisation of opponents.

The Al-Khalifa family monopolised power in Bahrain until the country gained independence from Britain in 1971, and in an effort to provide greater legitimacy for its rule introduced a constitution in 1973 and held the first elections for the National Assembly in December of that year. The experience was, however, short-lived. Parliament's challenging of government, and particularly its rejection of government proposals for summary powers to arrest those holding views considered to be a threat to the 'security of the state' in 1975, meant that the Emir dissolved the body and suspended the constitution in August of that year. The suspension of the parliament was a defining point for many opponents of the regime. Between 1994 and 1999, dissatisfaction with the political system combined with frustration over social and sectarian inequality, and specifically discrimination against the Shiite majority, to create a prolonged period of violence and unrest in Bahrain. The government's response was to detain demonstrators and exile opposition leaders, with suggestions of torture, intimidation and harassment rife (International Crisis Group 2005: 2–3).

The accession of Hamad bin 'Isa Al-Khalifa in 1999 and his promise of reform defused many of these tensions. Within months he opened dialogue with opposition leaders, released detainees and allowed exiled Bahrainis to return. Politically, the King suggested a return to the 1973 constitution and established special committees to develop reform proposals, published in December 2000. The resultant 'National Action Charter' stated that Bahrain should become a constitutional monarchy, with the powers of the king kept in check through a new bicameral legislature: the Nuwab (Council of Representatives) would be directly elected while the Shura (Consultative Council) would be appointed. The charter was, however, 'uncomfortably vague' on that process of appointment, and indeed on the relationship between the two chambers, causing some concern among leading reformers (Peterson 2009: 162). Nonetheless, the subsequent referendum on the constitutional changes in February 2001 resulted in overwhelming approval, with 98.4 per cent of Bahrainis voting in favour.

This though proved to be the high point of the reform process. The implementation of the constitution in February 2002 contained various amendments, inserted by the King, which retained certain key powers to the ruler, including full control of the government and the right to dissolve parliament. Then, in July, the provisions for parliament were published which clarified the relationship between the two chambers of parliament, determining that the 40-person Nuwab would be complemented by a 40-person Shura - appointed by the King and which could include members of the ruling family. Critically, in the event of disagreement between the two houses, the Shura would have the casting vote. With limited ability to scrutinise ministers and initiate legislation the Nuwab would be a pale imitation of its predecessor. It was not the return to the 1973 constitution that the King had promised. The changes, and the manner in which they had been implemented, revived concern and distrust among reformers. The immediate effect was the decision by four key political groups to boycott the elections scheduled for October.

Controlled pluralism – politics without parties

Like Kuwait, Bahrain has no formal political parties, but again de facto parties exist as 'political societies'. The main societies tend to be Islamist movements, of both Shia and Sunni origin, but less ideologically driven than counterparts elsewhere, and have shown an ability to work with each other, especially by the need for greater political reform. The four societies that boycotted the elections were the predominantly Shiite Islamist groups Al-Wefaq and the Islamic Action Society, along with the liberal secular National Democratic Society and the secular Progressive National Bloc.

Unsurprisingly, the electoral turnout at just over 53 per cent reflected the absence of the key groups. Moreover, the most significant debates in the subsequent parliament between 2002 and 2006 mainly pitted the Sunni Islamist groups against each other. Although neither offered any substantial opposition to government, the parliament did in that period push for greater powers, albeit with limited results. However, it was activities of groups outside parliament that set the tone for the subsequent election in 2006. During that period Shia and Sunni political societies pressed for a return to the 1973 constitution, an increase in parliamentary power and a reduction in the influence of the Shura. But it was the government's adoption of a political parties law in 2005 which provided the biggest catalyst. The law was designed to restrict further political activities and meant that political societies had to register or be deemed illegal. In the event, the biggest Shia society, Al-Wefaq, decided to register and contest the subsequent elections in 2006. (A more hardline splinter group, Al-Haq, broke away from Al-Wefaq at this point and remain formally outside the law.)

Turnout in 2006 was markedly higher at 72 per cent and the Shia Islamists did relatively well, picking up 18 of the 40 seats. However, given that the Shia have a clear majority in the population, the fact that Sunni representatives took the remaining 22 seats has more to do with the way in which the government influenced both the electoral system and the campaign itself, than the clear expression of voter preferences. Government manipulation of the electoral process, as explained below, is one of the dominant characteristics of the Al-Khalifas' managed political reform.

The constellation of forces in parliament did change its dynamic after 2006, making it a more rumbustious arena for political debate. This is partly a result of their frustration at the limited opportunities to influence policy and Sunni opposition to measures tackling anti-Shia discrimination meant Al-Wefaq occasionally resorted to walking out of the chamber in order to make the plenary inquorate and prevent decisions taking place. However, the societies have shown that where they do work together they can be more effective, and did so towards the end of the parliament, especially in tackling government corruption. Yet the limited parliamentary powers held by the Nuwab continue to undermine their overall effectiveness.

Bahrain's managed reform

Aside from the constitutional limits placed on parliamentary power, the Al-Khalifas' style of controlled pluralism is characterised by three main elements, namely, the manipulation of the electoral system, harassment of opponents and restricting civil society activity.

The gerrymandering of electoral constituencies to ensure Sunni domination of the parliament has been one of the most contentious issues since the 2006 election. Although Shia citizens account for more than two-thirds of the population, they won less than 50 per cent of the seats in parliament. This was a direct result of the way in which the constituencies are drawn, with the 40 electoral districts varying greatly in size: the largest district contains over 12,000 people, in a mainly Shia area, and the smallest – largely Sunni – has only 500 voters.[4] In addition, the government has sought to expand the Sunni population by granting citizenship to expatriates from Jordan, Yemen, Iraq, Syria and Saudi Arabia. The size of this exercise was revealed in the 2008 census results, which suggested that Bahraini citizens had increased by 42 per cent (Lawson 2010: 5) and Shia opposition groups claim that between 65,000 and 100,000 additional Sunnis have been added to the electoral roll between 2000 and 2010.[5]

Second, harassment of opposition candidates and supporters was a significant feature of both the 2006 and 2010 election campaigns. Government tactics gained particular prominence just before the election in 2006 when a report compiled by a former adviser to the Ministry for Cabinet Affairs, Salah Al-Bandar, was released suggesting a concerted effort by government to rig the voting system. It claimed that the government had spent around $6 million to fund anti-Shia, and specifically Al-Wefaq, campaigning. Reports of vote-buying, intimidation of voters and destruction of campaign offices were common in both 2006 and 2010. However, the level of repression appeared to increase a notch during 2010, with opponents arrested, their houses fire-bombed and the alleged torture of detainees by the authorities.[6]

Third, although Bahrain has a more lively civil society than other countries in the Gulf, the government has sought to place strict limits on that activity – particularly those that seek to monitor government. Most visibly, the security services have gone after various human rights groups in Bahrain, and in 2004 abolished the Bahrain Centre for Human Rights after a string of critical reports. In addition, journalists critical of government are frequently arrested and operate within tightly defined laws. But international organisations promoting democracy have also been prevented from operating in Bahrain. The US National Democratic Institute (NDI) had its licence revoked in the run-up to the 2006 elections, and although it was able to operate from 2007 onwards, it was again effectively thrown out shortly before the 2010 poll. According to another Bahrain-based human rights organisation, the NDI's eviction was due to the authorities' fear that they would want to monitor the conduct of the next election and were training local Bahrainis how to do so.[7]

Conclusion – limited pluralism and targeted repression

At the time of King Hamad's accession there was a widespread optimism that he might usher in a new era of reform, but there is much speculation as to Hamad's true motives. One argument is that he is a genuine reformer but was blown off course by having to manage other powerful and conservative interests within the ruling family, not least Sheikh Khalifa bin Salman, his uncle and Prime Minister. This is compounded by Saudi Arabian influence, which supplies Bahrain with 140,000 barrels of oil per day[8] and is nervous of an emergent Shia presence in Bahrain. Others suggest that the promise of reform was simply a political tactic designed to manage civil unrest in the short-term but maintain absolute control of the political sphere (see Peterson 2009; Khalaf 2008).

After the turmoil of the 1990s the promise of political reform did much to ease sectarian tension between the Shia and Sunni population. However, those expectations were undermined when details of the new constitution emerged and by the way in which the King has used those powers subsequently. It appears that Bahrain is now settling into a cycle of repression which reaches its peak during the election campaign but then eases off while the parliament is sitting.

The fragmentation of opposition in parliament means it offers only a limited challenge to the regime and the King has successfully exploited the divisions between his opponents. When the societies have coordinated their efforts they have had some success, but coherent opposition to government has been only a fleeting occurence. The difficulty of opposition is captured in the continuing dilemma facing Al-Wefaq: does it again boycott elections and remove any opportunity to challenge government ministers direct, and thus open itself up to charges from government of complicity with hostile outside forces? Or does it continue to participate in the political process, but run the risk of co-option, providing legitimacy for the parliament but disappointing its core support by achieving very little? Any disillusionment with Al-Wefaq simply benefits the harder line Al-Haq, which continues to operate outside the system. It is just one example of how the regime has managed to play its various opponents off against each other and place itself 'in the comfortable political centre between the Sunni Islamist societies... and a divided Shia Opposition' (Ottoway and Hamzawy 2009: 21–2). How the parliament develops following the 2010 election will depend on the extent to which the different groups can coalesce to provide a united opposition to the government.

Oman

By comparison with Kuwait and Bahrain the process of political liberalisation in Oman has proceeded in a slow, quiet and linear fashion. It is an exercise in extreme top-down reform whose pace is determined almost entirely by the ruling Sultan Qaboos, and with little evidence of external pressure for change. The dynamics of change in Oman are governed by two distinct features. The first is the Sultan himself. Qaboos came to power in 1970 when he overthrew his father, having been under virtual house arrest since the mid-1960s, seizing power with the tacit support of the British government. However, the accession was contested by his uncle Sayid Tariq bin Taymur, who wanted to establish Oman as a constitutional monarchy, while Qaboos wanted untrammelled monarchical power. Although Tariq was made Prime Minister, he had resigned by the end of 1971 and central authority as well as the legitimacy of the state was concentrated in the person of the Sultan (Valeri 2006: 187). Although widely regarded as a benign ruler, there could be no confusion that the state was to be run as an autocracy. The Basic Law (effectively the constitution) established in 1996 enshrined leadership in the Sultan and stated that public activities remained 'the prerogative of the state' (Siegfried 2000: 372).

Second, the political culture is infected at every level with the 'Omani way' which, broadly, means that any change is consistent with Omani culture and tradition (Jones and Ridout 2005; Rabi 2002). On its own this means that reforms proceed slowly, but that pace is further tempered by the overarching emphasis on consultation and consensus. It is not a coincidence that Oman's principal representative body is the Majlis A'Shura (Consultative Council), rather than the Majlis Al-Nuwab (Council of Representatives) favoured in Kuwait and Bahrain. Ultimately, the legitimacy of the institutions comes 'not only from the principle of representation but also from consultation, which, in Oman, also functions as principle, or an end in itself' (Jones 2007: 169).

The first steps towards representation took place in 1991 when the Majlis A'Shura was formed with representatives of 59 constituencies (*wilayah*) chosen by notables in each of those areas. Although with very limited powers, ministers

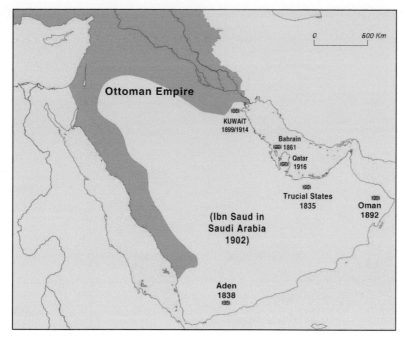

PLATE 1   Britain's presence in the Gulf, 1835–1971

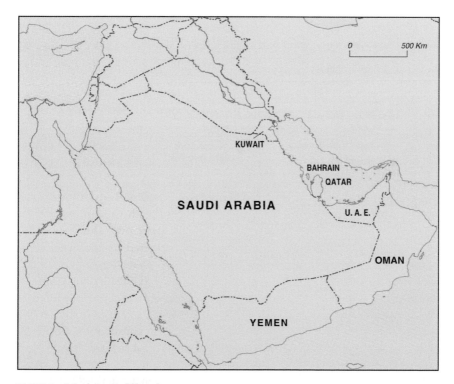

PLATE 2   Modern Gulf borders

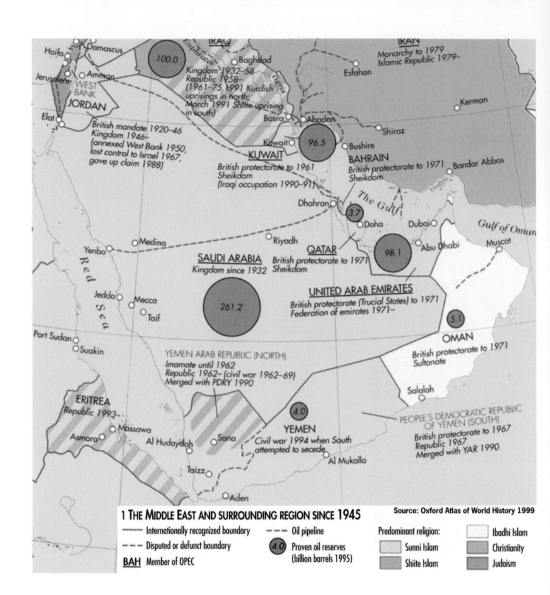

Haifa · Damascus
Jerusalem · Amman
WEST BANK
JORDAN
Elat
British mandate 1920–46
Kingdom 1946–
(annexed West Bank 1950, lost control to Israel 1967, gave up claim 1988)

IRAQ
100.0
Baghdad
Kingdom 1932–58.
Republic 1958–
(1961–75, 1991 Kurdish uprisings in north;
March 1991 Shiite uprising in south)
Basra · Abadan
Kuwait
KUWAIT
British protectorate to 1961
Sheikdom
(Iraqi occupation 1990–91)

IRAN
Monarchy to 1979
Islamic Republic 1979–
Esfahan
Shiraz
Kerman
Bushire
BAHRAIN
British protectorate to 1971 · Bandar Abbas
Sheikdom

96.5

Dhahran
3.7
The Gulf
Doha · Dubai
Gulf of Oman
Muscat
Abu Dhabi

Medina
Yenbo
Riyadh
QATAR
British protectorate to 1971
Sheikdom
98.1

SAUDI ARABIA
Kingdom since 1932

UNITED ARAB EMIRATES
British protectorate (Trucial States) to 1971
Federation of emirates 1971–

Red Sea
Jedda
Mecca
Taif
261.2

5.1

Port Sudan
Suakin

OMAN
British protectorate to 1971
Sultanate

YEMEN ARAB REPUBLIC (NORTH)
Imamate until 1962
Republic 1962– (civil war 1962–69)
Merged with PDRY 1990

Salalah

ERITREA
Republic 1993–

Asmara · Massawa
Al Hudaydah
Sana
Taizz
Aden

4.0
YEMEN
Civil war 1994 when South attempted to secede
Al Mukalla

PEOPLE'S DEMOCRATIC REPUBLIC OF YEMEN (SOUTH)
British protectorate to 1967
Republic 1967
Merged with YAR 1990

1 THE MIDDLE EAST AND SURROUNDING REGION SINCE 1945

Source: Oxford Atlas of World History 1999

— Internationally recognized boundary
––– Disputed or defunct boundary
BAH Member of OPEC
––– Oil pipeline
(4.0) Proven oil reserves (billion barrels 1995)

Predominant religion:
Sunni Islam
Shiite Islam
Ibadhi Islam
Christianity
Judaism

PLATE 3   The Middle East and surrounding region since 1945

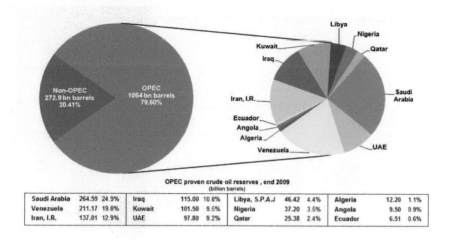

OPEC proven crude oil reserves, end 2009 (billion barrels)								
Saudi Arabia	264.59	24.9%	Iraq	115.00	10.8%	Libya, S.P.A.J	46.42	4.4%	Algeria	12.20	1.1%
Venezuela	211.17	19.8%	Kuwait	101.50	9.5%	Nigeria	37.20	3.5%	Angola	9.50	0.9%
Iran, I.R.	137.01	12.9%	UAE	97.80	9.2%	Qatar	25.38	2.4%	Ecuador	6.51	0.6%

PLATE 4 OPEC share of world crude oil reserves 2009

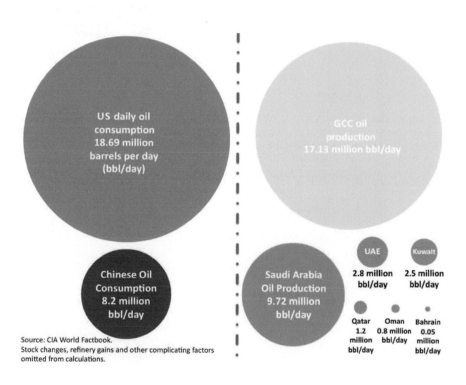

Source: CIA World Factbook.
Stock changes, refinery gains and other complicating factors omitted from calculations.

PLATE 5 Oil consumption and production

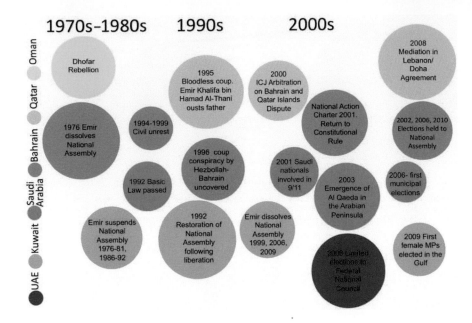

1970s–1980s   **1990s**   **2000s**

Oman

Dhofar Rebellion

Qatar

1995 Bloodless coup. Emir Khalifa bin Hamad Al-Thani ousts father

2000 ICJ Arbitration on Bahrain and Qatar Islands Dispute

2008 Mediation in Lebanon/ Doha Agreement

Bahrain

1976 Emir dissolves National Assembly

1994–1999 Civil unrest

1996 coup conspiracy by Hezbollah-Bahrain uncovered

National Action Charter 2001. Return to Constitutional Rule

2002, 2006, 2010 Elections held to National Assembly

1992 Basic Law passed

Saudi Arabia

2001 Saudi nationals involved in 9/11

2003 Emergence of Al Qaeda in the Arabian Peninsula

2006- first municipal elections

Kuwait

Emir suspends National Assembly 1976-81, 1986-92

1992 Restoration of National Assembly following liberation

Emir dissolves National Assembly 1999, 2006, 2009

UAE

2006 Limited elections to Federal National Council

2009 First female MPs elected in the Gulf

PLATE 6   GCC political conflict and reform

would be obliged to report to the Shura on their activity for the first time. The electorate was gradually expanded over the course of the next decade until 2003, when the first full elections were held under universal franchise. By the 2007 elections the Shura had 84 members who competed on the basis of names only, but were for the first time able to employ campaign techniques such as posters and advertisements. The Shura was complemented by the creation of the Majlis A'Dawla in 2000, as an upper, appointed body, although in contrast to Bahrain, the institution was broadly welcomed. This reflected the dynamics of change in each country – in Oman, the Shura had less to lose, but the Dawla also presented less of a direct threat to the elected lower house, being seen as a deliberative body to address issues of national importance rather than a competitor for decision-making power (Kechichian 2006: 55–6).

However, the powers of the Shura Council are effectively limited to economic matters. It cannot initiate legislation, has limited ability to comment on government bills and the key offices of state – which reside with the Sultan – such as defence and foreign affairs, remain beyond the purview of the institution. The turnout for elections has been relatively poor, at around 30 per cent, perhaps because, in the words of one author, the Shura resembles 'a depoliticised local council' (Rabi 2009: 216).

Although Oman's political development appears remarkably limited there are three important trends which are likely to determine the future course of representation in the Sultanate. First, the move towards greater representation came from the Sultan himself, who faced no obvious public pressure for such moves. According to Kechichian it was a recognition that emancipation would need to come at some stage, that it would not happen quickly and that it was better controlled by the Sultan, but 'that once such a step was initiated, it would be impossible to set the process back' (Kechichian 2006: 51). Progress may have been slow, but this controlled evolution has not been marked by the sorts of regressive and repressive steps taken in Kuwait and Bahrain – and there are few signs that it is likely to happen.

Second, Oman has one of the highest rates of population growth in the world, estimated at around 3.5 per cent a year. This presents a challenge on the political front as the political expectations of this younger generation, particularly those educated in the West, may outstrip the speed of reform in Oman (Rabi 2009: 217). But it also presents an economic challenge to the rentier model. Although oil is still the mainstay of its economy, accounting for around half of the country's GDP, its natural resources are far lower than its neighbours and the country has gone further in privatising and diversifying the economy.[9] But it is estimated that the number entering the job market each year will increase by 212 per cent by 2035 and that the economy will need to find 700,000 new jobs in that period (Kechichian 2006: 87). With structural unemployment estimated at somewhere between 12 per cent and 15 per cent, economic performance is likely to have a strong bearing on the politics of Oman in coming years.

Third, anticipating these difficulties may explain the form of 'atypical rentier' state that Sultan Qaboos has sought to create. In contrast to other Gulf states where the merchant elites were excluded from power, in Oman business interests ensured that the government did not swallow them up (Allen and Rigsbee 2000: 218) but were instead absorbed into the state's representative institutions. As Marc Valeri suggests, political liberalisation started 'as a means for the ruler to neutralise emerging socio-political forces by co-opting them into a game he controls, thereby recognising their existence without taking any political risks' (Valeri 2006: 202).

The Shura Council has thus played an important role in economic diversification in a way that is unusual in the Gulf, and the institution has extended that role since its inception in 1991. However, the limitations on the Shura Council's powers combined with the continuing absence of political parties means that elections are relatively meaningless, offering citizens only a choice between local dignitaries rather than competing visions of government. Given the economic pressures brewing in Oman, it is unlikely the Shura Council will provide a legitimising function for the regime or an outlet for social concerns in the future unless the pace of reform quickens.

Conclusion

As Lisa Anderson has noted, the analysis of 'Arab exceptionalism' in recent decades has been distorted by a disciplinary bias towards democracy, at times appearing to assume that democratisation is, ultimately, inevitable (Anderson 2006: 209). Several authors have compared the political development of some GCC countries to the evolution of Europe's nation-states into constitutional monarchies (e.g. Herb 2009b: 134–5) suggesting, implicitly, that the current phase is a transitional one from which a broader form of representative democracy will eventually flow.

Although there are signs that the political balance might be slowly shifting, political liberalisation in the Gulf remains a process of top-down, managed reform which preserves the power and position of the autocrats who rule these countries. At the turn of the twenty-first century the parliamentary institutions in Kuwait, Bahrain and Oman have undoubtedly progressed and extended their role, albeit in a slow and sometimes haphazard fashion. But all of them are struggling to find a distinctive role within their respective political systems. At present they have neither entirely convinced the public of the benefits that they bring, nor have they created a role in the administration of the state which gives them a unique and clear authority. That said, it is difficult to imagine any of those parliamentary institutions being abolished entirely. They were established to provide new sources of legitimacy for the regime and outlets for public concern or tension, and although that legitimising role is somewhat attenuated, without them those rulers would face increased difficulties in governing and managing internal tensions.

There are three factors worth highlighting from this brief analysis which will continue to have a bearing on the development of the parliaments in Kuwait, Bahrain and Oman. First the quality of parliamentary performance has much to do with the underdeveloped nature of political parties in the region. Political parties should provide the connective tissue that links government policy and the public, offer a distinct choice for voters at elections and form the basis for the organisation of parliamentary business. In practice, the fact that they are formally disallowed in each of the states means that they struggle to achieve any of these tasks well. Although de facto parties exist in Kuwait and Bahrain, they are mostly poorly organised and ill-disciplined in parliament. This, in turn, plays into the hands of the ruling autocrats. As Brumberg notes, the survival strategies for autocratic rulers are designed to prevent the emergence of any effective political society (Brumberg 2002: 64), allowing them to split the opposition and undermine the effectiveness of the parliamentary institution as a whole. In turn, this further weakens the claims of the parliament and the political blocs to political and public legitimacy. The dilemma is described by Ottoway and Hamzawy who conclude that across the Arab region 'opposition movements have not proven themselves able to capitalise on the regimes' need to burnish their democratic credentials to wrest concessions or enlarge the political space within which they are allowed to operate.' (Ottoway and Hamzawy 2009: 11).

Second, the presence of the Islamist movements is shaping the process of reform. The ruling regimes are playing on the fear of Islamist movements in each of these countries. In Kuwait and Bahrain, the rulers play the blocs off against each other, while in Oman two apparent challenges to Qaboos' regime were widely reported to have been inspired by Islamists (although this appears to have been exaggerated). Still, the Islamists appear to have been the main beneficiary of the process of political liberalisation in Kuwait and Bahrain. This stems partly from their extra-parliamentary activities, providing support and welfare services to the less affluent areas. But it also reflects their ability to provide an alternative vision of society. In liberalised autocracies, where to oppose the government is often conflated (deliberately by the regime) with opposing the state itself, the nuanced message of secular parties often gets lost. In short, Islamists provide the opposition. Yet, in all three countries none of these political movements is demanding a republic – they are all committed to working within the system to achieve greater political liberalisation under a constitutional monarchy (even the plotters in Oman). Indeed as Peterson has noted, they have shown how effective Islamist movements can be as forces for political reform in Bahrain and Kuwait (Peterson 2009: 183–5). They may thus continue to play an important role in the development of these parliamentary institutions.

Third, the legitimacy of these parliaments and their importance in governance will depend on the extent to which the private sector thinks they can represent their interests. The need for economic liberalisation is one of the most pressing domestic issues in all three countries. Yet the parliaments in each have had a marginal influence on the debate, due either to a preoccupation with preserving the rentier model, a focus on political battles at the expense of economic reform or simply because of their limited powers. Economic liberalisation will change the dynamics. It will alter the relationship between citizen and state and the traditional tight relationship between the bureaucratic and private sector middle class, which have both so far limited demands for democratisation. This could work for or against the extension of parliamentary power, but it will depend on how well the parliaments adapt to the demands by new groups for new sorts of representation.

As Ghassan Salame suggested in 1994, political liberalisation is not so much the result of the struggle for democracy than the end product of complex social phenomena (Salame 1994: 16). Political change in the Gulf region and across the Arab world in coming years will be determined not so much by arguments about forms of governance than by questions of identity, religious and ethnic politics, economic development and the dynamics of the rentier state (Anderson 2006: 209). The role of parliaments in each of these countries will depend less on their ability to secure more formal power for themselves than on the way they use those powers – and the role they play in shaping each of those key debates.

Notes

1. The terms 'parliament' or 'parliamentary institution' are used as generic terms throughout to cover the range of national representative, legislative and consultative bodies that exist within the region. A distinction is made between the *Majlis A'Shura* and *Majlis Al-Nuwab* later in the chapter.
2. International Institute for Strategic Studies, *Strategic Comments: Kuwait – Signs of Revival*, July 2010.
3. Ibid.
4. Bertelsmann Transformation Index, 2010, Bahrain Country Report.
5. 'Crackdown in Bahrain Hints of End to Reforms', *New York Times*, 26 August 2010.
6. 'Shut Up the Shias', *The Economist*, 9 September 2010.
7. 'Preventing the Director of the NDI from Entering Bahrain', Bahrain Centre for Human Rights, 12 May 2010.
8. BTI, op cit., p. 19.
9. 'Analysis: Oman racing against time with depleting oil reserves' *Business Intelligence Middle East*, 12 November 2008.

References

Abdelkarim, A. (ed.) (1999) *Change and Development in the Gulf*. Basingstoke: Macmillan.
Allen, C. and Rigsbee, W.L. (2000) *Oman Under Qaboos: From Coup to Constitution 1970–1996*. London: Frank Cass.
Anderson, L. (2006) 'Searching where the light shines: studying democratisation in the Middle East', *Annual Review of Political Science*, 9: 189–214.
Brown, N.J. (2007) *Pushing Towards Party Politics? Kuwait's Islamic Constitutional Movement*, Carnegie Endowment for International Peace, Middle East Series, Number 79,

January.

Brumberg, D. (2002) 'Democratisation in the Arab World? The trap of liberalised autocracy', *Journal of Democracy*, 13(4): 56–68.

Brumberg, D. (2003) *Liberalisation Versus Democracy: Understanding Arab Political Reform*, Carnegie Endowment for International Peace Working Papers, Number 37, May.

Crystal, J. (1989) 'Coalitions in oil monarchies: Kuwait and Qatar', *Comparative Politics*, 21(4): 427–43.

Crystal, J. (2009) 'Economic and political liberalisation: views from the business community', in J. Teitelbaum (ed.), *Political Liberalisation in the Persian Gulf*. New York: Columbia University Press.

Diamond, L. (2010) 'Why are there no Arab democracies?', *Journal of Democracy*, 21(1): 93–104.

Diamond, L., Plattner, M.F. and Brumberg, D. (eds) (2003) *Islam and Democracy in the Middle East*. Baltimore, MD: Johns Hopkins University Press.

Ehteshami, A. (2003) 'Reform from above: the politics of participation in the oil monarchies', *International Affairs*, 79(1): 53–75.

Ehteshami, A. and Wright, S. (2007) 'Political Change in the Arab Oil Monarchies: From liberalisation to enfranchisement', *International Affairs*, 83(5): 913–32.

Herb, M. (2002) 'Emirs and parliaments in the Gulf', *Journal of Democracy*, 13(4): 41–7.

Herb, M. (2009a) 'A nation of bureaucrats: political participation and economic diversification in Kuwait and the United Arab Emirates', *International Journal of Middle East Studies*, 41: 375–95.

Herb, M. (2009b) 'Kuwait: the obstacle of parliamentary politics', J. Teitelbaum (ed.), *Political Liberalisation in the Persian Gulf*. New York: Columbia University Press.

Huntington, S.P. (1993) *The Third Wave: Democratisation in the Late Twentieth Century*. Norman, OK: University of Oklahoma Press.

Ibrahim, H.T. (2006) *Political Reform in the Gulf Co-operation Council States*. Dubai: Gulf Research Centre.

International Crisis Group (2005) *Bahrain's Sectarian Challenge*, Middle East Report No. 40. Brussels: ICG.

Jones, J. (2007) *Negotiating Change: The New Politics of the Middle East*. London: I.B. Tauris.

Jones, J. and Ridout, N. (2005) 'Democratic development in Oman', *Middle East Journal*, 59(3): 376–92.

Katz, M.N. (2004) 'Assessing the political stability of Oman', *Middle East Review of International Affairs*, 8(3): 1–10.

Katzman, K. (2010) *Bahrain: Reform, Security and U.S. Policy*. Washington: Congressional Research Service.

Kechichian, J.A. (2005) *Political Participation and Stability in the Sultanate of Oman*. Dubai: Gulf Research Centre.

Khalaf, A. (2008) *The Outcome of a Ten-Year Process of Political Reform in Bahrain*, Arab Reform Brief No. 24. Dubai: Gulf Research Centre.

Khalaf, A. and Luciani, G. (2006) *Constitutional Reform and Political Participation in the Gulf*. Dubai: Gulf Research Centre.

Lawson, F.H. (2010) 'Bahrain', *Freedom House: Countries at the Crossroads*, on line at: http://www.freedomhouse.org/template.cfm?page=140&edition=9&ccrpage=43&ccrcountry=177 (accessed 11 August 2011).

Ottaway, M. and Hamzawy, A. (2009) *Getting to Pluralism: Political Actors in the Arab World*. Washington, DC: Carnegie Endowment for International Peace.

Peterson, J.E. (2002) 'Bahrain's first steps towards reform under Amir Hamad', *Asian Affairs*, February.

Peterson, J.E. (2004) 'Oman: Three and a Half Decades of Change and Development', *Middle East Policy*, XI(2): 125-37.

Peterson, J.E. (2005) *The Emergence of Post-Traditional Oman*, Durham Middle East Papers – Sir William Luce Publication Series, Paper No. 5. University of Durham.

Peterson, J.E. (2006) *The Arab Gulf States: Further Steps Towards Political Participation.* Dubai: Gulf Research Centre.

Peterson, J.E. (2009) 'Bahrain: Reform, promise and reality' in J. Teitelbaum (ed.), *Political Liberalisation in the Persian Gulf.* New York: Columbia University Press.

Rabi, U. (2002) 'Majlis A'Shura and Majlis al-Dawla: weaving old practices and new realities on the process of state formation in Oman', *Middle Eastern Studies*, 38(4): 41–50.

Rabi, U. (2009) 'Oman: say yes to Oman, say no to the tribe!' in J. Teitelbaum (ed.), *Political Liberalisation in the Persian Gulf.* New York: Columbia University Press.

Salame, G. (1994) *Democracy Without Democrats: The Renewal of Politics in the Muslim World.* London: I.B. Tauris.

Salem, P. (2007) *Kuwait: Politics in a Participatory Emirate*, Carnegie Papers No. 3. Carnegie Middle East Centre, Carnegie Endowment for International Peace, June.

Siegfried, N.A. (2000) 'Legislation and legitimisation in Oman: the basic law', *Islamic Law and Society*, 7(2): 359–96.

Teitelbaum, J. (ed.) (2009) *Political Liberalisation in the Persian Gulf.* New York: Columbia University Press.

Valeri, M. (2006) 'Liberalisation from above: political reforms and sultanism in Oman', in A. Khalaf and G. Luciani (eds). *Constitutional Reform and Political Participation in the Gulf*, Dubai: Gulf Research Centre.

Waterbury, J. (1994) 'Democracy without democrats? The potential for political liberalisation in the Middle East', in G. Salame (ed.), *Democracy Without Democrats: The Renewal of Politics in the Muslim World.* London: I.B. Tauris.

Wright, S. (2006) *Generational Change and Elite-Driven Reforms in the Kingdom of Bahrain*, Durham Middle East Papers No. 7 – Sir William Luce Publication Series. University of Durham.

2

NATIONALISM IN THE GULF STATES

Neil Partrick

Introduction

The ruling elites of the independent states that make up the Gulf Cooperation Council (GCC), the six-member association of countries founded in 1981, are paying increasing attention to *haweeya al-watani* (national identity) and *turath* (heritage) within their countries. However, the concept of nation in the Gulf Arab countries is underdeveloped to the extent that the emergent public debate about ways to protect national identity has not yet defined what is meant by 'national'. According to one UAE academic, 'The national identity assertion doesn't mean Emirati identity so much as indigenous identity, being from this area, [being one of] the indigenous people' (al-Kitbi 2008).

In the current context of internal disquiet about foreign population numbers, Iran's rising regional prominence and sectarian sensitivities within some GCC states, 'national' identity is increasingly being employed as a state-building tool. However, steps to boost national identity do not necessarily create coherent national communities. As the state-led reinvention of national tradition is stepped up, usually without reference to disparate and sometimes disputatious groups, inclusion is not being felt across the national communities. While progress has arguably been made in some GCC states in at least addressing the limitations to national coherence, nationalism in the Gulf remains a highly contested notion, liable to promote as much as conceal national division.

This chapter will argue that a narrow conception of the nation predominates in Gulf Arab countries in which sub-state tribal and sectarian fealties are strong and loyalties to a larger national entity beyond the state are lacking. As such the state is a vehicle for narrow, pre-state, interests that command allegiance on the basis of sectional rather than national loyalties. Thus the debate on national identity obscures some very different conceptions of belonging above and beyond a shared sense of threat from those who for the most part do not claim national membership.

While the GCC states are the principal political communities within the area, what it means to be a member of these national communities remains unclear. The national identity debate does not reflect a struggle for national self-determination as seen in other parts of the Middle East, nor the national chauvinism and expansionism associated with some European nations in the nineteenth and twentieth centuries. In the modern state era, these countries do not seek territorial aggrandisement, although there are residual territorial sensitivities between some GCC states, ongoing fears of Iran and a historic wariness of Saudi Arabia. Kuwaiti nationalism, long fed by fears of Iraq (Partrick 2006), deepened after the state was effectively extinguished in 1990–1. However, the Gulf Arab states tend not to construct their national identity in hostility to a neighbour, nor have increased external fears united these relatively disparate polities.

Nationalism is a word avoided by those leading the identity debate in the GCC states. Findlow cites the UAE as an example of states that do not fit the 'defined by the other' assumption of traditional notions of nationalism (Findlow 2000). She argues that UAE nationalism represents a 'positive turning inward' as opposed to a 'negative turning outward' (ibid. 16). However, this turning inward throughout the GCC states can include a nationalism expressed in the 'ethno politics' (Longva 2006) of chauvinism toward non-national residents and even fellow nationals judged inadequate by the 'blue blooded' standards of the 'in' community within the nation. (In the Kuwaiti context this can include contempt for the relatively newly naturalised tribes on the part of members of the old urban merchant elite, who themselves were drawn from leading Kuwaiti tribes.)

The image of the nation presented by various state heritage projects since the 1980s has yet to be superseded by a debate that has properly addressed the histories of those sub-communities whose identity is not part of the 're-imagined tradition' of the state. The 'National Dialogue' launched by King Abdallah in 2003 notably attempted to 're-imagine' tradition (Hobsbawm and Ranger 1992) by projecting a new image of Saudi Arabia as inclusive of its different communities. The 'Saudi national' debate, however, has since reached the limits of both political symbolism and the actual basis of power in the country, which prevents too profound a challenge to the internal al-Saud partnership with the clerics.

More widely in the GCC, a national identity debate has been sparked by acute socio-economic concerns about demographic imbalances and existential concerns among a number of Gulf leaders about the internal and regional influence of Iran. While economic downturns periodically ease demographic imbalances, rentier politics and the expansion of the service sector economy in many of these states means that population trends are unlikely to fundamentally change. However, periodic downturns also emphasise political vulnerabilities among rulers who forged a social contract in the oil era through which political acquiescence among nationals was rewarded with social and economic security. At present, with the partial exception of Bahrain, there is limited evidence that this acquiescence is under particular strain. However, national cultural and related regional political sensitivities are likely to remain.

Defining what constitutes the nation presents a number of difficulties related to the historical trajectories and the manner in which each of the different Gulf states arrived at independence. One of Saudi Arabia's founding national myths, for example, is what the Saudi state officially describes as the 'freeing' of Riyadh in 1902, after the symbolic wresting of control of the Masmak fortress (Al-Rasheed 2004: 186). This victory, secured for the al-Saud by *muwahiddun* (unitarian), or so-called 'Wahhabi'[1] fighters, was understood as that of a religious cause and was not conceived as the liberation of a newly born nation. Port cities such as Kuwait, Abu Dhabi, Bahrain, Qatar and Dubai had an identity and distinctiveness underlined by the protection, however imperfect, given by Britain to the ruling sheikhs from potential *muwahiddun* invasion. The consolidation of control over territorial space that local ruling families had begun on the southern shore of the Gulf in the eighteenth and nineteenth centuries also helped to identify the people of these territories with the land (Crystal 1990: 20). Tribal sheikhs in the pre-oil and early oil era had shown wavering loyalties at a time when a ruler sought to use external British protection to aid internal territorial consolidation (Onley and Khalaf 2006). By the time of independent statehood most occupants of these lands had developed identifications with both the ruling sheikh and the territory over which he sought authority, therefore placing the ruling family at the heart of the emergent state-building project. This developing awareness of belonging to a defined physical territory under a local leadership created nascent nations, albeit nations whose identity was problematically bound up with one family.

Saudi Arabia

In common with many states, the Saudi leadership has partly defined the Saudi state in terms of what its founders were opposed to. There was opposition to both the Ottomans and their Arabian allies, and later to British attempts to constrain al-Saud power in the Peninsula. Despite the successful unification of the Hijaz, Asir and Eastern Province under the al-Saud, distinct regional traditions are maintained, with sometimes sharply contrasting social norms (Yamani 2004). Arguably the more important battles of Arabia cannot be commemorated even in the cautious manner of the marking of the 'freeing' of Riyadh because Saudi rule is viewed in some parts of the country as essentially 'Najdi' (Al-Rasheed 2004: 195). Furthermore, heroic victories on the battlefield are not presented in the official historiography as the bloody birth pains of the new Saudi nation, even if some 'pre-state' poetic references expressed the determination to defend the *watan* (nation or country) (al-Dakheel 2009).

The Saudi National Museum in Riyadh presents the expansion of the Kingdom at the expense of other local leaders' territories, as the growth of Islamic belief and in particular of *tawhid*: unity of God. The unification of territory and of peoples, and the expunging of 'polytheistic' belief and practice, is presented as an emancipatory act for Islam, not for the Saudi nation. The partnership between the *muwahiddun* and the Al-Saud is portrayed as the marriage of religious reform and of religiously sanctioned leadership. The clerics are what Sami Zubaida has called 'main legislators' (2003) in that they control the process of *ijtihad* (interpretation) of religious law and therefore need to sign off any government policy innovations that could be interpreted as having Islamic implications.

The religious mission in Saudi Arabia is officially presented as something akin to nation-building in that the Islamically unacceptable *fitna* (lawlessness) wrought by tribal division is supposedly overcome by the unifying effect of restoring 'correct' practice under religiously sanctioned leadership. Religion's contradiction of national imagining, however, lies in the limits it can sometimes put on the nation as an inclusive community. While a Gulf Arab state's imagining of nationals as well as the nation will usually ignore issues that may divide the national community by sub-group (Khalaf 2008: 66), Saudi Arabia's highly conservative Sunni *ulema* (clerics) effectively define who is a member of 'in' and 'out' groups in the Saudi state, helping to prioritise the Sunni sect at the expense of the Shia, and the conservative Najdi tradition over that of other regions, thereby undermining the effectiveness of a state-led conception of the nation.

According to Saudi analyst Turki al-Rasheed, 'Any ruler will use two swords – the sword of religion and of tribalism' (al-Rasheed 2009). However, religion in Saudi Arabia undermines the building of a coherent national community by representing a parallel loyalty to that of the nation and by legitimising the leadership of the state rather than the importance of the state per se. To Saudi academic Khalid al-Dakheel '. . . the notion of religion [as an identifier] tends to dilute the nationhood identity [within the] realm of the state' (2009). So much so that the commemoration of the seizing of the Masmak fortress in Riyadh from the al-Rasheed tribe, which was marked very publicly outside the Kingdom in 1991 as a pivotal national event, was a low-key internal affair due to the judgment by the senior *ulema* that only the Islamic festivals of Eid al-Fitra and Eid al-Adha should be celebrated. The founding of the modern kingdom in 1932 only became a public holiday as recently as September 2005, indicative of an incipient, state-led, Saudi nationalism liable to continue to struggle to downplay the importance of contradictory, non-state forces.

While the state is constrained in marshalling national sentiment, religion is used to bolster the authority of the royal family. The location of the *haramain* (Mecca and Medina) within the territory of the state is an important part of this legitimacy as is the emphasis on the title *khadim al-haramain* (custodian of the two holy places). Repeating a quote attributed to Ibn Saud, the former Saudi judge al-Gassim observes that, 'Religion is like the falcon, he who captures it will hunt with it' (al-Gassim 2007). However, al-Dakheel draws a distinction between the expansionary religious mission of the *muwahiddun* and the statecraft of Ibn Saud who helped to fix the idea of the Saudi state within defined territories by making agreements with neighbouring states at the behest of the British. Through this process Ibn Saud also crushed what al-Dakheel presents as a challenge to state authority, the 1926–9 'Ikhwan' revolt of two key tribes. Had their demands for political power and financial reward for their role in the *muwahiddun* been accommodated, the authority of the nascent Kingdom would have been weakened. Facing down their challenge represented the victory of an alliance that bound together the al-Saud family, loyal tribes and religious fighters.

Loyalty in the Kingdom today, argues al-Dakheel, is to the Saudi state or to a tribal sheikh and not to the royal family. A sense of nationhood within Saudi Arabia and all the GCC states has been bolstered by the relative neutrality of the state's welfare provision and by the state's increasing 'imagining' of national tradition. However, the identity of the state and loyalty to it remains bound up with the identity of, and loyalty to, the ruling family. According to Turki al-Rasheed, in Saudi Arabia and the wider region 'loyalty [is] to the person and not to the state; this is the major weak point' (2009). This is exemplified by Ibn Saud's practice of extending support from key tribes, including those drawn from the country's disparate regions, through repeated marriages to the daughters of senior tribal elders, while retaining the option of divorce as a tool of alliance building (Al-Rasheed 2004).

Tribal solidarity

In the Gulf Arab states of today, tribes are still central to national leadership and are presented by that leadership as part of the national construct. In fact the leaderships within the Gulf are the dominant families of ruling tribes that emerged in the struggle for authority in the pre-independence phase or, in the Saudi case, a ruling family aligned with powerful, religiously inspired, warriors.[2] The de facto al-Saud partnership with the 'religious establishment' means that the latter have their own 'sub-state' interests as senior clerics with a political and economic relationship to the state.

In the Saudi state, and the smaller Gulf states, ministries are used as patronage networks, with tribal configurations sometimes repeated in official guises. Authority in Gulf Arab societies – pre- and post-independence – needed financial credibility to underscore the effectiveness of its practice of *asabiyya* (solidarity). 'Rent' was therefore as much a feature of pre-state leadership as it is a key characteristic of the mostly energy-rich Gulf Arab states of today. So, rather than nationally integrated bodies, the Gulf Arab states emerged with new structures that replicated the old tribe and kinship basis of authority. Van der Meulen cites the example in Saudi Arabia of a new 'state class' that, like the private sector, would distribute largesse on the old tribal basis (1997: 64–5).

Although the state is often used by tribal as well as other sub-national leaders to enhance their own patronage powers, the tribe is seen by some as more reliable than the state. Turki al-Rasheed says there is an attitude of 'I go back to the tribe because I feel more secure – it will secure me more than a country or civil society' (Al-Rasheed, 2009). Sectarian identities can also be enhanced when the state struggles to meet expectations, as reflected in the sense of economic injustice motivating Shia oppositionists in Saudi Arabia and Bahrain,[3] for example. Attempts to constrain aspects of the social contract at times of economic duress have in the past been popularly resisted in Saudi Arabia,[4] suggesting that a sustained challenge to a Gulf state's patronage capabilities could test national coherence and further deepen different sub-national identities.

Tribalism in the smaller Gulf states

Unlike Saudi Arabia, the use of tribal authority in the smaller Gulf states is combined with a relatively light Islamic touch. Carefully managed religious leaderships sanction the authority of the rulers who do not overtly draw on religious legitimation (Van der Meulen 1997). Underpinning this maintenance of *asabiyya* is the use of state machinery to selectively disburse patronage to maintain alliances based on family, tribe and region. The politics of patron–client relations exist alongside the formally neutral role of the stage. In Abu Dhabi in the late 1960s the Zaab tribe were added to the Al-Nahyan's circle of allies, lending their name to a district in the city and taking up a significant number of foreign ministry jobs, having previously been loyal to, and located in, Ras al-Khaimah, an emirate ruled by a branch of the al-Qassimi. The Shehi tribe originated in the Omani Musandam Peninsula but have acquired Emirati nationality in recent years, and many have settled in neighbouring Ras al-Khaimah.

In the Sultanate of Oman a neo-traditional,[5] or perhaps 'neo-tribal', state is still in evidence where tribal sheikhs, even lower-level sheikhs, are appointed by the Sultan. While Oman and its neighbours are not wholly traditional entities, the incorporation, management and even direct intervention in the affairs of tribes as one of the tools of a (state) leader's rule suggests that this is less nation-building statecraft than pre-state style 'sheikh-craft' in, what Tibi would call, a state guise. According to an Omani academic, this is about 'manipulating old traditional leaders and behaviour in a political way. [The state] looks modern but deep down it's traditional' (Omani academic 2008).

These examples suggest that what is being publicly imagined by the state as a national community is operating under a non-invented tradition of leadership that has transferred itself to the state, whereby the means of patronage and influence can be operated with more sophistication than at the pre-state tribal level.

Arab nationalism

Arab nationalism as a construct still has some residual force in the region. In the Gulf Arab state context this is expressed in the language of unity (*wahda*), which is ambiguous enough usually to allow policies of solidarity with Palestine and other symbols of Arab brotherhood to suffice. However, this is tested when regional divisions in recent years have helped to fracture the Palestinians, making the expression of solidarity problematic for foreign Arab governments.

In the past, ideational delegitimisation in the form of Arab nationalist criticism could come from within and without although largely took the form of nationalist propaganda attacks from Iraq. This only accentuated the importance of a legitimate local identity bound up in the two established factors of local rule: *asabiyya* and Islam. The latter became more important, however, with the growth of political Islam, a construct that re-imagined the Islamic past to proffer an alternative political future based on new political structures (Tibi 1990: 118) that seemingly would have no place for the ruling sheikhs. Saudi Arabia was better placed to try to cope with this tide, although all Gulf countries asserted a more conservative domestic order in response.

Islam and the national polity

As elsewhere in the Arab world, Islamists had been promoted in public life in a number of the Gulf states in the 1970s in response to changing regional politics and in order to counterbalance ongoing pressure from leftists and Arab nationalists. Following the Iranian Revolution it appeared more risky to be giving domestic Islamists a public role that effectively helped to legitimise ideas that would, at minimum, reorder the state. However, it was assumed that the public engagement of Islamists by inclusion in the Kuwaiti parliament, for example, and as officials in the *awqaf* (Islamic affairs), education and justice ministries in the UAE, would incorporate them both politically and, by extension, aid the state in its projection of a conservative and Islamic image. For most Gulf Arab leaders, a correct Islamic image, at least, was and continues to be promoted while the substance is largely resisted.

Islam is plainly not exclusive to the national culture of any one Gulf Arab state, despite the impression created at the Saudi National Museum. The GCC states, collectively and individually, all emphasise Islamic fealty in policy statements and public projects, and all have emphasised Islam as part of the recent focus on national identity. States have also been anxious to ensure that a 'government-friendly' Islam is nurtured through control of Friday sermons, and there has been a growth of public broadcast Quran recitation contests in the UAE.

Bedouin exclusiveness

One of the difficulties for the GCC countries in their efforts to strengthen national identity is that they remain wedded to a selective re-imagining of the past that emphasises a tribal identity. Efforts within the UAE during its 'Year of National Identity' in 2008 included the construction of bedouin-style tents in the airports of a number of the separate emirates that provided traditional style hospitality. Sensitivities over the impact of large-scale immigration into the

UAE have encouraged an emphasis on chronicling oral history and educating both nationals and non-nationals about the traditions of the country. The heritage industry is now thriving throughout the GCC, with a state funding boom in recent years that, in some cases, has literally reconstructed old *souq* areas in order to provide nationals as well as visitors with a connection to a re-imagined past. Although this reconstruction is often selective and avoids explicit references to differences within the nation, it does not prevent the communication of the preferred version of local history. For example, the Arabian bedouin desert traditions extensively on show in the UAE's heritage areas do not have much to say to the large proportion of the Dubai population whose forefathers originated in Iran and among whom speaking Persian at home is not uncommon (nor is it among other *hawala* ('returnees') or so-called *ajam* (or 'Persian') communities in the Gulf).[6] In the context of growing fears about Iran this is not unsurprising, but this has long been common practice in the GCC, and emphasises what is generally a difficulty about publicly embracing internal aspects of a country's past that do not fit with the preferred national identity projected by its leadership.

Tribe and federation

This emphasis on a bedouin-style cultural past, even though nationals are overwhelmingly part of settled communities, is interesting given the importance of tribal alliances that remain important features of the authority of local emirate rulers within the UAE. This, in turn, underscores the separate identity and history of the individual emirates for which the notion of the wider Emirati nation is a construct with a short-lived history by definition. It was said of the UAE in 1979 that 'political loyalty to one's tribe has not as yet given way to loyalty to the state as an abstract political concept' (Khalifa 1979: 99). That the state is made even more abstract by being made up of seven emirates in an ambiguous and ill-defined relationship with each other plainly does not help. Emirati academic Abdulkhaleq Abdulla asserted in 2008, 'To the credit of the [UAE] state, they managed to make an Emirati identity the overriding identity' (Abdulla interview 2008). National Day in the UAE is celebrated with growing popular enthusiasm – in contrast to the more muted atmosphere seen in Bahrain, for example. However, Abdulla and other Emirati nationals concede that 'localism' has been on the rise throughout the UAE. The extent of Abu Dhabi financial support through formal and informal support for other emirates suggests that localism may be coming to an end. However, Dubai is unlikely to radically alter its external relations and comparatively open economic platform, not least for Iran. A federation that could only agree on a loose association after very drawn out constitutional deliberations, and which to this day is managed more by informal cooperation based on mutual interest than institutional development, seems unlikely to cohere too deeply.

Tribe and state

The importance attached to tribe within a number of the GCC states permeates those for whom tribal practice is also a less vivid part of their lives than for their forefathers. Qatar and UAE national students, for example, emphasise the importance of tribe as something long-standing.[7] By contrast, national identity is much more contemporary and correspondingly can seem less significant Exasperation with the importance given to tribe as one of several sub-state identities can often be found among Gulf intellectuals keen to disassociate their country from the backward image that, for some, tribe suggests. However, it is also acknowledged that state weakness in the Gulf and, more widely, in the Arab world reflects the difference between an 'elite' who form part of the inner circle and are, therefore, protected and consequently 'champion the national cause', and those who are outside and therefore see themselves more in terms of family or tribe. This is not loyalty to the state but to the sheikh (Qatari academic 2008). Lawtaya argues that in Oman '. . . there are different loyalties to that of the state: everybody knows this is [an] inhibiting force in the evolution of society' (Lawtaya 2008).

Citizenship

The founding of the state in the Gulf, argues al-Najjar, is, as yet, an 'incomplete process', where the notion of equal and active citizenship is not fully understood. Citizenship is not 'established in the practice of the state nor in the attitude and practices of the people' (al-Najjar 2008). This official conception of *muwatina* (citizenship) is therefore indistinguishable from *jinsia* (nationality) and promotes what officially speaking is an inclusive notion of national community that contradicts officially sanctioned inequalities in citizenship.

Even when the territorial boundaries are largely concurrent with the 'nation', the idea of a national community can be a problematic concept when issues of defining and equally applying nationality enter the equation. While some notions of nationalism, including what became the dominant Arab nationalist discourse, can be ethnically exclusive and inherently anti-democratic (Tibi 1997), the national imaginings of individual Gulf Arab states promote an inclusive agenda, at least among those who hold nationality. However, holding the *jinsia* of a given country does not necessarily translate into being a full 'citizen', and even where it does there are concerns about equality in terms of political and economic opportunities. In Qatar there are effectively two classes of citizenship. So-called 'naturalised' Qataris, representing an estimated two-thirds of the population, are judged to have settled in the country since 1930. They differ from so-called 'native' Qataris in that they have no automatic right to be candidates or to vote in municipal or potentially national legislative elections. Classifying the majority of the population as effectively second class reflects the state leadership's distrust of many of its 'citizens'. Specifically it excludes a perceptibly errant tribe, the al-Murra, some of whom were willing to work with Saudi Arabia in a 1996 plot to restore the former Qatari ruler Sheikh Khalifa, who had been overthrown by his son, the current Qatari ruler Hamed, in 1995. More significant in numerical terms, the 1930 cut-off also ensures that a number of those thought of as 'Persian' are excluded from a stronger voice in national affairs.

'Persians', or so-called *ajam* in the Gulf states, can, in some popular referencing, include *hawala* or 'returning' Sunni Arabs, some of whom went to Iran in search of work four and five generations previously. Others are ethnically Persian. This separate but apparently equal factor applies in the UAE where most national passport holders enjoy a full and undifferentiated national status. However, only a small proportion can vote in elections to the UAE's consultative body, the Federal National Council. Furthermore a significant minority throughout the GCC states are either not in possession of the full entitlements of nationals, frequently those referred to as *ajam*, or are *bidoon* (literally 'without', i.e. stateless). The latter can represent anywhere between 1 and 10 per cent of the national populations of GCC countries, and are usually descendents of those who in the twentieth century emigrated from neighbouring countries. In the Kuwaiti case, the *bidoon* issue overlaps with historic sensitivities about Iraqi influence inside the emirate, with many who continue to be denied Kuwaiti nationality believed to have originated from Iraq.

There are major sensitivities around the issue of belonging, even among those with full nationality. These sensitivities often revolve around whether certain groups are considered to be what one Emirati thinker termed the 'pure Arab thoroughbred stallion' (al-Qassimi 2008). The issue of national belonging is plainly being distorted by these other perceptions of belonging, while legal measures effectively enforcing inequality suggest that the state itself is not based on a conception of national inclusion. This legal and perceptual problem is particularly controversial in Bahrain. Political polarisation prevents common legal norms, and procedures for the operation of family law (Toumi 2009), periodic violence involving those Shia highly critical of the reform process and occasional arrests of figures alleged to be involved in plots against the government make it difficult to talk of a coherent national community, let alone a nationalism that reflects and/or entrenches a common identity. The Kuwaiti national identity suffers from a comparable if less starkly polarising dynamic with the estimated one-third plus of its population who are Shia periodically having their loyalty questioned by sections of the Sunni majority.

Whose tradition is being imagined?

In Bahrain the national image in the media and education on the one hand papers over the country's diverse traditions by talking of one community (former official, Ministry of Education 2008). On the other hand the official national heritage revival, as represented at the Bahrain National Museum, stresses the importance of pearling to the country's origins. However, many of the indigenous Shia of Bahrain (*Baharna*) did not engage in pearling, and agriculture, which they were more liable to have conducted, is ignored (Louer 2008). Official Bahraini renovation projects emphasise both historic settlement and the country's more contemporary culture where the role of elite, Sunni and often ruling family figures are highlighted (Nawwab 2008).

In Kuwait pearling is also central to the imagining of national identity (Khalaf 2008) and is also relatively exclusive, effectively cutting out the bedouin who were not present in the country when the pearling industry was at its height. Subsequent nationality reforms made it easier to incorporate the bedouin into the ruling family's internal political balancing. However, the 1920 cut-off year that defines a 'native' Kuwaiti can be problematic for *bedu* Kuwaitis, who in any case are seen less favourably by those *hadharis* (settled) who contributed that year to a key national myth: the Battle of Jahra, when Saudi Wahhabi fighters were repelled with the aid of the British. The *hadhari*s include a number of the Kuwaiti Shia, however, helping their assertion of being an in-group. Kuwait's politics of descent parallels official differences in citizenship in Qatar and elsewhere in the GCC, creating what Longva argues is a 'civic ethnocracy' in which there is a societal downgrading of those nationals without pure descent. (Longva 2006: 119). This politics of descent also feeds into the non-nationality of an estimated 100,000 Kuwaiti *bidoon*, who are 'without' Kuwaiti (or any other) nationality. While Gulf states manipulate the sense of difference among *hadhari* and *bedu*, the extent to which there are also common entitlements has led Longva to argue that, in the case of Kuwait at least, there is 'a nationalisation of tribe, rather than the tribalisation of the nation' (Longva 2006: 181). Indicative of the common entitlements that can create state loyalty, in Kuwait and the UAE, for example, there are financial incentives for a national male to marry another national as his first wife. Such intra-national marriage is further encouraged by the patriarchal feature of denying nationality to the children of a national woman who marries a non-national. Set against the 'nationalisation' thesis is the evident selective patronage of tribe throughout the Gulf, and the limits to welfare-generated loyalty shown at previous periods of fiscal stress (ibid.).

Political reform and national inclusion

Legislative bodies could theoretically assist the state's ability to embody national identity, providing perhaps an institutional strength in the face of other non-state identities such as religion or tribe. However, they tend to function as a platform for sub-state interests. The dominant role of tribal representatives in the Kuwaiti parliament, for example, emphasises how it has changed from being a platform for institutionalising the authority of senior merchants to promoting the tribal allies of the ruling al-Sabah family. With the exception of Saudi Arabia, all the other GCC countries have moved over the last decade or so toward setting up partly elected legislative bodies. However, their powers are relatively limited, ranging from a solely consultative role (UAE) to a constrained legislative role (Oman, Bahrain). Saudi Arabia responded to the very divergent pressures within and without the Kingdom after the 1991 Gulf War by taking, from the *ulema*'s perspective, controversial steps to effectively constitutionalise the powers of the al-Saud, the authority of Islam and Islamic law (and therefore of the clerics themselves), and the newly proposed *majlis al-shoura* (consultative council). The *majlis* draws in the Wahhabi religious establishment and the relatively liberal business and academic elites, but only by appointment, and it remains a purely consultative body. With limitations on both electoral participation and authority, the importance of these legislative bodies as 'national' institutions is in doubt.

Shia exclusion

The Saudi religious establishment's position as a major stakeholder in the Saudi political system has a direct correlation with the relatively disempowered position of the Shia. A number of influential Shia leaders, both clerical and non-clerical, returned in the 1990s after being exiled in Iran and the UK in the 1980s. From the vantage point of relative political exclusion, they proved themselves more willing than many of the majority Saudi Sunni community to open up the debate about how a more meaningful notion of *watan* – homeland or nation – could be constructed. Some leading Saudi Shia thinkers argued that citizenship is not simply about being a national but implies rights as well as responsibilities (Ibrahim 2006: 223–5). This has implications for whether sovereignty is vested in the monarch or, at least partly, in the nationals, ultimately affecting what is meant by 'nation'. If the idea of nation is inherently bound up in that of the al-Saud ruling family and their (pre-state) alliances, then this is not a nation-state that embodies national culture and identity.

These arguments appear to confine the previous Saudi Shia Islamist conceptions of many such activists to the history books. For example, a separation of mosque and state is envisaged by these Saudi Shia for all Saudi citizens, made perhaps more feasible by the demand that the focus of Shia religious loyalty (*marja'*) be allowed by the Saudi state authorities to be within state boundaries rather than in Najaf or Qom (Saudi Shia political leader 2007). In the Saudi leadership and among some Saudi Sunnis there remain high levels of distrust of the Shia minority and a tendency to see local incidents through the prism of regional tensions.

Inward-facing chauvinism

The growth of identity politics generally, including that seen in emergent nation-states worldwide, is, argue some, related to the impact of globalisation. This suggests that globalisation does not so much threaten national identity as facilitate the communication of a variety of identities, among which national identity, enjoying the everyday 'banal' advantages of public media and constant repetition, is able to fend rather well (Tomlinson 2003: 270–5). The 'inward-facing' nationalism identifiable in the GCC states is not inclusive as 'national' identity is partly measured against internal demographic 'threats'; however, this chauvinism is not defined outwardly against other nations. This can be related to the fact that they do not have what Emirati writer Mishaal Gergawi calls the 'colonial baggage' of some Arab states (Sharjah Museums Department 2008). However, a significant part of the current UAE drive to deepen awareness of national identity is caused by population inflows without a correspondingly 'inwardly' defined sense of what national culture, and therefore the nation, actually is. The director of Sharjah Museums Department, Manal Attiyah, has urged the government to connect museums with schools and universities in order, as she revealingly puts it, 'to create a collective memory' (ibid.).

It does, at least, appear to be clear what is meant by 'national' in this growing debate. For one thing some of the old terminological ambiguities have gone. The word that is being used in official government discourse is *watan* or *watani*, i.e. nation or national, with its clear emphasis on the existing territory of the separate states, rather than the ambiguities of an Arab or Islamic 'nation' (*umma*) for example. However, the component parts of what is, say, Emirati or Kuwaiti that are often cited in the national imagining – Arab and Islam – are constructs that previously, and to some extent today, offer alternatives to the local nationalisms. Arabism has been reduced in the Gulf, although the extent to which it was ever much more than state-led financial generosity and exceptional and well-managed Palestinian solidarity demonstrations is questionable. However, the Arabic language is a key definer of what it means to be Arab, and the demographic pressures experienced in the UAE and Qatar, especially, have reduced it to an effective second language in an increasing portion of national life. The UAE reacted to this in the 2008 'Year of National Identity' by promoting Arabic as the 'official' language, and has proven cautious about the extensive use of English seen in government schools in Qatar and Oman for example (Partrick 2010). Yet English is increasingly spoken within those Emirati and Qatari households whose children attend private schools in which the language of instruction is invariably English, thereby reducing the Arabic capabilities of younger nationals (ibid.).

Islam offers a loyalty beyond state boundaries in relation to which the traditional construct of the secular nation comes perhaps a poor second. However, tackling national (local) needs through a deepening of education reform and the (related) promotion of entry into the non-public sector job market (nationalisation) necessarily requires further de-emphasising of Arabic and, in Saudi Arabia at least, a reduction in the amount of attention given to Islam in the education sector. Yet it is the Arab and Islam constructs that are central to the official local narratives about what 'national' means.

Non-imagining of the 'Other'

'Civic ethnocracy' contains group divisions but when the majority of the inhabitants of the country are not nationals and are therefore a perceived 'external threat [this] ensures group solidarity', argues Longva (2005: 127). In the UAE the national identity debate largely deals with the majority population as a threat to 'nationality'. A senior Emirati academic commented, 'The mix of the country creates nationhood, not the nationhood of Emiratis alone; this is simply the falsification of reality' (Emirati academic 2008). However, even modestly accommodating steps would be taken very warily in the UAE. Nor is it likely that any such moves in this direction would occur in neighbouring Kuwait, for example, where the enforced departure of Palestinian, Yemeni and other long-term residents in 1991 reflected the Gulf state's profound distrust of the long-term foreign Arab community. The Gulf crisis of 1990–1 encouraged a shift in the GCC states to draw in foreign workers from non-Arab countries. Despite sometimes coming from countries that were historic trading partners, these workers were much further away in cultural terms and therefore judged to be politically safer in addition to being cheaper.

A *Khaleeji* nation?

The invasion of Kuwait by Iraq and the subsequent reliance upon the US as the principle bilateral defence partner of the Gulf Arab states underlined contradictions with the Arab and Islamic constructs that these states used when presenting themselves to both domestic and regional audiences. It also confirmed that a growing set of Gulf (*Khaleeji*) institutions through the mechanisms of the GCC itself were a reflection of a top-down construct that had not fundamentally altered an essentially realist, state-orientated way of managing their individual affairs. GCC agreement in 1986 on a limited collective defence capability ('Peninsula Shield') proved that the states were prepared to go beyond the narrow state interests envisaged by realism. However, the fact that a larger force could not be agreed and that Oman, the strongest advocate for such a body, wanted to constrain its cross-border authority due to fears of Saudi encroachment, suggests limited interdependence. It has been argued that, prior to 1991 at least, the GCC, while failing to be a coherent 'security community' that sought collective solutions to a defined common threat perception, was making progress in the 'institutionalisation of collective decision-making' on security matters, reflecting a joint concern at the overlap between external Iranian and Iraqi threats and their own internal stability (Barnett and Gause 1998: 177). However this 'institutionalisation' did not bind the members of the GCC, even if the 'norms' of GCC activity in the 1980s required a post-facto collective signing off on individual initiatives (ibid.: 175). This is what one Emirati academic called '...projecting an image...of a somewhat collective foreign policy' (Abdulla 1999). The development of the GCC promoted the notion of *haweeya Khaleeji* (Gulf identity) as a conscious alternative to the delegitimising radical Islamism of the newly born Iranian Republic and of the rival resurgent assertions of Arab nationalism being expressed by Iraq as a tool of its own national interests. However, as a political construct this was not felt among the nationals of the GCC states. There is a sense of a *shakseeya Khaleeji* (Gulf personality, i.e. common cultural traits). However an Emirati journalist and academic argues that this 'is a minor thing', in political terms 'a manifesta- tion of shared history' reflected in pearling and shared cultural and familial experiences (unattributed interview 2008). Says UAE academic al-Kitbi, 'The GCC didn't create a feeling between the people . . . [rather] it is something we feel [for example] when we travel outside the country' (Al-Kitbi 2008). Others have pointed to similarities in dress codes, noting also, however, that the obligation to dress in 'Khaleeji' styles, with local variations, has become much stronger since the Iranian Revolution.

The GCC was not founded as a 'security community' that would pool sovereignty to advance common defence needs, even if it provided a symbolic reassurance until 1991. The GCC's founding charter describes the organisation as an 'institutional embodiment of a historic, social and cultural reality' reflected in what it calls 'deep religious and cultural ties' that link the six states, and given that 'strong kin relations prevail among their citizens'. According to Abdulkha- leq Abdulla, the GCC has 'already passed the point of no return' in terms of deepening economic cohesion (Abdulla 2008). However, in May 2009 the UAE joined Oman in opting out of the planned common currency. Jealously guarded sovereignty and inter-GCC competition continues to constrain economic integration, just as it has limited political and security cooperation. The deepening of the bilateral relationship with the US after 1991, with whom (in addition to the UK and France) all the GCC states except Saudi Arabia signed a formal defence agreement, underlines their separate state identity. However, this strategic relationship can also conflict with the terms in which that identity is locally and regionally expressed. The GCC states were not 'imagined' as the embodiment of resistance to a foreign power, as seen in the national myth that underpins Syrian and Iraqi identity, for instance. As such, their relations with the US, while sometimes difficult and embarrassing domestically and regionally, do not feed local nationalism. Rather, unpopular US regional policies can encourage state leaderships, mindful of local and to some extent Arabist sensitivities, to distance themselves from Washington, just as fear of Iranian regional gains helps to underscore the value they place on the bilateral defence relationship with the US.

Conclusion

Historically speaking, single-state nationalism has not been a driving force in the politics of the Gulf Arab states. Local rulers kept faith with local norms, whether upholding the legacy of the Saudi political compact with the *ulema* or the general requirement to adhere to Arab and Islamic identities. Even in its heyday, Arab nationalism was largely an instrument constraining local foreign policy options due to fear of ideological delegitimisation by more powerful neighbours. Today, Arabism requires Gulf states to keep some distance from unpopular US policies and to downgrade or avoid engagement with Israel. To some extent, this fits naturally with a critical stance toward Iran. However, Iran's increased regional influence is handled differently by each of the GCC states as a mixture of strategy, domestic political and religious opinion, US influence, and business interests affect attitudes to Tehran. Iran's more assertive regional posture has been one of the factors feeding the more active national imagining of recent years as state leaders have, as they did in the 1980s, responded to regional insecurities by reinventing tradition.

The question of national identity in the GCC today centres on an increased desire on the part of local leaderships and, to a lesser extent, other local elites to emphasise the national above other competing identities, assert a claimed indigenous culture and, commensurate with what are mostly market-friendly economies, to put some limit to the inflow of foreign nationals. State leaders remain central to national concepts and therefore, as in the pre-oil age, remain at the centre of authority construction through alliances and the telling of the national narrative. The rulers' sensitivity to sub-national groups within the community whose identity does not fit the traditionally constructed national narrative has also encouraged them to intensify state coherence but without addressing some often controversial and disputed histories. As a consequence, rulers have sometimes deepened resentments among perceptibly 'out' groups.

Preferred histories can exclude key communities, while claimed distinct national cultural trademarks offer a fairly limited variation in what are largely standard *Khaleeji* social traits and (recently reinvented) dress codes. These social aspects relate to whether the policing of Islamic virtue is pronounced (Saudi Arabia) or relatively soft-pedalled (elsewhere) and dependent on maintaining respect for essential norms. To some extent, this reflects how much Islam and Islamists have a role in the public space of each GCC state. To different degrees a public platform for clerics or identifiable Islamists can be found in all GCC states, although Saudi Arabia is exceptional in giving the *ulema* a de facto partnership role in governance. As such even the public commemoration of 'national' events is problematic in the Kingdom. Elsewhere in the GCC, a largely inward-looking and state-led nationalism preoccupies itself with protecting and deepening a national identity that focuses on Arab and Islamic norms, as seen through the specific prism of the local states, and educational and employment reforms to facilitate the entry of greater numbers of nationals into the work-force. Underlining these concerns is nationalist-style sensitivity to the impact of foreign residents, who are perceived as diluting local identity but whose significant numerical presence is unlikely to fundamentally alter. In short, existential fears are deepening the state-building efforts of largely new nations whose leaders are 'inventing' the national community without regard to the sometimes contradictory elements that underpin authority and the differing sub-communities who are not being equally 'imagined'. National identity in the Gulf, it seems, is set to remain a diffuse and contested notion.

Notes

1. Named after the eighteenth-century cleric who aligned with the al-Saud, Mohammed ibn Abdel-Wahhab.
2. Bassam Tibi draws on a key concept of the fourteenth-century philosopher Ibn Khaldoun to write of 'new *asabiyya*s in nation state guises' (Tibi 1990: 132) when modern Arab polities also practice group (i.e. tribal) solidarity (*asabiyya*) but repackage it as leadership of a national community. Tribe in this reading has not gone away. Ibn Khaldun argued that *asabiyya* and Islam were the two key instruments of leadership by Arab rulers.
3. Interviews with Shia figures, Saudi Arabia (2005, 2007, 2009) and Bahrain (2008).
4. Opposition in Saudi Arabia in 2000 caused the government to back down from a proposed major hike in subsidised electricity prices. Electricity and water remain subsidised for nationals throughout the GCC countries.
5. For the argument that the Gulf states were neo-traditional and are now 'post-traditional', see Peterson, (2005).
6. Although notably one of the heritage showpieces in Dubai, the Bastakia, reinvents an Emirati past in an area whose very name is taken from the town of Bastak in southern Iran that some Dubaian Emirati nationals can trace their family's origins to and whose distinctive wind towers were first developed on the other side of the Gulf. This is not denied in some local press reporting e.g. 'Historic district sees a century of change,' *Khaleej Times*, 17 July 2010.
7. Based on author's discussions with students in UAE and Qatar in October and December 2008 respectively.

Interviews (selected)

Abdulla, Abdulkhaleq (2008), professor of political science, Emirates University, October.
Abdul-Malik, Ahmed (2008), media researcher, Doha, December.
Al-Dakheel, Khalid (2009), professor of sociology, King Saud University, Riyadh, February, Dubai.
Al-Gassim, Abdulaziz (2007), former judge; and managing partner, Abdulaziz al-Gassim Law Firm, Riyadh, June.
Al-Harrasi, Abdullah (2008), chairman, Omani Encyclopaedia Committee, Muscat, October.
Al-Kitbi, Ebtisam (2008), Dubai, political science professor, Emirates University, May.
Al-Mahmoud, Abdel-Aziz, chief editor, *Al-Arab* daily newspaper, Doha, December.
Al-Mahruqy, Mohammed (2008), member consultative commission, Supreme Council of the GCC, Muscat, October.
Al-Mukhaini, Ahmed (2008), former consultant, Majlis al-Shoura, Muscat, October.
Al-Najjar, Baqer (2008), professor of sociology, University of Bahrain, Manama, December.
Al-Qassimi, Sultan (2008), writer and chairman, Young Arab Leaders Forum, Dubai, May.

Al-Rasheed, Turki (2009), director, Golden Grass Incorporated, and analyst, Riyadh, February.
Al-Saif, Tawfiq, political analyst (2007), Eastern Province, June.
Al-Shayeb, Jafar, head, Qatif Municipality (2007), Eastern Province, June.
Al-Saif, Tawfiq, political analyst (2007), Eastern Province, June.
Ali, Jassim and Fairouz, Jawwad (2008), members, Bahraini Assembly lower house, Manama, November.
Emirati analyst (2008), Dubai, June.
Fadel, Mohammed (2008), journalist, Manama, December.
Ghobash, Mohammed (2008), executive director, *Al-Alam* newspaper, Dubai.
Heard-Bey, Frauke (2008), Abu Dhabi Authority for Culture and Heritage, Abu Dhabi, May.
Lawtaya, Sadeq (2008), consultant, Oman Research Council, Dubai, November.
Mushaimer, Hassan (2008), Al-Haq leader, Manama, December.
Omani academic (2008).
Qatari academic (2008), Doha, December.
Former official (2008), Ministry of Education, Manama, December.
'The Role of Museums and their Collections in the Formation of Emirati Identity' (2009), debate including Manal Al-Attiyah, director, Sharjah Museums Department; and writers Sultan Al-Qassemi and Mishal Al-Gergawi, Sharjah Museums Department, January.

Secondary sources (selected)

Abdulla, A. (1999) 'The GCC: nature, origin and process', in M. Hudson (ed.), *Middle East Dilemma: The Politics and Economics of Arab Integration*. New York: Columbia University Press.
Abdulla, A. (2008) 'UAE's demographic imbalance', *Gulf News*, 14 April [Dubai, UAE].
Al-Fahad, A. (2004) 'The Imama vs the Iqal: Hadari–Bedouin Conflict in the Formation of the Saudi State', in M. Al-Rasheed and R. Vitalis (eds), *Counter-Narratives – History, Contemporary Society and Politics in Saudi Arabia and Yemen*. New York: Palgrave Macmillan.
Al-Rasheed, M. (2004) 'Historical imagination in Saudi Arabia', in M. Al-Rasheed and R. Vitalis (eds) *Counter-Narratives – History, Contemporary Society and Politics in Saudi Arabia and Yemen*. New York: Palgrave Macmillan.
Barnett, M. and Gause, G. (1998) 'Caravans in opposite directions', in E. Adler and M. Barnett (eds), *Security Communities*. Cambridge: Cambridge University Press.
Crystal, J. (1990) *Oil and Politics in the Gulf – Rulers and Merchants in Kuwait and Qatar*. Cambridge: Cambridge University Press.
Findlow, S. (2000) *The United Arab Emirates: Nationalism and Arab Islamic Identity*. Abu Dhabi: Emirates Center for Strategic Studies and Research (ECSSR).
Hobsbawm, E. and Ranger, T. (1992) *The Invention of Tradition*. Cambridge: Canto.
Ibrahim, F. (2006) *The Shi'is of Saudi Arabia*. London: Saqi.
Khalaf, S. (2008) 'The nationalisation of culture', in A. Alsharekh and R. Springborg (eds), *Popular Culture and Political Identity in the Arab Gulf States*. London: Saqi.
Khalifa, A.M. (1979) *The United Arab Emirates: Unity in Fragmentation*. London: Croom Helm.
Longva, A.N. (2005) 'Neither autocracy nor democracy: citizens, expatriates and the social political system in Kuwait', in P. Dresch and J. Piscatori (eds), *Monarchies and*

Nations: Globalization and Identity in the Arab States of the Gulf. London: I.B. Tauris.

Longva, A.N. (2006) 'Nationalism in pre-modern guise: the discourse on hadhar and bedu in Kuwait', *International Journal of Middle Eastern Studies*, 38: 171–87.

Louer, L. (2008) *Transnational Shia Politics: Religious and Political Networks in the Gulf.* New York: Columbia University Press.

Nawwab, N. (2008) 'The social and political elements that drive the poetic journey', in A. Alsharekh and R. Springborg (eds), *Popular Culture and Political Identity in the Arab Gulf States.* London: Saqi.

Okruhlik, G. (2004) 'Struggles over history and identity', in M. Al-Rasheed and R. Vitalis (eds), *Counter-Narratives – History, Contemporary Society and Politics in Saudi Arabia and Yemen.* New York: Palgrave.

Onley, J. and Khalaf, S. (2006) 'Shaikhly authority in the pre-oil Gulf – an historical-anthropological study', *History and Anthropology*, 17(3): 189–208.

Partrick, N. (2006) 'Kuwait's Foreign Policy: Non-Alignment, Ideology and the Pursuit of Security'. Unpublished thesis, London School of Economics.

Partrick, N. (2010) 'Investment in human resource development in the Gulf', in *Human Resources and Development in the Arabian Gulf.* Abu Dhabi: Emirates Centre for Strategic Studies and Research.

Peterson J.E. (2005) *The Emergence of Post-Traditional Oman*, Sir William Luce Fellowship Paper No. 5, Durham Middle East Papers No. 78. University of Durham.

Tibi, B. (1990) 'Old tribes and imposed nation states', in P.S. Khoury and J. Kostiner (eds), *Tribes and State formation in the Middle East.* Berkeley, CA: University of California Press.

Tibi, N. (1997) *Arab Nationalism: A Critical Enquiry.* London: Macmillan.

Tomlinson, J. (2003) 'Globalization and cultural identity', in D. Held and A. McGrew (eds), *The Global Transformations Reader.* Oxford: Wiley-Blackwell.

Toumi, H. (2009) 'Top Shiite scholars oppose family law draft', *Gulf News*, 4 January.

van der Meulen, H. (1997) 'The Role of Tribal and Kinship Ties in the Politics of the UAE'. Unpublished PhD thesis, Tufts Fletcher University.

Yamani, M. (2004) *Cradle of Islam: The Hijaz and the Quest for an Arabian Identity.* London: I.B. Tauris.

YouGovSiraj Survey Results (2008) National Identity, *The National* (newspaper), Abu Dhabi, September, online at http://www.national.ae (accessed 1 October 2008).

Zubeida, S. (2003) *Law and Power in the Islamic World.* London: I.B. Tauris.

3

MIGRATION POLITICS IN THE ARABIAN PENINSULA

John Chalcraft

Introduction

Historians and social scientists writing on the changing fate of monarchy in the Arabian peninsula have done remarkably little to address the political significance of migration. Research focusing on the ruling families has emphasised how they have overcome the dilemmas of modernisation and, more *sotto voce*, the contradictions of capitalism, through great power support, the crafting of states and building of coalitions (using rents where possible), and on how rulers have identified themselves as generous father-figures, authentic yet modernising guardians of national, Arab and Islamic traditions and values (Anderson 1991, 2000; Ayalon 2000; Beblawi 1990; Crystal 1990; Davidson 2008; Entelis 1976; Halliday 2000; Huntington 1968; Khalaf 1992, 2000; Kostiner 2000; Luciani 1990; Maddy-Weitzman 2000; Mahdavi 1970; Okruhlik 1999; Owen 2004; Ross 2001; Zagorski 2009). Research focusing on migrants has mainly analysed them as 'manpower' required for 'economic growth'. Here, expert planners and responsible authorities either succeed or fail in implementing migration policies that will guarantee the undistorted operation of the market – while paying due attention to local 'cultural' and 'demographic' concerns (Bhagwati 1984; Birks and Sinclair 1980; Fergany 1982; Kapiszeswki 2001; Seccombe 1983, 1987; Seccombe and Lawless 1986; Serageldin et al. 1983; Sherbiny 1981, 1984). This latter approach occludes both its own politics and those of migrant 'manpower' by making the profoundly unequal and consequential control over *persons*, their livelihoods and social and political relations appear merely as the neutral and technocratic management of *things*. The relative lack of overall attention to migration politics is perhaps surprising given that in six of the eight surviving monarchies in the Arab world, the workforce is between one half and nine-tenths foreign.

Migrants have been given a minor role in some of the literature as those who operated to divide and defeat the challenge posed to monarchy by the emergent forces of a socialist working class (Disney 1977: 22; Franklin 1985; Halliday 1977a, 1980, 1984; Khalaf 1985; Lackner 1978: 194, 197, 216). Or they have been viewed in passing as an 'apolitical', 'transient' and 'disposable' workforce convenient for patrimonial rulers trying to overcome the dilemmas of modernisation. These theses are not straw men, but they suffer, arguably, from endogenous socio-economic determinism: they rely on determinist, materialist and teleological expectations regarding the identity, politics and subjective orientation of workers and migrants. Migrants/workers are supposed to spring, fully formed, from the socio-economic base, and then enter the political superstructure in order to enact certain pro/anti-monarchical positions.

The literature treating migrants as acculturated and political subjects, however, is growing (Abu Lughod 1985; Choucri 1986; Kapiszewski 2001; Lackner 1978; Longva 1997; Louër 2008; Russell 1988, 1989; Russell and al-Ramadhan 1994; Vitalis 2007; Weiner 1982). This paper aims to build on such work to develop a distinctive argument about the political role of migration in the Arabian peninsula from the 1950s to the present. The premise is to refuse to define migrants/workers wholly in terms of demographics, manpower, wage-labour, capital, rents and economic growth, and to situate them in changing cultural, ideological, political and transnational contexts.

Monarchy under siege

In the 1960s, the ruling families in the Arabian peninsula had strong reasons to be anxious about their future. Britain and the United States reaffirmed their at least covert support for monarchy with the British–CIA coup of 1953 in Iran (Abrahamian 2001). But 'protection' from the imperialist camp had not saved other monarchs – whether in Egypt in 1952 or Iraq in 1958. Western geopolitical support could be a liability where the charge of 'puppet' stuck. Revolutionaries in Oman, for example, were inspired by the belief that '[King] Feisal [of Saudi Arabia] is [President Lyndon] Johnson's ass' (Halliday 1974: 384). Diplomatic support, arms and money from the Soviet Union, on the other hand, as well as from the republican and sometimes revolutionary states of the Non-Aligned Movement (led by Egypt, India, Ghana and Yugoslavia) usually went to the opponents of monarchy.

The world communist movement depicted monarchy as a feudal and imperialist anachronism. Third Worldist discourse condemned Arabian amirs and sheikhs as the reactionary and economically dependent puppets of neo-colonialism (Khalili 2007; Malley 1996). In the West, Leftist critics heralded the way combined and uneven capitalism would engender anti-monarchist and socialist revolution (Halliday 1974: 29). On the Right, policy-influencing political scientists were convinced that monarchs worldwide were due to fall. Samuel Huntington argued in the 1960s that monarchy would never be able to survive the acute 'king's dilemma' it faced: monarchy needed to centralise power in order to deliver reform, but this would make 'difficult or impossible the expansion of the power of the traditional polity and the assimilation into it of the new groups produced by modernization.' The outlook for these monarchs was 'bleak' and the only real questions concerned 'the scope of the violence of their demise and who wields the violence' (Huntington 1968: 5, 177, 191; cf. Halpern 1963). The British diplomatic records for Saudi Arabia emphatically confirm that British officials held similar views until 1971, when it was decided that the prospects for monarchical survival were improving (Burdett 1997, 2004).

The regional stage was even less comforting. In Morocco, the monarchy lurched from crisis to crisis in the 1960s and early 1970s (Waterbury 1973). Jordan's King Hussein was nearly unseated in 1956–7 and faced a further crisis in 1970 (Ashton 2008). All the other Arab monarchs had been overthrown: King Farouk of Egypt in 1952–3, Muhammad VIII al-Amin of Tunisia in 1956–7, the Hashemites of Iraq in 1958, the Imam of Yemen in 1962 and King Idriss of Libya in 1969.

The republican and revolutionary governments in the region voiced loudly their opposition to monarchs and appeared to hold the political initiative in terms of their identification with ascendant Third Worldism, pan-Arab liberation, economic development, social justice and modernisation. In Egypt, the Free Officers declared that the whole nation was 'unanimous in wishing to see the monarchical regime disappear forever'. Closer to home, the Yemeni Revolutionary Council which deposed the Imam defined the primary goal of the revolution as putting 'an end to those things that have blocked all progress in Yemen – tyranny, reaction, corrupt government, and the evil system of monarchy' (Ayalon 2000: 34). These regional governments were ready to support – with troops, arms, money and/or propaganda – anti-monarchical opposition movements in the peninsula, from North Yemen to Bahrain (Halliday 1980: 215–17).

Arab migrants

After the Second World War, Arab migration to the peninsula greatly increased. Until the 1940s, most migrants were from India (Seccombe and Lawless 1986: 573). This changed during the 1950s and 1960s. The break-up of the British empire and national independence played an important role. On the one hand, Indian independence in 1947 loosened ties to South Asia. On the other hand, the passing of direct rule in Mandate Palestine was the crucial backdrop to the mass dispossession of the Palestinians at the hands of Zionist settlers, which resulted in the exile to other Arab states of about 1.5 million Palestinians (Halliday 1984: 4). Moreover, the development and leadership imperatives occasioned by national independence were part of the rationale behind development projects that would employ migrants.

By 1975, 90 per cent of the non-national workforce of Saudi Arabia was comprised of Arab migrants – the largest groups being Yemenis, Palestinians and Egyptians (Birks and Sinclair 1980: 97, 115). In Kuwait, Arab migrants totalled around 400,000, comprising about four-fifths of the total non-national workforce in 1975. Almost half of the Arab migrants were Palestinian or Jordanian, and most of the rest were either Egyptian, Syrian or Iraqi (Birks and Sinclair 1980: 34, 44, 48–50; Joukhadar 1980; Russell 1989: 27). In Bahrain, in 1971, around half the non-national workforce was Arab, two-thirds of these from Oman (Birks and Sinclair 1980: 158, 168, 171). The absolute numbers involved in Qatar were smaller, but Arab migrants – mostly Palestinians, Jordanians and Egyptians – comprised just over a quarter of non-nationals (Birks and Sinclair 1980: 57–8, 70).

Socio-economic development plans and associated employment were developed later (from the late 1960s onwards) in the UAE and Oman – but, especially in the early stages, they also employed Arab migrants in large numbers. Egyptians and Palestinians were teaching in schools in Dubai in the 1950s. In the UAE in 1975, a quarter (62,000) of all migrant workers (251,500) were Arab, the most numerous being Palestinian or Jordanian, Omani and Egyptian (Birks and Sinclair 1980: 73, 89). In Oman, almost half the workforce was probably non-national in 1975, an unknown but significant proportion of these being Arab (Birks and Sinclair 1980: 177, 186; Seccombe and Lawless 1986: 573).

Migrant politics

Arab migrants were not just manpower; they also brought politics. In Bahrain, Syrian teachers caused a stir as early as 1929 by organising a teacher-student strike in 'the Egyptian manner' (Bahrain Government 1924–1956, Vol. 2: 28–9; Mdairis 2004: 13–14). In the 1940s and 1950s, Arab migrants and return migrants (educated in Egypt and the Mashriq) were active in underground political parties, the politicised cultural and sporting clubs, and the press. Much to the irritation of Charles Belgrave, the British Adviser, they spread ideas of pan-Arabism, Ba'athism, Nasserism, and liberalism, playing a role in the round of non-sectarian, nationalist, constitutional, and labour protest during 1954–6 against British imperialism and the ruling Khalifa autocracy (Khuri 1980: 198; Mdairis 2004: 12, 14). Iraqi activists exiled to Bahrain – among others – lent their experience in labour organising to Bahraini nationalists in the 1950s (Khalaf 1985: 25). The rights of Arab (but not Indian) labour were championed in the Bahraini press. It was declared that Arabs were brothers, not foreigners, for whom even passports were unnecessary (Khuri 1980: 198; Mdairis 2004: 15–16).

In Kuwait, Arab migrants were more numerous and active. Palestinians especially were involved in Kuwait's cultural and political clubs, in the press and in student activism and the underground political parties – especially the Movement of Arab Nationalists (MAN), founded at the American University of Beirut in 1951 and in Kuwait by return migrants shortly thereafter – and in labour organising and unionisation (Brand 1988: 127; Ghazali 2007: 428–33; Lackner 1978: 94; Al-Mdairis 2004: 22). Palestinians – who brought 'experience of labour organization and . . . progressive political consciousness' (Smith 1984: 172–3) – were permitted to form labour unions in Kuwait under the auspices of the PLO (Brand 1988: 128–9). Fatah – the long-dominant faction of the PLO after 1969 – was founded in Kuwait by Yasser Arafat and others in the late 1950s. Arab and Palestinian labour and national rights were championed in the press, and foreign and non-Arab companies – above all the oil companies – were attacked for exploiting their Arab labour (Mdairis 2004: 15–16). Migrants and return migrants were involved in leadership and rank-and-file roles in the strikes and protests associated with Suez and the Tripartite Aggression in 1956, the United Arab Republic in 1959 and the defeat of 1967. After 1963, opposition Arab nationalist deputies in the National Assembly 'supported by the large Jordanian/Palestinian immigrant population' (Weiner 1982: 23) urged the Amir to loosen the harshly exclusive citizenship laws for Palestinians and Arabs and pressed for a more pan-Arab role for Kuwait in the region (Halliday 1984: 6; Russell 1989: 34, 37; Russell and Ramadhan 1994: 584). Indeed, one of the reasons for the suspension of the constitution, censorship and the closure of the Assembly in 1976 was the ruling family's alarm at the strength and outspoken-ness of the Arab nationalist bloc and its Arab and Palestinian supporters (Russell 1989: 37; Weiner 1982: 23).

While the Republican *coup d'état* on the Nasserist model in North Yemen in 1962 owed something to the activities of Nasserist Egyptian officers training the forces of the soon-to-be deposed Imam, migrants were involved in much larger numbers in the labour movement and anti-colonial struggle that evicted the British from Aden and South Yemen in 1967. The British had recruited North Yemeni migrant labour for work in the port of Aden for political reasons – fearing any disruption of the social structure in the hinterland of South Yemen itself (Halliday 1974: 183). Nonetheless, these North Yemeni migrants went on strike in their thousands from March 1956 onwards in what became one of the most radical and sustained waves of labour protest in the Arab world in the postwar period (Halliday 1974: 86; Watt et al. 1962). These protests at points paralysed the port and played an important role in making the colony ungovernable from the British point of view, contributing to the decision to withdraw completely. The Saudi ruling family, fearing for their throne, complained to the British that just when they had closed the door to revolution in North Yemen, the British had opened it again in South Yemen (Burdett 2004, Vol. 3: 288).

In the desert kingdom of Saudi Arabia itself, republican, liberal, Leftist and labour opposition developed in various ways in the Hijaz, the oilfields of the Eastern province, and the armed forces. Arab migrants – Palestinian, Yemeni and Egyptian – played important roles. In the Hijaz, existing regional and ideological opponents of the House of Saud were joined by journalists and politicised elements in the sizeable community of Arab migrants – especially Egyptians and Palestinians – who started to work in numbers from the late 1940s in Saudi Arabia and the Hijaz in the oil industry, in education, journalism and administration. While clubs and unions were generally banned, migrants writing in the press worked to stitch together a pan-Arab consciousness, and ideas of administrative reform, representative institutions and socio-economic development (Abir 1993: 28–9, 35). Especially between 1958 and 1960, in addition to pamphleteering by opposition organisations, the Saudi press – 'dominated by Egyptians and the Hijazi intelligentsia' – openly defied censorship and frequently published articles promoting Arab nationalism – and indirectly attacking the regime (Abir 1993: 40). In the 1960s, the Saudi regime made moves to censor and reorient the press, deport journalists and reduce numbers of Egyptian teachers who were thought to be importing Arab nationalist ideas (Lackner 1978: 192–3; Kapiszewski 2001: 133–44).

The most important round of worker mobilisation (petitions, demonstrations, boycotts and strikes) in Saudi history began at Aramco in March 1953 and continued until June 1956. Thousands of workers – most of the Aramco workforce – participated (Vitalis 2007: 127–93). As elsewhere on the peninsula, workers' demands combined social and economic issues with nationalist, Nasserist, communist and pan-Arab politics (Abir 1993: 35; Rasheed 2002: 99–100; Smith 1984: 173). Although Vitalis underplays their role, Palestinians, Yemenis and others were involved as activists and participants (Halliday 1984: 7; Lackner 1978: 94–5). While this evidence must be used carefully, deportations of migrant workers from Aramco in November 1953 included 'three Palestinians, a Bahraini, and a naturalized Saudi citizen from Aden... who was stripped of his citizenship before being exiled' (Vitalis 2007: 154–5). By the end of 1954, more than 160 Palestinian workers had been arrested and deported. Another 100 Palestinians, suspected members of the Parti Populaire Syrien and the Ba'ath Party, were arrested in 1955 (Lackner 1978: 193; Smith 1984: 173; Vitalis 2007: 152, 161).

The third main site of opposition in Saudi Arabia was the army and the air force. There was an attempted coup by a small group of Free Officers in 1955, a number of acts of sabotage (such as the explosions of November 1966 to February 1967), several assassination attempts on leading members of the royal family and at least one other serious coup attempt in 1969. In 1967, members of the armed forces and the police were accused of organising, joining in with, or at the very least failing to prevent demonstrations and crowd actions. Certainly the British assessment from the mid-1950s until 1971 was that a coup was a definite possibility and even a likelihood (Burdett 1997, 2004). The point to note here is that those who carried out acts of sabotage seem often to have been Palestinian or Yemeni migrants. For example, an arms cache was discovered hidden in the king's palace in Riyadh in April 1957. A Palestinian confessed to having secreted them under the instructions of the Egyptian military attaché, Lt Col Khashaba (Vitalis 2007: 189). Sketchy details in the British documents of a plot to kill Faisal in January 1965 involved Palestinians (Burdett 1997, Vol. 5: 23). The bombs of November 1966 to February 1967 were initially blamed on Egyptian-trained Yemenis and 17 Yemenis were executed publicly in March

1967 (Burdett 2004, Vol. 2: 507–19). The Saudis arrested and beat a number of Palestinians in the wake of a few explosions on 2 June 1967 at American targets in Jedda (Burdett 2004, Vol. 2: 847, 857). Finally, South Yemenis from the South Yemeni National Liberation Front and the Hadramaut, Egyptian military instructors, and a least one Lebanese were among those arrested during the clampdown following the coup attempt of 1969 (Burdett 2004, Vol. 4: 4ff.; Burdett 2004, Vol. 5: 59–64).

Pan-Arabism and development

Migration as an idea, and migrants themselves as a social group, were linked materially and affectively to pan-Arabism. The idea that the borders of the Gulf states had been fixed artificially by the colonial powers to dominate an Arab nation divided into statelets (*dawliyyat*) was a central artefact of widely popular pan-Arab ideology. Some form of unity, it was held, would enable the Arab nation to achieve liberation from colonial divide and rule, and economic dependency, to punch its weight on the world stage and to reverse the catastrophic expulsion of the Palestinians of 1948. Migration was bound up with this pan-Arabism. It was imperative that Arabs should be able to migrate to live and work in any 'region' of the Arab homeland without restriction or discrimination. Many in the peninsula were profoundly attached to the idea that new arrivals from the Arab world should be welcomed as brothers from different parts of the homeland. In Kuwait 'appointing Palestinians came to be viewed as a national obligation', during a 'honeymoon period' for both communities who were 'swept up in the Arab nationalist fervor of the time' (Brand 1988: 124, 144). Restriction and discrimination transgressed the pressing need for political unity in the face of colonial and Zionist divide and rule; offended against the principle that friendship, brotherhood and cooperation should characterise relations between Arabs; and weakened the very forms of cultural exchange and solidarity that free movement was intended to promote.

Some argued that the inclusive and egalitarian movement of labour was an important element in the *economic* development of the Arab nation. For Arab nationalists such as the Saudi official Abdallah al-Tariqi, who played an important role in the founding of OPEC but who was exiled in the early 1960s (Vitalis 2007: 133–4), oil wealth represented an opportunity wherein Arab states with different endowments in population, natural resources and capital could cooperate with one another, and complement one another's strengths in an overall project involving not the distribution of rents, but the 'expansion of the productive base of the economy through industrialization and the diversification of sources of income' (Naqeeb 1990: 83, 101) in an enlarged regional bloc to escape dependency and subordination. For the sending Arab countries to receive the full economic benefit of movement across regional borders, a number of voices argued that the receiving countries should not discriminate in socio-economic terms against their fellow Arabs. This would restrict opportunities for migrants, lower remittances, diminish migrants' ability to acquire skills in the receiving countries, and/or bring them back to the sending countries. Likewise, for the receiving countries, discrimination and restriction was inimical to socio-economic development, for it would only create a class of unproductive rentiers in the oil-rich states who could rely on expatriates to do all the productive and menial labour (Sayigh 1972: 293–4, 298–9). 'True reform', the Kuwaiti academic Shamlan Alessa wrote, 'and more efficiency in the bureaucracy cannot occur unless there is equality of treatment and pay for all workers, regardless of country of origin' (Alessa 1981: 55). Under the banner of pan-Arabism, then, locals and migrants could identify themselves as 'brothers' with similar interests.

Monarchy remade

The six monarchies of the Arabian peninsula overcame the opposition that beset them. By the 1990s, they were more secure and stable than ever before. The international and regional context changed fundamentally during these decades. The United States – a supporter of monarchy – was increasingly powerful internationally, and after 1991 became the world's only superpower with a major military presence in the Gulf to boot. Neo-liberal economists either bracketed politics as a market distortion or offered their consultancy services to the ruling families, or both. Monarchy was increasingly applauded as 'politically balanced, economically developmental, yet traditional and socioculturally integrative' (Kostiner 2000: 10). Emerging human rights activism tackled individual violations of codes to which rulers had signed up, not the ruling system as such. The Non-Aligned Movement ran out of steam, split over the Soviet invasion of Afghanistan in 1979. China turned to 'market reform' in the late 1970s. The USSR broke up in 1991. The theory of the rentier state, which started out very much as a Leftist critique of the nugatory economic effects of rentierism, became, with the demise of this kind of developmentalist economics, a rather elitist and determinist explanation for the power of monarchs to repress or co-opt. Pan-Arab unity schemes failed, and the Arab radical republics were crushingly defeated at the hands of Israel in 1967. In 1974, Sadat turned toward Washington Consensus economics and signed a separate peace with Israel in 1979. The 'revolutionary' republics, weighed down with high energy prices and debt, started to compare unfavourably with the Gulf monarchies, boosted by the quadrupling in the oil price in 1973, in terms of delivering physical and social infrastructure and raised disposable incomes to their national populations. Opposition movements in the peninsula were now severed from international material or affective support, and the banners of pan-Arabism, developmentalism and regional radicalism looked increasingly tattered.

Migration politics

In this new context, migration to the oil-rich monarchies of the Gulf Cooperation

Council (GCC) from the formerly radical republics became a potent symbol of the changing balance of power and wealth, and transmitted ideas and practices to the poorer states that undermined the hegemony of pan-Arabism, Nasserism and leftist developmentalism, and promoted the neo-liberal dispensation (Halliday 1984: 3). The regional governments that had formerly held the progressive initiative and appeared almost to lay siege to the peninsula in political terms, approached the Gulf monarchs in matters of migration as subordinates, increasingly spoke the language of market forces and mostly competed with each other to send the cheapest and most obedient labour force (Halliday 1984: 10). Pan-Arab migration had been seen as a way to break the bonds of dependency; it now became, through remittances sent home to cover indebted governments' spiralling energy bills and balance of payments crises, a sign and mediator of a powerful new form of dependency – that of the formerly radical republics on their monarchical 'elder brothers' (Alnasrawi 1991: 155–66).

Halliday argued that return migration encouraged 'the spread of capitalist relations into the poorer developing countries affected by the oil boom' (Halliday 1980: 226). Certainly, the World Bank and other US-sponsored international development agencies discovered (in the 1970s) the entrepreneurial virtues of the 'informal sector' (Elyachar 2005), itself very much a creature of the tens of billions of dollars in remittances that Gulf migrants sent home to the Arab world and beyond (Harik and Sullivan 1992; Ibrahim 1982). Migrants themselves were supposed to be, and sometimes aspired to be, the micro-entrepreneurs so lauded in neo-liberal economics. In fact, skills useful for sending countries were not learned in menial jobs in the Gulf, and remittances drove up inflation, encouraged imports and were spent on survival and privatised consumption often centred on the nuclear family. Migration drove a wedge into statist developmentalism and organised national labour, and acted to reinforce the very patterns of dependency that market theories centred on economic growth claimed they would reverse. Instead of the mutually beneficial cooperation between oil-rich and population-rich countries envisaged by pan-Arabism, these years witnessed 'increased inequality and deterioration in the productive and human resources of the Arab world . . . between the oil-rich and population-rich states' (Halliday 1984: 3).

Re-composition and diversification

The re-composition of the migrant workforce in the GCC monarchies between the 1970s and the 1990s drove a coach and horses through the material and affective links that had bound migrants through pan-Arabism to allies in the receiving country. The central features of this were the turn to Asian labour from the mid-1970s (Choucri 1986), the growing restrictions on Palestinian labour in the 1970s, followed by the mass expulsions of Palestinian and Yemeni labour from Kuwait and Saudi Arabia in 1991–2, and policies of 'diversification' thereafter.

Ruling families had long made use of Asian labour to head off challenges to their rule. In Bahrain, the British favoured Indians over Iranians (Seccombe 1983: 6–7), and Palestinians had faced restrictions there (Weiner 1982: 28; Franklin 1985: 12). In Oman, the preference for Baluchi and other South Asian labour over Arabs 'suspicious' for political reasons was also well-known (Halliday 1977: 10). In the 1970s, however, the turn to Asian labour was dramatic. By 1985, the percentage of migrants in the GCC countries accounted for by Arabs had fallen to 56 per cent (from 72 per cent in 1975). Contrarywise, whereas non-Arabs made up only 12 per cent of all workers in the Gulf in 1970, by 1985 Asians comprised some 63 per cent of the Gulf workforce (Kapiszewski 2006: 7). Certainly there were economic reasons to employ Asians. But their political advantages were important too. They 'were unlikely to make claims for citizenship... were alien and could continue to remain disenfranchised. They were regarded as more likely to be passive observers of political processes ...than as potential activists or claimants on social services' (Choucri 1986: 252; Halliday 1984: 5; Kapiszewski 2006: 6–7; Weiner 1982: 28). They were 'removed from the currents of Arab nationalism and Islamism' (Humphrey 1993: 7). Indeed, the guardians of pan-Arabism were threatened by the turn to Asian labour. They usually wrote of(f) Asian migrants as aliens strange in nationality, culture, colour and manners (Fergany 1983). This view worked to divide and fragment the labour force (Halliday 1984: 6). Asians also came without intra-Arab and regional entanglements, which, it was thought, made them easier to expel (Weiner 1982: 12). Some Asians, recalling the fate of their compatriots expelled from East Africa by populist governments, supported monarchy as a guarantor of a segmented society (Kostiner 2000: 4–5; Weiner 1982: 9).

The two countries where the re-composition of the resident population was most violent and far-reaching were those which had received the largest numbers of Arab migrants, and which had experienced the most political opposition to monarchy from them. In Kuwait, the turn to Asian labour in the 1970s was in part aimed at defusing Arab nationalism. In this period, 'Jordanians and Palestinians were the only group that experience[d] reductions in rates of immigration across all sectors' (Russell 1989: 36–7; cf Choucri 1986: 262–3, 266). Efforts to deport, imprison or execute Palestinian or Yemeni radicals had been pursued for years in Saudi Arabia, where Palestinians had been restricted from working on 'sensitive installations and in the oilfields' (Smith 1984: 173; cf. Brand 1988: 127). But the real change came with the invasion and occupation of Kuwait by Iraq in 1990. The PLO refused to condemn Saddam Hussein's actions and some 300–400,000 Palestinians were expelled as a result from Kuwait during 1991–2 (Russell and Ramadhan 1994: 569, 581). Yemen attempted to remain 'officially neutral' (Okruhlik and Conge 1997: 559) and Yemeni workers in Saudi Arabia paid the price: 750,000 to 1 million Yemenis were forced to leave in the few months following September 1990 (Hartmann 1995; Sadowski 1991). The re-composition of the migrant population was far-reaching. In Saudi Arabia, the percentage of Arabs in the foreign population fell from 91 per cent in 1975 to 33 per cent in 2004; in Kuwait 'the decline was from 80 per cent in 1975 to 30 per cent in 2003' (Kapiszewski 2006: 8). Migrants were unable to resist their expulsion, while regional governments sat on their hands (Gause 1993: 161–2). Even lip-service to the idea that Arab migrants were preferred (Weiner 1982: 28) was now dropped, and Kuwait openly declared a policy of diversification, which would 'consider nationality and ethnicity to prevent any one group from controlling the labour market' (Russell and Ramadhan 1994: 580).

Segregation and rotation

Meanwhile, receiving countries devised new forms of geographical, workplace and legal segregation and rotation designed to insulate migrants from nationals. First, many of the development projects inaugurated in the 1970s were located in enclaves at some distance from existing urban centres, minimising contact between the migrant workers who built them and nationals. Shuaiba (in Kuwait), Umm Said (in Qatar), Jebel Ali (Dubai), Ruwais (Abu Dhabi), Yenbo and Jubail (Saudi Arabia) were all on desert sites away from major centres of population (Birks and Sinclair 1980: 151). Second, contractors who imported, housed, fed and then removed all the labour required for particular projects were increasingly given preference (Birks and Sinclair 1980: 151; Kapiszewski 2006: 7; Lackner 1978: 194). This 'self-sufficient' contracting system was designed to nullify the social or political footprint of migrant labour in the receiving country (Disney 1977: 23–4). The increased use of South Asian domestic labour, along with passport-withholding and virtual imprisonment within private households, more or less guaranteed the exclusion of such women from political activity. Migrants had long been subject to summary deportation and denied nationality, citizenship and civil and social rights (Khalaf 1992: 72). New legal and administrative measures were now devised to ensure segregation and rotation. In the UAE, for example, a law of 1980 required 'foreign workers to leave the country for six months before changing jobs'. This measure was designed to prevent the 'trouble' that the presence of unemployed migrants might provoke and shore up the system of rotation (Choucri 1986: 263; Winckler 2000: 246).

Local nationalism

Migration had long been a lightning rod for local politicisation on nationalist lines. In 1936 in Kuwait, the British Political Representative reckoned that 'an influx of Indians would be liable to lead to trouble' among the local population (Seccombe 1983: 14). Or, in July 1951, in Qatar, workers at Petroleum Development Qatar went on strike demanding the dismissal of 150 Dhofaris working for the company (Seccombe 1983: 12). In both cases, however, protests couched in nationalist terms were understood to threaten local rulers who were identified with British imperialism in general and Indian subjects in particular. The difference after decolonisation, when overt imperial 'protection' was no longer a target, was that nationalist mobilisation was turned to monarchical advantage. Ruling families and their allies have invented and made use of 'authentic' culture, nationalism, and 'traditional' values – such as the extensive and selective use of 'camel culture' in the UAE – in order to identify themselves as the guardians of supposedly genuine Arab values and traditions, and thus bolster the 'dynastic political structure' (Khalaf 2000: 244; see also Khalaf 1992). In Kuwait, local nationalists sought to preserve the 'traditional' ideological bases of Kuwaiti identity: 'loyalty to the patriarchal leadership of the monarch and adherence to the principle that anyone who was not a member of one of the original tribes is an alien with no legitimate claims on the rights or prerogatives of tribal membership' (Russell 1989: 31). In this view, migrants, Arab and non-Arab, were seen as outsiders and competitors in the labour market. Local nationalism, suitably rearticulated in conservative terms, could serve sheikhly rule.

This rearticulation set the stage for a new insistence on and particular definition of the double threat posed by migrants. First, migrants were said to be threatening because they made nationals a 'minority in their own country'. This characterisation of the threat that was heavily dependent on the attrition of pan-Arabism which was more expansive on the definition of who was indigenous, the attrition of Leftist political or economic critique (which went well beyond demography), and the complete closure of any route to citizenship or nationality which ensured that foreigners would stay foreigners and 'locals' remain a minority. Second, again and again, migrants were said to be threatening – by rulers and subjects alike – because they might change the much-cherished traditions, customs and values of the Gulf countries (Kapiszewski 2006: 8). In short, the monarchic, conservative nationalist dispensation was reinforced by the notion that migrants posed a demographic and cultural threat to the Gulf countries. As long as nationalist anxieties about migrants were channelled into these terms, they were a force which underpinned 'national consensus' (Fuccaro 2008: 3–4) and the position of the ruling families.

Nationalisation policies, ostensibly intended to replace the foreign workforce with suitably trained nationals, had their origins in the economic slowdown attendant on falling oil revenues in the 1980s. The slowdown created discontent, triggered a search for scapegoats, and stoked the fires of local nationalism. One of the main goals of Saudi Arabia's fourth Five Year Development Plan (1985–90) was ostensibly to reduce the number of foreigners in the kingdom by 1.2 million. Oman imposed restrictions on certain occupational categories in 1987. A Bahraini programme was initiated in 1989 (Winckler 2000: 246). But given that for more than a quarter of a century nationalisation policies have been almost completely unsuccessful in that the foreign proportion of the workforce has only increased (Winckler 2000: 246–8, 251–2), it makes sense to question whether the ostensible aim of these programmes is the only matter at stake. If it was then why would these failed policies be continually reimplemented? It seems plausible instead to view these programmes at least partly in the light of the hegemonic functions they serve. Perhaps they in some way work to win the consent of the dominant bloc and that of various subaltern social groups on the national stage. Certainly when nationalisation policies threatened widespread interests, such as the legislation in Kuwait restricting according to wealth the number of foreign maids that households could employ, an outcry followed and the law was quickly rescinded. It may be that nationalisation programmes, and the flurry of conferences, panels, lectures, press articles and discussion that surrounds them, while making little difference to the composition of the workforce, do repeatedly affirm the unity of nationals against foreigners, ingrain the interpellation of migrants as demographic and cultural threats, and provide an important justification for the patronage-enhancing policy of the rotation of 'guest-worker' migrants: if migrants are supposedly to be replaced, sooner or later, by nationals, there need be no provision for their assimilation.

By barring assimilation, rulers kept the population of patronage claimants low, increasing per capita the amount of patronage to be dispensed and thus enhancing its political impact. As Khalaf has it, '[t]he state, personified by the ruling family... has produced in the eyes of its subjects an image of a paternalistic, all-powerful, all-providing, and all-giving father' (Khalaf 1992: 64). This image and practice was far easier to sustain where the recipients of such paternalism were two or three times less numerous than they might otherwise have been.

Neo-liberalism

The final major element in the exclusion of migrants from national politics was the selective use of neo-liberal policy. The manpower planning assumptions associated with a gathering Washington Consensus, and implicit (and explicit) in numerous World Bank publications, consultancy reports and academic tracts (Birks and Sinclair 1980; Bhagwati 1984; Fergany 1982; Kapiszeswki 2001; Seccombe 1983, 1987; Seccombe and Lawless 1986; Serageldin et al. 1983; Sherbiny 1981, 1984), were fundamentally at odds with the statist and developmentalist economics associated with radical pan-Arabism. Whereas the aim of the developmentalists had been a diversified project of productive and regionally balanced industrialisation and economic development linked to the strength of the Arab nation, the aim of neo-liberal economics was national 'economic growth' measured by Gross Domestic Product. This formulation was thoroughly wedded to local nationalism. Whereas the developmentalists had insisted that development necessarily implied an inclusionary and egalitarian policy with regard to Arab migrants, this kind of politics was irrelevant to neo-liberal consultants, who were only interested in whether the national state was creating the conditions for the undistorted operation of supply and demand in the labour market (cf. Bin Talal 1984: 612). This perspective was congenial to rulers: it enabled a view of migration in apparently apolitical, non-pan-Arab and local nationalist terms.

With regard to 'expatriates' and 'economic growth', the new economists operated with a very simple assumption based on World Bank manpower planning models: '[t]he tougher the population policy, the greater the reduction of future economic growth' (Sherbiny 1984: 655). However dubious the economic sense of a prescription that totally ignored the question of productivity per head, the point here is that neo-liberal economists told Gulf rulers that the more migrants they allowed to their shores, the higher the economic growth they could expect. This was a policy prescription enacted from on high, not a 'free market' force on the ground that prevented Gulf rulers in spite of their best intentions from nationalising the workforce, as some assume (Kapiszewski 2006: 7–9). Further, given that local rulers sought to retain the power of patronage by keeping their national populations small but to deliver economic growth to win consent and insure themselves against the vagaries of the oil market, the implication for migration policy was clear. They should allow as many migrants as possible to work in their territories, while minimising costs (such as unfavourable 'dependency rates') and excluding migrants from the benefits of nationality as far as possible. The thinking here was the exact opposite of the developmentalist prescriptions on inclusion and non-discrimination, and totally ignored their critique of rentierism and exploitation which implied far-reaching socio-political change. In complete contrast, neo-liberalism delivered, under the circumstances, a powerful prescription for the maintenance of the status quo through exclusion, segregation and discrimination.

These assumptions could be readily internalised by important national sectors in the Gulf. Who did not want to see economic growth? Or, more to the point, who, from householders to businessmen, wanted to be told that they could not import cheap, abundant and menial labour? At the same time, few wanted to see their slice of the oil rent pie cut more thinly by policies of assimilation, and so nationals had a stake in the segregation and exclusion of migrants – a self-interested view that was authorised by the individualistic neo-liberal vision. Neo-liberalism, further, offered a view of migrants as faceless, maximising, and even opportunistic individuals who chose to come to the Gulf because that was where they could make the most money (Davidson 2008: 187). This view was a potent solvent of solidarities between nationals and migrants.

Strikes and protests

Even under harsh conditions of exclusion, segregation, state violence and deportation, and bereft of allies in the receiving country or meaningful support from sending governments, migrants of virtually all nationalities have continued to hold a strong sense of grievance about pay, conditions and exclusion. As a Pakistani taxi-driver told me with some feeling in April 2009 in Dubai: 'We are social slaves here!' Indeed, migrants have organised protests from the 1970s to the present. From the Korean strikes in Saudi Arabia in 1977 to clashes of Indians with their employers in Oman in 1978 (Halliday 1984: 7; Weiner 1982: 21–2), to the mass protests of Bangladeshi cleaners in Kuwait in 2005 and the new rounds of protest in the Gulf more generally since that time, migrants have continued to interpret their condition and try to change it for the better. But these strikes and protests, in stark contrast to those in which migrants were involved in the 1950s and 1960s, have put forward only economic-corporate demands. Indeed, many protests have only involved desperate rearguard actions by workers to obtain wages promised to them in contracts but never paid. These protests have not been identified with any larger oppositional politics. They have ceased, there-fore, for the time being, to be part of any broad-based political challenge to ruling families of the GCC.

Conclusion

This chapter has suggested a way in which migration can be written into the analysis of the changing fate of monarchy on the Arabian peninsula. I have argued that migration played a role in both the challenge to and the consolida-tion of family rule. On the one hand, in the particular international and regional context of the 1950s and 1960s, migration was an element in a challenge to the rule of beleaguered monarchs in the peninsula. In the decades following 1947–8, Arab migrants – especially Palestinians, Egyptians and Yemenis – transmitted international and regional anti-monarchical pressures. They played a role in 'the revolutionary, Arab nationalist tide which inundated the Gulf and Arab peninsula region in the 1950s' (Naqeeb 1990: 101). They formed an important component in protest movements inspired by republicanism, Leftism and pan-Arabism in which a wide variety of other groups were involved. From the 1970s onwards, however, in a completely changed international and regional context, migrants became an adjunct rather than a challenge to the resurgent power of patrimonial ruling families in the region. They mediated via remittances a new international and regional balance in which Gulf monarchs became more powerful vis-à-vis increasingly indebted and divided Arab and Third World sending countries, especially the formerly 'revolutionary' single-party states. In the receiving countries, migrants of ever more varied national origins lost their place in oppositional movements which fell apart with the attrition of radical pan-Arabism and Leftism and the rise of local, conservative nationalism and neo-liberalism. Alienated from local allies, understood as a demographic and cultural problem, and facing market forces, segregation and exclusion, migrants were now only able to lodge protests in corporate-economic terms, and the political challenge to monarchies of which they formed a part was defeated.

Two points are worth underlining. First, this analysis avoids strong tenden-cies to the teleology, materialism and determinism of modernisation theory on the one hand and of Marxism on the other. Monarchs did not via migration overcome an inevitable King's Dilemma, or fragment a socialist working-class, because the dilemmas of modernisation and the rise of working-class socialism were not and are not inevitable or automatic. Much depended instead on the transnational cultural, political and ideological sphere. No inherent telos prevailed, history, context and contingency mattered, and there was real scope for the role of ideas in identifying diverse interests.

Second, the argument aims to illustrate how in comparative politics the meaning and effect of a given factor – in this case migration – is not constant and stable. The political world depicted here is not a clock-like mechanism comprised of levers and springs, cogs and hands (dependent and independent variables), with each having assigned or predictable effects, or operating as constant or even probabilistic causes (Almond and Genco 1977). Instead the effect of migration, and the meaning, form and politics of migration itself, varied fundamentally (although not in an endlessly fluid or random way) according to history, context and the (re)construction of movements of opposition.

The foregoing implies, finally, that the present state of migrant political demobilisation may not last. It is possible that in the coming years an oppositional politics linking the interests, ideas and aspirations of various groups – second (and even third) generation migrants (often professionals) excluded from citizenship, exploited workers, those in marriages between nationals and non-nationals, *bidun* groups, rights activists, and disaffected nationals, for example – will emerge on the basis of new ideas to challenge the status quo anew.

References

Abir, M. (1993) *Saudi Arabia: Government, Society and the Gulf Crisis*. London: Routledge.

Abrahamian, Ervand (2001) 'The 1953 Coup in Iran', *Science and Society*, 65(2): 182–215.

Abu Lughod, Janet (1985) 'Recent migration in the Arab World', in S. E. Ibrahim and N. S. Hopkins (eds), *Arab Society: Social Science Perspectives*. Cairo: American University in Cairo Press.

Al-Rasheed, M. (2002) *A History of Saudi Arabia*. Cambridge: Cambridge University Press.

Alessa, Shamlan Y. (1981) *The Manpower Problem in Kuwait*. London: Kegan Paul International.

Almond, Gabriel and Genco, Stephen (1977) 'Clouds, clocks, and the study of politics', *World Politics*, 29(4): 489–522.

Alnasrawi, Abbas (1991) *Arab Nationalism, Oil, and the Political Economy of Dependency*. New York: Greenwood.

Anderson, Lisa (1991) 'Absolutism and the resilience of monarchy in the Middle East', *Political Science Quarterly*, 106: 1–25.

Anderson, Lisa (2000) 'Dynasts and nationalists: why monarchies survive', in Joseph Kostiner (ed.) *Middle East Monarchies: The Challenge of Modernity*. Boulder, CO: Lynne Rienner.

Ashton, Nigel (2008) *King Hussein of Jordan: A Political Life*. New Haven, CT: Yale University Press.

Ayalon, Ami (2000) 'Post-Ottoman Arab Monarchies: old bottles, new labels?', in Joseph Kostiner (ed.), *Middle East Monarchies: The Challenge of Modernity*. Boulder, CO: Lynne Rienner.

82 John Chalcraft

Bahrain Government Annual Reports, 1924–1956 (1986) 5 Vols. Gerards Cross: Archive Editions.

Beblawi, Hazem (1990) 'The rentier state in the Arab world', in Giacomo Luciani (ed.), *The Arab State*. London: Routledge pp. 85–98.

Bhagwati, J. (1984) 'Incentives and disincentives: international migration', *Weltwirtschaftliches Archiv*, 120(4): 678–700.

Bin Talal, Hassan (1984) 'Manpower migration in the Middle East: an overview', *Middle East Journal*, 38(4): 610–614.

Birks, J.S. and Sinclair, C.A. (1980) *Arab Manpower: The Crisis of Development*. London: Croom Helm.

Brand, Laurie A. (1988) *Palestinians in the Arab World: Institution Building and the Search for State*. New York: Columbia.

Burdett, A.L.P. (1997) *Records of Saudi Arabia, 1961–1965*, 5 vols. Chippenham: Archive Editions.

Burdett, A.L.P. (2004) *Records of Saudi Arabia, 1966–1971*, 6 vols. Chippenham: Archive Editions.

Choucri, N. (1986) 'Asians in the Arab World: labor migration and public policy', *Middle Eastern Studies*, 22(2): 252–73.

Crystal, Jill (1990) *Oil and Politics in the Gulf: Rulers and Merchants in Kuwait and Qatar*. New York: Cambridge University Press.

Davidson, Christopher M. (2008) *Dubai: The Vulnerability of Success*. London: Hurst.

Disney, Nigel (1977) 'South Korean Workers in the Middle East', *MERIP*, 61 (October): 22–4, 26.

Elyachar, Julia (2006) *Markets of Dispossession: NGOs, Economic Development, and the State in Cairo*. Durham, NC: Duke University Press.

Entelis, John P. (1976) 'Oil wealth and the prospects for democratization in the Arabian peninsula: the case of Saudi Arabia', in Naiem A. Sherbiny and Mark A. Tessler (eds), *Arab Oil: Impact on the Arab Countries and Global Implications*. New York: Praeger.

Fergany, Nader (1982) 'The impact of emigration on national development in the Arab region: the case of the Yemen Arab Republic', *International Migration Review*, 16(4): 757–80.

Fergany, Nader (ed.) (1983) *Al-'Ummala al-Ajnabiyya fi Aqtar al-Khalij al-'Arabi/Foreign Workers in the Gulf Countries*. Beirut: Centre for Arab Unity Studies.

Franklin, Robert Lee (1985) *The Indian Community in Bahrain: Labour Immigration in a Plural Society*. Unpublished PhD Dissertation, Harvard University.

Fuccaro, Nelida (2008) 'Pearl Towns and Early Oil Cities: Migration and Integration in the Arab Coast of the Persian Gulf'. Unpublished paper.

Gause, F. Gregory III (1993) *Oil Monarchies: Domestic and Security Challenges in the Arab Gulf States*. New York: Council on Foreign Relations.

Ghazali, Salah Muhammad 'Aisa Al- (2007) *Al-Jama'at al-Siyasiya al-Kuwaytiya fi Qarn 1910–2007: Dusturiyin, Islamiyyin, al-Shi'a, al-Qawmiyyin/Political Organizations in Kuwait, 1910–2007: Constitutionalists, Islamists, Shi'a and [Arab] Nationalists*. Kuwait: n.p.

Halliday, Fred (1977a) 'Migration and the labor force in the oil producing states of the Middle East', *Development and Change*, 8: 263–91.

Halliday, Fred (1977b) 'Labor migration in the Middle East', *MERIP Reports*, 59 (August): 3–17.

Halliday, Fred (1980) 'The Gulf between two revolutions: 1958–1979', in Tim Niblock (ed.), *Social and Economic Development in the Arab Gulf*. London: Croom Helm.

Halliday, Fred (1984) 'Labor migration in the Arab World', *MERIP Reports*, 123 (May):

3–10, 30.

Halliday, Fred (2000) 'Monarchies in the Middle East: a concluding appraisal', in Joseph Kostiner (ed.), *Middle East Monarchies: The Challenge of Modernity*. Boulder, CO: Lynne Rienner, pp. 289–303.

Halliday, Fred (2002 [1974]) *Arabia without Sultans*, 2nd edn. London: Saqi Books.

Halpern, Manfred (1963) *The Politics of Social Change in the Middle East and North Africa*. Princeton, NJ: Princeton University Press.

Harik, Iliya and Sullivan, Denis J. (1992) *Privatization and Liberalization in the Middle East*. Bloomington, IN: Indiana University Press.

Hartmann, Rainer (1995) 'Yemeni exodus from Saudi Arabia: the Gulf conflict and the ceasing of workers emigration', *Journal of South Asian and Middle Eastern Studies*, 19(2) (Winter).

Humphrey, Michael (1993) 'The political economy of population movements in the Middle East', *Middle East Report*, 23(181) (March/April).

Huntington, Samuel P. (1968) *Political Order in Changing Societies*. New Haven, CT: Yale University Press.

Ibrahim, Saad Eddin (1982) *The New Arab Social Order: A Study of the Social Impact of Oil Wealth*. Boulder, CO: Westview Press.

Joukhadar, Abdul-Halim (1980) 'Les Etrangers au Koweit', *Population*, 35(1) (January–February): 57–82.

Kapiszewski, Andrzej (2001) *Nationals and Expatriates: Population and Labour Dilemmas of the Gulf Cooperation Council States*. London: Ithaca Press.

Kapiszewski, Andrzej (2006) *Arab versus Asian Migrant Workers in the GCC Countries*. Paper Presented to United Nations Expert Group Meeting on International Migration and Development in the Arab Region. Beirut (15–17 May), pp. 1–20.

Khalaf, Abd ul-Hadi (1985) 'Labor Movements in Bahrain', *MERIP Reports*, 132 (May): 24–9.

Khalaf, Suleyman N. (1992) 'Gulf societies and the image of unlimited good', *Dialectical Anthropology*, 17: 53–84.

Khalaf, Suleyman N. (2000) 'Poetics and politics of newly invented traditions in the Gulf: camel racing in the United Arab Emirates', *International Journal of Cultural and Social Anthropology*, XXXIX(3) (Summer): 243–262.

Khalili, Laleh (2007) *Heroes and Martyrs of Palestine: The Politics of National Commemoration*. Cambridge: Cambridge University Press.

Khuri, Fuad I. (1980) *Tribe and State in Bahrain*. Chicago: Chicago University Press.

Kostiner, Joseph (ed.) (2000) *Middle East Monarchies: The Challenge of Modernity*. Boulder, CO: Lynne Rienner.

Lackner, Helen (1978) *A House Built on Sand: A Political Economy of Saudi Arabia*. London: Ithaca Press.

Longva, Ahn Nga (1997) *Walls Built on Sand: Migration, Exclusion and Society in Kuwait*. Boulder, CO: Westview Press.

Louër, Laurence (2008) 'The political impact of labor: migration in Bahrain', *City and Society*, 20(1): 32–53.

Luciani, Giacomo (1990) 'Allocation vs production states: a theoretical framework' in Giacomo Luciani (ed.), *The Arab State*. London: Routledge.

Maddy-Weitzman, Bruce (2000) 'Why did Arab monarchies fall? An analysis of old and new explanations', in Joseph Kostiner (ed.), *Middle East Monarchies: The Challenge of Modernity*. Boulder, CO: Lynne Rienner.

Mahdavi, Hossein (1970) 'The patterns and problems of economic development in rentier states: the case of Iran', Michael Cook (ed.), *Studies in the Economic History of the*

Middle East. Oxford: Oxford University Press.

Malley, Robert (1996) *The Call from Algeria: Third Worldism, Revolution, and the Turn to Islam.* Berkeley, CA: University of California Press.

Mdairis, Falah Abdallah Al- (2004) *Al-Harakat wa-l-Jama'at al-Siyasiyya fi-l-Bahrain 1938–2002/Political Organizations and Movements in Bahrain 1938–2002.* Beirut: Dar al-Kunuz al-Adabiyya.

Naqeeb, Khaldoun Hasan al- (1990) *Society and State in the Gulf and Arab Peninsula: A different perspective*, trans. L.M. Kenny. London: Routledge.

Okruhlik, Gwenn (1999) 'Rentier wealth, unruly law, and the rise of opposition: the political economy of oil states', *Comparative Politics*, (Spring): 295–315.

Okruhlik, Gwenn and Conge, Patrick (1997) 'National autonomy, labor migration and political crisis: Yemen and Saudi Arabia', *Middle East Journal*, 51(4) (Autumn): 554-65.

Owen, Roger (2004) *State, Power and Politics in the Making of the Modern Middle East.* London: Routledge.

Ross, Michael L (2001) 'Does oil hinder democracy?', *World Politics*, 53(3): 325-61.

Russell, Sharon Stanton (1986) 'Remittances from international migration: a review in perspective', *World Development*, 14(6): 677–96.

Russell, Sharon Stanton (1988) 'Migration and political integration in the Arab world', in Giacomo Luciani and Ghassan Salamé (eds), *The Politics of Arab Integration.* London: Croom Helm.

Russell, Sharon Stanton (1989) 'Politics and ideology in migration policy formulation: the case of Kuwait', *International Migration Review*, 23(1) (Spring): 24–47.

Russell, Sharon Stanton and Muhammad Ali al-Ramadhan (1994) 'Kuwait's migration policy since the Gulf crisis', *International Journal of Middle East Studies*, 26(4) (November): 569–87.

Sadowski, Yahya (1991) 'Arab economies after the Gulf War: power, poverty, and petrodollars', *Middle East Report*, 21(3) (May/June).

Sayigh, Yusif A. (1971) 'Problems and prospects of development in the Arabian peninsula', *International Journal of Middle East Studies*, 2 (January).

Seccombe, Ian J. (1983) 'Labour migration to the Arabian Gulf: evolution and characteristics 1920–1950', *Bulletin of the British Society for Middle East Studies*, 10(1): 3–20.

Seccombe, Ian J. (1987) *Work Camps and Company Towns: Settlement Patterns and the Gulf Oil Industry.* Durham: Centre for Islamic and Middle Eastern Studies.

Seccombe, Ian J. and Lawless, R.I. (1986) 'Foreign worker dependence in the Gulf, and the international oil companies: 1910–50', *International Migration Review*, XX(3) (Autumn): 548–74.

Serageldin, Ismail (1983) *Manpower and International Labor Migration in the Middle East and North Africa*, A World Bank Publication. New York: Oxford University Press.

Serageldin, Ismail and Li, Bob (1983) *Tools for Manpower Planning: The World Bank Models*, Vol. 1, World Bank Staff Working Papers No. 587. Washington, DC (May).

Sherbiny, Naiem A. (ed.) (1981) *Manpower Planning in the Oil Countries.* Greenwich, CT: JAI Press.

Sherbiny, Naiem A. (1984) 'Expatriate labor flows to the Arab oil countries in the 1980s', *Middle East Journal*, 38(4) (Autumn): 643–67.

Sherbiny, Naiem A. and Tessler, Mark A. (eds) (1976) *Arab Oil: Impact on the Arab Countries and Global Implications.* New York: Praeger.

Smith, Pamela Ann (1984) *Palestine and the Palestinians, 1876–1983.* New York: St. Martin's Press.

Vitalis, Robert (2007) *America's Kingdom: Mythmaking on the Saudi Oil Frontier.* Stanford, CA: Stanford University Press.

Waterbury, John (1973) 'Endemic and planned corruption in a monarchical regime', *World Politics*, 25(4) (July): 533–55.

Watt, D.C. (1962) 'Labour relations and trade unionism in Aden, 1952–60', *Middle East Journal*, 16: 443–56.

Weiner, Myron (1982) 'International migration and development: Indians in the Persian Gulf', *Population and Development Review*, 8(1) (March): 1–36.

Winckler, O. (2000) 'Gulf monarchies as rentier states: the nationalization policies of the labour force', in J. Kostiner (ed.), *Middle East Monarchies: The Challenge of Modernity*. Boulder, CO: Lynne Rienner, pp. 237–56.

Zagorski, Paul W. (2009) *Comparative Politics: Continuity and Breakdown in the Contemporary World*. London: Routledge.

4

GENDER AND PARTICIPATION IN THE ARAB GULF

Wanda Krause

Introduction

The chapter seeks to understand the political roles of women in government-supported organizations in the Gulf states. With reference to the governmentality literature discussed here, it investigates the positions women occupy to support state objectives and influence change. The process of a specific type of governmentality, called rentier governmentality in the Gulf, will be discussed. Such an enquiry is important on three fronts. First, dominant theoretical frameworks in the Arab Gulf, in particular rentier state theory, inadequately explain or capture important developments. Second, it is essential to understand what processes are shaping the kinds of individuals which support state objectives and the participation of women. Thirdly, women have been viewed as tangential to political action and depicted as passive actors within the Gulf and the Middle East in general. Appreciably, we can gain a better understanding of the significance of women's participation through an unconventional approach to studying the Arab Gulf. To this end, this research relies on five years of field research in the Gulf states, particularly in the UAE and Qatar, and applies the literature on governmentality to the rentier state. To reiterate, this chapter focuses only on the role of government-supported organizations as opposed to the various other forms of organization that do exist for women in the Arab Gulf states.

Governmentality

Governmentality was first introduced by Foucault to describe how government regulates the conduct of others or oneself (Hindess 1997: 106; Dean 1999: 17, 18), or in other words "the conduct of conduct" (Dean 1999: 10). It is concerned with the different mentalities of government (Dean 1999: 16) and the various ways in which human conduct is influenced. Importantly, governmentality is not characterized only by discipline and regulation; rather, it emphasizes a productive dimension (Ferguson and Gupta 2002). This means that instead of punishment and direct coercive measures, as described in most of the literature, the state can use various other mechanisms, such as the entitlements and welfare allocations typically found within the Gulf countries. Foucault was interested in the mechanisms of government found within state institutions and outside them, or that transcend state, civil society and the family (Ferguson and Gupta 2002). Here, I use the concept to signify the diffusion of modes of governance, such as state feminism, beyond the boundaries of the state and the "imbrication of all kinds of social actors such as GONGOs" (Sharma 2006: 62). As such, I seek to understand what role women acquire and how they conduct themselves through partaking in activities, here government-run organizations.

More recently, "governmentality" has been used to describe a process of neo-liberalism in which a transfer of government operations to non-state entities occurs "that can produce a degree of 'autonomization' of entities of government from the state" (Barry et al. 1996: 11, 12). A new modality of government is operative: the state creates mechanisms that work on their own to achieve results. One would need, however, to understand that the process of govern-mentality might look different in contexts outside the West.

As Dean (1999: 67) notes, programs of empowerment are particularly clear examples of neo-liberal governmentality that seek to operationalize a decen-tralization of power. Although the governmentality theorization is borne out of Western contexts where a decentralization of power is said to occur and may be viewed as specific to those contexts, the corporatist models applied to the Gulf are insufficient for analyzing the productive dimension within individual conduct in line with fulfilling state objectives. As such, we look at how the process of a decentralization and "empowerment" may actually give greater powers to the state, and especially that of a welfare or rentier state, while at the same time empowering women. How are different groups hierarchically con-nected with one another, and what problems are to be solved and objectives sought (Dean 1999: 30)? What practices, strategies, and forms of influence are used by way of solving these problems or reaching these objectives? Thus how do the GONGO (government-organized non-governmental organizations) associations function as institutions that assist government? One needs to investigate how state and society is produced and developed through not only bureaucratic practices, but also the interaction between state and societal actors, public cultural representations, and the support of organizations.

The rentier state

As the Gulf countries have characteristics of the rentier state, being oil-wealthy and with low populations, how the rentier state is produced is of special interest here. Rentier state literature is concerned with the political consequences that result from a state's reliance on natural resource exports, such as oil. Such a state is concerned domestically with "distribution,' "circulation," or "allocation" (Ayubi 1999: 227). Here, and in brief, a rentier state is defined as one that obtains at least 40 percent of its Gross Domestic Product (GDP) from foreign sources or "rents" (van der Meulen 1997: 7, 51).

Rentier state scholarship forms two categories – one considers the political effect of rents, and the other concerns the economic effect of a state's dependence on natural resource exports. Subsequently, with the first category, the principal claims suggest oil wealth is an obstacle to civil society; with the second, its scholars suggest that oil wealth is an impediment to effective economic development. Economic restructuring can have a direct effect on women's social development if, as individuals and members of their community, their well-being and autonomy are enhanced (Yamani 1997: 274).

The Gulf states are criticized based on their rentier state status of squashing civil society and providing obstacles to political and economic development. The argument is that oil allows the state to subdue and contain civil society activism by providing the services that they would normally perform or that they had performed in the past. As generally is the case in the region, a rentier state often provides resources to its citizens, from jobs or free housing to electricity and water. In many of the Gulf states, citizens may be provided land for housing or business activities. It is, however, a narrow and inaccurate view to categorize rentier states as merely suppressive of individual capacities, a result and consequence of an over-reliance on rentier theory literature.

The study of women in government-supported organizations will be discussed in reference to the literature on the rentier state since it is claimed that rentierism has had a considerable influence on the politics and economics of the Gulfian societies (Meulen 1997: 6); yet, it is important to also include theories of governance for a broader perspective. Rentierism has produced what is called a "rentier society," in which citizens are said to have an income without sometimes working. In this thinking, a kind of "rentier mentality" may be expected to prevail in such a society (Ayubi 1999: 227).

Problems with the rentier state theory

Discussions concerning the rentier state in the Gulf states are dominated by the view that associational life is ineffective, if it is even present at all. The problem with this is that rentier state theory cannot account for how a rentier state can witness openings created by civil society actors, nor really any other meaningful processes in the other direction. However, if changes are manifesting, the theory cannot stand alone explaining the political processes of the Gulf region.

Some scholars are pointing out that other variables have been excluded. The Gulf is a difficult place to test the claim that oil is an impediment to civil societal expansion because almost all oil-rich Middle Eastern governments have been highly authoritarian since gaining independence (Ross 2001: 331). Herb (2002) reminds us that all Gulf rentier states have emerged from a background of poverty. Furthermore, rentier state theory "ignores" the possibility that oil revenues might have positive effects on civil society. Moreover, there is evidence that civil society sectors are not subdued. If bottom-up activism is a factor in changing dynamics, then not only should these be given due attention but also how the state responds to various groupings and collaborations. Concerning the assumption that meaningful activism has "shut down" inside the rentier state, Curtis (2001: 45) notes how "[t]he unfortunate corollary of this has been the development of the rentier state model that regards 'societal' influence on decision-making as an irrelevance."

Therefore, the greatest problem for the discussion on women's government-supported organizations in the Gulf is in the focus of mainstream rentier state theorists on the state. A complete picture of state–societal interaction must include analysis of spheres found outside the statist formulation of the state. Rather than focusing on the state in order to understand change, it is imperative to also look at sectors that may produce the state itself and achieve state goals, as well as on sectors that communicate with, bargain, pressure, and respond to the state. As power is not the sole domain of the state, it is essential to study how power manifests itself in spheres that are depoliticized because they have been allocated a place outside the imagined boundary of the state. As Navaro-Yashin (2002: 135) notes, "[t]he state . . . is also generated from within the agencies of what is called (and reified as) society."

Rentier state theory is excluding significant components for a comprehensive understanding of political reconfigurations. Therefore this chapter diverges from the mainstream view within rentier state theory that the state perpetuates itself and its interests through recognized state apparatuses (Navaro-Yashin 2002). To illustrate the paucity of such a dominant framework, the chapter focuses on a major locus for control and change – government-supported women's organizations.

Rentier governmentality

The following sections are concerned with the programs and strategies used to influence conduct that may be possible due to but not limited to oil wealth. The Gulf states govern and construct themselves and society through the implementation of policies and importantly the choosing to prioritize supporting specific goals through specific venues. This process of rentier governmentality is illustrated here through the agency of the state's official women's organizations. Employing the terms of verticality and encompassment,[1] the chapter delineates how the state and official women's associations (re)configure the state and civil society sectors in terms of hierarchy and space.

Within the larger theoretical development in which GONGO associations have been viewed as part of the neo-liberal process and in which the nation-state cedes power to what are usually state-developed agencies and institutions, this study shows that GONGOs are, in most ways, empowered to fulfill functions of the welfare (specifically rentier) state. As Rose (1996: 46) explains:

> Political forces seek to give effect to their strategies, not only through the utilization of laws, bureaucracies, funding regimes and authoritative State

agencies and agents, but through utilizing and instrumentalizing forms of authority other than those of the 'State' in order to govern – spatially and constitutionally – 'at a distance'.

Yet, in contrast with the theoretical underpinnings of neo-liberal governmentality, which I maintain are not necessarily occurring in the West in practice, a decentralization of power is also not always at stake in the case of the Gulf states. In fact, the state can gain greater powers through the vertical encompassment[2] of civil society sectors, made possible largely through rentierism and strategies of governmentality, while supporting human and society capacity building.

Authoritarian governmentality, in general, occurs when the state "does not rely on the choices, aspirations or capacities of the individual subject" (Dean 1999: 145). Egypt and Tunisia are examples of authoritarian governmentality; to varying degrees, Syria, Libya, and Yemen embody a mixture of authoritarian governmentality and cult mentality. Power in the Gulf states is, however, exercised most predominantly through resources controlled by the ruling elite and which have been used to simultaneously build a "modern" society within very little time. In this context, state leaders embrace the potential of women by providing large amounts of funding for their activities and address women as pivotal to development. It could be said that the oil money these Gulf states have at their disposal provides a unique case. In some ways, it does make for an interesting case; however, it is often ignored that leaders of states, such as Libya and Egypt, had huge amounts of money at their disposal that could have been channelled in earnest to development, including the development of women. Indeed, "Egypt" was never poor. As such, it is not oil money that uniquely enables the channelling of resources to women's GONGOs but rather concerted policies and priorities. Hence, strategies of "rentier governmentality" are not unique because of the "rents" used for a particular form of governance, although oil wealth does form an essential mode of governance.

The status of women and their public presence

To best contextualize the participation of women, I first provide an overview of women's status in the Gulf. The following discusses women according to general study and work conditions, recent gender reforms, and personal status laws comparatively. Women have made significant strides in areas of literacy and university education. In most of the countries, women have reached the same or better literacy levels and enrollment numbers in higher educational institutions than their male counterparts. For example, adult male illiteracy in the UAE exceeded female illiteracy 25 percent to 21 percent in 2000 (UNDP-POGAR 2006). In Qatar, 96 percent of girls and 95 percent of boys were enrolled in primary education already in 2000. Adult illiteracy in Qatar was 19.6 percent for men and 15.6 percent for women in 2002 (UNDP-POGAR 2006).

As a further example, in Kuwait, women comprise two-thirds of university-level students. Over 67 percent of Kuwait University graduates are women (UNDP-POGAR 2006). Also, in Bahrain 72 percent of the students at the Arabian Gulf University are women (Ahmed 2009: 23), and in Qatar 68 percent graduating from post-secondary education are women (Breslin and Jones 2009: 75). These statistics are similar to the UAE in which 75 percent of the student body at the National University in Al-Ain is female. However, directly after 2001 when males returned from overseas because of 9/11 the number of males at universities grew significantly, and in some cases the enrollment was even slightly greater for males. Thus the larger proportion of women enrolled in higher education is in part due to more men traveling overseas for study.

Compared to the other Gulf countries, illiteracy remains a national problem in Oman; however, a dramatic shift in literacy is evident and women have achieved gender parity with men in education. In 1970, there were no schools for girls in the country and in 1984 84 percent of adult women were still illiterate. As of 2002, that had reduced to 34.6 percent (UNDP-POGAR 2006).

Participation rates in the workforce are increasing across all Gulf countries at varying rates. The vast majority of women employed are in the public sector. With comparatively high rates of participation in the workforce, in 2001 Kuwaiti women constituted 31.8 percent (UNDP-POGAR 2006) and in 2007, 51 percent (Kelly 2009: 8). In Bahrain women constituted 21 percent in 2000 (UNDP-POGAR 2006) and 31 percent in 2007 (Ahmed 2009: 23); and in the UAE, 15 per cent in 2000[3] and 41 percent in 2007 (Kelly 2009: 8). In Oman women comprised 18 percent of the labor force in 2007 (al-Talei 2009: 51). Even though in Oman female participation in the workforce and female university enrollment is comparatively low, on the ground, female youth tend to express much higher aspirations for participation in public life than their counterparts across the border in the UAE. As of 2010, women comprise 36 percent of the labor force (Attwood, online). Al-Talei (2009: 51) found that the majority of Qatar's citizens oppose women taking an active role in public life; however, this view is rapidly changing. Like in the other Gulf states, however, women in Qatar may exercise more decision-making power in the home as compared to their sisters in other Arab countries, a phenomenon little understood within Western feminist epistemology.[4]

Women do not generally receive equal pay for equal work in private sector jobs, and cases of discrimination in this sector abound, such as the receipt of various perks and benefits. Discrimination in promotion is still reported in the public sector. Education and most workplaces generally remain segregated by sex. However, segregation is also a means by which women are encouraged to take part in public life. In other words, without segregation at universities and in the public sector there would be a much smaller percentage of women studying and entering the workforce.

According to the UNDP's assessment, Kuwait has made greater progress towards improving women's political rights (UNDP-POGAR 2006). Significantly, on 16 May 2005, the Kuwaiti parliament approved a law giving Kuwaiti women full political rights including electoral rights. Previously, Kuwait received international attention on female suffrage in 2003 when the cabinet approved draft legislation granting women full rights to vote and run as candidates in elections. The legislation was blocked, however, given the predominance of conservative Islamists and other social conservatives in the legislature. Similarly, the parliament had blocked a decree issued in 1999 by Emir Sheikh Jaber al-Ahmad al-Sabah granting women the right to vote and run for office in the 2003 parliamentary elections.

Thus, although Kuwaiti women have made greater advances, they do have greater challenges with this Islamist influence. Some reformists attest the best strategy with dealing with both "extremist" Islamists and "traditional" members of government is dialogue to shift perceptions and notions. The argument is that changes must necessarily occur from the inside out. Other women try to build consensus through gathering international support and the help of lawyers and male activists. Certainly, the series of protests, and especially the organized demonstrations of March 2005 against the exclusion of women from politics, attracted the international attention needed to put enough pressure on the parliament when, two months later, women achieved full political participation.

Gains in the government sector remain steady. On 12 June 2005, for the first time in Kuwait's history, a woman was appointed minister of planning and administrative development and later appointed minister of health. A second female was appointed minister of education and higher studies. That year, two further women were appointed to the 16-member municipal council. In 2007, a woman was appointed minister of education and higher studies, and in 2008 a woman was appointed minister for housing and administrative planning. In 2009, four women were finally elected to the national parliament. Such developments are statistically notable, although they have brought simultaneously numerous other challenges to women which are beyond the scope of this paper.

Until 2002, Bahraini women had no political rights. They could not vote or stand in elections. The constitution was amended in 2002 so that women were allowed to run in the 2002 municipal and parliamentary elections, although none won seats. One female candidate won uncontested a parliamentary seat, becoming the first elected Bahraini female deputy in parliamentary elections held on 25 November 2006. In 2004, a woman was appointed as minister of health, in January 2005 a second was appointed minister of social affairs, and in 2008 a woman was appointed minister of culture and information. Significantly, Sheikh Hamad bin Khalifa al-Thani issued a decree on 26 April 2007, appointing a woman as a judge in the constitutional court. Bahrain had appointed its first female judge on 6 June 2006. Furthermore, in June 2006, when Bahrain was elected head of the United Nations General Assembly, a woman was appointed as the Assembly's President, becoming the first Middle Eastern woman and the third woman in history to take the post. However, political gains in Kuwait and Bahrain have also been made with grassroots pressures.

Political gains in the UAE and Qatar have been largely led by the rulers and, in particular, the wives of the rulers, Sheikha Fatima bint Mubarak, wife of the late Sheikh Zayed, and Sheikha Moza bint Nasser, wife of Qatar's Emir, Sheikh Hamad. Although women had long held positions in the parliament of a local government, Sharjah, the UAE had been one of the slowest to include women in key federal government positions. In 2004, the UAE appointed a woman as minister of economy and trade. A woman then became the first elected to the Federal National Council, and eight more were appointed in 2007, representing 22.5 percent of the parliament and instantly sweeping the UAE up to a ranking of having one of the highest number of female parliamentarians in the world! Following Bahrain, beginning in 2008 women could also be judges and public prosecutors. In March 1999, Qatar held the first elections in the nation's history although no women won seats. The first female official was elected in the second municipal elections held in April 2003 and then a female was appointed minister of education. Previously, Sheikh Hamad's sister held the highest position given to a woman as deputy chairman of the Higher Committee for Family Affairs. In 2007, a woman won a seat in the Central Municipal Council.

Oman had been one of the forerunners in support of women in public office in the Gulf region. Nonetheless, the parliamentary elections for the Majlis al-Shura (Consultative Council) in October 2003 were the first in which women were free to participate without restrictions; yet, none won and the two female incumbents were both re-elected, keeping the female representation the same. Sultan Qaboos appointed to his 70 member Majlis ad-Dawla[5] 14 women in November 2007 (al-Talei 2009: 52). In 2003, the sultan appointed Oman's first female minister; currently women fill three other ministerial posts,[6] and women served as ambassadors as early as 1999.

Progress is being made in regard to personal status law across the Gulf but women continue to face legal inequality. The Family Law that the Emir of Qatar, Sheikh Hamad al-Thani, promulgated on 29 June 2007 is made up of 301 articles addressing domestic issues not based entirely on Islamic law nor confined to interpretations of one Islamic school of law. The law gives the wife the right to end the marriage under certain conditions and, significantly, banned "temporary marriages."

Aside from unequal citizenship rights, women face practical obstacles and discrimination in divorce and inheritance decisions. Women's testimony is given equal value in court proceedings only in Oman, as of 2008. Generally, women take up employment with the permission of a male guardian. In cases of divorce, custody laws differ, but a woman usually loses her right to custody upon remarriage. A man need not have a reason for divorce, and recently women are controversially being divorced by SMS (texting). Although divorce is increasingly initiated by women, they must still provide specific reasons and often undergo a lengthy process, or else give up certain often substantial entitlements through provision of *khula* (divorce initiated by a woman). In none of the countries are women officially allowed to confer citizenship to their spouses or children. In fact, women can risk losing their citizenship upon marriage to a non-GCC foreigner, although in the UAE and, recently, Bahrain sheikhly or emiri decree allowed the passing of citizenship for confined cases. Discrimination occurs normatively in rulings between persons of different status, such as with a rich woman and a poor woman or a local and a domestic servant.

In Bahrain and Kuwait, differences exist in the personal status code for Sunni and Shia women. For example, Shia women are treated more equitably in divorce and inheritance proceedings than their Sunni counterparts, who receive more favorable custody verdicts. Only the Sunni needs to have a male guardian sign a marriage contract. In Kuwait, Shia women face less favorable custody outcomes than Sunni women do. However, oftentimes divorce decrees and procedures are solely dependent upon the personal approaches or prejudices of the judge presiding over the case. Furthermore, personal status laws are not always enforced in practice.

Marrying foreign women is argued to be a problem in the Gulf states of stability, and is obviously a challenge for local women who face obstacles, in terms of norms, familial acceptance, and government laws.[7] In 1998, 28 percent of marriages in the UAE were between UAE men and foreign women. Marriage of one man to more than one woman continues to be a challenge to many women. Although varying, according to the emirate, 50 percent of marriages of locals in the UAE are to more than one wife; in particular many marriages are not registered (Krause 2007: 101,102), a phenomenon that exists across the Gulf albeit with usually lower numbers.

Violence against women continues to be a pressing issue. Extremely few local women report spousal abuse to the police and it is often kept within the family, or more recently sometimes discussed in great secrecy with appointed women within some of the GONGOs. There are many reports of women being sent home from police stations to reconcile. Due to the belief that some of these officers hold that men have authority over their wives, women are sometimes denied protection. Spousal rape is not a criminal offense in any of the countries. Across the Gulf there are, furthermore, reports of violence against, and rape of, domestic servants. They rarely report incidences because their livelihood depends on their employment with the host family, as well as those they support in their home countries. Furthermore, a recent Freedom House report (2009: 14, 19, 20, 24, 56, 73, 74, 91, 92, 93, 111, 112) found forced prostitution of young women brought over on false passports or lied to over work descriptions to be an "increasing" problem that GCC governments have made efforts to address. Due to the existing interpretations of Islamic law and other reasons, ratification of the CEDAW has been with reservations on some points. Kuwait ratified the CEDAW in 1994, Bahrain in 2002, the UAE in 2004, Oman in 2006, and Qatar as of 2010.

An overall assessment that women have in some cases few and other cases some adequate human rights protections and that they do face gender-based discrimination is also observed by Freedom House (Freedom House 2009: 138–

41).[8] The statistics offered by Freedom House, however, could do better to factor in the violations of freedoms and rights among three specific sectors of women although authors of country studies have made a commendable effort to note some of these issues. These violations are among the increasing volume of tens of thousands of women trafficked into these countries, the hundreds of thousands of domestic workers and staff from South-East Asia in other low-paying jobs, and the *bedoon* (i.e. local residents without citizenship). Although Gulf states have issued recent laws to tackle these specific challenges, there still exist too many loopholes allowing trafficking to grow and employers to continue mistreatment. Interviewees from among these sectors have made abundantly clear that violations of their personhood are extreme and continue to be widespread.

A Human Rights Watch report (1995), among others, brought to light thousands of *bedoon*, who have no legal status and thus have lived without any legal rights within these countries. As of July 2009, Kuwait has drawn up proposals to address the issue.[9] An accurate analysis of human rights for women must necessarily factor in all living within the area for which conclusions are drawn.

Overview of government-supported women's organizations and their activities

In the Gulf, there are various forms of organizations, a number of which do receive some form of funding by the state. There are, furthermore, numerous kinds of women's organizations, ranging from the various expatriate organizations to differing Islamic and a few Islamist groupings. Networks are also a growing form of organization. Many forms of organization are informal and, therefore, remain unregistered with government. How they all differ is primarily in their relationship to government. Again, this chapter is interested specifically in women's GONGOs.

In Kuwait, the merchant class founded two women's associations in 1963 – the Cultural and Social Society (CSS) and the Arab Women's Development Society (AWDS) – which remained the only two for a decade, with the government dismantling the AWDS in 1980. Although the two had a brief union, the CSS (Women's Cultural and Social Society, WCSS) saw its role in terms of providing entertainment for its members and charity for the poor, whereas the AWDS tried to modernize society and raise the status of women. In 1975, the Girls Club was established, including members mostly from the al-Qinaie family. In the early 1980s, two Islamic women's organizations were founded – Bayader al-Salam and the Islamic Care Society, the latter formed by the prime minister's wife. The largest associations today are the WCSS and the Federation of Kuwaiti Women's Associations. The Kuwaiti government supports and regulates the Federation, the only women's group allowed to represent Kuwait internationally (UNDP-POGAR 2006).

The United Arab Emirates has the largest volume of government-run women's associations. There are six main UAE women's organizations which had already become modalities of governance by 1979 when they were subsumed under Sheikha Fatima's umbrella organization in Abu Dhabi, the al-Ittihad al-Nisa'i (Women's Union), making seven. Each emirate organization is led by a sheikha (or sheikhas) of the emirate in which it is located, and each has branches located in other cities or villages of its respective emirate, amounting to around 33. Lessons, lectures, conferences, and seminars within associations focus on four main areas: religion, health and beauty, family issues, and general skills development.

The first women's association in Qatar was created in 1982, the women's branch of the Red Crescent Society called the Qatari Women's Association, funded by the state. In 2002, Sheikha Moza, wife of the emir of Qatar, established the Supreme Council for Family Affairs, an umbrella organization. This council presides over six organizations, including the Family Consultation Centre and the Qatari Foundation for the Protection of Women and Children. The Family Consultation Centre offers the same services as the UAE women's associations. The Qatari Foundation for the Protection of Women and Children offers a legal framework for the rights of women and children, to protect women's constitutional, legal rights, to address domestic abuse, and to provide social awareness. It coordinates activities with other women's GONGOs in the region.

In Bahrain, four new women's organizations, including the Union of Bahraini Women and the Bahrain Women's Society, were founded in 2001, adding to others that had already existed. Currently, the total number is 19, although 12 are really part of the umbrella Bahraini Women's Union, created in 2006. These associations help illiterate mothers by providing daycare facilities for their children, and contribute to educational activities at literacy centers. The Supreme Council for Women in Bahrain announced a "national strategy for advancement of Bahraini women" in 2005, which aimed to increase participation of women in the workforce, leadership and decision-making positions, and raise awareness of discrimination.

In Oman, the Ministry of Social Affairs, Labor, and Vocational Training is responsible for women's issues at the governmental level. The Ministry supports women's affairs by funding and supporting the Oman Women's Association (OWA) and grassroots women's organizations. The ministry, furthermore, provides services through the OWA.[10] The OWA reportedly has 23 branches all over the country with a membership of 3,000 women (UNDP-POGAR 2006). OWA activities are very similar to those of the UAE and Qatari associations. The OWA provides an informal counseling role for women with divorce-related difficulties, but also for girls forced to marry against their will and women and girls suffering from domestic abuse. There are also 50 affiliated groups throughout the country (UNDP-POGAR 2006).

Stability and development

Given the rapid development over recent decades and the heavy force of globalization shifting many local practices, legitimacy and identities are generally fragile. All Gulf states have embarked upon strategies to take control over internal security, economic threats, and perceived attacks on local culture, largely imposed by the high volume of expatriates and what are often deemed foreign practices. Foremost of these initiatives is engaging in a discourse of unity and nation-building. This is achieved notably through women's educational empowerment, establishing the framework within which women are expected to take up public roles, and the various resources and practices of rentier governmentality. However, a productive dimension to women's participation also includes a forward vision beyond the containment of negative influences, such as that espoused in particular state visions, for example the Qatar 2030 vision for the development of the individual, economy, society, and environment.

Unity and nation-building

There is a need, as Davidson (2005: 77) argues, to legitimize and reinforce rulership. In the face of globalizing forces, it is furthermore essential to restore and embellish the past in order to anchor and strengthen a local identity. Relying upon a balance of personal, patrimonial, cultural, and religious resources (Davidson 2006: 11), the state must utilize a number of strategies of governmentality.

Such an endeavor involves the application of various symbols and a "controlled consociationalism" (Ayubi 1999: 245). Visual symbols bring the past into a collective consciousness. For example, in the middle of several cities across the Arab Gulf one can find roundabouts decorated with sculptures of oysters with pearls, dedicated to the memory of pearl diving. The pearling industry's history is also captured through sculptures of vessels and the restored ships that line the harbors within cities. Within the cities and along the coasts, traditional forts and towers have been restored.[11] Museums have been given a greater role in reviving an imagined past in the face of globalizing forces. As Khalaf argues, there is now a crucial need for the development of "living museums" and "imagined communities" (cited in Davidson 2005: 78) or what Davidson calls the production of "living memories." Examples may be found at the Dubai Heritage Village, the Pearling Village, and the Hatta Heritage Village in the UAE or Souq Waqif in Qatar. Camel racing, a sport unique to the region, is a further symbol that has an emotive quality and thus functions as a unifying force for the Gulf countries. To preserve part of the Bedouin heritage, the rulers have invested in racing circuits, prizes, and racing camels (Davidson 2005: 78). As Abu 'Athira noted, "Camel races used to be run [only] on special occasions such as weddings; now they are sponsored by governments to help people keep their camels and not lose their traditional way of life" (quoted in Davidson 2005: 78).

Allied groups have occupied different locations within a vertical order comprising the ruling families at the top and then other tribal, commercial and professional groups, previously predominantly the merchant class (Davidson 2005: 78). Governance is exercised through pacts and laws. In this context, strict laws regulate self-organizing groups, delineating how they will pursue interests or debate social issues that may conflict with the interests of the leaders. For example, in the UAE, under law all organizations are registered by a national; in Qatar, some exceptions have been made to this rule beginning in 2010; and in Kuwait, the state retains the decision-making power over who may control an association. According to al-Mughni (1997: 195), who has researched women's associations in Kuwait, the current control of women's groups by elite women is by no means accidental, having together worked to exclude women from lower classes even creating associations.

The Islamic groups have also comprised part of such allied groups. The state incorporates those Islamic groups whose aspirations fit neatly with traditionalist views on a range of issues, especially women's issues, and especially so with increased concern over globalizing influences. However, the more extreme, and violent, Islamic groups are among the major political threats to the ruling elite. At the same time, some of these associations, among female leaders, have found strategies of inclusion of particularly less conservative or even reformist Islamic thinkers useful.

The Gulf states have embraced capitalism and economic liberalization as an inevitable process, with Kuwait, Dubai, and Qatar embarking on strategies to take full advantage of globalization. As Davidson suggests, this path upsets the patrimonial, cultural, and religious resources that make up the "ruling bargain" between the state and its citizens (Davidson 2006: 11). Among those who have long opposed any form of liberalization that serves Western interests, one can hear individuals questioning the benefit of the capitalist or democratic path.

Oil has been instrumental in enabling the state to structure existing groups into a patron–client order (Ayubi 1999: 247). A rentier-based "ruling bargain" is forged between the elite state actors and the technocrats of the new middle class that are typical of Gulf countries. Relative autonomy is accorded to the technocrats by expanding their role towards the promotion of modernization. Importantly, however, this ordering is meant to ensure a source of legitimacy (Ayubi 1999: 247). Incorporating mainstream Islam also includes funding the building of mosques and overseeing and controlling the lessons that take place. Importantly, there is funding for lecturers and speakers who, for example, highlight issues that are deemed "apolitical" in substance. Simultaneously, certain Islamic orientations will be sidelined through the unbalanced distribution of funding. Bahrain is an extreme case in point.

As has been recognized by allied groups, support of organizations related to family issues is one of the most effective means of securing security and stability. The most effective are women's organizations. Much of the literature uses state feminism to refer to the process by which the state takes on women's interests normatively through women's organizations. State feminism, as exercised largely through the state-run women's associations, illustrates conflicting practice and outcomes. And although the organizations are set up and funded to serve strategic interests, the women participating do not all share the same commitments and actually may use these avenues to subvert the frameworks within which they are working.

Large investments or laws enable growth of organizations to support government objectives. Especially in Oman, the UAE, and Qatar, women's organizations often receive substantial amounts of money for the development of facilities. In Oman, for example, women's associations are able to register somewhat more quickly because the associations require approval only by the Minister of Social Development, as opposed to the Council of Ministers for all other forms of organization.[12] In both Oman and the UAE, no other organizations extend in the way that these women's associations do from urban areas into very rural regions, with their numerous branches subsumed under each country's umbrella women's organization. In Bahrain, Shia are generally hindered from forming formal organizations in which they can promote ideological perceptions or organize on a social level. Shia women are, therefore, suppressed from expressing their experiences of social injustice through formal organization (Seikaly 1997: 140) and have been forced to take to the streets, culminating in the 2011 protests which also illustrated the violence the Bahraini state is prepared to use as strategy of containment.

"Women's issues" in identity building

Although Bahrain's sweeping and repressive actions illustrate the diverging strategies that differentiate a Gulf state from others, in general women's government-supported associations across the Gulf share many striking similarities, especially in the means of supporting security and stability. Aside from the by-laws that state that associations may not engage in political activity, most government-supported women's associations direct their activities to areas they regard as "apolitical."

Islamic knowledge is significant. As evinced in the various GONGOs, women attend regular lessons on Qur'an recitation and *hadith* (prophetic narration), and speakers have included influential scholars. Topics vary, but often include women's familial roles, society, the environment, *da'wa* (Islamic call), prayer, mysticism, charity, fasting, and child-raising. Women are producers of the nation and pass down knowledge.

In addition, there are lectures and courses in the area of "health and beauty." These aim to raise women's awareness of illnesses, children's nutrition and general well-being, drug administration or use, vaccination, and breastfeeding. Beauty courses are offered on make-up, henna, or tips for hair. More significant in numbers and emphasis are the conferences and lectures dealing with women's roles, parenting, and how to be a good spouse. General skills development is achieved through literacy classes, learning computer skills, painting, drawing, cake decorating, baking, etiquette, fruit carving, cooking, or flower arranging. Significant also is the initiative to revive "traditions," through learning to make handicrafts, dresses, and other sewing or stitching activities.

Unlike associations in many developing countries that have embarked upon programs focusing on rights and specifically naming them as such, the majority of associations, especially in the UAE, Qatar, and Oman, articulate their work within the term "development." Kuwait's associations have otherwise been more direct in referring to rights. Reference to women's rights has been linked to Western feminism and viewed as destructive. More recently, "empowerment" is finding greater significance in state discourse on women. However, a Bahraini, Ghada Jamsheer (listed as one of the top ten most effective women in the Arab world in 2006 by *Forbes Magazine*), has called Bahrain's reforms "artificial and marginal" in its quest to use the family law issue, which remains unconsolidated, as a bargaining tool with opposition Islamic groups. She further points to the High Council for Women, headed by the King's wife, as the means through which the state has hindered non-governmental women's associations from forming or functioning.[13]

There is increasing tension between roles as defined by Western feminism and traditional roles. A vigorous attempt has emerged to develop and protect local practices, religion and tradition. State leaders do have reason to worry that their traditions and identity (in its ongoing formulation) will evaporate with the large non-local population found throughout the Gulf. A "plan," i.e. the Bahrainization or Kuwaitization Plan, in this endeavor is implemented through the media and associations to produce the type of individual supportive of state and societal development.

The head of state, typically seen as the nation's "father," leads his "children" to prosperity and the good life within the national "family" that transcends the private and public. Through these associations, a specific model is promoted as the ideal woman along with her ideal roles and propensities. Thus the state and women's GONGOs direct women to embody a desire that has been fashioned within a discourse on *watan* and duty. "[I]ndividuals are to fulfil their obligations not through their relations of dependency and obligation to one another, but through seeking to *fulfil themselves*" (Rose 1996: 57).

Important in the endeavor for stability and national development is education. In the UAE, Sheikh Zayed established the view that women were indispensable to the development of the country and the preservation of its heritage and identity:

> Education is like a beacon lighting your way in the darkness. It teaches you many things, the most important of which is to know your duties towards your nation, homeland, families, and the realities relating to your present, future, and your past . . .
>
> *(quoted in al-Hamed 2002: 262)*

Establishing women as "mothers of the nation" with responsibility for "maintaining the traditional family structure" (Dresch 2005: 24) is one of the crucial means through which the emirates pursue identity building.

Beyond education, the "stable family" has also been a project aimed at social development and identity building. Finding suitable marriage partners for local women has been fraught with difficulties. The project for stable families has alleviated some of these difficulties by making marriage to local women financially easier through inducements. The funding for marriages in the UAE, Qatar, and Bahrain encourages national men to marry national women, to lessen the burden of expensive weddings, and help promote stable families (since no funding is provided for subsequent marriages). As Dresch (2005: 148) has noted:

> The Fund represents a massive attempt at social engineering. Nor is it just 'top-down'... [I]t does a remarkable job not just of organising talks and seminars but of intervening as a social service and mobilising other services to solve family problems.

By organizing society's private sphere, the state has made private interests public matters.

Just as the state consists of persons who implement the goals of the rulers while pursuing other agendas, one must also recognize women within these associations as individuals whose agency is a product not only of state-led programs, but also of other influences and priorities. While some women give priority to ruling tribal clans in their activism within the associations, others base their participation on allegiance to less powerful tribes, economic circumstance, a sense of a common good that extends past a good formulated for nationals, or Islamist group embeddedness.

As Al-Oraimi (2004: 316) points out for the case of the UAE, while the majority of elite women (most often not from the ruling class) do not feel they can effect change through these associations, some attempt to work through these organizations to promote their goals of "bringing about the new balance of political power." They do this by taking a non-confrontational stance with government, and using the organization as "a hub for positive leadership." Islamist women in some of these associations sometimes demonstrate a "quiet" disavowal of the nationalist agenda, a view that has been awakened by the fact that their identities as women or Muslims have not provided a cause for solidarity with their elite co-participants. Such women pursue Islamist activities at the expense of the state, enabled through the very mechanism by which the state seeks to influence society and maintain legitimacy.

Some of those women wanting greater political reform opt to use other means, such as protest. Instances of protest are, however, very limited in comparison to those occurring in the other parts of the Middle East, such as recently in Egypt, Tunisia, Libya, and Syria. The Arab Spring affected Bahrain; however, the political dynamics, fractures within society, and state reaction cannot be generalized for the Gulf states. Moreover, the front lines of protest in these instances have gone far beyond women's issues only. There are the instances of protest for women's rights in Saudi Arabia in 1991, again in 2011 with women driving, or Kuwait in 1999. At the time, these protests garnered international support more than anything else. In Kuwait, women gained greater political rights in 2005, but only because of the combined efforts of males and females, activists, lawyers, and politicians.

Protest has not been a fundamental strategy for women to garner specifically women's rights as rights for women as a group. In fact, for the goal of empowering women the means have included being actually nudged through state prerogatives where leaders, such as Sheika Moza or Sheikha Fatima and many other powerful women, have argued for women's participation and pursuance of freedoms. It should not be ignored or underestimated that there are not just "pockets of resistance" within society to embracing a form of development that encompasses women's empowerment or the entrance of women into the "public" sphere. Other means include using the services of organizations, including those that are government-funded, that address fundamental structures of marginalization, such as poverty or (indirectly) class.

Conclusions

The modality of governmentality has enabled women to acquire some form of greater independence and self-development. Indeed, the leading figures and organizations have helped women to enjoy education and work possibilities, and important competencies. Some of the women who have been part of these organizations have moved on to take up prominent positions of responsibility outside the organizations. There are often among the sheikhas those who have a vision for genuine reform. There are also other emerging organizations for capacity building, especially among the business community, for women to develop. In recent years, there are also a few organizations, such as in the UAE and Qatar, that address human rights abuses, such as the trafficking of women.

The official women's organizations direct women's activities towards state goals although they differ sometimes in strategies and focus. Bahrain's and Kuwait's official organizations have also been steered by merchant class families and have often had an additional mixture of class-based and rights-based focus, different in many ways to Qatar's, Oman's and the UAE's. State supported organizations sometimes have large provisions of state funding, operating under an individual or elite class members. Sometimes management is organized through the appointment of ministerial employees. Salaries are normally included as an incentive for the majority of "participants." Furthermore, strategies involve the shaping of role, purpose, and identity. While such shaping produces empowered women in many ways, corporatist politics are also at work. As such, a process is occurring in which human, societal and economic development is enhanced, simultaneous to a reconfiguring of the state.

The women's GONGO organizations are invaluable because, despite the ambitions for better conditions for women, the strategies of the state provide a crucial means of "governing at a distance." The conventionally defined boundaries of the state are shown to collapse as these associations reconfigure state powers. This chapter has focused on the participation of women in state-led initiatives. A broader and more comprehensive understanding of civil society development and participation is, of course, informed by the study of all actors – those within state-funded and non-state-funded forms of organization.

Notes

1. "Verticality" refers to the state as an institution that is somehow "above" civil society, the community, and family. State planning consequently will be top-down and state actions directed from above, while grassroots actions are contrasted with those of the states because they are initiated from below. With the idea of "encompassment" the state is located within an ever-widening ripple of circles, starting with family and local community and ending with the system of nation-states (Ferguson and Gupta 2002: 982).
2. The ways in which the state represents itself as a reified entity with particular "spatial" properties through specific sets of metaphors and practices (Ferguson and Gupta 2002: 981, 982).
3. Women's Developing Role in the UAE (online). Available at: http://sjw.hct.ac.ae/html/students/noorah/personal6.htm (accessed 9 November 2003).
4. Interest in this phenomenon has culminated in discussions with Qatari women and men via informal interviews, London 2009. See also Jill Crystal (2005) "Women's Rights in the Middle East and North Africa: Citizenship and Justice, Qatar," Freedom House (online). Available at: http://www.freedomhouse.org/template.cfm?page=181 (accessed 28 April 2009).
5. The Majlis ad-Dawla serves as an advisory body that reviews draft laws proposed by the government.
6. Ministry of Information, Sultanate of Oman (online). Available at: http://www.omanet.om/english/social/dev2.asp?cat=hist (accessed 9 January 2009).
7. Across the Arab Gulf concerns are increasing over women unable to find marriage partners.
8. Saudi Arabia receives a much lower assessment. Saudi Arabia is excluded from this study, as it requires greater discussion apart from the other Gulf countries due to greater political controls over women's participation and much greater variance in participation with the rest of the Gulf.
9. Kuwait Times, "New Solution for 'Bedoon' Problem" (online) Available at: http://www.kuwaittimes.net/read.news.php?newsid=NTg4NDY1NTQ2 (accessed 13 July 2009).
10. US Department of State, "Oman: Country Reports on Human Rights Practices – 2006" (online). Available at: http://www.state.gov/g/drl/rls/hrrpt/2006/78860.htm (accessed 9 January 2009).
11. Davidson found that some of these sites, such as the fort on Futaisi Island off the coast of Abu Dhabi, were prefabricated. See Davidson (2005: 78).
12. US Department of State, "Oman: Country Reports on Human Rights Practices – 2006" (online). Available at: http://www.state.gov/g/drl/rls/hrrpt/2006/78860.htm

(accessed 9 January 2009).
13. Ghada Jamsheer, cited in Chan'ad Bahraini, "Women's Rights in Bahrain" (online). Available at: http://chanad.weblogs.us/=516 (accessed 15 December 2008).

References

Ahmed, Dunya Ahmed Abdulla (2009) "Bahrain," in Sanja Kelly and Julia Breslin (eds), *Women's Rights in the Middle East and North Africa: Gulf Edition*. New York: Freedom House.

al-Hamed, Mowza bint Mohammed bin Butti (2002) *Zayed. The Millennial Legend*. Dubai: Bin Dasmal.

al-Mughni, Haya (1997)"From gender equality to female subjugation: the changing agendas of women's groups in Kuwait," in Dawn Chatty and Annika Rabo (eds), *Organizing Women: Formal and Informal Women's Groups in the Middle East*. Oxford: Berg.

al-Oraimi, Suaad Zayed (2004) *Gender and Development: The role of Women in the Formal Economic and Political Spheres in the United Arab Emirates*. PhD dissertation, American University of Washington.

al-Talei, Rafiah (2009) "Oman," in Sanja Kelly and Julia Breslin (eds), *Women's Rights in the Middle East and North Africa: Gulf Edition*. New York: Freedom House.

Attwood (ed.) (2010) "Female Participation in Qatari Workforce Grows – Study," *Arabian Business*, 26 August (online). Available at: http://www.arabianbusiness.com/female-participation-in-qatari-workforce-grows-study-344713.html (accessed 11 August 2011).

Ayubi, Nazih N. (1999) *Over-stating the Arab State: Politics and Society in the Middle East*. London: I. B. Tauris.

Barry, Andrew, Thomas Osborne, and Nikolas Rose (eds) (1996) *Foucault and Political Reason: Liberalism, Neo-liberalism and Rationalities of Government*. Chicago: University of Chicago Press.

Breslin, Julia and Jones, Toby (2009) "Qatar," in Sanja Kelly and Julia Breslin (eds), *Women's Rights in the Middle East and North Africa: Gulf Edition*. New York: Freedom House.

Crystal, Jill (2005) "Women's Rights in the Middle East and North Africa: Citizenship and Justice, Qatar," Freedom House (online). Available at: http://www.freedomhouse.org/template.cfm?page=181 (accessed 28 April 2009).

Curtis, Shaun (2001) *Globalization, Countertrade and Privatization in the Arabian Gulf*. PhD dissertation, University of Toronto.

Davidson, Christopher M. (2005) *The United Arab Emirates: A Study in Survival*. Boulder, CO: Lynne Rienner.

Davidson, Christopher M. (2006) *The Emirates of Abu Dhabi and Dubai: Contrasting Roles in the International System*. Paper presented to conference on "The Global Gulf," Institute of Arab and Islamic Studies, University of Exeter (July).

Dean, Mitchell (1999) *Governmentality: Power and Rule in Modern Society*. London: Sage.

Dresch, Paul (2005) "Debates on marriage and nationality in the United Arab Emirates," in Paul Dresch and James Piscatori (eds), *Monarchies and Nations: Globalisation and Identity in the Arab States of the Gulf*. London: I. B. Tauris.

Ferguson, James and Akhil Gupta (2002) "Spatializing states: toward an ethnography of neoliberal governmentality," *American Ethnologist*, 29(4): 981–1002.

Herb, Michael (2002) *Do Rents Cause Authoritarianism?* Paper presented at the annual meeting of the Middle East Studies Association (November).

Hindess, Barry (1997) *Discourses of Power: From Hobbes to Foucault*. Oxford: Blackwell.

Human Rights Watch (1995) *Human Rights Watch World Report 1995 – Kuwait*, 1 January. Available at: http://www.unhcr.org/refworld/docid/467fcab623.html (accessed 24 June 2011).

Jamsheer, Ghada, cited in Chan'ad Bahraini, "Women's Rights in Bahrain" (online). Available at: http://chanad.weblogs.us/=516 (accessed 15 December 2008).

Kelly, Sanja (2009) "Recent gains and new opportunities for women's rights in the Arab Gulf States," in Sanja Kelly and Julia Breslin (eds), *Women's Rights in the Middle East and North Africa: Gulf Edition*. New York: Freedom House.

Kelly, Sanja and Breslin, Julia (eds) (2009) *Women's Rights in the Middle East and North Africa: Gulf Edition*. New York: Freedom House.

Krause, Wanda (2007) *Civil Society in the Arab Gulf: A Case Study on Women's Activism in the United Arab Emirates*. PhD dissertation, University of Exeter.

Meulen, Hendrik van der (1997) *The Role of Tribal and Kinship Ties in the Politics of the United Arab Emirates*. PhD dissertation, Fletcher School of Law and Diplomacy, USA.

Ministry of Information, "Sultanate of Oman" (online). Available at: http://www. omanet.om/english/social/dev2.asp?cat=hist (accessed 9 January 2009).

Navaro-Yashin, Yael (2002) *Faces of the State: Secularism and Public Life in Turkey*. Princeton, NJ: Princeton University Press.

Rose, Nikolas (1996) "Governing 'advanced' liberal democracies," in Andrew Barry, Thomas Osborne, and Nikolas Rose (eds), *Foucault and Political Reason: Liberalism, Neo-Liberalism and Rationalities of Governmentality*. Chicago: University of Chicago Press.

Ross, Michael L. (2001) "Does oil hinder democracy?" *World Politics*, 53 (April): 325–61.

Seikaly, May (1997) "Bahraini women in formal and informal groups," in Dawn Chatty and Annika Rabo (eds), *Organizing Women: Formal and Informal Women's Groups in the Middle East*. Oxford: Berg.

Sharma, Aradhana (2006) "Crossbreeding institutions, breeding struggle: women's empowerment, neoliberal governmentality, and state (re)formation in India," *Cultural Anthropology*, 21(1): 60–95.

UNDP-POGAR (2006) "Gender and Citizenship Initiative" (online). Available at: http://gender.pogar.org/countries/country.asp?cid=15 (accessed 9 January 2009).

US Department of State (2006) "Oman: Country Reports on Human Rights Practices – 2006" (online). Available at: http://www.state.gov/g/drl/rls/hrrpt/2006/ 78860.htm (accessed 9 January 2009).

Yamani, Mai (1997) "Health education, gender and the security of the Gulf in the twenty-first century," in David E. Long and Christian Koch (eds), *Gulf Security in the Twenty-First Century*. Abu Dhabi: Emirates Center for Strategic Studies and Research.

5

THE ARAB GULF MOMENT

Abdulkhaleq Abdulla

Introducing the Gulf moment

This is the Arab Gulf moment in contemporary Arab history. The six mostly small but oil-rich states of Kuwait, Bahrain, Saudi Arabia, Qatar, Oman and the United Arab Emirates (UAE) have come a long way from their once relative remoteness and peripheral status, and now wield enormous power, as they assume the center stage of Arab politics and the forefront of international finance (Bin Huwedin 2009: 213–51). What sets the Arab Gulf States (AGS) apart is their political stability, relative prosperity, consistent moderate ideology, and determination to achieve full economic and monetary integration and create their own internationally recognized regional organization.[1]

The AGS have a high standard of living and enjoy a comparatively good quality of life; the World Bank has classified their economies among the best performing, with an average of 5.8 percent annual growth during the first decade of the twenty-first century (World Bank 2009). The 2009 Arab Knowledge Report indicates that generous investment in human capital, economic reform, and the building of information technology infrastructure during the past ten years has increased the AGS's readiness for the knowledge economy.[2]

Yet even if it continues to flourish and assume a greater role in Arab politics, the Gulf moment is not entirely without its challenges and shortcomings. The small AGS remain highly vulnerable to regional tensions and dependent on foreign protection, mostly American, as they have been since 1971. Rapid socioeconomic change and the double-digit economic growth policy have come at a daunting social cost, whereby the citizens of these states are becoming a disappearing minority in their own countries. The fast pace of globalization, spearheaded by ambitious cities like Dubai and Abu Dhabi, has raised legitimate concerns regarding the concept of citizenship, issues of authenticity and national identity, and ultimately the social sustainability of their economic growth strategies. The real challenge facing the Gulf moment is closely related to the growing middle-class demand for good governance and greater participation. The prevailing political stagnation may yet prove to be the Achilles heel of the Gulf moment in history.

This chapter examines some of the key sociopolitical issues that are at the forefront of the intellectual and academic debate in the AGS at this moment in their historical unfolding. It shifts the focus of attention toward internal issues, i.e. the domestic debates within, rather than the external debates about, the AGS. The central questions revolve around how durable is the Gulf moment, and how much of the new thinking is, in essence, old thinking. What accounts for the suppressed popular demand for political reform? How did the business-friendly UAE model manage to outshine the more politically empowering Kuwait model of development? Have the AGS finally transcended their unhealthy dependence on oil?

How the AGS handle these pertinent questions will determine the authenticity of the New Gulf and the longevity of the Gulf moment and its future directions.[3]

The context of the Gulf moment

The current Gulf moment is deeply rooted in the historical turning points of the past half century, beginning with the discovery of oil in the 1940s and 1950s, political independence in 1971, the oil boom of 1973, the turbulent years of the 1980s, the establishment of the Gulf Cooperation Council (GCC) in 1981, the Iraqi invasion of Kuwait in 1990, the acceleration of globalization during the 1990s, and the tragic events of 11 September 2001, which exposed the AGS to severe global scrutiny. These truly epochal developments have contributed in great measure to the emergence of the Gulf moment. Since the end of the Second World War, the Gulf has experienced four major historical turning points: pre-modernity (1950–70), the first stage of modernity (1971–90), the second stage of modernity (1990–2010), and finally the global moment of 2010 onwards.

The starting point of the Gulf moment is the British colonial legacy in the Gulf and their withdrawal in 1971. The pre-modernity phase is interlinked with the nearly 150 years of British involvement in Gulf affairs.[4] Britain was the sole power which unilaterally changed the social and political realities in the region. It changed rulers, imposed artificial borders[5] and basically preserved the existing tribal order (Qasim no date). When Britain suddenly decided to remove its direct military presence from the Gulf in 1968, it instantly created a power vacuum and a politically fragmented region full of small states that also happened to be massively oil rich (Crystal 1990). The immediate task confronting the vulnerable AGS was the challenge of nation-building. They had to learn from scratch how to deal with the political, social, and economic intricacies of the modern world.

The years from 1971 to 1990 mark the first phase of modernity for the AGS. The sharp oil price increase in 1973 was the main catalyst for this second historical turning point. The policy emphasis was on nation-building, modernizing the infrastructure, and setting up a generous welfare state using the available oil revenue (Bulloch 1984). The massive wealth associated with an oil price increase of 400 percent transformed the societies of the AGS beyond recognition. The scope of the socioeconomic changes was far-reaching. But, while triggering rapid socioeconomic changes, oil wealth has ironically led to political rigidity, and consolidated the one-family political system. The combination of oil wealth and colonial legacy are the root cause of the personalization of authority in the AGS. Change and continuity remained the constant issue, with its logical contradiction of doing things in new ways while at the same time preserving the fundamentals of the old system.

The first phase of modernity also witnessed the downfall of the Shah in 1979 and the gradual consolidation of the revolutionary Islamic Republic in Iran, which represented an unwanted challenge to the status quo in the more conservative AGS (Saikal 1980). The 1980s was rightly characterized as "the turbulent decade" in Gulf history (Graz 1990). It was also a decade of lost opportunity as the price of oil dropped sharply, causing financial strain for the AGS. These states had to reorder their sociopolitical agendas, curtail important features of the generous welfare programs, and concentrate on defence and security matters, as Iran and Iraq engaged in eight years of escalating military conflict. This war, dubbed "the longest war" (Hiro 1990), was the deadliest conflict in Gulf history, and confirmed the proposition that, when it comes to the Gulf, tensions and wars are the rule whereas cooperation and peaceful coexistence are the exception.[6]

The Iraqi invasion of Kuwait confirmed this rather pessimistic view of the Gulf region. The invasion on 2 August 1990 shattered the political innocence of the AGS. It raised immediate concerns and lasting questions regarding the territorial integrity and political viability of small states in the region, exposing the vulnerability of not just Kuwait but the other AGS, including Saudi Arabia. However, the 1990s and 2000s were also the years of the second phase of modernity in the Gulf, fueled by the new oil boom. The primary policy imperative of these decades was quality education, a consumer economy, media and information technology advancement, and the seeking of direct foreign investment and expertise.

Two sociopolitical issues dominated the debate during this phase of modernity. The first was the gradual retreat of Kuwait, which had played a pioneering role during the first era of modernity, and the rise of the UAE/Dubai development model as the new trendsetter. The emergence of Dubai as the new hub and center of growth, innovation, and modernity captured the regional imagination, and heightened competition among the AGS for a fresh round of fast-track economic growth. The second issue was the rising demand for political reform and foreign pressures, mostly American, for greater democratization following 9/11. These two issues, as with the previous ongoing dichotomy of change and continuity, were never satisfactorily settled. The first decade of the new millennium brought its own opportunities and concerns, mostly associated with the forces of globalization. This is the global moment for the AGS, which has added yet another set of sociopolitical issues on top of the old ones.

No account of the Gulf moment is complete without an adequate understanding of the lasting impact of these turning points that have shaped the public consciousness, created many of the existing opportunities, influenced government decisions, and sharpened societal issues in the AGS. These states have had to face daunting socio-political challenges, which indicate that the last four decades have not been luxurious but have, in fact, been extremely tough. Hence, the conventional wisdom that the AGS have had an easy time, acquiring massive wealth and enjoying a prosperous standard of living while others were undergoing many hardships, is a gross misunderstanding of the complexity of the Gulf moment.

Issues of the Gulf moment

Four issues stand out as the issues of the moment for the AGS.[7] These are the issues of change and continuity, political reform and stagnation, the local and the global, and finally the contrast between the UAE versus the Kuwaiti model of development. These issues are historically specific and delineate different phases of the Gulf moment. They also vary in intensity of debate and societal significance from one AGS to another.[8]

Change versus continuity

Of these four issues, change and continuity is the oldest and by far the most intricate.[9] It is almost self-evident that the AGS have gone through massive socioeconomic transformations that have permeated all aspects of life. Yet, and despite the fact that change is seemingly so obvious and so pervasive, there are still those who strongly believe that hardly anything meaningful or substantial has changed. Despite the abundance of change, a much greater degree of continuity is also visible in the Gulf moment. Change, as is abundantly clear, is also ironically in doubt. Many aspects of life have undoubtedly changed, and changed beyond recognition. The AGS have been experiencing more systemic and stressful changes than the rest of the Arab countries. On the other hand, many aspects of life, including values, institutions, and power relations, have resisted the forces of change. Therefore, when it comes to continuity versus discontinuity (what has and what has not changed in the AGS in recent history), the issue is vigorously debated, and is legitimately surrounded by considerable controversy.

The continuity perspective, which asserts that hardly anything worthwhile has changed, is the more popular view. This line of thinking assumes that the Gulf moment is essentially at its pre-modern stage of development, as it has been for centuries. The AGS are still, in essence, traditional societies wrapped in a facade of modernity. Traditionalism primarily governs political relations and determines social structure and the way these states attend to their daily business. Indeed, the net impact of the oil wealth of the 1970s and the 1990s has been the consolidation of the existing order. Oil, in its own unique way, has strengthened the socio-political status quo and the old frames of reference, including the typically conservative and old-fashioned mode of thinking. Continuity, rather than change, has emerged as the most desirable wisdom and popular choice of the moment.

According to this view, the politically conservative regimes of the AGS have become more conservative. That is also why the religiously inclined societies of the AGS today appear more religious than they were during the pre-modernity phase. Furthermore, the seemingly traditional sociopolitical settings of the AGS are now stronger and more enduring, denying, in the process, the early pessimistic predictions regarding their longevity and stability. When it comes to the AGS, it seems as though "the old way is the best way."

The hallmark of continuity is the centuries' old ruling families of the AGS, who have survived tough challenges and proved to be adept in the art of survival and ruling. Keen scholars are forced to revisit their previous propositions, and are now asserting that "While a generation ago scholars were forecasting the demise of the Gulf monarchies, more recent interpretations have come to appreciate the political strength of this form of government and are now predicting its longevity" (Springborg 2008: 13).

Gulf monarchies seem to be more powerful today than they were in previous generations. Their legitimacy is hardly in doubt. In essence they still use Islam, tradition, charisma, and tribalism as symbols of legitimacy, as much as they rely on oil, socioeconomic achievements, modern administration, and bureaucracy, including a state-of-the-art security apparatus. The Al Saud ruling family of Saudi Arabia is more than two and a half centuries old. Both the Al Sabah in Kuwait and the Al Khalifa in Bahrain established their rule in the late eighteenth century. The Al Nahayan of the UAE came to power in Abu Dhabi in the 1760s. The Al Said family is part of a ruling dynasty which ruled Oman as far back as 1700. The Al Thani of Qatar is the AGS monarchy with the shortest history in power, going back to 1868. Gregory Gause, the author of *Oil Monarchies* (1994), says "It would be a serious mistake to underestimate their staying in power or to assume that the only support for their rule is the protection of the US" (Gause 1994: 146).

But the continuity viewpoint, while carrying some elements of truth, drastically underestimates the existence of formidable forces of change in the Gulf moment. These forces are rapidly gaining momentum; it is no longer convincing to argue that hardly anything changes in the AGS. Indeed, it is not feasible to conduct "business as usual" in what have become the highly open, globalized, and massively modernized (if not post-modernized) societies of the AGS. This is the essence of the second perspective on the issue of change and continuity. This view claims that changes in the AGS have not only been massive, but have occurred at a tremendous pace. Change was inevitable after a series of important developments, from the discovery of oil to the onset of globalization. These have unleashed a set of awesome socioeconomic forces that have profoundly "turned the AGS once and for all away from tribalism to modern state" (Redha 1992).

The net result has been impressive. The largely traditional and conservative ways of life have been more or less completely replaced. Old-fashioned uniformity has been superseded by a vigorous and prosperous diversity. A more modern, urban and distinctly affluent society is coming into being. Relatively diversified economies are now in full operation, with extensive links to global financial and commercial markets. Importantly, there is now a better quality of life for the fast-growing national population of the AGS.

Change has been most visible in the rise of an entrepreneurial middle class, which represents a fundamental rupture from the past. Sociopolitically there has been already a discernable structural shift of social power away from old tribal leaders and business oligarchies, which are still around, but have lost much ground as a social force for continuity. The existence of a well-established middle class is the most concrete proof of structural change in the AGS.

The new Gulf is predominantly a middle-class Gulf. This class, which barely existed in the pre-modern phase, is expanding exponentially in size and influence. In terms of societal impact, the members of the middle class tend not only to act as the drivers for modernization, democratization, globalization, social mobility, and entrepreneurship, but also inject a dose of political stability into the economic prosperity of the Gulf moment.

Numerically, this class is the largest indigenous social group within Gulf society. They make up nearly 80 percent of the total citizens in the AGS. The majority of the Gulf middle class are salaried bureaucrats and technocrats, heavily employed by government enterprises. But, above all, the Gulf middle class enjoys government affiliation, status, and privileges. They prefer job security and take prosperity for granted. That is why they are just as politically loyal to the regime and to the ruling families as the old tribal class and the older generation. Indeed, they are becoming even more indispensable for the "outcome legitimacy" of Gulf monarchies and the stability of the Gulf moment.

No other class can generate as much of the needed resources as members of the burgeoning middle class, who are often the first in their families to be fully literate.[10] They are active agents in the realm of the production of ideas, yet are not homogenous, with clear social and political agendas or roles in society. The middle classes in the AGS are made up of the new bourgeoisie, prosperous businessmen and entrepreneurs, bureaucrats, military and security officers, the intelligentsia, and professionals of all types, such as teachers, doctors, and lawyers.[11]

As for their attitudes and role in society, a recent survey reveals that the majority of the Gulf middle class think they are better off materially than the generation before, and feel secure in their jobs. They are generally confident and upbeat in their outlook about the future. Surprisingly, members of this class are satisfied with the education and health services provided by the state, are mostly positive about internal changes, and believe that hard work pays and brings achievements. In addition, the Gulf middle classes exhibit a high sense of national pride and tend to identify more closely with their own country than with Arabs or Muslims in general.[12] However, the Emirati middle class exhibits the most satisfaction and greatest social recognition from employment, feeling that hard work and ambition can bring career advancement. The Saudi middle class appears to be the most financially secure. The Bahraini middle class is "less well off, less optimistic and less confident and certainly the most troubled" among their middle class counterparts in the other AGS.[13]

As the AGS economies have grown more prosperous over the last two decades, the sizeable Gulf middle class has also produced its own new generation, which is visibly more global in its lifestyle, IT skills, aspirations, spending habits, and, above all, place of work. It is responsible for integrating the AGS into the global age; hence, whereas the previous generation were the pioneers of the modernity phase, the new generation are agents of the global moment in AGS history. In addition, the new middle class seems to prefer private-sector and knowledge economy jobs linked to the global economy, rather than being salaried bureaucrats and technocrats employed by the government.

Over time, as the economies of the AGS change, many basic values of the new Gulf middle class also appear to change. They start to acquire a set of similar sociopolitical views shared by the global middle class, such as assigning more importance to individual liberties, considering religion less central, holding more liberal social values, and expressing more concern about the environment and democratic institutions.[14] However, it is not yet clear that this global middle class will be more receptive to the significantly large noncitizen community of the AGS. The dynamics of the evolving power relationships between these two social segments will determine the AGS's political future, including the notion of national identity and the issue of democratization. The possibilities are endless, including a unique experience in the "blending of cultures", multicultural society, and the creation of global citizens with variations such as "Global Emirati."[15] Ultimately it is not the old or the new middle class but the Gulf monarchies that shape the future course and decide issues of change and continuity; they still remain the bedrock of continuity in the AGS.

Political reform versus political stagnation

The second sociopolitical issue of the Gulf moment is political reform versus political stagnation, intrinsically linked to the "change and continuity" debate in the AGS. These issues are two faces of the same process, except that political reform is confined to the political sphere rather than the larger societal space. Structurally, it is an immediate concern for the Gulf middle classes, who value democratization but are politically impotent to carry it to its logical conclusion (Abdulla 2001). The first true historical opening for political reform appeared when a younger generation of Gulf monarchies assumed power in the 1990s. These younger rulers, lacking the charisma of the older generation, recognized the need for institutional legitimacy to complement traditional and charismatic sources of legitimacy. They also found it politically convenient to respond positively to outside pressure, emanating mostly from Washington, following 9/11.

Yet the political reform process turned out to be extremely mute, patchy, and halting. Public demand never went beyond scattered articles, occasional conferences, and a few cases of petitions signed by a handful of academics, intellectuals, and human rights activists. Saudi Arabia has seen several high-profile petitions explicitly demanding constitutional reform.[16] They were promptly brought to the attention of the reform-minded King Abdulla bin Abdul Aziz, who responded favorably by initiating an ongoing national dialogue and taking the timely decision to go ahead with the first ever municipality election in Saudi Arabia during 2005.[17] That was the full extent of political reform seen in Saudi Arabia, although the 86-year-old monarch has "set in train radical changes which are nothing short of revolutionary"[18] in other areas, such as the media, women's empowerment, civil liberties, education, and economic and financial reform. In Bahrain, the better organized opposition movements have the longest history of petitions and agitation, and forced the government of the newly crowned King Hamad Al Khalifa to declare a national accord and agree to establish a bicameral legislative body, one of which is fully elected.[19] Both Qatar and the more inward-looking Oman have seen similar cases of popular petitions and the occasional burst of local demands for constitutional reform, but little has happened apart from a few cosmetic institutional openings. As for the more globally disposed UAE, demand for political reform has always been flat, and the government has never taken democratization seriously (Abdulla 2001).

The Gulf political reform movement soon lost its momentum and is unlikely to pick up traction in the near future. Even the global financial crisis of 2008–9 did not lead to any visible political agitation in the AGS. External interest in democratization evaporated just as fast as it had bubbled up. The meager political changes introduced by the Gulf monarchies during the second modernity phase did not yield any significant institutions of democracy. The younger generation of Gulf monarchs now feel secure and sufficiently legitimate to ignore early promises of democratic openings. The spring of democracy in the AGS, and indeed throughout the Arab world, has turned out to be short lived.[20] Except for Kuwait, a return to the old nondemocratic political systems and paternalistic political culture appears as strong as ever. The prevailing thinking is that there is no genuine domestic appetite for political reform and a preference for the status quo. The AGS can afford to postpone democracy as long as they deliver on socioeconomic development and adhere to the welfare programs as policy priorities.

The logic of the governing system is simple: why enact political reform when the old social contract is still binding, and almost all of life's necessities, such as prosperity, security, and stability, are amply provided for? There are no grounds for political reform when 86 percent of citizens in a country such as the UAE express strong satisfaction with their lives and feel optimistic about the future.[21]

Hence, where there is no demand, there is no policy response and outcome; governments throughout history have not voluntarily initiated policies and undergone reform if the demand was lacking. It is commonly believed in the AGS that democracy is divisive and destabilizing; it breeds conflict and is proving to be synonymous with political instability (Muntada al Tanmeya 2001). It is this innate popular fear of political instability that quietens demand for reform in the Gulf. The majority do not want to tamper with political and economic stability, even if it implies an indefinite postponement of democratic transformation. To put it succinctly, why scratch where it does not itch?

It is not political reform, but rather political stagnation, that is the prevailing order in the AGS. According to the Arab Human Development Report, the AGS suffer from a chronic freedom deficit. The report shows that the gap between the human development index and the political freedom index is larger in the AGS than it is in other Arab states.[22] The AGS scored badly on the good governance index, which includes accountability, rule of law, and level of corruption, political stability, and government efficiency. Kuwait is considered the best, and Saudi Arabia the worst case in the region. Bahrain is the front runner when it comes to political participation, which includes political associations, frequency of election, and freedom of civil society. The 2010 Freedom House report classifies all the AGS as not Free States, except for Kuwait, which is classified as partially free.

Undoubtedly, the AGS "made enormous strides on social and economic modernization but have almost totally neglected the political leg of modernity."[23] Kuwait, Qatar, Bahrain, and the UAE rank among the top 50 countries in the 2010 Human Development Report. However, when it comes to freedom, democracy,and political participation, the AGS have an embarrassingly dismal standing. This invites the perennial question as to what explanation there is for political stagnation, and why is there no cogent popular demand for reform in the AGS?

It should be noted, however, that while the AGS are not democratic states, they are by no means despotic or overly repressive authoritarian regimes. They do not rely on unmitigated coercion. Rather, the preferred approach is through cooptation, which has been remarkably effective in preempting opposition and demand for reform. Despite the lack of political reform and a lukewarm attitude towards democratization, these states are in essence benevolent and paternalistic. The largely obedient tribal culture, which is unlikely to disappear soon, is heavily used by the Gulf monarchies to keep political loyalty to the sheikhs, emirs, sultans, and kings of the AGS. In addition, the AGS value highly their internal stability, which often mitigates against any call for radical change of the political status quo. Democracy seems to have been wittingly traded off for domestic stability. This is greatly helped by the abundance of social liberty, especially in the smaller AGS.

While these factors are very relevant, it is also possible that lack of active demand for political change in the AGS could also be due to fear of the security apparatus. This is especially true in the case of Saudi Arabia. The heavy handedness of the secret police looms large and impedes reform throughout the region. According to the 2004 Arab Human Development Report, "the central role of the secret police force, with its stealthy and octopus-like reach, is the single biggest impediment to political reform throughout the Arab world."[24] Certainly the security-conscious AGS have prevented the emergence of political opposition, nongovernmental organizations, human rights associations, and labor unions. Lately, Islamist intellectuals and organizations, in particular, have been the main target of the security apparatus. This, in turn, has scared other activists, who have become decidedly timid in their demand for political change.

Demand for reform has experienced an additional setback as a result of the general dissatisfaction toward the perceived negative outcomes associated with the ongoing democratization transformation in places such as Lebanon, Iraq, Palestine, and even Kuwait and Bahrain. These regional democracies have revived sectarianism and produced violence, domestic instability, political strains, social setbacks, and the occasional economic gridlock. The fruits of the first wave of political reform in the region have not been particularly appealing. Since democracy trickles down by example, the existing models have not provided a positive incentive. Iraq, which ran a successful election in 2010, stands out as the scariest case of democratic transition. Lebanon is a unique case of confessional democracy that cannot be emulated by the AGS. Turkey is becoming an attractive case of Muslim democratization in the region, but it is demographically large and geographically too far away from the Gulf region. As for neighbouring Iran, its theocratic democracy is not attractive for the mostly Sunni AGS.

When it comes to political reform, what has been badly needed is one credible case of democracy in the region. In the absence of a successful democratic role model, it is difficult for political reform advocates in the AGS to make a strong case for democracy. Ironically, the role model in the region is not Kuwait, the oldest democracy, but rather the more global UAE, which according to the 2005 Gulf Strategic Report is "the least democratic of the AGS."[25] The supposedly best case of democracy, Kuwait, and the worst case of political participation, the UAE, have further complicated the issue of political reform in the AGS.

Kuwait versus the UAE

In the AGS region, Kuwait has the greatest political mobility, but it is the UAE that has the most dynamic economy. The developmental gap between these two AGS is deepening by the day, yet both models have a profoundly negative impact on the political reform movement throughout the region.

Kuwait is admired for having the best written constitution among the AGS. Its lively democracy is the oldest and the most institutionalized, and the 50-seat Kuwaiti parliament is setting the standard for accountability, transparency, and democratic maturity. No one doubts Kuwait's democratic credentials. Its cogent political opposition is nearly always in full operation, and uses the interpellation mechanism to extend parliamentary oversight over the executive branch, which has always been the exclusive domain of the ruling family.[26]

However, democracy has exposed this previously progressive country to renewed political, tribal, and sectarian tensions. Kuwait appears exhausted by internal bickering and occasional governmental paralysis. The "no confidence" parliamentarian tool has been over-used, and even abused, to score personal gains at the expense of national priorities.[27] Worse, Kuwait's celebrated political mobility is preventing economic progress. Contrary to modernization theory, democracy in Kuwait has not generated corresponding economic reform. The apparent setback of the Kuwait model is not confined to the economic sphere, but is all encompassing. The country looks far more conservative socially and more sectarian and tribal than it did during the 1970s.

Kuwait is still one of the most striking examples of democracy in action in the Arab world, but the behavior of its legislators has made democracy appear perplexing.[28] While Kuwait is the role model for democratization, the UAE has evolved as a trendsetter for rapid economic growth, and stands as a sharp contrast to Kuwait, as its ostensibly successful economic reforms have not led to any genuine democratic openings. The UAE has focused very clearly on business alone. The result has been impressive. It has, followed closely by Qatar, emerged as the fastest growing economy in the Gulf, with GDP exceeding $200 billion in 2010.

The UAE's economic success is in no doubt, but it has little to show in terms of political reform. Its ageing Federal National Council (FNC) "is a big political liability for a supposedly progressive county like the UAE."[29] Even after the limited election introduced in 2006 and the appointment of several women as members, the FNC remains embarrassingly the weakest legislative body in the Gulf region.[30] The UAE is an economic power engine but looks more like a political dwarf. The country that claims to be the leader in economic prosperity is also the last in constitutional and political reform.

> Despite their deep historical and socioeconomic similarities, Kuwait and the UAE have taken diametrically opposing paths to economic and political modernity. However, neither of these two models make a strong case for democratization in the Gulf. Each in its own unique way makes political reform a very complicated affair. However, for the AGS the choice is clear, it is the UAE, not Kuwait, which is the preferable model at this global moment in Gulf history. The economics of modernization and globalization win over the more dicey political modernity.[31]
>
> *(Abdulla 2009)*

The global versus the local

Aside from asserting its economic credentials, the UAE is also branding itself as "Global Emirates" (al Nahayan 2009) and acting as the epicentre of the global moment in the Gulf. It also finds itself struggling the most with the issue of "global versus local," the latest of the hotly debated sociopolitical issues of the moment.

The Globalization Index has continuously ranked the AGS as the most globalized Arab states. The UAE is the most globalized among the AGS, at thirty-fifth worldwide.[32] These rankings confirm that the AGS are no strangers to global attention, and signs of globalization are found all over the region. Some of the AGS are among the most integrated within the world market, and open to privatization and free market ideas, the essential tenets of economic globalization.

It is therefore no accident that the AGS are well ahead in their initial response to globalization, and showing greater confidence in dealing with its prospects and risks. This is due in part to their history and geography, but, more importantly, is also related to oil. Oil has forced the AGS to become directly involved in global affairs and exposed to global influence. Because of oil, their vitality and centrality to global economics and politics remains high, and is only bound to increase measurably in the near future.[33] Saudi Arabia was the only Arab state invited to join the Group of Twenty (G20),[34] established in 1999 to bring together systemically important industrialized and developing economies to discuss key issues in the global economy and finance. The AGS had their first encounter with forces of globalization during the Gulf crisis of 1990–1. This crisis epitomized how, in a densely interconnected world system, local decisions and regional actions could trigger global responses, and how the fate of a small Gulf state, Kuwait, became intrinsically linked with the politics of superpowers thousands of miles away (Abdulla 2006a: 124).

The AGS have realized that globalization is immensely beneficial and often glamorous. The economic gains of globalization are undoubtedly impressive, but there are also heavy costs to going global. This is especially true with regard to the tremendous impact on the social fabric and the cultural identity of the AGS. The city of Dubai typically exemplifies the extremes of the global moment.

Dubai is emerging as the forefront of the booming global cities of the Gulf. Until recently the city, called by some the "City of Gold" and by others the "Kingdom of Bling" (Barrett 2010), was one of the world's fastest-growing cities. Dubai steadily developed from a remote fishing enclave to a prominent regional financial, trade, and tourist hub in less than half a century. It overcame the challenges of its past to join a short list of the world's most successful cities.

Essential to its far-fetched dreams is Dubai's attempt to establish the first post-oil economy in the midst of the largest oil-producing and exporting nations in the world. Oil currently accounts for only 7 percent of Dubai's gross domestic product (GDP), as opposed to 43 percent in 1992.[35] It became clear that the more oil declined, the more Dubai was forced to diversify its economy. In fact, Dubai eventually discovered that it was relatively better off without oil. Signs of modernity, globality, and affluence are more visible in non-oil Dubai than they are in Riyadh, Kuwait, Doha, Abu Dhabi, and other Gulf cities still heavily reliant on oil revenues. More significant, the city developed a reputation for being a pioneer in utilizing knowledge and innovative thinking. Its Internet and media cities, as well as the more than 20 specialized free zones, are now replicated all over the region.

In terms of identity, Dubai is no longer what it was just a short time ago – Emirati, Gulf, Arab, Islamic or Middle Eastern. It has hurriedly become a global city that is intricately connected to the economic, financial, and commercial global network. The globalization of the city is reflected in indicators such as multinational companies and international banks headquartered in Dubai, as well as the city's vast links with international commercial and financial centers. Based on these indicators, Dubai was ranked twenty-seventh in a list of the most globalized cities compiled by the 2010 Global Cities Index.[36] Many of these palatable global gains came to a sudden halt during the severe 2008 global financial crisis, when it was revealed that the city had accumulated a debt of more than $80 billion, which had mostly been used to inflate the real estate sector. This proved to be the weakest link in the Dubai project.[37] Being one of the most globalized economies in the region, it was inevitable that Dubai was hit the most by the global financial crisis of 2008–9. The GDP dipped into negative growth for the first time in 15 years and the vibrant local stock market lost more than 70 percent of its value.[38] The global credit crunch brought a pause to some of Dubai's wildest ambitions to build the tallest, the biggest, and the largest of everything. The city had to learn the hard way that high dependence on the global economy has disadvantages as well as advantages. However, in moments of crisis the pains may prevail. The crisis was momentarily a humbling experience for Dubai and the other regional advocates of globalization. But while the crisis exposed the city's global vulnerability and forced it to be financially more responsible, it was not decisively crippling. All vital signs indicate that the city is slowly inching towards economic growth, while its infrastructure and economic diversification plans leave it irreplaceable as a regional business hub.[39]

The gains and pains of going global are not limited to Dubai or the UAE. Other AGS cities have feverishly joined the global moment and are emulating the essentials of the Dubai model, especially building new alternatives to oil-based economies. The 2009 Arab Knowledge Report indicates that the AGS are leading in the four pillars of the knowledge economy: education, innovation, ICT, and economic incentives and institutional regime. The UAE leads the AGS and the rest of the Arab World in terms of readiness for the knowledge economy, followed closely by Kuwait, Bahrain, and Qatar (Arab Knowledge Report 2009).

The economic benefits are impressive, but Dubai is discovering that the social cost of globalization is also massive. It appears that the more global the city, the more it has lost touch with everything that is local, including the "loss of identity and the erosion of the ruling bargain" (Davidson 2008: 193). In the case of Dubai, the clearest manifestation of this dialectical process of the global versus the local is the demographic issue, which is so alarmingly skewed that it is virtually unsustainable. The citizens of Dubai are becoming a disappearing minority in their own city. Officially, they make up 15 percent of the total population. Worse is to come, as the percentage is expected to drop as low as 5 percent by 2020, alongside the prospect of a zero percent local population by 2025. This zero percent eventuality is viewed as one of the most daunting pains of globalization. This situation is not limited to Dubai and the UAE, with citizens in Qatar, Kuwait, and Bahrain comprising 18 percent, 31 percent and 50 percent of the population respectively.

Sociologically, the demographic imbalance means that the city is made up of a small local minority and a large foreign majority. While on the surface there appears to be social harmony between the two communities, it is a different story underneath. The central social contradiction has to do with the fact that the minority enjoys all the privileges, while the majority does not get the privileges they would expect in modern societies. From the perspective of democratic theory, this does not appear a healthy situation if the majority of the people living in a country do not have a voice, while the minority, whether citizen or otherwise, have the right to determine the country's future.

Similarly, the national minority is growing deeply bewildered. On the one hand, many are materially well off and feel proud of the city's global successes. Yet there is also deep fear of losing it all to the expanding expatriate population of 180 different nationalities occupying key positions in nearly all of the strategic sectors of the Dubai global economy.

Hence pride and fear live inside the disappearing citizens of Dubai and the UAE, as well as the other AGS citizens, who are going through a serious identity crisis, and often raise the question of the sustainability of the Dubai model, and therefore of the future of the whole Gulf moment.

The Gulf moment: the road ahead

The future direction will largely be decided by how successfully Dubai and the AGS deal with these complex sociopolitical issues and challenges: the global and the local, change and continuity, the old and the new, political reform and stagnation, and the evolving relationship between the entrenched Gulf monarchies and the modernizing Gulf middle classes.[40] The AGS have managed to maneuver their way through these contentious issues remarkably well in the past four decades. How these pending sociopolitical issues are handled could determine their transition, not just toward good governance and a more prosperous post-rentier society, but ultimately their eventual emergence as a major centre of economic power, shaping the shifting landscape of Arab politics in the first half of the twenty-first century.[41]

The AGS have all the attributes to advance their current regional preeminence and assert their geoeconomic and geopolitical leadership. In a region full of violence, extremism, and self-doubt, the AGS are the exception in terms of visible human capital advancement, social achievement, political stability, economic reform, and regional and global vitality.[42] In addition, they sit on top of nearly 40 percent of the world's oil reserves. At current production rates, this oil is presumed to last until 2160, and is figuratively worth $40 trillion, more than the total GDP of the USA, China, and the EU combined. It is also projected that the AGS will accumulate a net surplus of more than $3.5 trillion by 2015, and, based on IMF calculations, their collective GDP is expected to reach $2 trillion by 2020. The World Sovereign Wealth Fund Institute lists the Abu Dhabi Investment Authority as the largest sovereign wealth fund by asset in the world in 2010, and estimates that the combined sovereign wealth fund of the AGS stands currently at $1.3 trillion.[43] Furthermore, these states are ahead in human development measures and readiness for the knowledge economy. In terms of social and material well-being, the continuous prosperity of the AGS is in little doubt, and the road ahead for the Gulf moment seems promising. It is also reasonable to expect that the Gulf middle class will, over the next ten years, demand a modicum of institutional and political reform. This will enhance economic prosperity, internal order, and stability, and further consolidate the Gulf moment in Arab history.

It appears that the Gulf moment is here to stay, and to flourish for a long time to come. Over the next decade, the AGS will continue to draw the world's attention, not just because of its huge energy potential, but also its global financial clout, expanding capital markets, innovative cities, and growing regional impact. Even the 2008 global financial crisis did not shake the ambitious developmental plans of the AGS.[44] They have made it to this point, and there is no reason why they cannot attend to the critical issues and challenges of the global phase of the Gulf moment in Arab history.

Notes

1. David Ottaway in his new article "The Arab tomorrow" (2010) observes that "Not only has the center of Arab wealth moved to the Gulf, so too, has the source of new initiatives and thinking."
2. United Nations Development Program and Mohammed bin Rashid Al Maktoum Foundation, *Arab Knowledge Report* (2009).
3. May Yamani makes a clear distinctions between Saudi Arabia which she calls a "frozen state" and the other smaller AGS she labels as "flourishing states." She says

> Frozen states include Saudi Arabia where democracy is omitted from political discourse, even limited partial elections have been put on hold, and the royal succession remains a secret kept from the population. Frozen states appear more stable in the short term, as oil revenues still buy the subservience and submission of

most of the subjects, but stability coincides with the possibility of increased violence and civil unrest, owing to widespread grievance over sectarian rule. The small AGS are flourishing states that have joined the global economy through political and economic reform. Managing social and political inclusion is not difficult for states blessed with an advantageous position along one of the world's major trade routes, tradition of cosmopolitanism and commerce, massive oil wealth, and small national population.

See May Yamani, "The Middle East's challenge," *Gulf News*, Friday, 30 December 2009.

4. Raymond Barrett asserts that

The level of control the British Empire exerted over the local rulers was astounding. The political agent dictated who the local rulers could talk to, what countries they could visit, even what kind of goods could be imported into each princely domain

(2010: 56).

5. John C. Wilkinson states that 'For most of the history of defining territories in Arabia, Britain has been the sole arbiter of boundaries', in Schofield (1994: 95).
6. Abdulla (1994: 1–13).
7. While most of the sociopolitical issues discussed in this part of the chapter are applicable across the board, they are, however, more relevant to the smaller AGS. Hence reference to Saudi Arabia, which deserves a separate treatment of its own, is noticeably infrequent. It is also worth mentioning that the aim is to introduce these issues as debated with limited effort to connect them analytically.
8. This part of the chapter depends heavily on issues discussed during the annual meetings of the Muntada al Tanmeya al Khaleeji (Gulf Development Forum (DF)). Most of these discussions are available in more than 20 books published in Arabic over the past 30 years. For more on the DF see: http://www.df.ae (accessed 11 August 2011).
9. The issue of change and continuity was the topic for discussion in the 13th annual conference of Markaz al Emirat Ll Dirasat wal Buhuth al Stratejeyah, (The Emirates Center for Strategic Studies and Research), Abu Dhabi, 2008. The papers are published by the Center under the title *Al Khaleej al Arabi beena al Muhafazhah wa al Taghayeer.*
10. There are some 110,000 students from the AGS enrolled in American, European, and Australian colleges and universities, 80,000 of them from Saudi Arabia, and as of 2010, 30,000 of which are women.
11. The Gulf middle class mostly would fit the Western description of white-collar workers.
12. Zogby (2007: 31–7).
13. Ibid., p. 36.
14. The Pew Global Project Attitudes (2009), "The Global Middle Class: Views on Democracy, Religion, Values and Life Satisfaction in Emerging Nations".
15. "Blending of cultures in the UAE", *Gulf News*, 12 June 2010.
16. The first of these petitions was the "Mudhakkarat al Nassiha" (Memorandum of Advice) presented to King Fahd by 107 liberals and Islamists human rights activists in 1992.
17. Abdulkhaleq Abdulla, "Maarakat Al Isslah fi Al Saudia", *Al Khaleej*, 3 February 2004.
18. Patrick Seale, "Saudi Arabia's royal revolution," *Gulf News*, Friday, 26 March 2010, p. 8.
19. Lately even the reform minded Bahrain "appears to be reconsidering its decade-long flirtation with reform." See Thanassis Cambanis, "Crackdown in Bahrain hints of end to reform," *New York Times*, 26 August 2010.
20. This is the final verdict of the second Arab Reform Initiative titled "The State of Reform in the Arab World 2009–2010" which covers democratic transitions in the

ten Arab states of Algeria, Egypt, Jordan, Kuwait, Lebanon, Morocco, Palestine, Saudi Arabia, Syria, and Yemen.

21. Wahdat al Darasat, Al Khaleej, Itajahat al Raae Nahwa al Qadhaya al Watanaya, al Khaleej newspaper, 2004.
22. United Nation Development Program, Arab Human Development Report 2004.
23. Abdulkhaleq Abdulla, Al Boa'ad al Seyasi ll Tanmeya al Bashareyah: Halat Dowal Majlis Attaawun' in al Tanmeya al Bashareyah fi Dowal Majlis Attaawun; al Najahat wa al Ekhfaqat. Muntada al Tanmeya, 2003.
24. United Nations Development Program, Arab Human Development Report 2004, "Towards Freedom for the Arab World." See also Neil MacFarquhar, "Heavy hand of the secret police impeding reform in Arab world," *New York Times*, 14 November 2005.
25. Al Taqreer al Strateeji al Khaleeji 2004–2005.
26. Salih (2006).
27. Kam Salih states that

In the last ten years it was alleged that the exercise of interpellation was abused to the extent that it lost credibility as an effective supervisory instrument. It is generally observed that the majority of interpellations initiated in this period either focused on marginal issues or targeted certain personalities. This generated some instability and negatively affected the democracy process

(2006: 44).

28. Ghanim Al Najar, *Nashaat wa Tatawor el Democrartiyah fi al Kuwait*. Paper presented to the 31st Annual Meeting of the Muntada Al Tanmeya, Bahrain, February 2010.
29. Abdulkhaleq Abdulla, *Al Islah al Seyasi halat al Emarat*. Paper presented to the Gulf Research Center Political Reform Workshop, Dubai, 2005.
30. Abdulrahim Shaheen, *Tajrubat al Majlis al Watani al Itihadi Mihafizah um Muawaqah lel Tanmiyeh*. Paper presented to the 31st Annual Meeting of the Development Forum, Bahrain, Febuary 2010.
31. Even though Kuwait ranked higher than the UAE in the 2010 Newsweek list of the Best Countries in the World. See *Newsweek*, "Overall ranking of the best countries of the world," 23 August 2010, pp. 34–5.
32. http://globalization.kof.ethz.ch/static/pdf/rankings_2008.pdf (accessed 11 August 2011).
33. Majid Al Manief, *Al Naft wa al Oulama*. Paper presented to the 21st Annual Conference of the Development Forum, Dubai 2000.
34. In *The Arab Tomorrow*, David Ottaway (2010) asserts that

Saudi Arabia is the one new Arab powerhouse to have emerged as a player on the international scene. Its status as the world's central oil bank – it has the largest reserves (267 billion barrels) and production capacity (12.5 million barrels a day) – and holder of massive dollar reserves ($395 billion in mid-2009) puts it in a unique position among the Arab states. The kingdom is the only Arab country in the Group of 20, the organization of the world's major economic powers.

35. Dubai Municipality, Dubai Essential Statistics 2010.
36. These include 24 metrics across five dimensions, namely: business activities, human capital, information exchange, cultural experience and political engagement (*Foreign Policy Magazine*, 25 August 2010).
37. Sultan Sooud Al Qasimi, "Dubai's financial woes in context," *Financial Times*, 30 November 2009).
38. Abdulkhaleq Abdulla, "The post crisis UAE," *Gulf News*, Saturday, 3 October 2009.

39. Abdulkhaleq Abdulla, "Dubai diversification leaves it well placed," *Financial Times*, 7 January 2009.
40. The future of the AGS was the topic of the 28th Annual Meeting of Muntada al Tanmeya held in Bahrain in February 2008. The conference discussed the various future scenarios of the AGS put forth by the world economic forum. The full proceedings are published in Mohammed Rumayhi (ed.) (2010) *Al Khaleej 2025: Derasat fi Mustaqbal Majlis Attaawun*. Beirut: al Saqi.
41. Raghda El Halawany, "Shifting roles in the Middle East: the Gulf states, individually or collectively, are now important international players," *Gulf News*, Friday, 19 June 2010, Weekend Review, pp. 4–7.
42. *Markaz al Emirat Ll Dirasat wal Buhuth al Stratejeyah*, al Mawarid al Bashareya wa al Tanmeya fi al Khaleej al Arabi, Abu Dhabi, 2009.
43. SWF Institute, Funds Ranking 2010. Also see *Gulf News*, Saturday, 24 April 2010, p. 29.
44. See the following official documents available on the Internet: *The Abu Dhabi Economic Vision 2030*; *Bahrain 2030*; *UAE National Charter 2021*.

References

Abdulla, Abdulkhaleq (1994) "Gulf War: the sociopolitical background," *Arab Studies Quarterly*, 16(3): 1–13.
Abdulla, Abdulkhaleq (1999) "The Gulf Cooperation Council: nature, origin and process," in Michael Hudson (ed.), *Middle East Dilemma: The Politics and Economics of Arab Integration*. New York: Columbia University Press, pp. 151–70.
Abdulla, Abdulkhaleq (2000) *The Arab Gulf States: Old Approaches and New Realities*. Abu Dhabi: Emirates Center for Strategic Studies and Research.
Abdulla, Abdulkhaleq (2001) *Mutatalabat wa Tahadayat al Tahawal al Democrati fi Dawal Majlis Attaawun, Muntada al Tanmeya*. Paper presented to Muntada al Tanmeya, Bahrain.
Abdulla, Abdulkhaleq (2006a) "Dubai: an Arab city going global," *Journal of Social Affairs*, 23(92).
Abdulla, Abdulkhaleq (2006b) *Al Nedham al Aqlaimi al Khaleeji*. Dubai: Markaz al khaleej ll Abhath.
Abdulla, Abdulkhaleq (2009) *Political Reform in Arab Gulf States*. Paper presented to the Conference on Gulf and Europe, Madrid, 2 November.
Al Kawari, Ali (2002) *Inaakasat al Hadi min Septambar ala dawal al khaleej ala Arabi*. Dubai: Markaz al Khaleej ll Abhath.
Al Naaimi, Abdulrahman (2002) Al Bahrain: *Maodhooaat Alislah Alsiyasi*. Beirut: Dar Alkunooz.
Al Nageeb, Khaldoun (1987) *al Usul al ijtimaiyah lil dawlah al tasallutiyah fi al Mashriq al arabi*. Beirut: Markaz al wahdah al Aarbia.
Al Nageeb, Khaldoun (1996) *Sara'a al Qabeela Wa al Democratiyah: Halat al Kuwait*. London: al Saqi.
Al Nahayan, Nahayan Mabarak (2009) *Global Emirates: An Anthology of Tolerance and Enterprise*. Dubai: Motivate.
Al Rumayhi, Mohammed (2010) *Al Khaleej 2025: Derasat fi Mustaqbal Majlis Attaawun*. Beirut: al Saqi.
Al Rumayhi, Muhammadi (1995) *Al Khalij Laysa Naftan: Dirasah fi Ishkaliyat al Tanmeya wa l Wahdah*. Beirut: Dar al jaded.
Arab Knowledge Report (2009), United Nations Development Program and Mohamad bin Rashid Al Maktoum Foundation, Dubai.
Barrett, Raymond (2010) *Dubai Dreams: Inside the Kingdom of Bling*. London: Nicholas Brealey.

Bin Huwedin, Mohammed (2009) "Dawr Dual al Khaleej fi Qayadat al Alam al Arabi fi al Qarn al Hadi Walashreen," *Journal of the Gulf and Arabian Peninsula Studies*, 132(35).
Bulloch, John (1984) *The Persian Gulf Unveiled*. New York: Congdon & Weed.
Crystal, Jill (1990) *Oil and Politics in the Gulf*. New York: Cambridge University Press.
Davidson, Christopher M. (2008) *Dubai: The Vulnerability of Success*. London: Hurst.
Dhaher, Masoud (2008) *al Estomrar wa al Tagheer fo Tajrobat al Tahdeeth al Omanieh, 1970–2005*. Beirut: al Farabi.
Duderstandt, Michael and Schildberg, Arne (2006) *Dead Ends Transition: Rentier Economics and Protectorates*. New York: Campus Verlag.
Fox, John W., Mourtada-Sabbah, Nada, and al Mutawa, Mohammed (eds) (2006) *Globalization and the Gulf*. London: Routledge.
Gause, Gregory (1994) "Oil monarchies: domestic and security challenges," in *The Arab Gulf States*, New York: Council on Foreign Affairs.
Graz, Liesl (1990) *The Turbulent Gulf*. London: I.B. Tauris.
Hiro, Dilip (1990) *The Longest War*. London: Paladino.
Hudson, Michael (2006) "Engulfing the Gulf," in John W. Fox, Nada Moutada-Sabbah, and Mohammed al Mutawa (eds), *Globalization and the Gulf*. London: Routledge, p. 148.
Krane, Jim (2009) *Dubai: The Story of the World's Fastest City*. London: Atlantic Books.
Muntada al Tanmeya (1998) *Qadhaya wa Homom al Mutjamaa al Madani fi Dawal Majlis al ttaawun*. Kuwait: Dar Qurtas.
Muntada al Tanmeya (1999) *al Khaleej al Arabi wa Furas wa Tahadeyat al Qarn al Wahid wa al Aashroon*. Kuwait: Dar Qurtas.
Muntada al Tanmeya (2000) *Dawal al Khaleej wa al Aawlamah*. Kuwait: Dar Qurtas.
Muntada al Tanmeya (2001) *Mutatalabat wa tahadeyat al Tahawal al Democrati fi Dawal Majlis al al ttaawun*. Kuwait: Dar Qurtas.
Muntada al Tanmeya (2002) *al Khaleej al Arabi wa al Moheet al Asiwi*. Kuwait: Dar Qurtas.
Muntada al Tanmeya (2003) *al Tanmeya al Bashareya fi Dawal Majlis al ttaawun*. Kuwait: Dar Qurtas.
Muntada al Tanmeya (2005) *al Walyat al Mutahida al Amerikiya wa al Khaleej*. Kuwait: Dar Qurtas.
Muntada al Tanmeya (2006) *Etijahat al Shabab fi Dawal Majlis al ttaawun*. Kuwait: Dar Qurtas.
Muntada al Tanmeya (2007) *al Aallam fi Dawal al Khaleej*. Kuwait: Dar Qurtas.
O'Sullivan, Edmund (2008) *The New Gulf: How Modern Arabia is Changing the World for Good*. Dubai: Motivate.
Peterson, J.E. (1988) *The Arab Gulf States: Steps Toward Political Participation*, Washington Papers. Washington, DC: Center for Strategic and International Studies.
Qasim, Jamal (n.d.) *Alkhaleej al Arabi fi Asr al Tawasou'a al Uroubi al Awal*. Cairo: Dar al fikr al Arabi.
Redha, Mohammed Jawad (1992) *Sara'a al Dawlat wa al Qabeela fi al Khaleej al Arabi*. Beirut: Markaz Darasat al Wehda al Arabia.
Saikal, Amin (1980) *The Rise and Fall of the Shah*. Princeton, NJ: Princeton University Press.
Salih, Kamal O. (2006) "Parliamentary control of the executive: evaluation of the interpellation mechanism, case study Kuwait National Assembly, 1992–2004," *Journal of South Asian and Middle Eastern Studies*, 29(3).
Schofield, Richard (ed.) (1994) *Territorial Foundations of the Gulf States*. New York: St. Martin Press.
Springborg, Robert (2008) "Introduction," in Alanoud Alsharekh and Robert Springborg (eds), *Popular Culture and Political Identity in the Arab Gulf States*. London: Saqi.
World Bank (2009) *Global Outlook*. Washington, DC: World Bank.
Zogby, James J. (2007) "Shedding light on the Gulf's middle class," *McKinsey Quarterly*.

PART 2

Economic reforms and evolution of governing structures

6

GOVERNING MARKETS IN THE GULF STATES

Mark Thatcher[1]

Introduction

Since the 1990s, several Gulf states have sharply altered the governance of their markets by adopting institutions widely used in other countries, notably the United States and Western Europe. They have ended legal monopolies, established rules for competition and delegated powers to regulatory agencies. The spread of such institutions is a puzzle: why should GCC countries, despite their considerable wealth, adopt reforms that run counter to their traditional market and governmental institutions? Moreover, to what extent have GCC countries adopted similar reforms in the face of international pressures and opportunities?

This chapter focuses on why Gulf states have created 'independent regulatory agencies' (IRAs). IRAs are a crucial example of wider changes in the governance of Gulf markets. Establishing IRAs involves legal separation of public agencies from governments by formal delegation of powers and setting out explicit statutory objectives and powers. Yet Gulf states have no administrative or political tradition of IRAs or similar structures. Hence IRAs are a real innovation and represent an importation from abroad that is closely linked to other policies of reforming domestic markets such as liberalisation, privatisation and attracting non-Gulf inward investment.

The chapter examines the establishment of IRAs in two sectors – stock exchanges for company securities trading and telecommunications. Both are economically and politically strategic. They lie at the heart of new strategies by GCC states of attracting inward investment and developing domestic markets, both directly and through their linkage to other sectors, such as banking, tourism and information technology. Indeed, they offer a form of 'critical case' for the extent of change in market governance institutions in the Gulf because they are the most likely sectors to experience reform.

The central argument is that IRAs have spread in telecommunication and stock exchanges in GCC countries. But they have also spread unevenly, with some states not adopting them, or only creating agencies that lack sufficient formal/legal independence from governments to qualify as IRAs. This pattern of the partial adoption of formal Western institutions is best explained by an internationalisation model that analyses interactions between specific international forces and domestic factors, based on the 'second image reversed' (see Gourevitch 1978 and Katzenstein 1978). Early work examined how changes in the costs and benefits of cross-border economic exchanges affected incentives to alter domestic policies (see Milner and Keohane 1996; Frieden and Rogowski 1996). More recent studies have argued that 'policy forms' of internationalisation can also be crucial, such as the policies and institutions of powerful overseas nations or supra-national regulation (Thatcher 2007; Simmons et al. 2006; Braithwaite and Drahos 2000). At the same time, responses to internationalisation are strongly influenced by domestic factors as national policy-makers enjoy margins of choice, as they can interpret and use overseas experiences, giving rise to differences in processes of reform, strategies and/or outcomes (Katzenstein 1985; Gourevitch 1986; Hallerberg and Basinger 1998; Thatcher 2007).

The key international forces in the governance of stock exchanges and telecommunications have been the desire to attract non-GCC investment and expertise, cross-national learning and 'modelling' from overseas institutions from outside the Gulf. However, domestic factors have been central to whether, when and how such learning and modelling takes place and its institutional impacts. Thus IRAs have been created when national policy-makers, notably unelected rulers, have developed focused strategies, often because they feared a lack of energy wealth and were very keen to attract inward investment. There is a paradox that strong leadership by unelected rulers can aid swift change, whereas stronger, more independent legislatures can limit new institutions. Equally, high energy reserves can limit the perceived need for reforms. Hence, international factors have been crucial for the spread of IRAs, but their impacts also depend on domestic conditions.

It is important to define an IRA, as many different types of regulatory agency are possible. An IRA is a regulatory organisation separated from government ministries and from suppliers. It is given powers under public law, its head has a degree of tenure, and it possesses its own organisational resources. These minimum institutional features mean that in formal institutional or legal terms, IRAs enjoy a degree of independence both from governments, which cannot simply dismiss the head of an IRA or remove its resources, and from suppliers, who face a body with its own legal and organisational resources.[2] It is also crucial to note that these institutional features refer to the formal independence of IRAs as distinct from their independence in practice. This chapter focuses on decisions to create IRAs, rather than their performance or effects on economic outcomes, because the very sharp change in institutions governing markets is in itself an important political and governmental phenomenon to be understood before looking at subsequent developments.

This chapter looks at the creation of IRAs for stock exchanges and telecommunications before offering discussion about the ways in which an internationalisation model explains the pattern of the establishment of IRAs and wider changes in the governance of markets in GCC states.

The uneven spread of IRAs for securities trading in Gulf states

Until the 1980s, there were no formal stock exchanges in GCC countries. Instead, very small informal over-the-counter markets existed, often in shops or markets. Attempts were made in the 1980s to expand stock markets, in order to aid the private sector and reduce dependence on governments.[3] In particular, the official Kuwait Stock Exchange was established after the 1982 Al-Manakh crash involving the existing over-the-counter market, the Bahrain stock exchange was set up in 1987 and the Oman exchange in 1989 (World Bank 2004; for Oman see Allen and Rigsby, 2000: 112–13; *Financial Times*, 12 July 1988). The stock markets were usually publicly owned. Often they were 'regulated' through broadly drafted laws and very loose rules drawn up and enforced either by the central bank (for instance Bahrain after 1987) or by a combination of the finance ministry and 'self-regulation' by an association of traders (for instance, the Kuwait Stock Exchange). Trading was very limited in volume[4] and stocks were domestic, dominated by government-owned companies since most privately owned companies were family owned. There were very few rules governing trading – for instance, insider trading was not an offence.

The period from the late 1990s onwards saw pressures and opportunities for reform of stock exchanges. Wealth was concentrated and much held outside the region.[5] But obstacles emerged to investment and transfers of funds in Western countries, with much greater suspicion of Islamic banks, especially after 9/11. This offered incentives to find regional opportunities for Gulf investors. At the same time, private companies faced difficulties raising finance from local stock markets, and were highly dependent on governments or banks or otherwise international financial markets which, in turn, demanded state guarantees.[6] Other Arab states began to seek to develop stock markets with IRAs in order to attract capital, offering regulatory competition to GCC states; in particular, Jordan set up an IRA for securities in 1997. Meanwhile, a major boom in GCC stock markets during the late 1990s and early 2000s due to loose credit provided by banks (which also profited from share sales) was followed by a large downturn in 2005-6 that led to losses for investors, with many markets falling by 25–50 per cent.[7] Strong discontent arose about the lack of rules on matters such as insider trading, with public demonstrations in some countries.[8]

In this new context, Gulf states began to reform their stock markets. They sought to develop alternative sources of investment for citizens and finance for firms. But several also aimed to attract non-GCC capital to build up a strong international financial sector and some set up IRAs.[9] Table 6.1 summarises whether an IRA has been established, the date of its creation and its key institutional features. Within the United Arab Emirates (UAE) it examines the two largest emirates, Abu Dhabi and Dubai.

TABLE 6.1. IRAs for stock markets in GCC states

GCC country	IRA	Date created	Key institutional features
Bahrain	No: the central bank (Bahrain Monetary Agency) is the regulator.		
Kuwait	Under discussion – bill passed 2010.		
Oman	No: the Capital Market Authority (CMA), established in 1998, is a government authority responsible for organising and overseeing the issue and trading of securities in the Sultanate.		
Qatar	Qatar Financial Centre Regulatory Authority (QFC).	2005: QFC Law (Law No. 7 of 2005) was by the Emir of the State of Qatar on 9 March 2005 and became effective on 1 May 2005.	Regulates financial services firms that conduct regulated activities in, or from, the QFC. Has an appeal body, the QFC Regulatory Tribunal. Plan to have unified financial regulator overseeing banking and securities by 2008/2010.★
Saudi Arabia	Capital Market Authority – 'government organization with financial, legal and administrative independence. It reports directly to the Prime Minister.'	2003: the Capital Market Law (CML) was issued by Royal Decree number m/3 dated 31 July 2003.	Board composed of five members, who shall be natural Saudi Arabian persons. Financial budget submitted to ministry of finance.
UAE federal level	Emirates Securities and and Commodities Authority – although it has a legal personality it is not an IRA because it is headed by representatives of ministries.	2000: Federal Law No. 4 of 2000 concerning the Emirates Securities and Commodities Authority and Market.	Regulates UAE domestic securities market, e.g. Abu Dhabi securities and Dubai financial market.

Dubai	Dubai Financial Services Authority (DFSA).	Dubai Law No. 9 of 2004, Law establishing the Dubai International Financial Centre.	Regulates the international market, Dubai International Financial Centre (DIFC), including Dubai International Financial Exchange (DIFX), acting under a separate legal system.

* See *Financial Times*, 17 July 2007.

Table 6.1 shows that three states (Dubai, Qatar and Saudi Arabia) have created fully fledged IRAs. Kuwait is currently legislating for an IRA. However, three states have followed alternative institutional reforms – the UAE and Oman, which have agencies that lack sufficient formal independence to qualify as an IRA, and Bahrain, which has given regulatory functions to the central bank.

The earliest and most far-reaching reforms were in Dubai. Lacking large oil revenues, it has sought to develop itself as a hub or international 'world city', with high-class infrastructure (cf. Marchal 2001 and Davidson 2007). In the field of finance, following a change in the UAE (federal) constitution in 2004 allowing individual emirates to establish free trade zones,[10] Dubai created the Dubai International Financial Centre (DIFC) (launched 2002 and legally established in 2004).[11] The initiative to create the DIFC was taken by the then Crown Prince Sheikh Mohammed Bin Rashid Al Maktoum (now Ruler of Dubai) (Interviewees 9, 10 and 12). The ambition was to create a regional financial centre aimed at international investors from outside the GCC countries.

The creation of the DIFC involved substantial changes in regulation. A separate stock market – the Dubai International Financial Exchange (DIFX) – was established for international investors and stocks. The DIFX is regulated by an IRA established specifically for the purpose, namely the Dubai Financial Services Authority (DFSA).[12] In contrast the existing local exchange, the Dubai Financial Market (formally established in 2000) remained a domestic market regulated by the Emirates Securities and Commodities Authority (ESCA), the board of which is chaired by the minister of finance and commerce and hence is not sufficiently legally separate from the government to be an IRA. Moreover, Dubai has established an international financial and legal 'island' to attract overseas investors and trading. Almost all dealing within the DIFC was made exempt from UAE civil law and a special judicial system for the DIFC was created under the DIFC Judicial Authority.

The creation of the DFSA followed a study in 2001–2 by the consultant group McKinsey that argued for a special financial services regulator to help attract international capital and to ensure high standards of corporate governance (Interviewees 9 and 12). In addition, policy-makers wished to meet the principles of IOSCO (the International Organisation of Securities Commissions), which state that 'The regulator should be operationally independent and accountable in the exercise of its functions and powers' (IOSCO 2003: Interviewee 8). The Crown Prince and his advisors looked at overseas examples, notably Britain, the United States and Hong Kong (Interviewees 10 and 12). But the British Financial Services Authority (FSA) was the 'primary model' for the DFSA (Interviewee 9). Indeed, the DFSA was largely planned by Philip Thorpe, a former managing director of the FSA, and Ian Hay Davidson, former managing director of Lloyds of London, who became respectively its chief executive and chairman. There was little opposition to the idea of a separate regulator within Dubai, in large measure because the DIFC was an international zone with a separate market for regional players; only business parts of the DIFC expressed some opposition, being used to conducting business in a traditional manner (Interviewee 9).

The creation of an IRA with substantial legal independence is far from easy. In June 2004, Thorpe and Hay-Davidson were dismissed from their posts at the DFSA. Reported reasons included their desire to be independent from the DIFC and the application of rules to land deals conducted by members of the DIFC board (Interviewees 8 and 9, *Financial Times,* 28 June 2004; 13 July 2005). After pressure from the DFSA board, the then Crown Prince decided to pass legislation (Law No. 9 of 2004) that granted the DFSA substantial independence as well as placing the DIFC under its own separate legal system, modelled on Anglo-Saxon structures and principles (Interviewees 8 and 9). The legislation gave the DFSA considerable legal autonomy and powers. Thus it gave the DFSA its own legal personality. It made the DFSA the sole body responsible for the regulation of financial services in the DIFC, able to carry these out 'without interference from any other body' and accountable only to the DIFC president/ governor who is appointed by decree by the Emir of Dubai. The DFSA is headed by a regulatory council appointed for fixed terms and only open to dismissal for cause in accordance with the DIFC's laws and regulations. The DFSA's tasks include proposing legislation to the DIFC's president, making policies, issuing regulations and carrying out 'solely and in an independent manner the licensing, registration and supervision' of DIFC establishments.

Interestingly, Qatar followed Dubai in establishing the Qatar Financial Centre (QFC) in 2005.[13] It included an IRA for financial services, the QFC Regulatory Authority (QFCRA). The provisions were very similar to those in Dubai, and the QFCRA enjoys considerable legal independence and powers. Such similarities were perhaps not accidental as, following his exit from the DFSA, Philip Thorpe went on to head the Qatar authority. However, unlike Dubai, Qatar did not establish a separate international stock exchange but instead is seeking to develop the Doha exchange, which it had set up in 1995–7, notably by allowing non-Qataris to buy up to 25 per cent of companies quoted on the Doha exchange in 2005.

Saudi Arabia also set up an agency to regulate financial services, the Saudi Arabia Capital Markets Authority (CMA), in 2003.[14] It followed concerns that the United States was no longer as good a destination for Saudi investments, especially after 9/11, and the creation of the Saudi Stock Exchange as a corporate body, separate from the Saudi Arabian Monetary Agency (SAMA), the country's central bank (*Financial Times*, 22 August 2002; *Middle East Economic Digest*, 14 November 2003). The institutional design of the CMA took elements of the British FSA and the US Securities and Exchange Commission (SEC). Hence the CMA is a government organisation, headed by a board of five full-time persons, each appointed for a fixed term of five years, renewable once. It has legal personality, powers to issue rules and regulations, and legally specified duties to ensure the development and proper functioning of the exchange. But the extent of delegation and internationalisation is less than in Dubai and Qatar; the CMA reports to the prime minister, and its members must be Saudi nationals. Equally, there has been no move to introduce a separate legal system.

While Dubai, Qatar and Saudi Arabia have radically reformed their regulatory institutions by establishing sectoral IRAs, other GCC countries have followed different paths. Bahrain has moved away from self-regulation, but has chosen a supervisory model based on the central bank being a single regulator for the entire financial sector. Thus in 2002 responsibility for supervising the Bahrain Stock Exchange and the insurance sector was transferred from the minister for commerce and agriculture to the Central Bank of Bahrain (CBB).[15] However, the CBB is not separate from the Bahrain Stock Exchange, as its head sits on the Exchange's board. Nor is it formally independent from the government despite new legislation in 2006, its board includes a representative of the ministry of finance.[16]

There were several reasons why Bahrain chose not to create an IRA for securities. One is that no single dominant international model had yet developed in the period 1999–2002, when reforms were being debated (Interviewee 15). The British FSA was new and not yet tested, and indeed a single European institutional model had not emerged. There were alternative models and, instead, Bahrain looked at Singapore, where the central bank supervises the entire financial services sector, as a good example of a dominant regional financial centre using human capital despite lacking natural resources. However, a second factor was the strong resistance by the CBB to losing any of its powers, a position that was supported by the Prime Minister and the Crown Prince. It argued that a separate IRA for securities would have meant duplication, higher costs and, perhaps more importantly, finding skilled staff. A third reason was that Bahrain has a strong banking sector but a much smaller securities one, and hence there seemed good reasons to keep regulation of the two together. In any case, the government and the CBB invited the IMF and the World Bank to assess the position. Its report in 2006 was largely favourable toward the central bank's regulatory activities (IMF 2006a: esp. 13–16). Moreover, Bahrain joined IOSCO, which validated the model of the CBB as regulator. Hence, while international pressures favoured the separation of operations and regulation, they did not point unambiguously to creating an IRA, while domestic actors favoured a powerful central bank.

Kuwait offers an interesting counter-example to the other states. It illustrates the obstacles to reform and the importance of both central leadership and the perceived economic necessity for the creation of powerful IRAs. Kuwait had the oldest GCC stock market, the Kuwait Stock Exchange (KSE). Since the reforms of the early 1980s the KSE has been regulated by a Market Committee, but this is not an independent body; instead, it includes several representatives from the government and, indeed, from the regulatee, the KSE.

There have been powerful pressures to reform the regulatory system and recognition that an IRA is needed, because of the Market Committee's lack of sufficient independence from the KSE and possible conflicts of interest due to its members being regulators and market participants (Interviewees 3 and 6). The Central Bank of Kuwait and the finance ministry wish to develop the KSE and invited the World Bank and outside consultants (McKinsey and the International Securities Consultancy (ISC)) to undertake studies in order to gain outside support for change (Interviewees 1, 3 and 5). The 2004 World Bank report argued that the Market Committee was inadequate, saying that it 'has not been delegated appropriate powers and responsibilities to enable it to act as an independent regulatory agency or to oversee the development of an efficient, fair and transparent securities market' (World Bank 2004: 5). A report by the IMF in 2006 again criticised regulatory arrangements and suggested 'establishing comprehensive oversight of the stock exchange' (IMF 2006b and 2006c). Similarly, the consultants pointed out that Kuwait's regulatory institutions were insufficient (Interviewees 3 and 6). Another pressure for change was the desire to meet IOSCO's requirements concerning the independence of the regulator. Moreover, the KSE has faced the danger of capital outflows to other GCC stock exchanges, and has attracted fewer international investors than other exchanges. One reason for this is believed to be the weaknesses of supervision in Kuwait, especially not meeting international standards (Interviewees 1, 3 and 7; *Emirates Business*, 24 July and 6 October 2008). Finally, there was considerable domestic discontent when, following a large-scale boom, there was a sharp crash in 2005–6, when allegations of market manipulation were made (Interviewee 1; *Zawya*, 8 November 2007).

In response to these pressures, Kuwaiti policy-makers began discussing the creation of an IRA in 2005. An academic, Dr Amani Bouresli, from the University of Kuwait, made detailed legislative proposals that envisaged a Capital Market Authority, closely modelled on the US SEC and the British FSA (Interviewee 1). They included the CMA being headed by a board appointed for terms of five years, renewable once, with removal being difficult. They suggested the CMA should have strong powers, notably to punish malpractice, and its own budget funded by the government. The KSE leadership is also keen to 'catch up international standards' and adopt 'best practice',[17] and commissioned a report from ISC which also recommended an IRA. The legislative committee of the parliament began to look at proposals.

Yet, despite these forces in favour of an IRA, passing legislation was very slow. One reason was the plethora of proposals – no fewer than five were made to the legislative committee as the KSE and reformers failed to agree a common position, and the Kuwait government did not offer a strong lead. But another reason was the strong opposition to reforms by brokers who feared that the new rules would be too strict (Interviewees 3, 4 and 5; *Zawya*, 8 November 2007). Finally, the parliamentary system, involving considerable debate and opportunities for delay, has made progress slow. As a result, legislative proposals were discussed for several years, and only in 2010 did a Bill to establish a Capital Markets Authority pass its first two readings, although it has not yet been implemented (as of June 2010).

In conclusion, several GCC states have set up or are moving towards IRAs for stock exchanges. International factors have been crucial for change. The desire to attract overseas investors by establishing new institutions has been a central element in the strategies of GCC policy-makers. Moreover, overseas examples and international organisations have provided models, norms and impetus for reform. They have aided the adoption of institutions that differ radically from the small, informally regulated exchanges that until very recently were seen in GCC states.

However, important national differences remain: while some GCC states have established IRAs, others have agencies that lack sufficient independence to qualify as IRAs, while alternative institutional models to agencies have been followed, notably by Bahrain and Kuwait, which do not have regulatory agencies for their stock exchanges. International factors have interacted with domestic ones. Thus, while overseas examples have been important for change, learning from abroad has been selective, as national policy-makers chose the examples from which to learn. As for international organisations, they have often been invited to provide advice, which has usually supported the strategy of GCC leaders. In addition, international norms have been sufficiently flexible to accommodate different institutional arrangements (e.g. the IOSCO norms were compatible with both IRAs and regulation in Bahrain by a non-independent central bank). Moreover, the analysis shows that a suitable domestic environment is essential for reform. Indeed, the case of Kuwait would seem to indicate a paradox: a stronger elected legislature and more scope for political contestation have led to barriers to institutional reform. In contrast, where strong political leadership has been present, notably from unelected rulers, change has been more rapid.

The partial spread of IRAs in telecommunications

Until the 2000s telecommunications services were a state legal monopoly in GCC countries. They were usually supplied by a government ministry, often the posts and telecommunications ministry. The same ministry held regulatory powers over the sector. Yet since 2000, IRAs for telecommunications have been established in several GCC countries. The first was Bahrain, which created the Telecommunications Regulatory Authority (TRA) in 2002, followed by the UAE (which regulates telecommunications at the federal level) in 2003.[18] Three other states (Oman, Qatar and Saudi Arabia) have also set up sectoral agencies, but because of the powers that remain in the hands of ministers, they do not have sufficient legal independence to qualify as fully fledged IRAs. Table 6.2 summarises the spread of IRAs across GCC states.

TABLE 6.2 IRAs in telecommunications

GCC	Sectoral IRA	Date created	Key institutional features
Bahrain	Telecommunications Regulatory Authority (TRA).	2002	Strong formal independence, e.g. powers vested in General Director, appointed for one term, but this is renewable and General Director is difficult to dismiss.
Kuwait	Under discussion – planned for 2008; at present the regulator is ministry of posts and telecommunications.	2002	Three full-time members but chaired by minister of transport and communications.
Oman	No: Sultanate of Oman Telecommunications Regulatory Authority is chaired by a minister.		
Qatar	No: ictQATAR.	2004 and 2006: a 2004 emiri decree gave ictQATAR the authority to regulate the country's telecommunications market. Decree Law Number 34 of 2006 gives ictQATAR a full range of powers to regulate the telecommunications market in Qatar.	ictQatar headed by the Supreme Council for Communication and Information Technology, chaired by the minister.
Saudi Arabia	No: a sectoral body, the Communications and Information Technology Commission (originally called Saudi	2001 Telecoms law.	The Commission's Board is chaired by the minister, and includes 'representatives' from

	Communications Commission), lacks sufficient independence to qualify as an IRA.		post, telegraph and telecommunications, the ministry of finance and national economy and the ministry of commerce.
UAE federal level	Telecommunications Regulatory Authority (TRA) of the United Arab Emirates.	UAE Federal Law by Decree No. 3 of 2003, Telecom Law.	Managed by a board of directors, comprising five board members, including the chairman and the Director General. The board is appointed by resolution of the Supreme Committee for a period of four years renewed for similar periods; its dismissal is only possible on grounds stated in the law.

Several reasons lie behind the decision to create IRAs. One has been overseas examples. By the 2000s, all EU countries and many others, from Latin America to South-East Asia, had a telecommunications IRA. Other Arab states began to establish them (e.g. Jordan in 1995 and Egypt in 2003). GCC states looked to overseas examples, both directly and through consultants and foreign experts. Indeed, there are often striking similarities between GCC IRAs and those in Western countries, especially the United Kingdom. The IRAs are usually given legal personality and consist of a board of several members who cannot be dismissed except for reasons generally specified in the governing law.[19] They have duties, which cover both competition and objectives such as achieving some form of 'universal service' and developing telecommunications activities.[20]

In addition, international norms created incentives for setting up an IRA. The World Trade Organisation (WTO) agreements on telecommunications and information technology were signed by several GCC countries by the mid-2000s (*Financial Times*, 22 June 2005). Thus Bahrain and Saudi Arabia, for example, have signed the WTO Information Technology agreement, while Oman joined the WTO in 2000, making commitments to liberalise the entire sector and to having an independent regulator that was 'separate from, and not accountable to, any supplier of basic telecommunications services' (WTO 2000). The United States has put pressures on GCC states to alter governance arrangements (Interviewee 13; *Financial Times*, 22 June 2005). One element has been the signature of bilateral free trade agreements with the United States (for instance by Bahrain in 2004 and by Oman in 2006) which specify that both sides must have an IRA.[21]

A third reason for the spread of agencies has been the liberalisation of telecommunications markets, often in response to growing demand for new services from both households and businesses (Interviewee 13). An IRA is useful in dealing with liberalisation by offering an impartial body which also has the technical expertise to deal with issues that may be politically difficult and/or purely technical, such as interconnection costs or tariffs, especially in GCC countries where incumbent telecommunications operators remain state-owned (Interviewee 13).

A fourth reason, closely related to liberalisation, has been the desire to attract inward investment, especially in new services. Third-generation mobile services provide the clearest example: almost all GCC states have encouraged overseas bidders for new licences. Several bids have involved consortia of Middle Eastern and Western companies.[22] An IRA is able to handle competing bids and can be seen to be impartial. It can increase the credibility of state commitments in the eyes of overseas entrants, who can worry either that their bids will not be fairly treated or that regulatory conditions will change once they have made their investment.

Gulf states in telecommunications have therefore changed their telecommunications policies in ways similar to those for stock exchanges. They seek the development of the telecommunications market as part of wider strategies of attracting inward investment and economic diversification. They have therefore ended monopolies and sought to create regulators that are seen as impartial. They have given licences to overseas operators — both from other GCC states and from outside. In addition, their own incumbent operators have expanded abroad, especially in other GCC states, through overseas subsidiaries, the purchase of overseas operators and taking licences.[23]

The case of Bahrain offers a clear illustration of the reasons for the spread of IRAs in telecommunications. For Bahrain, a major question in the 2000s was how to become a business centre in the region in order to increase future revenue (Bahrain has few oil or gas revenues). A key sector is finance, and indeed banks pressed for the liberalisation of telecommunications (Interviewee 13). The government invited consultants and an international US-based law firm (White & Case), which recommended an IRA largely modelled on overseas IRAs, notably that of the United Kingdom (Interviewees 13, 16 and 17). One argument was the desire to meet international 'best practice'. Another reason was that Bahrain wished to sign a free trade agreement with the United States as part of a wider political relationship with, and recognition by, the United States, and that agreement required an IRA for telecommunications (Interviewee 17). The policy obtained support from the highest level, notably from the Crown Prince, who emphasised the importance of attracting international investment and telecommunications providers (Interviewee 16).

As a result, the Telecommunications Regulatory Authority (TRA) was created in 2002 as an independent legal entity.[24] The approach 'very much followed UK thinking', as Britain was seen as having a well-developed regulatory system (Interviewee 17). The TRA's duties and powers were remarkably similar to those of the British telecommunications IRA Oftel and its successor Ofcom. Thus the TRA was given duties of protecting the interests of subscribers and users over tariffs, ensuring service provision, quality of service and protection of privacy, promoting effective and fair competition and ensuring that licence applicants could provide the services for which they were applying. Equally, the TRA's structure has strong similarities with the chief executive and board structure used by Ofcom since 2000. The TRA has been given a degree of financial autonomy from the government in that it is funded from fees, fines and annual fees on licensees up to 1 per cent of their turnover, and it uses its funding to pay salaries and for operations. The minister's main role is to set policy through a three-yearly Telecommunications Plan, and can only intervene indirectly, such as through appointing the members of the TRA board, who in turn choose the TRA general director.[25] Hence, in formal institutional terms, the TRA has significant separation from the government. Moreover, many overseas personnel, notaby from Britain, have taken senior positions within the TRA – for example, the first general director, Andreas Avgousti, had worked for Oftel, while his successor, Alan Horne, had worked for British Telecom.

Three GCC states have sectoral agencies that are not IRAs. One is Saudi Arabia, which created the Communications and Information Technology Commission (CITC) in 2001 but left it insufficiently separate from the government to qualify as a fully fledged IRA. In particular, the communications minister chairs the board, which also includes 'representatives' from the PTT (Post, Telegraph and Telecommunications), finance and national economy, and commerce ministries. Similarly, Qatar created a specialised agency, ictQatar, in 2004, whose highest body, the Supreme Council for Information and Communications Technology, contains members of the government.[26] However, interestingly, the lack of an IRA has not prevented liberalisation. Thus, in Saudi Arabia, the CITC governor declared in 2004 that its aims were to encourage both foreign and domestic investment and to introduce competition into the sector (Interview, Mohammed Al-Suwaiyal, *Middle East Economic Digest*, 23 July 2004, pp. 30–5). Indeed, Saudi Arabia awarded a second GSM (Global System for Mobile Communications) mobile licence in 2005 to Mobily, a consortium led by the UAE telecommunications incumbent Etisalat, and a third in 2007 to the Kuwaiti/Bahrain supplier MTC (*Middle East Economic Digest*, 10 August 2007, p. 20). It also began the liberalisation of fixed-line telephony, involving ten bids for a second licence that led to three bids being recommended, all of them by consortia led by overseas suppliers.[27] The CITC ran the bidding process and made recommendations to the Saudi cabinet (cf. *Financial Times*, 15 July 2004; *Middle East Economic Digest*, 21 July 2004, 23 July 2004, 19 January 2007).

The experience of Saudi Arabia is interesting as it shows that a fully fledged IRA is not essential for policies of liberalisation and inward investment. Hence, a simple functionalist explanation that the establishment of IRAs follows changing market needs is insufficient. Equally, it shows the extent to which governance of the largest GCC market is developing and the strength of forces for change that apply even in an oil-rich and large country.

The most different case among the GCC states is Kuwait. Telecommunications remain regulated by the ministry of communications. An IRA has been discussed for some time and is strongly desired. One factor is the need to attract inward investment and boost investor confidence (Interviewee 2). Thus, for instance, Kuwait is undertaking liberalisation measures such as seeking bids for a third mobile licence. The need for reform was underlined when Zain, a large Kuwait-based new entrant with subsidiaries and stakes across the Middle East, announced in September 2007 that it would move the headquarters of its international operations unit from Kuwait to Bahrain; one reason for this may have been difficulties in Kuwait concerning legal regulatory barriers linked to the lack of an IRA (Interviewee 13; *AMEinfo*, 19 September 2007, reporting by Reuters, *Arab Times*, 1 October 2007). Another reason in favour of an IRA in Kuwait is to ensure that the market works properly (Interviewee 2). In particular, issues such as interconnection, monitoring of prices and frequency management are difficult, and it is argued that they would be helped by an IRA. (Interviewee 2; *Kuwait Times*, 14 November 2007, reported in TMC Net). A final reason is the desire to meet international norms. Kuwait is the only GCC state without an IRA for telecommunications. As one senior policy-maker put it, 'everybody is doing it' (Interviewee 2).

Discussions about creating a telecommunications IRA have been going on for some years in Kuwait and there is little opposition in principle. Yet no IRA has yet been set up. One reason appears to be that ministers have different views. Another may be that Kuwait is not looking at other countries as models or examples (Interviewee 2). An IRA was planned to coincide with the launch in 2008 of a third mobile network, empowered to implement policy, license services, enforce rules and deal with disputes (*Middle East Economic Digest*, 10 August 2007; *Kuwait Times*, 14 November 2007, reported TMC Net) but as of June 2010, none had been established.

Thus, overall, several GCC states have created IRAs for telecommunications due to the desire to attract outside investment and to regulate newly liberalised markets. These have been significant factors, as well as the influence of overseas examples and international norms and incentives. But other GCC states have established agencies that have only limited formal independence and hence do not qualify as IRAs, while Kuwait has continued with regulation by the posts and telecommunications ministries. The overall pattern therefore suggests that international factors offer incentives and reasons to create IRAs for telecommunications, but that domestic circumstances affect whether and when they do so or instead establish other forms of agency or continue with traditional regulatory structures.

Conclusion: changes in the governance of GCC markets

The governance institutions of securities trading and telecommunications markets in GCC countries have been radically reformed. New stock markets have been created, with formalised rules or even their own legal systems. Telecommunications suppliers have been transformed from ministries into legal corporations and supply has been liberalised. Overseas firms have been permitted to enter both stock markets and telecommunications. Most importantly, a key institutional reform has been the establishment of specialised sectoral agencies, and in particular IRAs, to regulate the two sectors.

This chapter has analysed the pattern of governance reform – not just the spread of IRAs but also other forms of agency and sometimes no agency – through the internationalisation approach. This suggests that international factors can play a crucial role in domestic reform, but also underlines their interaction with national circumstances. In GCC countries, the desire to attract non-Gulf capital through new institutions, and also the need to deal with difficult and technically complex issues such as regulating competition when markets are opened up (especially to foreign suppliers), have provided a rationale for IRAs. Equally, overseas reforms have provided examples to be copied or at least modelled. It is noteworthy that GCC policy-makers looked to Western countries, especially Britain, aided by consultants and senior personnel drawn from there. In addition, the recommendations of international organisations, such as the World Bank and IOSCO and free trade agreements with the United States have aided in legitimating reforms.

But it is important to recognise that these international factors are not decisive on their own. One reason is that international examples are numerous and often ambiguous, and therefore are open to selective learning. Hence in securities trading, for example, Dubai and Qatar looked mainly to Britain, whereas Bahrain chose to emulate Singapore. Second, the World Bank and the IMF were often invited by domestic officials to make reports, and perhaps unsurprisingly they often produced advice that was close to that desired by the policy-makers who had requested them. Thus these reports recommended IRAs in some countries but not in others (e.g. securities trading in Bahrain). Moreover, institutional alternatives to IRAs exist. Several countries have sought to attract inward investment and liberalised their markets without an IRA – for instance, Kuwait and Saudi Arabia in telecommunications. Others have found alternative institutional models, such as a central bank regulating stock exchanges (notably in Bahrain). Finally, although there may be pressures to establish an IRA in order to attract overseas capital or deal with complex issues, countries can resist those pressures or find alternative institutional responses. Hence, for example, Kuwait has not yet introduced IRAs despite looking to overseas reforms, while Saudi Arabia has chosen to establish agencies that are not IRAs.

Thus the impact of international factors is conditioned by domestic strategies and conditions. It varies according to the strategies of national leaders and their ability to overcome domestic opposition. Dubai's strategy of international development based on importing Western institutions such as IRAs stands in contrast with less dependent agencies created in Saudi Arabia, while Kuwait is engaged in a lengthy process of reform that involves several proposals and considerable discussion by the parliament. There is a paradox that Kuwait's relatively more independent legislature that is the subject of contested elections has been an important constraint on the adoption of IRAs, whereas strong leadership by non-elected rulers in other countries has aided the spread of IRAs. Indeed, the importance of strong support from such rulers has been clearly seen in Dubai and Bahrain. Finally, it is perhaps unsurprising that reforms to create IRAs and alter governance institutions have gone furthest in Dubai and Bahrain which lack substantial oil revenues, whereas they have been more limited and slower in Kuwait and Saudi Arabia which have massive energy reserves.

Establishing formally independent IRAs can be the first step in a process of developing rule-bound governance of markets that enjoy a degree of autonomy from short-term domestic interests. The economic crisis that has developed since 2007/8 will test the strength of IRAs and their ability to act independently of governments and domestic interests. More generally, it will open up questions about the strategy of attracting outside investment and the role of IRAs in the development of telecommunications and financial markets. If the internationalisation analysis offered in this chapter explains how, when and why IRAs have been created, we can also expect both that international factors will be crucial for the operation of IRAs and that domestic conditions will affect responses to such factors, so that there will continue to be significant variations across GCC nations.

Notes

1. I wish to thank three referees who provided comments on an earlier draft and especially the late Fred Halliday who generously provided help and encouragement; I also thank the interviewees for their time and assistance. The views expressed remain mine.
2. Thereafter, the degree of formal independence is a variable, depending on many factors, ranging from powers of reappointment to length of term and continuing government controls (Thatcher and Stone Sweet 2002 and Gilardi 2002).
3. *Financial Times*, 12 July 1988.
4. One estimate was that the Dubai OTC market had *c*.26 listed securities before 2000 and trading amounted to a few thousand dirham (Interviewee 10).
5. One estimate is that in 1998 the 350,000 wealthiest Gulf nationals representing 2 per cent of the region's population, owned $800 bn of assets, half of which were held abroad (*Financial Times*, 26 March 1998).
6. For instance, in 1998, state-owned Saudi Arabian Airlines failed to raise $4.5 bn capital from local stock markets and found that international markets demanded a sovereign guarantee (*Financial Times*, 26 March 1998).
7. Cf. *Middle East Economic Digest*, 24 November 2006, p. 88; for instance, the Tadawul all-share index for the Saudi Arabian stock market fell 52.5 per cent in 2006 (*LA*

Tribune, 30 January 2007).

8. Interviews; *LA Tribune*, 15 March 2006.
9. For data on stock market sizes, see Shochat (2008: 44–6).
10. Federal Law No. 8 of 2004, Regarding the Free Trade Zones.
11. UAE Federal Decree No. 35 of 2004, establishing the DIFC as a financial free zone in Dubai Middle East, and Dubai Law No. 9 of 2004, the Law Establishing the Dubai International Financial Centre; for a discussion see *Middle East Economic Digest*, 1 October 2004, p. 8.
12. In 2007 a holding company, Borse Dubai, was created to own both DIFX and the Dubai Financial Markets.
13. See Law No. 7 of 2005, On the promulgation of Law for the Qatar Financial Center.
14. Royal Decree No. (M/30) dated 2/6/1424 AH (16 June 2003).
15. Decree Law 21/2002 with respect to the amendment of some articles of Decree Law 4/1987 with respect to the establishment and organisation of the Bahrain Stock Exchange.
16. Central Bank of Bahrain and Financial Institutions Law 2006, Art. 5.
17. Quotations are from Interviewees 3 and 5; Interviewee 4.
18. Federal Law by Decree No. 3 of 2003, Telecom Law.
19. See, for example, for UAE, Federal Law by Decree No. 3 of 2003, Telecom Law, Art. 11.
20. See, for example, Chapter 2 Art. of the Qatar Telecommunications Law of 2006, or Art. 7 of Oman's Telecommunications Act of 2002.
21. See, for example, Art. 12 (7) of the Agreement between the Government of the United States of America and the Government of Bahrain on the Establishment of a Free Trade Area.
22. For example, Vodafone in Bahrain, or the Nordic operator TDC as part of Nawras in Oman.
23. One example is Etisalat, which has licences in other GCC states and bought stakes in other operators, e.g. the Pakistani operator Pakistan Telecommunication Company Limited, in 2005.
24. Legislative Decree No. 48 of 2002, promulgating the Telecommunications Law.
25. In addition, it owns a majority share in Batelco, the incumbent operator.
26. See notably Articles 2–5 of the Telecommunications Law of 2006.
27. Consortia led by Bahrain Telecommunications Co., Hong Kong's PCCW and US Verizon Communications (*Financial Times*, 12 March 2007; *Arab News*, 22 April 2007).

References

Allen, C. and Rigsby, W.L. (2000) *Oman Under Qaboos: From Coup to Constitution, 1970– 1996*. London: Routledge.

Braithwaite, J. and Drahos, P. (2000) *Global Business Regulation*. Cambridge: Cambridge University Press.

Davidson, C. (2007) 'The Emirates of Abu Dhabi and Dubai: contrasting roles in the international system', *Asian Affairs*, 38(1), pp. 588–611.

Frieden, J. and Rogowski, R. (1996) 'The impact of international economy on national policies: an analytical overview', in R. Keohane and H. Milner (eds), *Internationalization and Domestic Politics*. Cambridge: Cambridge University Press.

Gilardi, F. (2002) 'Policy credibility and delegation to independent regulatory agencies: a comparative empirical analysis', *Journal of European Public Policy*, 9(6): 873–93.

Gilardi, F. (2005) 'The institutional foundations of regulatory capitalism: the diffusion of independent regulatory agencies in Western Europe', *Annals of the American Academy of Political and Social Science*, 598: 84–101.

Gourevitch, P. (1978) 'The second image reversed: the international sources of domestic politics', *International Organization*, 32(4): 881–912.

Gourevitch, P. (1986) *Politics in Hard Times: Comparative Responses to International Economic Crises*. Ithaca, NY: Cornell University Press.

Hallerberger, M. and Basinger, S. (1998) 'Internationalization and changes in tax policy in OECD countries: the importance of domestic veto players', *Comparative Political Studies*, 31(3): 321–52.

International Monetary Fund (IMF) (2006a) *Kingdom of Bahrain: Financial System Stability Assessment*. Washington, DC: IMF.

International Monetary Fund (IMF) (2006b) *IMF Executive Board Concludes 2006 Article IV Consultation with Kuwait*, Public Information Notice No. 06/35, 29 March.

International Monetary Fund (IMF) (2006c) *Kuwait: 2006 Article IV Consultation*, April. Washington, DC: IMF.

International Organisation of Securities Commission (IOSCO) (2003) *Objectives and Principles of Securities Regulation*, May.

Katzenstein, P. (1978) *Between Power and Plenty: Foreign Economic Policies of Advanced Industrial States*. Madison, WI: University of Wisconsin Press.

Katzenstein, P. (1985) *Small States in World Markets: Industrial Policy in Europe*. Ithaca, NY: Cornell University Press.

Levi-Faur, D. (2003) 'The politics of liberalization: privatization and regulation-for-competition in Europe's and Latin America's telecoms and electricity industries', *European Journal of Political Research*, 42(5): 705–40.

Marchal, R. (ed.) (2001) *Dubai: Cité Globale*. Paris: FNSP.

Milner, H. and Keohane, R. (1996) 'Internationalization and domestic politics: introduction', in R. Keohane and H. Milner (eds), *Internationalization and Domestic Politics*. Cambridge: Cambridge University Press.

Radaelli, C. (2004) 'The puzzle of regulatory competition', *Journal of Public Policy*, 24(1): 1–23.

Rose, R. (1993) *Lesson-Drawing in Public Policy: A Guide to Learning Across Time and Space*. Chatham, NJ: Chatham House.

Shochat, S. (2008) 'The Gulf Cooperation economies: diversification and reform', *LSE Kuwait Research Programme on Development, Governance and Globalization*, February.

Simmons, B.A., Dobbin, F. and Garrett, G. (2006) 'Introduction: the international diffusion of liberalism', *International Organization*, 60: 781–810.

Thatcher, M. (1999) *The Politics of Telecommunications*. Oxford: Oxford University Press.

Thatcher, M. (2002) 'Delegation to independent regulatory agencies: pressures, functions and contextual mediation', *West European Politics*, 25(1): 125–47.

Thatcher, M. (2007) *Internationalization and Economic Institutions*. Oxford: Oxford University Press.

Thatcher, M. and Stone Sweet, A. (2002) 'Theory and practice of delegation to non-majoritarian institutions', *West European Politics*, 25(1): 1–22.

World Bank (WB) (2004) *Financial Sector Assessment Programme, Kuwait*. Washington, DC: World Bank.

World Trade Organisation (WTO) (2000) *Oman Schedule of Specific Commitments, GATS/SC/132*, 22 December.

Interviewees

Note: The order in which interviewees are given does not correspond to the numbering in the notes.

Ms Lubna Al Hajri, Vice-President, External Relations, DIFX.

Mr Jameel Al-Alawi, Senior Legal Advisor, Economic Development Board, Bahrain.

Mr Yousef O. Al-Mejalhem, Financial Controller, KFAS, and advisor to the Committee on Stock Exchange Regulation, Kuwaiti Parliament.

Mr Faleh A Al-Raqaba, Deputy Manager for Exchange Market Affairs, Kuwait Stock Exchange.

Mrs Wafa Mohamed Al-Rasheed, Director of Technical Bureau Department, Kuwait Stock Exchange.

Dr Nasser Al-Sanee, member of the legislative committee of the Kuwaiti parliament.

Eng. Abdulaziz M Alosaimi, Under-Secretary, Ministry of Communications, Government of Kuwait.

Mr Babu das Augustine, Business Banking Editor, *Gulf News*.

Mr Andreas Avgousti, General Director, TRA, Bahrain, 2002–6 (telephone interview).

Dr Amani Bouresli, University of Kuwait.

Ms Roberta Darfur, DFSA.

Mr Liam Gibbon, Capital Markets Supervision Directorate, Central Bank of Bahrain.

Mr Alan Horne, General Director, TRA, Bahrain.

Mr Zaal Ibrahim, Corporate Affairs Department, DIFX.

Ms Joyce Maykut, QC, General Counsel and Secretary of the Board, Dubai Financial Services Authority.

Mr Ali Salman Thamer, Director, Capital Markets Supervision Directorate, Central Bank of Bahrain.

Mr Keith Williams, Trading Sector consultant and project manager CMDP, Kuwait Stock Exchange.

7

THE DEVELOPMENT OF ISLAMIC FINANCE IN THE GULF COOPERATION COUNCIL STATES

Rodney Wilson

The Gulf Cooperation Council (GCC)[1] is at the heart of the Islamic world, with the two holiest shrines under the guardianship of Saudi Arabia, a kingdom that prides itself on being governed under *shariah* law. It might therefore be expected that the GCC states would be at the centre of the rapidly expanding Islamic finance industry, which encompasses retail and investment banking, insurance, fund management and the issuance and trading of *shariah*-compliant securities known as *sukuk*. This study appraises the extent of Islamic banking and financial development in the GCC. The size of the industry is examined, and the extent to which government policy on legislation and regulation has facilitated the development of Islamic finance is discussed. The deposits and financing offered by Islamic banks are also reviewed, including the adequacy of these facilities in meeting customer needs. Islamic investment banking is less developed than retail operations in the GCC, but there have been significant developments in recent years, notably in *sukuk* issuance. The GCC has seen a proliferation of financial centres, and Bahrain has become the major centre for Islamic banking, although questions about its sustainability remain. How far competition between different centres is helpful to or detrimental for Islamic finance will be considered.

GCC Islamic financial institutions are taking an increasingly global perspective. Al Rajhi Bank has established subsidiaries in Malaysia, where it has a network of 19 branches, and Kuwait Finance House (KFH) has expanded into Turkey, where it is the country's largest Islamic bank with 88 branches – more than it has in Kuwait. KFH started retail, commercial and investment banking operations in Malaysia in 2006 and it has opened representative offices in Singapore and Melbourne. Dubai Islamic Bank is rapidly expanding its branch network in Pakistan, and it purchased the Bank of Khartoum in Sudan as well as three real-estate companies in Egypt. It also owns offshore real-estate investment companies based in the Cayman Islands as well as leasing companies in the Bahamas and Ireland, and has a 27.3 per cent stake in Bosnia International Bank, 31 per cent of a bank in Northern Cyprus and 18.5 per cent of Saba Islamic Bank of Yemen. Dubai Islamic Bank also has a 43 per cent investment stake in real-estate companies in Turkey, Lebanon and the United Kingdom.

The significance of these developments is that what is starting to emanate from the GCC states is a new form of Islamic capitalism, where accumulation is free of *riba* (interest) and other elements of Western capitalism which are objectionable from an Islamic perspective (Wilson 2006). Some of the major takeovers funded by the GCC, such as the Dubai Ports World acquisition of P&O Ports, have been largely financed through the issuance of Islamic *sukuk* securities. The Saudi Arabia Basic Industries Corporation (SABIC), the largest non-oil company in the Middle East and the fifth largest petrochemical company internationally, has also funded its global expansion through *sukuk* issuances. By acquiring production facilities at Geleen in the Netherlands, Teesside in the United Kingdom and Gelsenkirchen in Germany, it has been able to secure captive markets for its basic petrochemical output.

The size of the Islamic finance industry in the GCC

The leading Islamic banks are headquartered in the GCC, with Al Rajhi Bank the largest stock market listed Islamic bank globally. Despite the small size of Kuwait, the Kuwait Finance House has become the second largest stock market listed Islamic financial institution globally, with Dubai Islamic Bank the oldest. It has been registered as a bank since 1975, making it the oldest commercial Islamic bank. Bank Melli of Iran, where all banks are Islamic, is larger in terms of assets than Al Rajhi Bank, but it is government-owned rather than being stock market listed, and the exchange rate used to convert the value of its assets into US dollars for comparative purposes is questionable.

The twelve leading Islamic banks in the GCC are listed in Table 7.1 which also shows their profitability and return on assets (ROA). The profitability of some of the institutions listed was adversely affected by the global financial crisis of 2007–8 and the subsequent recession in the more exposed GCC markets, but it is remarkable how profitable Al Rajhi and the Islamic banks in Qatar remained.

TABLE 7.1 Leading Islamic banks in the GCC by asset values (2009)

Rank	Institution	Country	Assets billion $	Profits million $	ROA
1	Al Rajhi Bank	Saudi Arabia	45.5	1,805	4.0
2	Kuwait Finance House	Kuwait	39.3	268	0.7
3	Dubai Islamic Bank	UAE	22.9	332	1.4
4	Al Baraka Group	Bahrain	13.2	221	1.7
5	Qatar Islamic Bank	Qatar	10.8	493	4.6
6	Bank Al Jazira	Saudi Arabia	7.3	59	0.8
7	Bank Albilad	Saudi Arabia	4.6	−6.6	−1.4

continued overleaf

Table 7.1 continued

Rank	Institution	Country	Assets billion $	Profits million $	ROA
8	Sharjah Islamic Bank	UAE	4.3	154	3.5
9	Kuwait International Bank	Kuwait	3.9	72	1.8
10	Boubyan Bank	Kuwait	3.9	6	0.1
11	Qatar International Islamic Bank	Qatar	3.5	138	3.9
12	Shamil Bank	Bahrain	2.8	1	0.0

Source: Top 1000 World Banks, *The Banker*, London, July 2010, pp. 184–260.

Government policy on Islamic finance and legislative provision

Historically in the countries that now comprise the GCC there was much suspicion of, indeed even antagonism to, interest-based banking, notably from King Abdul Aziz, the founder of modern Saudi Arabia (Young 1983), and Sheikh Isa ibn Al Khalifa, the ruler of Bahrain until he was deposed in 1932 by the British in favour of his son (Wilson 1987). There was, however, no Islamic banking model which could be applied to meet the financing needs of the region, and in the absence of this, conventional banking filled the vacuum, although few local citizens opened savings accounts which paid interest, instead simply maintaining current accounts which paid no return.

The Royal Decree of 1952 establishing the Saudi Arabian Monetary Agency (SAMA) was similar to other central banking laws, the main distinguishing feature being the designation 'monetary agency' rather than 'central bank'. The Saudi Arabian Banking Control Law of 1966, which still governs regulation in the kingdom, specifically mentions bank lending under Articles 8 and 9, which is not permitted under *shariah*, and Article 10 prohibits banks from engaging in wholesale or retail trade, which could be interpreted as ruling out *murabaha* transactions. Much of the emphasis during the oil boom years of the 1970s was on building up a modern banking system to serve the kingdom's financial needs, but the sensitive issue of *shariah* compliance was not really addressed by SAMA. There was nevertheless support for international Islamic finance initiatives, notably the establishment of the Islamic Development Bank. This opened in Jeddah in 1975, its aim being to serve as a development assistance agency for the Islamic world. However, those Saudis who wished to establish Islamic banks in the kingdom, notably Prince Mohammed bin Faisal and Sheikh Saleh Kamel, were frustrated in their efforts, and they subsequently turned their attention to promoting Islamic finance overseas.

Elsewhere in the GCC, there was a more supportive attitude from the authorities for those who wished to establish Islamic banks, as the Emir of Dubai passed a decree on 12 March 1975 authorising the establishment of Dubai Islamic Bank and Kuwait passed legislation on 23 March 1977 to allow the establishment of Kuwait Finance House, these being for over two decades the only Islamic banks in these states (Saeed 1999). Bahrain and Qatar followed, establishing Islamic banks in 1979 and 1982 respectively.

The developments might have been expected to influence the attitude of the Saudi authorities to Islamic banking, but they remained surprisingly cautious. Indeed, there was a reluctance to provide Al Rajhi Bank, today the world's largest listed Islamic bank, with a banking licence, the concern being that this might highlight the interest transactions of the conventional banks in the kingdom (Wilson 2002). Al Rajhi Bank was finally given a banking licence in 1987, largely because it already had significant deposits, and it was felt that it would be preferable to have it regulated by the SAMA. The danger was that if there had been a run on its deposits this could have severely damaged confidence in the whole banking system, including the regulated banks.

With the launch of Al Rajhi Bank, five out the six GCC states had Islamic banks, the exception being Oman, which for political reasons concerned with limiting the influence of the Ibadi sect, refused to award any Islamic banking licences. It is only recently that Islamic finance has become available in Oman, Sohar Aluminium raising $260 million for a smelter project through Citi Islamic Investment Bank in Dubai, but there is still no local Islamic bank (Alam 2006).

Other governments have been much more supportive in recent years, notably Kuwait, which in 2004 passed an amendment to the Central Bank Law 32 of 1968 bringing the Kuwait Finance House under the regulatory authority of the Central Bank of Kuwait. The new legislative framework aimed to ensure that competition within the Islamic financial sector was opened up, with other banks permitted to apply for Islamic banking licences.[2] As a result, the Kuwait Real Estate Bank converted to being an Islamic bank, changing its name to Kuwait International Bank. A new Islamic financial institution, Boubian Bank, was also awarded an Islamic banking licence. The legislation also contained provisions on Islamic financial governance, especially Articles 86, 87, 93 and 96, including a stipulation that each institution should have a *shariah* board with at least three members. Although Kuwait's legislative provision is only part of its wider banking law, there is more detail on specific Islamic banking issues than in Malaysia's dedicated Islamic banking law that created its dual system.[3]

In sum, the smaller GCC states apart from Oman have passed legislation which has facilitated the development of Islamic finance, and Kuwait in particular has updated and augmented its banking legislation to ensure healthy competition between Islamic banks in its domestic market. Bahrain's official support for Islamic finance is at the regulatory rather than the legislative level. Ironically, it is Saudi Arabia which has been the laggard as far as specific laws governing Islamic finance are concerned, with no mention of Islamic banking in its banking legislation, or even in the Capital Markets Law of 2003, although there have been *sukuk* issuances in the kingdom and all the mutual funds governed by the law are *shariah*-compliant. SAMA and the Capital Markets Authority have yet to issue a single document pertaining to Islamic finance, in contrast to Bank Negara and the Securities Commission of Malaysia, or even the Financial Services Authority in the United Kingdom, which have issued numerous documents and guidelines. SAMA is involved in the deliberations of the Kuala Lumpur-based Islamic Financial Services Board (IFSB), but this represents a continuation of the policy of being interested in international developments in Islamic finance but not in domestic matters within the kingdom.

Trade finance using *murabaha*

In the 1970s, Islamic banking in the GCC was largely focused on business clients, with institutions such as Dubai Islamic Bank – the first modern Islamic bank, which dates from 1975 – serving a clientele of pious Muslim merchants. Dubai was already taking advantage of the first oil price boom to build on its position as a leading trading centre. The Dubai Islamic Bank's main business was financing based on *murabaha* contracts, whereby the bank would buy imports on behalf of a merchant and resell them to the merchant for a mark-up. It was the mark-up rather than interest that represented the bank's profit, but what made the transaction *shariah*-compliant was the fact that the bank assumed temporary ownership of the imports; the legal responsibilities associated with this justified the returns. In other words, instead of lending on the basis of interest, the Dubai Islamic Bank was an active trading partner sharing some of the liabilities with the merchants for which it was entitled to be rewarded.

Not only could a case for *murabaha* be argued on religious and moral grounds, but from the client's perspective it had some financial advantages over conventional lending. Usually letters of credit are required by an exporter or the exporter's bank before goods are dispatched, as evidence that the merchant is creditworthy and is in a position to meet their financial obligations. Banks charge fees for letters of credit as, in the event of the merchant defaulting, they will be liable for any payment shortfall. With *murabaha*, since the bank itself is first purchaser, letters of credit on behalf of the client are unnecessary, eliminating the fees. Furthermore, if the bank bulk purchases on behalf of several merchants, it may be possible to obtain the goods at a discount, which will either contribute to bank profits or can be partially passed on to the merchant through a lower repurchase price.

As a result of its religious merits and financial advantage, *murabaha* took off from the 1970s and accounted for most Islamic bank finance in the GCC. The Kuwait Finance House, established in 1977 as already indicated, also relied on *murabaha*, as did the Bahrain Islamic Bank, which started operations in 1978. *Murabaha* was, however, much criticised both by the early advocates of Islamic finance and a sceptical wider public, who viewed the mark-ups charged as proxies for interest, and the trading transactions as serving no financial purpose, even if legally they were distinct from conventional trade lending. As the payments by the merchants were deferred, the similarities with lending became apparent (Ahmad 2005). This may explain why the new Islamic banks attracted only a small share of financial business initially, and increasing market share has been an uphill struggle, even in the highly religious GCC states.

Islamic bank deposit facilities

The pioneering efforts to develop Islamic financial principles for modern finance in Pakistan in the 1950s and Egypt in the 1960s involved the establishment of credit unions, with members contributing small amounts of savings in return for being potentially eligible for modest interest-free loans, referred to as *qard hasan* in Islamic financial parlance (Warde 2000). Those who joined were relatively poor farmers, comparable to the clientele of microfinance institutions, who are too poor to have bank accounts and are without collateral to offer for loans.

In contrast, in the GCC, where there is much more affluence and only a limited agricultural sector, microfinance was largely irrelevant. Instead, the early clientele for the new Islamic banks were middle- and upper-ranking government employees and business owners, who were often very affluent. They mostly already had bank accounts, but were potentially willing to place savings with Islamic banks, partly because they found the concept of *shariah*-based banking to be morally satisfying and a way of signalling to their peers that they were pious in their financial dealings, even if they retained their conventional bank accounts.

Unlike in many developing countries where weekly wages are paid in cash, in the GCC most employees, including all those working for government, are paid monthly salaries through bank transfers. This necessitated all employees opening bank accounts, and those who were uncomfortable with *riba*-based banks naturally turned to Islamic banks as an acceptable alternative. Hence from the 1990s when the move from cash to salary transfers gathered momentum, the number of Islamic bank-account holders increased rapidly. Social benefits to local citizens are now also paid into bank accounts, so that even those who are retired, ill or eligible for other government payments have to open and maintain accounts.

Paying with Islamic bank cheques might impress recipients, even though the current accounts from which the funds were drawn were identical to their conventional equivalents, with the important distinction that deposited funds could not be used to finance interest-based lending. As Islamic banks cannot provide overdraft facilities, clients had to maintain sufficient funds in their accounts to ensure that cheques were honoured. Whether this reassured cheque recipients was a debatable point, as the onus was on the payer, not the bank, to ensure that all financial obligations were fulfilled.

In practice, most Islamic bank depositors in the GCC maintained substantial funds in current accounts on which they earned no return, reducing substantially the costs of funding for the banks. As a consequence, Islamic banking in the GCC has been very lucrative, Al Rajhi Bank being by far the most profitable bank in Saudi Arabia. Elsewhere in the GCC, Islamic bank clients seem more concerned to receive a return on their deposits. In the Dubai Islamic Bank, only 20 per cent of deposits are held in current accounts, the remainder being held in savings or investment accounts where clients share in the bank's profits rather than receiving interest.[4]

Shariah-compliant consumer credit

A major criticism of conventional banks from an Islamic perspective is that they entice their personal clients into debt by encouraging consumption of unnecessary goods, and thereby promote the worst aspects of capitalism (Chapra 1985). However, in practice in the GCC, the Islamic banks have behaved in exactly the same way as conventional banks when providing consumer credit. Indeed, the major Islamic banks in the GCC are unapologetic; their business strategy is to focus on consumer rather than development finance. As the GCC states have become increasingly affluent consumer societies, Islamic banks have responded by offering financing products similar to their interest-based competitors and indeed to those of retail banks in the West. In other words, only the methods of financing are different, not the allocation of funds.

Initially Islamic banks only offered debit cards to their current-account customers, which meant that they could not go into debt, but more recently credit cards have been marketed, as their clients have sought to have more flexibility over their discretionary spending in the shopping malls of the GCC. There can be no interest charges on debit balances with Islamic credit cards, but, as with conventional credit cards, the issuers, in this case Islamic banks, receive a commission from the retailer proportionate to the amount of the transactions in return for a guaranteed payment. Some banks charge an annual fee, but, given the competition from other card issuers, Al Rajhi Bank and Dubai Islamic Bank no longer charge fees.

Indeed, incentives are now given to cardholders, such as a 'buy one main dish and get one free' offer by Dubai Islamic Bank which extends to restaurants throughout the UAE,[5] 4 per cent cashback when the Noor Islamic Bank card, also issued in Dubai, is used for food purchases in selected supermarkets,[6] cards with football logos by Al Rajhi Bank designed for sports fans in Saudi Arabia and free shopping vouchers with the Visa Laki ladies' card issued by Al Rajhi Bank.[7] Gambling is, of course, prohibited in Islam, but Kuwait Finance House has an awards programme for its cardholders offering KD 100,000 in prizes.[8] It seems that an Islamic designation for credit cards is no constraint on product development or on what incentives clients are offered, even if some of the incentives would appear to conflict with Islamic teaching and are morally dubious.

Islamic banks, like their conventional competitors, allocate their consumer finance in line with salary. Clients with high incomes are given platinum cards, and those of more modest means classic cards, while middle-income earners receive gold cards. These define the credit limits on the cards, reflecting perceived ability to pay. Often limits are set at high levels for promotional purposes, however, as with the Al-Tayseer Platinum Premier Package offered by Kuwait Finance House, where the credit limit is three times a person's monthly salary and outstanding credit obligations can be deferred for up to twelve months at no additional charge.

Islamic consumer credit also covers car purchases and home equipment and improvements such as new bathrooms, kitchens or furnishings. Car finance involves *murabaha*, the bank purchasing a car on behalf of the client and reselling to the client for deferred payments. Al Rajhi Bank offers up to 60 months to pay through instalments with no down payment required. Applicants must have been employed for at least six months with a minimum monthly income of SR 2,500. Leasing is also possible, with free roadside assistance in case of vehicle breakdowns. Car finance has become highly significant in the GCC, with most buyers no longer paying in cash. Al Rajhi Bank has its own car showrooms at 11 locations throughout Saudi Arabia, while Kuwait Finance House has two new and used car showrooms, as well representatives available at most car distributors in Kuwait who can advise on its financing packages. KFH has established a separate affiliate, KFH Trade, for its car financing business and warranties are offered on all vehicles sold for two years.

Real-estate finance

The fastest-growing sector in the GCC until 2008 was real estate and construction, and Islamic banks are heavily involved in all aspects of real-estate financing, from residential mortgages to the finance of major commercial property developments through *istisna* (project finance). In addition to mortgages for owner-occupied properties there is much buy-to-let activity, as only local nationals can own property in Saudi Arabia and Kuwait, and therefore the large expatriate workforce offers a captive market for landlords. Elsewhere foreigners can now purchase property, but only in designated zones.

Kuwait Finance House has been involved in real-estate finance for over 30 years and produces quarterly reports on the local market in Kuwait containing a detailed analysis of pricing trends.[9] It has a real-estate affiliate which provides *shariah*-compliant mortgages as well as an *ijara* – a leasing service that provides an ownership option for clients whose financial circumstances permit.

Housing finance is also a major Islamic financing activity in Saudi Arabia, as although the government-owned Real Estate Development Fund (REDF) provides interest-free finance to local nationals, it is inadequately capitalised and repayments are often deferred or not honoured by its beneficiaries. Consequently although since its inception in the 1970s REDF has provided 443,842 loans,[10] as the Saudi population has grown the waiting list for finance has increased, with applicants often having to wait for years for finance, fewer than 10,000 loans a year being approved on average in recent years.

The Islamic banks have aimed to fill this gap, with Al Rajhi Bank offering funds for villas and apartments through a *musharaka* partnership arrangement whereby the client pays at least 10 per cent of the initial purchase price and the bank pays a maximum of 90 per cent. The client pays rent to the bank for the share it owns, but at the same time buys out the bank's share on an instalment basis, usually over a 15- to 25-year period. Al Rajhi Bank also offers finance for land purchase and building homes through an *istisna* project finance facility, where the costs of materials supplied and construction are covered and the client repays over a period of up to 25 years.[11] This differs from a conventional loan, as the bank is financing costs directly on the basis of invoices supplied by the client.

Al Rajhi Bank also provides funding for up to ten years for investors who wish to acquire property for renting to expatriates working in the kingdom. Unlike in the UAE and Bahrain, foreign nationals are not allowed, as already mentioned, to own property in Saudi Arabia, but with over 6 million expatriates working in the kingdom, there is a captive market for landlords. In addition it is estimated that fewer than one-third of Saudi nationals own their own home, partly because they have insufficient income to afford to buy. A further handicap has been the absence of a mortgage law, which has hindered the development of a housing market. At present most of the Al Rajhi Bank finance is for newly built properties, not existing housing. A Mortgage Law was finally passed by the Shoura Council in July 2008, but it is unclear how this will affect the housing market (Ghafour 2008). There has at least been no sub-prime crisis in Saudi Arabia, as banks such as Al Rajhi have pursued cautious financing policies. However, there is no evidence that the availability of Islamic finance has helped local citizens to acquire property who would not have acquired it anyway.

Given the construction boom in Dubai, it is not surprising that the largest property finance company, Amlak Finance,[12] is based there. Originally an affiliate of Emaar, Dubai's largest construction company, it was floated independently on the Dubai Financial Market in 2004, and has subsequently expanded into Egypt, Jordan and Qatar. Amlak has a *shariah* board and designates itself an Islamic financial institution, but its fees and charging structures are little different to conventional banks, except that it cites an annual profit rather than an interest rate. It is admirably transparent over fee charges, the application fee being AED 6,000 for residents and AED 10,000 for non-residents, the other major upfront charge being a valuation fee. As the annual profit rate charged is 8.5 per cent, the financing is far from cheap and, unlike Al Rajhi Bank, no information is given on the product structures, for example whether the financing involves *murabaha*, *musharaka* or other forms of Islamic financing.

The construction boom in the GCC, which Islamic financial institutions have helped to fuel, has created temporary employment for millions of expatriate building workers, provided housing for richer expatriates and some locals, and changed the landscapes of the region's cities. It has also resulted in much speculation, with property bought and sold in the UAE, Bahrain and Qatar before it is ever occupied. There is a large amount of empty residential property, and the Islamic finance institutions have been unconcerned about the social impact of their financing or the sustainability of the developments. There is certainly much to criticise, raising questions as to how far the values of those engaged in Islamic finance are different from those in commercial banks. The major correction in the property market since 2008, especially in Dubai, has adversely affected Islamic financial institutions as well as their conventional competitors, and Amlak has been merged with Tamweel, another Islamic mortgage company, to establish a larger company with a strengthened capital base.

Islamic investment banking

There are 12 wholesale banks of significance in the GCC, of which Arcapita, Gulf Finance House and Unicorn Investment Bank[13] are the major institutions; however, these are investment companies focused on asset management and venture capital investment around the world rather than investment banks as understood internationally. Arcapita invests itself as a principal, the aim being to sell on its assets to its investor base of around 1,000 clients. Gulf Finance House originates from Kuwait, but its Bahrain activity is substantial, its focus being on infrastructure finance in the Middle East and North Africa. Unicorn Investment Bank is a relative newcomer, founded only in 2004, with a business model similar to Arcapita and Gulf Investment House, but its focus is on the wider Islamic world, including Turkey, Pakistan and Malaysia.

Investment banking is arguably more compatible with *shariah* than is retail banking, since much of its income is fee-based rather than accruing from lending and charging interest. During the first oil boom in the 1970s there was little investment banking in the GCC, as governments financed most major projects from their own budgets. In recent years governments and the largely autonomous state-owned companies have sought more sophisticated methods of financing, including syndicated project finance and security issuance, as well as equity finance through initial public offerings, rights issues and convertible stock. These are core investment banking activities, but neither the major conventional banks nor the Islamic banks in the GCC have much expertise or experience in these areas.

Much of the Islamic investment activity in the GCC has involved project finance, with the UAE as the most active market followed by Saudi Arabia, as Table 7.2 shows. Many of the arrangers have been major international banks such as HSBC, Barclays Capital and Standard Chartered, demonstrating that it is organisational skills and experience that matter most, not knowledge of Islamic finance. The larger Islamic banks in the GCC, are, however, starting to get involved in project finance, notably Dubai Islamic Bank and Al Rajhi.

TABLE 7.2 Islamic project finance in the GCC (2000–10)

Country	Number of projects	Value of projects US$ million
Bahrain	30	16,472
Kuwait	7	2,418
Qatar	34	10,598
Saudi Arabia	52	49,042
UAE	78	54,405

Source: Islamic Finance Information Service, London, July 2010.

Musharaka partnerships are used for project finance, as they involve profit and loss sharing, with profits shared in accordance with contractually agreed ratios between the partners and losses shared in proportion to the subscribed capital (Rosly 2005). The provisions are clear and there is no problem in drawing up legal contracts consistent with *shariah* principles for this type of financing facility (Siddiqi 1985). There have been relatively few *musharaka* deals, however, the largest being a facility worth US$1 billion for Emaar Properties, the Dubai developer, in February 2007. Most project finance has involved *murabaha* or *ijara* structures that provide financing at fixed or variable rates comparable to the terms and conditions of conventional finance, rather than the distinctive, but perhaps more risky, *musharaka* structures based on profit and loss sharing.

Sukuk securities issuance

The global trend towards using money and capital markets for finance could not initially be replicated for Islamic finance, as the instruments used, such as bills, bonds and notes, were interest-based. Islamic finance appeared to be more suited to a classical banking business model, where deposits covered the funding and there was no attempt at securitising assets or liabilities to create money and capital market instruments. Securitised Islamic financial instruments were first issued in Pakistan under the Mudaraba Companies Ordinance of 1981 (Lewis and Algaoud 2001) and, in Malaysia, securities that were approved as being *shariah*-compliant were traded from 1995.[14] Although the sale of debt instruments, *bai dayn*, is permitted by the Shafii School of Islamic jurisprudence that prevails in Malaysia and Indonesia, the more conservative *shariah* scholars in the GCC do not allow such trading on the grounds that the transfer of debt at a price other than its face value can result in *riba*. Furthermore, debt trading severs the relationship between creditors and debtors, resulting in debt being treated impersonally.

As trading in real assets is permissible, *sukuk* securities were developed in Malaysia, which provided the asset backing to financial instruments which would make them more acceptable to GCC investors, although the first *sukuk* of this type, launched in 2000, attracted only domestic investors. The initiative then switched to the Bahrain Monetary Agency, now the Central Bank of Bahrain, which issued the first sovereign *sukuk* based on an *ijara* structure in 2001. The aim was not only to provide a new funding vehicle for the government, but also to build Bahrain's reputation as an Islamic financial market by providing a negotiable liquid asset which could be held by Islamic financial institutions. The initiative proved successful, as Islamic banks eagerly took up the issue, which was worth US$100 million (Obaidullah 2007). This brought competition, however, from Malaysia, which issued its own sovereign *sukuk* worth US$600 million in 2002, over half of the capital being subscribed from investors in the GCC, including Islamic banks.

As Table 7.3 shows, Bahrain has subsequently been the most active of GCC countries in terms of numbers of *sukuk* issued, although this is only a small proportion of Malaysia's issuance of 1,604 *sukuk*, worth US$110,456 million. In the GCC the UAE is the leader in terms of the value of *sukuk* issuance, with high-profile *sukuk* such as that issued by DP World in 2006 for US$3.5 billion to finance its worldwide expansion with the takeover of P&O Ports, and an even larger *sukuk* issued by Nakheel, the Dubai-based international property development company. Investors in the Nakheel *sukuk* feared that they might not be repaid on maturity due to Dubai's financial difficulties, but there was a full redemption on schedule in December 2009, and since then market confidence has improved. Saudi Arabia is undoubtedly the GCC market with the most potential, however, with three major *sukuk* for the Saudi Arabia Basic Industries Corporation, the region's largest petrochemical producer. The Bin Ladin Group, the kingdom's leading construction company, has also raised finance through a *sukuk*, as well as through a *shariah*-compliant syndication based on a *murabaha* structure.

TABLE 7.3 *Sukuk* securities issuance in the GCC (2000–10)

Country	Number	Value US$ million
Bahrain	139	8,348
Kuwait	2	200
Qatar	2	1,043
Saudi Arabia	20	16,494
UAE	34	17,303

Source: Islamic Finance Information Service, London, July 2010.

GCC financial centres

The market for financial services in the GCC is very fragmented and, despite moves towards monetary union and the aspiration to a single GCC currency, there is little regulatory convergence (Saleem 2008). Each state has developed its own regulatory system for banks and other financial institutions, and in the UAE and Qatar the financial centres have their own laws and regulations since they are not regulated by the central banks. The regulatory regimes are not just distinctive in relation to conventional banking and finance, but also with respect to Islamic finance, where there has been no attempt at harmonisation. Indeed, there is much competition between GCC financial centres for *shariah*-compliant business, one issue being whether this competition is beneficial or detrimental to the development of Islamic finance and, indeed, financial services more generally.

The regional role of Bahrain in Islamic finance

Bahrain has functioned as a regional financial centre since 1976, keeping its market open to foreign banks, while Saudi Arabia and Kuwait licensed only majority locally-owned institutions. Bahrain has more Islamic financial institutions than any other centre, with 24 Islamic banks and eleven Islamic *takaful* insurance companies, most of which serve the regional rather than the local market.[15] It is very dependent on Saudi business, however, and as the latter opens up its financial sector there are competitive challenges to Bahrain, including in Islamic banking.

The Bahrain Monetary Agency, now renamed the Central Bank of Bahrain, has been very active in promoting Bahrain as an Islamic financial centre. The island has been the headquarters since its foundation in 1991 of the Accounting and Auditing Organisation for Islamic Financial Institutions (AAOIFI), which serves as a standard-setting body for financial reporting.[16] Most Islamic financial institutions worldwide are members of AAOIFI and many adhere to its standards, which build on rather than replace the International Financial Reporting Standards (IFRS) used by most conventional banks in Europe and Asia.

Bahrain also hosts the International Islamic Financial Market (IIFM), whose remit is to help Islamic capital and money markets through promoting common trading standards.[17] Its work is at an early stage, but it has support from the central banks of Bahrain, Brunei, Indonesia, Malaysia and Sudan, as well as from the Jeddah-based Islamic Development Bank. However, the central banks of other GCC countries are not members, preferring to focus their efforts on their own markets and institutions. The Bahrain-based Liquidity Management Centre[18] has also been slow to take off, its aim being to facilitate the placing of surplus funds of Islamic financial institutions in profitable traded instruments. The capital was subscribed by Kuwait Finance House, the Bahrain and Dubai Islamic Banks and the Islamic Development Bank, but they have used international investment banks for much of their own *sukuk* issuance rather than the Liquidity Management Centre. The other major role of the Liquidity Management Centre is to promote secondary-market trading of *sukuk*. Trading volumes have been limited however, with 11 buying and selling transactions in 2005, 25 in 2006, 15 in 2007 and none since.

The Central Bank of Bahrain has a detailed rulebook which governs all financial activity on the island, including Islamic banking. However, there are only two additional specific requirements for Islamic banks: each Islamic bank must have an independent *shariah* supervisory committee, and Islamic banks should adopt the AAOIFI standards for their financial reporting.[19]

It is debatable how far Bahrain's relative success in attracting Islamic financial institutions is due to a pull factor − the encouragement of the Central Bank of Bahrain − or a push factor − the past unwillingness of its neighbours to grant new licences to Islamic banks and *takaful* insurance operators. There are six Islamic retail banks catering for the local market in Bahrain, including Bahrain Islamic Bank and Shamil Bank, but these are all small financial institutions. Their sustainability in the long term is open to question, especially as Saudi Arabia has opened up its market for financial services since 2005 as a condition of its World Trade Organisation membership, although admittedly the nine new entrants, which include Deutsche Bank, BNP Paribas and JPMorgan Chase, have only a limited interest in Islamic finance.

The Qatar and Dubai financial enclaves

Unlike Bahrain, Qatar and Dubai have established financial centres in free zones governed by their own laws and regulations which are based on English common law as applied to finance. Both the Qatar Financial Centre and the Dubai International Financial Centre (DIFC) are separate jurisdictions, with disputes not subject to the civil law which applies outside the zones in Qatar and the UAE. Institutions functioning in the free zones are also outside the jurisdiction of the local *shariah* courts, although admittedly *shariah* arbitration is rarely used in banking disputes, the *shariah* court remit being largely confined to disputes within families over matters such as inheritance.

The Qatar Financial Centre has a detailed rulebook covering Islamic finance, including criteria for *shariah* supervision.[20] In Qatar a higher proportion of bank deposits are *shariah*-compliant than in any other GCC state, but institutions such as the Qatar Islamic Bank, Masraf Al Rayan and the Qatar International Islamic Bank focus on the domestic market, and despite the international designation of the last-named it is regulated by the Central Bank of Qatar rather than by the financial centre authority. The merits of a division of regulatory responsibilities in a small state such as Qatar can be questioned, and in July 2007 the government recognised this by signalling that it intended to establish a single regulatory authority (Thorp 2008).

The major commercial banks in Qatar have established Islamic affiliates, most notably the Qatar National Bank, which has an Al Islami subsidiary, the Commercial Bank of Qatar, with its Al Safa Islamic Banking subsidiary, and Doha Bank, with its subsidiary Doha Bank Islamic.[21] This increasing competition in a relatively small market is encouraging Qatar's Islamic banks to look overseas for diversification and expansion. The Qatar Islamic Bank owns the

London-based European Finance House and the Kuala Lumpur-based Asian Finance Bank. It also has subsidiaries in Lebanon, Bahrain, Yemen and Kazakhstan operating under its own name, and is undertaking feasibility studies of the Turkish, Egyptian and Indonesian markets. Masraf Al Rayan has established a consumer financing operation in Saudi Arabia and is seeking permission to open a branch in Libya, a wholly Muslim country with no Islamic banks to date.

The introduction of a single regulatory system in the UAE is unlikely, as the country is a federation in which each emirate enjoys considerable autonomy, although the Central Bank oversees the entire banking system with the exception of banks registered with the DIFC. The latter has the highest international profile in the region, but Islamic finance is somewhat marginal to its interests. As in Qatar, the major Islamic banks in the UAE are focused on the domestic market; indeed, the Dubai Islamic Bank and the Abu Dhabi Islamic Bank largely concentrate on their home emirates, although they have branch networks throughout the UAE.

Some of the challenges faced by Islamic banking in Dubai became apparent during 2008 through a corruption investigation involving former Dubai Islamic Bank employees in their dealings with Tamweel, a leading local Islamic mortgage finance company. The credit crunch and concern over prospects for the real-estate market in Dubai have also taken their toll. Amlak, the leading *shariah*-compliant home mortgage company in the UAE, has seen its share value collapse, while the share price of Dubai Islamic Bank has fallen from AED 11.2 in October 2007 to AED 1.95 by July 2010. The wider Islamic financial sector has also been caught up in the share price slump, with Shuaa Capital, a highly respected Islamic investment bank, seeing its price decline from AED 8.22 to AED 1.02 by July 2010.[22]

Competition can, of course, be helpful to financial development, but the emergence of rival centres in the Gulf has fragmented the Islamic finance industry and resulted in the licensing of many very small institutions which cannot benefit from economies of scale or scope. None of the Islamic banks in the Gulf is in the top 100 world banks in terms of assets, and as a consequence it is the major international banks such as HSBC, Deutsche Bank and Citibank that have moved into Islamic finance to fill the void, especially in investment banking, where capacity and capability are of critical importance. Although HSBC has based much of its Islamic banking operations in Dubai, the other investment banks conduct their Islamic finance business from London, where it is easier to recruit skilled professionals, rather than from the GCC states. The Financial Services Authority in the United Kingdom has made considerable efforts to accommodate Islamic banking within a conventional regulatory framework, providing a model which regulators in the GCC can in most respects follow (Ainley et al. 2007). However, the UK policy of guaranteeing investment deposits while putting the onus on depositors to ensure *shariah* compliance by voluntarily giving up their right to deposit protection is unlikely to be acceptable in the GCC.

Conclusions

It is apparent from this survey that Islamic financial institutions in the GCC are significant sources of capital and are contributing to the development of Islamic finance worldwide, especially in Asia. The GCC is well positioned at the heart of the Muslim world to serve as an Islamic finance hub linking Europe, Asia and Africa, and the spread of subsidiaries of GCC-based Islamic banks illustrates that this is starting to happen.

The popular preference for Islamic banking in the GCC indicates that it is more of a bottom-up than a top-down movement. Al Rajhi Bank in Saudi Arabia has more branches than any other bank in the kingdom, and despite the reluctance to grant it a licence in the 1980s, as discussed earlier, it has become the largest stock-market-listed Islamic bank in the world. Like the Dubai Islamic Bank – the oldest Islamic commercial bank – Al Rajhi has successfully developed a range of deposit and financing products that has attracted millions of clients. The aim of these institutions is to provide as wide a range of facilities as conventional banks, but through *shariah*-compliant products.

Critics of these institutions argue that they are simply imitating conventional banks and focusing on more affluent clients rather than playing a social role and assisting the poor. They are also accused of encouraging consumer indebtedness through their highly popular vehicle and home finance, but most GCC citizens take cars for granted and want to own the homes they live in, and indeed acquire additional property to rent to expatriates to enhance their current income. The poorest in the GCC are mostly migrant labourers rather than local citizens, and labourers only use banks for remittances.

The most popular Islamic financial products, notably *murabaha* and *ijara*, were pioneered and refined in the GCC, and although investment *mudaraba* deposits were first developed in Jordan, the concept soon spread to Kuwait, Bahrain, Qatar and the UAE. Al Rajhi Bank in Saudi Arabia did not embrace this concept; rather, in Saudi Arabia mutual funds became the preferred vehicle for those seeking returns on investment. As a result the kingdom was to become the pioneer of *shariah*-compliant funds, and although funds under management have been adversely affected by the global recession and the collapse of share prices, including in the GCC, there remain more funds invested in accordance with *shariah* in Saudi Arabia than anywhere else.

Some governments in the GCC have been very supportive of Islamic finance, notably the government of Bahrain, which has become the major centre for Islamic banking and *takaful*, and Kuwait, which has helpful legislation. Oman has been totally negative and Saudi Arabia surprisingly reluctant, although this has not prevented Islamic banking playing a major role in the kingdom's financial sector. Nevertheless, if SAMA and the Capital Markets Authority were to play a more proactive role, Saudi Arabia could potentially become the global leader in the Islamic finance industry worldwide, with significant benefits to its economy, not least in terms of employment creation in the King

Abdullah Financial District, where, although a grand mosque is included in the plans, there is no mention of Islamic finance in the vision.

As the major international banks have been weakened by the financial crisis of 2008–9, this undoubtedly presents an opportunity for GCC Islamic banks which have been less adversely affected. GCC-based investors in conventional banks, such as Prince Waleed's Kingdom Holdings, which holds 5 per cent of Citibank, and the Abu Dhabi and Qatar Investment Authorities, which hold significant stakes in Barclays, have seen the value of their investments plummet. In contrast, the value of Al Rajhi Bank and Kuwait Finance House investments in retail Islamic banking affiliates in Asia has been much more resilient. There are already proven synergies between the GCC and its Asian and African neighbours in Islamic finance, and these provide a platform for future developments.

Although the financial crisis has resulted in a large decline in oil prices and has reduced the profitability of all financial institutions in the GCC, including Islamic banks, it may also present opportunities. There has been much questioning of the values underpinning the conventional financial system, and the search for alternative means that Islamic banks are likely to receive more attention, especially as their *raison d'être* is morality in financial transactions, based on religious teaching. The increasing international respect for Islamic finance is noted in the GCC, and encourages local acceptance by both governments and bank customers, not least because no Islamic bank has failed in the crisis or required a substantial government bail-out. Furthermore, a global economic recovery is likely to benefit the GCC as oil and gas prices rebound, resulting in fresh liquidity being pumped into Islamic banks to fuel further expansion. Some opportunities may have been missed, but there should be many more to come.

Notes

1. The GCC member states are Bahrain, Kuwait, Oman, Qatar, Saudi Arabia and the United Arab Emirates.
2. Central Bank of Kuwait, Legislation, Safat, 2004, Section 10.
3. Laws of Malaysia, Islamic Banking Act, Government Gazette, Kuala Lumpur 1983, Act 276. Reprinted incorporating amendments A1145 in 2002.
4. Dubai Islamic Bank, *Consolidated Financial Statements*, 31 December 2007, p. 37.
5. http://www.alislami.ae/en/personalbanking.card.credit.htm (accessed 11 August 2011).
6. http://www.noorbank.com/cb-assets-cards.html (accessed 11 August 2011).
7. http://www.alrajhibank.com.sa/Individual/Solutions/CreditCards/Pages/cards.aspx (accessed 11 August 2011).
8. http://www.kfh.com/english/Promotions/2005/tayseer-p/p2.asp (accessed 11 August 2011).
9. KFH, Local Real Estate Report, second quarter 2008, pp. 12–29.
10. Real Estate Development Fund, Annual Report, Riyadh, 2008, at http://www.mof.gov.sa/en/docs/ests/sub.ests.dev.fund.htm (accessed 11 August 2011).

11. http://www.alrajhibank.com.sa/Individual/Solutions/Realestatefinancing/ (accessed 11 August 2011).
12. http://www.amlakfinance.com/html. (accessed 11 August 2011).
13. http://www.arcapita.com; www.gfh.com; and http://www.unicorninvestment bank.com (accessed 11 August 2011).
14. Securities Commission of Malaysia, *Resolutions of the Securities Commission Shariah Advisory Council*, 2nd edn, Kuala Lumpur, 2006, pp. 2–5.
15. Business Friendly Bahrain, Islamic Financial Services, at http://www.bahrainfs.com/FSInBahrainIslamicFinance.aspx.
16. http://www.aaoifi.com (accessed 11 August 2011).
17. www.iifm.net (accessed 11 August 2011).
18. http://www.lmcbahrain.com. (accessed 11 August 2011).
19. Central Bank of Bahrain, *Rulebook, Volume 2: Islamic Banks*, HC-1.3.15 and HC-1.3.16.
20. Qatar Financial Centre, *Rulebook on Islamic Finance*, Doha, 2005, pp. 1–22.
21. Oxford Business Group, Islamic Financial Services Overview, *The Report: Qatar*, 2008, pp. 64–6.
22. Data cited from the Dubai Financial Market.

References

Ahmad, Abdel-Rahman Yousri (2005) 'Islamic banking modes of finance: proposals for further evolution', in Munawar Iqbal and Rodney Wilson (eds), *Islamic Perspectives on Wealth Creation*. Edinburgh: Edinburgh University Press, pp. 32–3.
Ainley, Michael, Mashayekhi, Ali, Hicks, Robert, Rahman, Arshadur and Ravalia, Ali (2007) *Islamic Finance in the United Kingdom: Regulation and Challenges*. London: Financial Services Authority.
Alam, Mehre (2006) 'Islamic finance: going strong', *Oman Economic Review*, June, pp. 1–8.
Chapra, M. Umer (1985) *Towards a Just Monetary System*. Leicester: Islamic Foundation, p. 130.
Elewa, Ahmed A. (2008) 'UAE to issue new law on Islamic finance activities', *Gulf News*, 9 April.
Ghafour, P.K. Abdul (2008) 'Shoura council OKs mortgage law', *Arab News*, 3 July.
Lewis, Mervyn K. and Algaoud, Latifa M. (2001) *Islamic Banking*. Cheltenham: Edward Elgar, pp. 110–11.
Noor, Osama (2008) '*Takaful* in UAE: making its presence felt', *Middle East Insurance Review*, June, p. 28.
Obaidullah, Mohammed (2007) 'Securitisation in Islam', in M. Kabir Hassan and Mervyn K. Lewis (eds), *Handbook of Islamic Banking*. Cheltenham: Edward Elgar, p. 197.
Rosly, Saiful Azhar (2005) *Critical Issues in Islamic Banking and Financial Markets*. Bloomington, IN: Author House, pp. 181–5.
Saeed, Abdullah (1999) *Islamic Banking and Interest: A Study of the Prohibition of Riba and its Contemporary Interpretation*. Leiden: Brill, p. 14.
Saleem, Nadia (2008) 'Plans for Gulf monetary union on track', *Gulf News*, 22 September.
Siddiqi, Muhammad Nejatullah (1985) *Partnership and Profit Sharing in Islamic Law*. Leicester: Islamic Foundation, pp. 9–18.
Thorp, Philip (2008) 'The importance of being regulated', in *The Report: Qatar*. Oxford

Business Group, pp. 88–9.

Warde, Ibrahim (2000) *Islamic Finance in the Global Economy.* Edinburgh: Edinburgh University Press, pp. 73–4.

Wilson, Rodney (1987) 'Financial development in the Arab Gulf: the eastern bank experience, 1917–1950', *Business History*, 29(2): 178–98.

Wilson, Rodney (2002) 'Arab government responses to Islamic finance: the cases of Egypt and Saudi Arabia', *Mediterranean Politics*, 7(3): 143–63.

Wilson, Rodney (2006) 'Islam et capitalisme reconsidérés', *Maghreb-Machrek*, 187: 29–44.

Wilson, Rodney (2007) 'Concerns and misconceptions in the provision of *takaful*', in Sohail Jaffer (ed.), *Islamic Insurance: Trends, Opportunities and the Future of* Takaful. London: Euromoney Books, pp. 72–86.

Young, Arthur (1983) *Saudi Arabia: The Making of a Financial Giant.* New York: New York University Press, pp. 61–3.

8

ANATOMY OF AN OIL-BASED WELFARE STATE

Rent distribution in Kuwait

Laura El-Katiri, Bassam Fattouh and Paul Segal

Introduction

Oil has made Kuwait rich. Oil is Kuwait's largest productive sector by a long way, and oil rents are the foundation of even the non-oil economy. But wealth does not lead automatically to economic and social development. Kuwait's achievement is that it has, for the most part, used its oil income to provide a high standard of living for full Kuwaiti citizens, while to a much lesser extent also benefiting non-Kuwaitis. Oil wealth has transformed the country within decades from a modest trade-based desert emirate to a modern city-state. It has also created a relatively egalitarian economy based on an extensive distributive system that provides Kuwaiti citizens with essential services including free healthcare, education and social security. Therefore the most important fact about Kuwait's oil wealth is that it has been successfully used to benefit its citizens. This feat has been achieved through a broad distributive welfare state, developed over the decades since oil was discovered.

Nonetheless, Kuwait's policies of rent distribution have developed in an *ad hoc* manner into an uncoordinated system with substantial distortions, inefficiencies and institutional deficiencies. These include the long-term use of subsidies to energy and other utilities that lead to inefficient use and misallocation of resources, a highly segmented labour market whose ability to absorb large numbers of young Kuwaitis outside the public sector remains in doubt and an uncompetitive and deteriorating business environment that stifles private and foreign investment.

The main purposes of this chapter are to examine the effects of Kuwait's extensive welfare system and identify the various channels of rent distribution that underlie it.

Oil rent and the transformation of Kuwait

In an economy dominated by natural resources the management of the *rents* becomes one of the most important roles of the government. Here we take the standard economists' definition of rents as *payments to a factor of production over and above that required to induce it to do its work* (Wessel 1967). This definition implies that resource rents are any payments to the owner of a natural resource that remain once labour (including highly skilled labour), capital (including technology) and any other inputs to the extraction of the resource have been paid.[1] In most resource-rich countries these rents accrue to the government. In countries like Kuwait in which the modern state apparatus developed after or during the development of the resource sector, countries often referred to as rentier economies or rentier states, the development of the institutions and policies of the government are heavily influenced by its role as the manager and distributor of rents (Mahdavy 1970; Beblawi 1987; Karl 1997).

Kuwait's pre-oil economy

Kuwait's pre-oil economy was marked by three main features: first, the accumulation of early wealth in Kuwait during the eighteenth and nineteenth centuries through trade and trade-based activities, largely in the hands of the merchant families; secondly, the political stabilisation of the emirate of Kuwait under the family of the Al-Sabah, which provided the stability needed for successful trade; thirdly, the virtual absence in any form of the welfare state known in Kuwait today.

Kuwait was founded in the early eighteenth century by a group of tribal clans that had migrated from the Najd in Saudi Arabia. Owing to its rich coastal waters, its suitability at the upper edge of the western side of the Gulf as a natural harbour, as well as its strategic location between the mainland trade routes between Baghdad and Aleppo, Kuwait soon flourished as a trading hub between the East and the West. The economy's main business sectors – land-trade, seafaring and a lucrative pearl industry – laid the foundations for early wealth creation in Kuwait, primarily in the hands of the merchants and trading families of Kuwait (Crystal 1995: 19; Al-Sabah 1980: 23). Soon known throughout the Gulf region as Kuwait's powerful merchant elite, Kuwait's merchant families not only dominated economic life, but also constituted an important element in the political balance between the Emir, the Ruler of Kuwait, on the one hand, and the ruled on the other (Crystal 1995: 19).

Prior to the discovery of oil, the Emir remained financially dependent on taxes and customs duties collected from the population. In the nineteenth century the merchants, as the main providers of these funds, exercised a strong influence on policy-making under the Emir. In the early twentieth century as the Emir began to benefit from strategic rent paid by the British and from the first payments for oil concessions, the merchants sought to reassert their influence through a political movement that led to a short period of political confrontation and, briefly, to the creation of an elected assembly, the majlis, during the 1930s (Crystal 1995: 47).[2]

This period overlapped with a period of economic decline caused by developments partly outside of Kuwait's control: the 1920s began with a conflict over trade routes with Saudi Arabia, leading to many trade routes being blocked for much of the decade. The dependence of Kuwait's economy on international trade meant that the emirate's economy was severely hit by the global financial crisis of the 1930s. The collapse of the pearl industry in the Persian Gulf during this period, a result of a flooding of international markets with cheap mass products from East Asia, further compromised the economy. While most of Kuwait's merchant community proved to be resilient to the crisis, those working further down the hierarchy, such as pearl divers, boat builders and Bedouin tribes, faced increasing impoverishment (Al-Sabah 1980: 16–24; Khalaf and Hammoud 1988).

Kuwait's oil economy

Oil was first discovered in Kuwait in 1938, following a concession agreement between the state of Kuwait and Britain that allowed the British to explore and produce from Kuwaiti oil fields, with production starting in 1948. Kuwait's oil revenues grew substantially in the decades after oil was discovered, rising from US$760,000 in 1946 to US$567.5 million by 1965 and, following the oil price bonanza of the mid-1970s, US$9.8 billion in 1976, the equivalent of 2.3 times non-oil GDP, or 70 percent of total GDP (Ismael 1993: 135; Khouja and Sadler 1984: 39; authors' own calculations).[3]

Kuwait's oil revenues have always accrued directly to the state.[4] Until 1975, the mechanism was royalties and taxes on profits paid by foreign oil companies. In 1975, Kuwait nationalised the country's oil industry, and in 1980 placed both the upstream and downstream sectors under the control of its national oil company, Kuwait Petroleum Company. With such vast rent income, the state not only became extraordinarily wealthy, but also found itself in control of the majority of the economy's overall output. The removal of most taxes levied on the domestic economy since the early 1950s clearly signalled that the basic relation between the state and its citizens was no longer one of mutual financial dependence but one defined by the purely distributive role played by the state.

It became clear soon after the discovery of oil that the state, as the owner and distributor of such substantial parts of the economy's wealth, needed to modify its approach to the economy as a whole. In the absence of a central planning department during the 1950s and early 1960s, the government began to spend increasing sums on the country's social and economic infrastructure. Kuwait's first five-year plan, adopted in 1967, defined the state's long-term objectives: first, the diversification of Kuwait's economy towards a self-sustaining growth independent of oil revenues; secondly, ensuring an equitable distribution of income among Kuwaitis; and thirdly, the training of Kuwait's human resource base and the development of specialised skills (Ismael 1993: 135).[5]

As a result of its need to channel rent into the economy following these objectives, the role of the state in the economy grew. The mining and quarrying sector, since 1975 entirely state-owned, has accounted for more than half of the Kuwaiti economy's output continuously since the 1950s (Government of Kuwait 2008: 220, Table 139).[6] Various industries, such as the refining, petrochemicals and fertiliser industries, as well as other economic sectors such as transport and logistics, have been highly dependent on the country's oil sector. In addition, sectors such as banking and finance and real estate have benefited from the availability of large sums of capital in Kuwait due to oil rents. In this way much of Kuwait's economy outside the oil sector proper is dependent on oil. The private sector, alongside many public business sectors, benefit not only from direct transfers and subsidies, but also from the overall high living standards of Kuwaitis and high public investment in infrastructure. For these reasons the state in Kuwait has been described as the prime mover of the economy (Al-Sabah 1980: 72; Ismael 1993: 95 and 105; NBK 2003: 19).

The percentage of Kuwaiti nationals both in Kuwait's total population and in Kuwait's workforce has declined substantially since the 1950s. Today 1.3 million people living in Kuwait, or more than 60 per cent of the population, are expatriates, primarily from Asia and other Arab countries, while non-Kuwaitis comprise 82 per cent of Kuwait's workforce. Kuwaiti nationals thus constitute a minority in their own country, and their participation rate in the national labour force is extremely small by international standards, with only 42 per cent of the working age (15–64) population employed (Government of Kuwait 2008: 25, Table 24).[7] An important consequence of the dichotomy within Kuwait's overall population is that one would expect the distribution of rent by the government to be aimed primarily at Kuwaiti nationals as opposed to expatriates who have few legal rights and no legal claim on the country's oil wealth.

Channels of rent distribution

The primary economic question facing the Kuwaiti government is how to spend its oil revenues. The challenge in distributing government oil rents derives from the fact that there is no final consumer to whom they 'naturally' accrue (Segal 2011). In most economic activities the majority of value added gets distributed as wages and profits, most of which is then spent by the recipients in the private sector. In contrast, oil revenues flow directly into the treasury and their distribution is decided by political means. When resource rents substitute for taxation of the private sector, as in the case of Kuwait, then individuals also benefit according to how their actual tax bill compares with the counterfactual situation of the absence of the resource. Thus the elimination of taxation of the private sector is not a distribution-neutral tax policy: if taxation in the absence of the rents would be progressive, then the elimination of taxes is regressive. While we cannot identify the counterfactual of what the economy or fiscal policy would look like without rents, we can identify the policies and channels used by the government to distribute oil rents.

These channels comprise fiscal policies that determine the distribution of the current benefits of oil rents. But Kuwait, like a number of resource-rich countries, also saves a share of oil receipts in the form of a sovereign wealth fund (SWF), named the Reserve Fund for Future Generations (RFFG). SWFs are at heart also a component of distributional policy in that they distribute the benefits of today's oil revenues to future generations. We discuss SWFs in general and the RFFG in particular in more detail below.

In this section we identify eight main channels through which the Kuwaiti government distributes rents into the wider economy. These are domestic public investment, land purchases, public transfer payments, subsidies, public employment, intervention in the private sector, the regulation of Kuwait's FDI environment and, finally, investment abroad.

Domestic public investment

Since the beginning of the 1950s, the government has invested substantially in infrastructure, in the country's economic diversification programme and in social services including health and education – which can also be seen as benefits in kind received by the population. These investments serve multiple purposes, all of which relate to the government's three central objectives of helping diversify the economy, developing the country's skills base and channelling oil revenues to the population (Ismael 1993: 135). Although the efficiency and returns on some of these investment projects have been quite low, and achieving the objective of diversifying the economy remains elusive, public investment has been successfully used to benefit Kuwaiti citizens. Kuwait can look back at some important achievements in key areas such as literacy, education and health. This contrasts with some of the discourse in the 'oil-curse' literature where it is argued that weak institutional features such as poor governance structure, a lack of accountability in government spending decisions, corruption and a lack of long-term planning prevent citizens from benefiting from their oil wealth at all (Devarajan and Raballand 2010).

Fighting illiteracy and building a comprehensive education system accessible to all Kuwaitis were among the earliest priorities for the government's social programmes. The government invested heavily in the construction of schools, the hiring of rapidly increasing numbers of teachers – most of them from other Arab countries such as Egypt and the Palestinian territories owing to a lack of Kuwaiti teachers – and literacy programmes aimed at the then largely illiterate population. In 1966 Kuwait University opened its doors to both Kuwaitis and children of expatriates living in Kuwait (Al-Sabah 1970: 57–8). Kuwait's education system is still free to both Kuwaiti nationals and non-Kuwaitis, and includes free books, school uniforms, meals, transportation and, for low-income families, a parental allowance. University education includes free dormitories, meals, sportswear, transportation and field trips. Kuwait awards some of the Gulf's most generous state funding to provide high-achieving students with scholarships to study abroad (Crystal 1995: 57).

Expenditure on education in Kuwait has accordingly been one of the largest items on the government's budget, typically representing some 5 per cent of GDP and 13 per cent of total government expenditure, comparable to, if not higher than, spending in high-income OECD countries (MBRF and UNDP/RBAS 2009: 298, Table 29; World Bank 2009).[8] Kuwait has one of the highest literacy rates in the MENA region – more than 94 per cent – including the MENA's highest rate of literacy for women of 91 per cent,[9] and among the region's highest rates of gross school enrolment of 75 per cent (World Bank 2009; UNDP 2009: 253, Table 253). The style and content of Kuwait's education system have, however, been criticised along with those of other Arab states.[10]

The 1950s also marked the beginning of a comprehensive approach towards improving Kuwait's formerly non-existent medical infrastructure, with medical treatment now being free to both nationals and expatriates. Despite criticism, particularly with regard to its cost, Kuwait's health system is seen today as one of the best in the region. Where Kuwait does not possess the necessary medical expertise, medical treatment for Kuwaitis is paid for abroad in specialist clinics, with transportation as well as accommodation costs for patients and their relatives paid for by the state (Crystal 1992: 62).

Beyond these social programmes, the state also initially invested heavily in public infrastructure and the development of an industrial base in a state-led drive for economic diversification. Infrastructure in the form of roads, harbours and an airport were key to any future growth of economic activity outside the all-dominating oil sector. While such infrastructure projects were initially essential to Kuwait's progress, the limited returns of government investment in the industry soon became evident. A lack of planning behind parts of the infrastructure development projects during the 1950s and 1960s in particular have been criticised (Al-Sabah 1970: 110–11). Unsuccessful cases of national companies include Kuwait Airways, which has been running losses for several decades since its establishment in 1954 (Al-Sabah 1970: 63).

Land purchase

A second channel for the distribution of Kuwait's oil wealth, particularly during the 1950s and 1960s, was Kuwait's land purchase programme. Despite its name, the programme was essentially designed as a form of transfer system with the aim of channelling the state's rapidly growing rent income to the population, while also redistributing land ownership on a large scale (Khouja and Sadler 1979: 44; Al-Sabah 1970: 57). Under the land purchase programme during the 1950s up to the 1980s, the central government bought land that was not in use from Kuwaiti nationals at highly inflated prices, retained some for public buildings and sold the remainder back to the public at low prices. These transactions implied transfers of wealth to both sellers and purchasers of land. In the early 1960s, one quarter of total government expenditure went into the land purchase programme (Al-Sabah 1970: 57).

The land purchase programme, however, lost its momentum during the 1980s and 1990s. Today, less than 3 per cent of total government expenditure is on land purchases (Government of Kuwait 2008: 229, Table 145). The decline of the programme may partly be due to the decline in land available for purchase, but it may also have been a response to severe criticism aimed at the programme throughout the 1960s and 1970s. Some observers objected that the programme was a highly inequitable redistribution of wealth and a major distortion of the real estate market (IBRD 1965: 45; Al-Sabah 1970: 57; Crystal 1992: 62). A World Bank report from 1965 describes the land purchase programme as

> a rather indiscriminate and inequitable way of distributing the oil revenues. In addition, probably the largest share of these funds are invested abroad, so that the land purchase program fails to accomplish its main objective of invigorating the Kuwaiti economy.
>
> *(IBRD 1965: 4)*

Crystal argued that the main beneficiaries of the land purchase programme have been Kuwait's wealthy seafaring and pearl trading families who historically owned most of the land bought by the government. In many cases, the land was later bought back by the same families who had sold it, resulting in large net profits for those families, leading essentially to 'a transfer of wealth from the state to the rich' (Crystal 1992: 62). In addition, Ismael found that the programme profoundly distorted land and property prices and invited large-scale property speculation (Ismael 1993: 102–4). Inflated property prices as well as access to land for building have remained a problem in Kuwait until today, for both residents and the business sector (personal interviews, March 2010).

Public transfer payments and pensions

The 1950s also witnessed the beginnings of a rapidly expanding social security system based on transfers paid directly to Kuwaiti nationals or businesses. Initially these transfers were aimed primarily at poverty reduction and were thus conditioned on grounds such as low income, illness and disability, widowhood, divorce and unemployment. In subsequent decades Kuwait's transfer system became broader, and developed into the single largest item on the government budget, surpassing general development expenditure and land purchase allocations. As can be seen from Table 8.1, the item 'miscellaneous expenditure and transfers' constituted 43 per cent and 59 per cent of total government expenditure in 2007/8 and 2008/9 respectively. This category can be further broken down into miscellaneous expenditure, domestic transfers and external transfers. In 2009, domestic transfers constituted the bulk of this expenditure item accounting for close to 50 per cent of total government expenditure. The 2009 figures have been inflated by the dramatic increase in transfers made to the pension fund in that year (discussed below). However, the

2008 figures still reveal the importance of such transfers in the Kuwaiti welfare system. In 2008, domestic transfers accounted for 25 per cent of total government expenditure, similar to the expenditure on wages and salaries in that year.

TABLE 8.1 Government expenditure (in million KD) (2007/8–2008/9)

Type of expenditure	2007/2008	Per cent of total	2008/2009	Per cent of total
Wages and salaries	2,477	25.5	3,039	16.6
Goods and services	1,768	18.2	3,002	16.4
Vehicles and equipment	90	0.9	122	0.7
Projects, maintenance and land purchase	1,206	12.4	1,358	7.4
Miscellaneous expenditure and transfers	4,157	42.9	10,741	58.8
Miscellaneous expenditure	1,283		1,286	
Transfers (domestic)	2,509		8,920	
Transfers (external)	365		535	
Total expenditure	9,698	100	18,262	100

Source: Ministry of Finance 2008/2009.

Domestic transfers have evolved into a complex system of different forms of government support which include transfers to individuals, civil institutions and public institutions (which include the Public Institute for Social Security (PIFSS), the body responsible for administering and paying out public pensions), general subsidies, support for private-sector activity and businesses and support for the national labour force outside the public sector. In 2009, by far the most important component of domestic transfers has been pensions, which cost more than double the government expenditure on wages and salaries. In 2009, out of the 10,741 million KD spent on miscellaneous expenditure and transfers, social security payments cost 6,877 million KD, an enormous 38 per cent of total government expenditure.[11] This spending is the result of many decades during which a large share of the Kuwaiti national workforce has been in public employment. The extent of the cost of Kuwait's pensions programme prompted the unusual move by the government to levy a type of social insurance contribution on each national's wage, paid by employers of Kuwaiti nationals (10 per cent of the wage rate with a cap at KD 2,250) as well as by national employees (5 per cent of the monthly salary) (Government of Kuwait 2010). However, pension payments far surpass government social insurance receipts, implying that pensions are not just a form of saving for individuals but are another means for the government to transfer oil rents to individuals. Indeed, they clearly comprise the largest channel of rent distribution in Kuwait.

Other transfers to individuals comprise around 7 per cent of domestic transfers. They are very diverse and include annual housing loan forgiveness on the grounds of poverty or death, a marriage fund that enables young Kuwaiti men from low income families to pay the obligatory marriage dowry and irregular untargeted transfers. Examples include Amiri grants that are paid irregularly to each national as a fixed rate per head as a kind of bonus at times of high oil revenues,[12] and general loan forgiveness to Kuwaiti nationals, often used to write off capital or interest on the financing of home maintenance, holidays abroad or cars. Transfers to civil institutions include financial support to private education institutions, newspapers, clubs and unions. Though they fall under the category 'general subsidies', payments under this heading refer to transfers made to individuals and include items such as extra allowances to protect households against the rising cost of living. These general subsidies do not include other types of subsidies such as production subsidies to the electricity and water sectors. These are discussed in detail in the next section.

Figure 8.1 below shows the share of transfers out of total household expenditure by 15 income groups for Kuwaitis and non-Kuwaitis. As seen from this graph, for Kuwaitis the share of transfers in total households' expenditure does not follow a uniform pattern. It varies between 8 per cent and 13 per cent while the poorest group receives 15 per cent of its income in transfers.[13] For non-Kuwaitis the picture is different. As we move up the income ladder, the share of transfer in total household consumption expenditure increases unevenly up to the eleventh expenditure group, then declines slightly for the top four groups. Thus for non-Kuwaitis, transfers appear somewhat regressive in nature. The share of transfers out of total expenditure in the lowest income groups is greater for Kuwaitis, while in the higher income groups it is greater for non-Kuwaitis.

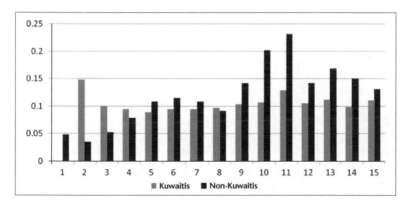

FIGURE 8.1 Share of transfers out of total expenditure by income group

Source: Government of Kuwait (2008), author's own calculation.

It may seem surprising that the Kuwaiti government would give transfers to non-Kuwaitis. Does it imply a 'pure' transfer of rent to non-Kuwaitis alone? While non-Kuwaitis seem to benefit from transfers, these transfers also benefit Kuwaitis indirectly by allowing businesses to pay immigrant workers a lower nominal wage. The same point applies to price subsidies which are also enjoyed by non-Kuwaiti residents.

Subsidies

The Kuwaiti government subsidises a number of goods and services, including electricity, water, food and housing. The measurement of subsidies is often a contentious issue, as one needs to compare the price charged to domestic consumers with some measure of cost. This, however, is not straightforward as there is more than one concept of cost (the average cost, the marginal cost and the opportunity cost) and it is not always clear which measure is used in the different studies.[14] This can, in part, explain the large divergence in estimates of subsidies between different organisations. Furthermore, some studies tend to treat transfers and subsidies in the same manner, which makes comparisons across studies meaningless. Nevertheless, regardless of the concept of cost used, subsidies are widespread in Kuwait, with electricity subsidies being the most important followed by education, health and water subsidies. According to a World Bank study, in 2003, subsidies accounted for 20 per cent of GDP though this figure includes some of the transfer payments discussed in the previous section (see Table 8.2).

TABLE 8.2 Estimated subsidies in Kuwait in 2003 (KD million)

Subsidy	Consumption subsidies			Production subsidies	Total subsidies	% of grand total
	Kuwaitis	Expatriates	Total			
Electricity	157.6	127.8	285.4	139.6	425	23.8
Water	71.7	48.5	120.2	39.4	159.6	8.9
Fuel	0.3	0.2	0.5	4.4	4.9	0.3
Housing loans	126.9	–	126.9	–	126.9	7.1
Renovation loans	7.4	–	7.4	–	7.4	0.4
Marriage loans	8.7	–	8.7	–	8.7	0.5
Industrial loans	–	–	–	4.1	4.1	0.2
Gov. housing	67.5	–	67.5	0	67.5	3.8
Gov. plots	49.7	–	49.7	271.2	320.9	18
Health care	70.2	91.8	162	–	162	9.1
Education	246.2	70.5	316.7	–	316.7	17.7
Transportation	0.4	6.7	7	–	7	0.4
Communications	8.6	4.6	13.2	4.4	17.6	1
Direct gov. aid	34.5	–	34.5	–	34.5	1.9
Basic food items	5.2	–	5.25	–	2	0.3
Cleaning and maintenance	54.7	35.9	90.6	26.2	116.8	6.5
Grand total	909.6	386	1295.6	489.3	1784.9	100
Ratio of subsidy to (%):						
Gov. revenues	17.4	7.4	24.7	9.3	34.1	–
Gov. expend.	22.7	9.6	32.3	12.2	44.5	–
GDP	10.2	4.3	14.6	5.5	20.1	–

Source: World Bank (2005: 59), Table 2.5.

Though provision of subsidies can be seen as an additional means to distribute the oil rent, subsidies are highly inefficient, leading to over-use of the subsidised good or service. Subsidies distort the allocation of resources by diverting part of oil from exports (sold at international prices, i.e. the opportunity cost of oil) toward domestic use in power generation or water desalination (sold at a fraction of international prices). They can also be regressive, in that in many instances richer households tend to capture the bulk of these subsidies. Finally, subsidies are entrenched in institutional barriers and lock-in mechanisms that make it difficult to abolish them. This is especially true in oil-rich countries where the local population considers access to cheap energy as their birthright.

Due to data limitations, this section will focus only on a few sectors were subsidies are highly prevalent, mainly electricity and water. According to Table 8.2, electricity consumption and production subsidies amounted to 425 KD million in 2003, around 6 per cent of total government revenues during that year. All residents, both nationals and expatriates, enjoy subsidised electricity prices. Electricity prices for the residential and industrial sectors in Kuwait are the cheapest in the Middle East, standing at around 0.7 US cents per kwh (see Figure 8.2). Subsidised prices are among the many factors – perhaps the most important one – that can explain why Kuwait has the highest electricity consumption per capita in the region (Figure 8.3).

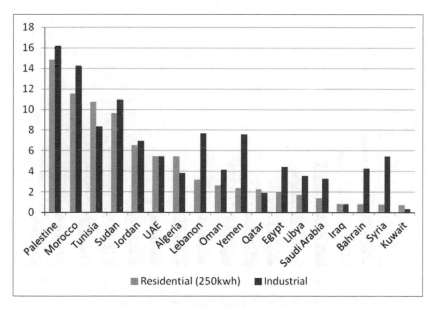

FIGURE 8.2 Residential and industrial electricity prices in selected Arab countries (US$)

Source: Arab Union of Producers, Transporters and Distributors of Electricity 2008. For Kuwait, data from Citory et al. (2007) for residential prices and Kuwait Ministry of Electricity and Water website for industrial prices (refers to subsidised industrial prices).

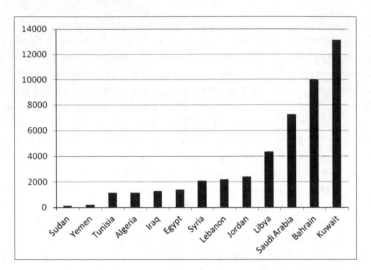

FIGURE 8.3   Electricity consumption per capita in selected Arab countries (2008) (kWh)

Source: Arab Union of Producers, Transporters and Distributors of Electricity 2008: Table 17.

As in the case of electricity, water tariffs are very low and do not come close to covering the cost of production. In 2002 the water tariff ranged between US$0.18/m^3 and US$0.57/m^3, depending on the end user, while the cost stood at around US$1.98. The resulting subsidy therefore amounted to about US$830 million in 2000, about 2.4 per cent of GDP and 5.9 per cent of oil export revenue (World Bank 2005). As seen in Figure 8.4, both Kuwaitis and non-Kuwaitis benefit from water subsidies directly through consumption subsidies and indirectly through production subsidies.

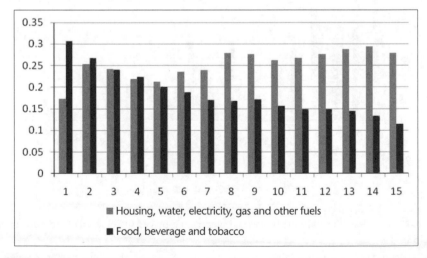

FIGURE 8.4   Expenditure on category out of total expenditure by income group (2007/08)

Source: Government of Kuwait (2008).

In addition to electricity and water subsidies, the government provides food subsidies on certain basic items, such as rice, sugar and cooking oil, through the use of ration cards. Based on Table 8.2, these subsidies are relatively small and benefit Kuwaitis only.

Married Kuwaitis that meet certain criteria are also entitled to housing subsidies. These can be used to purchase plots or houses from the National Housing Authority at prices well below cost, though the scheme has a long waiting list. While waiting, eligible Kuwaitis are entitled to rent smaller houses from the housing authority at a fraction of the market rent. The government also subsidises construction material for houses built on land purchased from the National Housing Authority.

Figure 8.4 shows the share of housing, water, electricity, gas and other fuels out of the total household budget for 15 income groups of nationals. As seen from this figure, the share for this category out of total expenditure does not show any significant pattern. Apart from the lowest income group, the shares are quite similar across the various income groups. This suggests that universal subsidies on electricity, water, housing and fuel will not have any strong distributional impact. In contrast, the share of food, beverages and tobacco in total expenditures is declining in income, following Engel's Law, with the poorest group spending nearly three times as much as the richest group in proportional terms. This implies that food subsidies are likely to be progressive.

There are two arguments that can, in the right circumstances, be used in favour of subsidies. First, if the social cost of a good is lower than the private cost – for instance, if a positive externality implies that there is some social benefit to consuming the good that is not reflected in its price – then it will be efficient to provide a subsidy that brings its private cost or price down to the level of its social cost. In this case the subsidy will increase efficiency, not reduce it. Second, even if the subsidy is inefficient, it may be a 'second best' way to distribute income to certain groups, if direct distribution of cash is not feasible. Thus subsidising low-quality foodstuffs consumed predominantly by the poor can be a way of reducing poverty if targeting direct transfers at the poor is difficult, as it may be since the poor are typically hard to identify (Cornia and Stewart 1993).

We have just seen that food subsidies are progressive in that they benefit the poor proportionately more than the rich, which may justify their use. In the case of housing, water, electricity and other fuels, however, it appears that the subsidies have no clear distributional impact and tend to benefit more those households in the high income group and hence are regressive. It also seems clear that there are no positive externalities associated with the consumption of these goods. On the contrary, environmental considerations would suggest that there are *negative* externalities associated with the consumption of fuel and power. These subsidies therefore are wholly inefficient.[15]

Public employment

A job in the public sector is guaranteed to Kuwaiti nationals and comes with attractive salaries and benefit packages. In consequence, 91 per cent of the Kuwaiti national labour force works in the public sector, while 98 per cent of private sector jobs are occupied by non-Kuwaitis (calculated from numbers from Government of Kuwait 2008: 113, Table 71). Government expenditure on wages and salaries is typically about 20 per cent of total expenditure, the second largest budget item after transfers (Government of Kuwait 2008: 224, Table 142).[16] Wage discrimination between Kuwaiti nationals and expatriates further adds to the perception by many Kuwaitis that their job is a form of entitlement based on nationality (Al-Sabah 1970: 116; personal interviews, March 2010).

There is a widespread perception that GCC governments' policy of distributing rents through provision of employment in the public sector has led to 'overstaffed bureaucracies' and an 'overgrown public sector whose omnipresence in the economy stifles the private sector, distorts work incentives, and leads to extreme dependence on governments to provide jobs' (Eifert et al. 2003). Given that most public sector output does not have an observable market value and hence cannot be measured in an uncontroversial way, there is no straightforward method to test such claims. Nevertheless, evidence suggests the existence of a highly segmented Kuwaiti labour market induced by an implicit guarantee of employment in the government sector. Due to the substantial size of oil rents, the Kuwaiti government has been able to afford relatively high wages, job security, social allowances and generous benefits for public employees. As a result, the gap between the private and public sector wage remains wide (especially if one takes into account the non-wage benefits), leading to high reservation wages for Kuwaitis. Thus there is little incentive for nationals to take on employment in the private sector. Unlike other countries in the GCC where the private sector accounted for the bulk of employment growth, the Kuwaiti public sector continues to be the major source of employment generation for nationals, accounting for more than three-quarter of employment growth in Kuwait during the period 1996–2000 (Fasano and Rishi 2004).

If it is true, as most observers appear to believe, that a significant share of Kuwaiti public sector employment is not productive, then the drawback of public employment as a form of rent distribution is that it prevents public sector employees from doing productive work in the private sector. It presents the employee with the following choice: be unproductive in the public sector and be rewarded with oil rents, or be productive in the private sector and not be rewarded with oil rents. Moreover, beyond the immediate problem of currently unproductive workers, over-employment in the public sector can lead to a failure to develop skills that would lead to growth and higher productivity. In this way, public employment as a form of rent distribution distorts incentives to produce, creating an inefficient and segmented labour market.

The Kuwaiti government has, however, partly responded to this problem by subsidising Kuwaiti labour in the private sector. KD200 million are annually channelled to private sector employers who employ nationals, in addition to government campaigns promoting the Kuwaitisation of the private sector. In 2008 another KD138 million went to the National Labour Support programme which subsidises Kuwaiti nationals' wages in the private sector with an average of KD180 per month with additional payments for spouses and children, adding up to the same benefits paid by the state to public sector employees (Ministry of Finance 2010: Table 15; NBK 2001: 9; personal interviews, March 2010). While subsidising Kuwaitis to work in the private sector helps to reduce the distortion that draws Kuwaitis into the public sector, such subsidies may create the additional distortion of encouraging private sector employers to employ Kuwaitis over better-qualified non-Kuwaitis.[17]

Transfers to the private sector

While employing less than 10 per cent of the Kuwaiti national labour force, Kuwait's private sector employs more than 75 per cent of the country's total labour force, including expatriates (Government of Kuwait 2008: 113, Table 71). The private sector dominates sectors such as services, manufacturing, catering, transportation and logistics, community and social work, but also the quickly evolving banking and finance sectors, real estate and trade (Government of Kuwait 2008: 112–3, Table 71). If Kuwait is to avoid having to create more unproductive public employment the private sector will have to absorb the next generation of Kuwaitis entering the job market – more than half of Kuwait's national population is below the age of 20 and will flood the job market in coming decades (Government of Kuwait 2008: 48, Table 21). At the same time, the development of Kuwait's private sector is key to Kuwait's economic diversification strategy.[18] The state has thus channelled large funds into the private sector in an effort to safeguard the latter's growth.

The government's provision of the public infrastructure and services that business requires, while not charging personal or corporate income tax, is one of the principal channels of indirect rent distribution to the private sector.[19] All sectors of the economy have benefited from large government expenditure on infrastructure projects including roads, electricity, water projects and other public works, particularly in recent years of high oil prices (NBK 2007: 25). Other measures used throughout the past fifty years include technical aid and preferential government purchases. Low-interest or interest-free loans provided by institutions created by the government, such as the Industrial Bank of Kuwait, were designed to fund the expansion of the private sector (Crystal 1992: 52). Transfers also include bail-outs to private investors and institutions, the most controversial of which was the bail-out of private investors during the Suq Al-Manakh crisis of 1982.

Foreign investment

Foreign investment in Kuwait is highly regulated, with the aims of protecting jobs for Kuwaiti nationals, ensuring Kuwaiti control over natural resources and generating additional rents to Kuwaiti nationals. Several sectors remain closed to FDI, including the emirate's all-important hydrocarbon sector. Foreign ownership of companies is restricted to 40 per cent in most sectors, though a recent change in the law has introduced 100 per cent foreign ownership in some sectors (*Arab Times Kuwait*, 7 February 2008; NBK 2010: 28). Foreign companies opening business branches or wishing to import into Kuwait also need a Kuwaiti agent (NBK 2010: 30, 35). This legal framework assures the involvement of Kuwaiti nationals as sponsors, agents and business partners in every business deal involving foreign investors, generating additional rents for Kuwaiti nationals.

This creation of artificial barriers is inefficient and one would expect it to deter investment. Unsurprisingly, therefore, Kuwait's share of FDI into the GCC has historically been low, and is in fact today the lowest in the region by far. In 2008, Kuwait was able to attract merely US$56 million, a tiny amount if compared with the GCC average of above US$10 billion; Bahrain, the second smallest market for FDI in the GCC, by comparison attracted nearly US$1.8 billion (UNCTAD 2009: 149). In 2010, Kuwait ranked 61st out of 183 economies in the Ease of Doing Business index compiled by the World Bank/ IFC, placing Kuwait far behind other GCC members such as Saudi Arabia (rank 13), Bahrain (rank 20) and Qatar (rank 39) (World Bank/IFC 2010). The amended corporate tax law of 2008, which reduced foreign corporate tax from a 5–50 per cent range to a flat rate of 15 per cent tax (NBK 2008: 34), seems to have failed in improving the foreign investment climate.

More worrying for Kuwait is investors' perception of widespread corruption in private and public institutions. In 2009, Kuwait dropped for a second consecutive year in the global corruption index produced by Transparency International, placing Kuwait at 66th place out of 180 countries. Kuwait is currently perceived by investors to be the most corrupt country in the GCC. While oil rents are not directly responsible for the general deterioration in the business environment, rents may create the impression that Kuwait does not need, or does not feel the urgency, to improve its business and regulatory environment in order to attract foreign investment.

Kuwaiti investment abroad

While most of its distributive policies aim at channelling oil rent to various target groups, Kuwait was also one of the first oil-rich countries to start investing oil revenues abroad rather than channelling them immediately into its domestic economy. The limited absorptive capacity of Kuwait's economy, due in part to the lack of potential for industrial development, and the prospects of higher returns for the resulting capital surplus through investment abroad, led the state to embark on a gradual increase of its foreign investments (Crystal 1992: 52). At the same time, the idea of keeping money safely abroad for bad times in the future began to win ground.

The establishment of the General Reserve Fund (GRF) in 1960 was a first step that marked the beginnings of Kuwait's foreign investment programme. Following the 1973 oil price hike and the resulting dramatic increase in revenues, Kuwait decided to lock away part of its annual oil revenues in the form of a Reserve Fund for Future Generations (RFFG), thereby ensuring the distribution of the country's current wealth to future, potentially post-oil generations. In 2005, the RFFG was estimated at KD35 bn or US$114 bn (NBK 2005: 34).[20] In 1982, the government established the Kuwait Investment Authority (KIA), which holds stakes in big corporations such as DaimlerChrysler and BP, Citigroup (sold December 2009) and Merrill Lynch (sold September 2008) (*Financial Times*, 7 December 2009; 19 November 2009).

Sovereign wealth funds such as the RFFG have two different fundamental purposes. The first, as the name suggests, is to save wealth for future generations, in anticipation of the exhaustion of oil reserves. A resource-rich but capital-poor, low-productivity and low-income country such as Nigeria or Bolivia might find that the best way to serve future generations is to invest most of their savings in human and physical capital at home, if they are able to do so effectively. For high-income countries, however, where the capital–labour ratio is high and where there is already sufficient investment in education, further domestic investment is likely to yield very low returns. In these cases, there is a strong incentive to seek higher-yielding investments abroad.

The second purpose of an oil income fund is to act as a 'stabilisation fund' to smooth incomes to oil producers in the face of highly volatile prices. Typical commodity stabilisation funds smooth government expenditures by taking a view on the long-run price of the commodity, with government expenditures kept at the sustainable level, estimated on the basis of predicted long-run average income. Such funds have a poor track record globally, however, because it is very difficult to correctly estimate the long-run price. In addition to this technical challenge, governments in need of finance have an incentive to overestimate the long-run price in order to justify extracting funds in the short run, leading to unsustainable expenditures and long-run indebtedness. In the case of Kuwait, however, the fact that the country is saving so much wealth, in addition to attempting to smooth its income, implies that it is very unlikely to suffer from this problem.

Assessment

Oil rents and living standards

What is the net effect of the complex system of transfers described above? We find no explicit targeting, and in particular there appears to be no effort to direct social benefits specifically at the poor. Unlike in countries that do not have large resource incomes, in Kuwait social benefits and other transfers distribute income, but they do not *re*-distribute income: they are financed from oil rather than by taxing individuals or businesses. The role of the fiscal system is thus not to adjust an existing distribution of income but, rather, to ensure that all Kuwaitis gain from oil rents.

The net effect appears to be a very egalitarian distribution in the economy, as indicated in household expenditure survey data presented in the government's Annual Statistical Abstract.[21] On the basis of these data we estimate a Gini coefficient of 21.8 for the Kuwaiti national population alone. This is an exceptionally low level of inequality, lower, indeed, than any recently recorded Gini coefficient for any whole country.[22] For the whole population we estimate a Gini coefficient of 28.0, also a very low level of inequality and similar to that of egalitarian northern European countries such as Germany. However, the household survey data are problematic: they imply a level of aggregate household consumption that is only 42 per cent of that reported in national accounts data, and in our view the above are likely to be underestimates of the true level of inequality (Anand and Segal 2008).

The shortcomings of the data make it difficult to estimate the level of poverty in Kuwait. Since Kuwait does not report an official poverty line, we use a US-based poverty line as used by the OECD (2008b: 152), which is US$8,087 per capita. If we take the household survey data at face value then we find that 27 per cent of Kuwaitis and 58 per cent of non-Kuwaitis live below this poverty line. If we scale up the survey-reported expenditures so that household consumption equals that reported in the national accounts, then no Kuwaitis, and only 6 per cent of non-Kuwaitis, live below this poverty line. The widths of these ranges reflect the inconsistencies in the data.

Beyond the share living below a poverty line, we can also use household survey data to investigate how well household expenditures reflect the magnitude of oil rents. We estimate adjusted per capita oil rents for consumption of KD9,634, while mean per capita expenditure in the household survey is KD2,856.[23] According to the data, it appears that most, if not all, Kuwaitis are consuming much less than per capita oil rents. Where is the money going? Households save some share of their incomes, and if this share is large then their expenditures would be substantially lower than their incomes. It is highly unlikely, however, that they would save more than two-thirds of their incomes on average. It is also possible that the survey data are broadly correct except for the very top of the distribution, in which case there may be a very small share of Kuwaitis, who do not take part in the survey, who receive the lion's share of the oil rents. If this is the case then Kuwait is far more unequal than the data suggest and we cannot rule out the possibility that the majority of Kuwaitis are not benefiting from their oil to the extent that they should.

Distortions and inefficiencies

An advantage of taxing oil rather than the population is that it is not economically distortionary. However, we have seen that Kuwait's government expenditures typically are distortionary. Subsidies to utilities are highly inefficient, leading to over-use of the subsidised good or service. Kuwait's system of general loan forgiveness has been criticised for rewarding risky expenditure on unnecessary goods (e.g. *Wall Street Journal*, 4 November 2005). We also saw that public employment as a means of rent distribution distorts the labour market, discouraging Kuwaitis from taking up potentially more productive jobs in the private sector. All of these inefficiencies derive from the basic fact that, when the goal is the distribution of rents to citizens, any attempt to achieve it through indirect distribution policies will end up distorting people's incentives in one way or another. In addition to these inefficient expenditures the government also creates artificial barriers to foreign investment into Kuwait, deterring such investment and potentially reducing longer-run growth.

Conclusions

Since the middle of the twentieth century Kuwait has successfully used its oil revenues to improve the living standards of its people. While data problems preclude firm conclusions, it seems reasonably clear that all Kuwaitis enjoy substantial benefits from their oil. They receive generous public services in addition to a variety of mechanisms that distribute oil income among the population. While many benefits are aimed at Kuwaitis alone, Kuwait's oil wealth has attracted large numbers of immigrants who enjoy, at least, the employment opportunities it creates. Kuwait should therefore be considered broadly a success story. It has certainly avoided the perils that some resource-rich countries have faced, and oil has unquestionably improved the lives of Kuwaitis. Nevertheless, some of Kuwait's policies of rent distribution such as subsidising utilities and providing public employment have resulted in substantial distortions, inefficiencies and institutional deficiencies and thus there remains substantial scope for improvement.

Notes

1. This follows from the definition because there is no opportunity cost to extracting natural resources: since they are worth nothing in the ground, any payment left over after extraction counts as rent.
2. A *majlis* is a traditional form of assembly usually comprising tribal elders, but in this format also includes representatives of leading families, gathering with the Amir and discussing policy issues.
3. Khouja and Sadler (1984: 39) and authors' own calculations. GDP shares are at domestic prices.
4. Until the 1962 constitution, the recipient of oil royalties was the Amir of Kuwait.

This changed with the introduction of a written constitution which made Kuwait one of the first country's in the Gulf to formally declare all of the country's natural resource revenues to belong to the state rather than the ruler. Kuwaiti Constitution, Part 2, Art. 21, available online at: http://www.kt.com.kw/ba/dostour.htm (accessed 11 August 2011).

5. These aims have been reiterated throughout Kuwait's development plans, the most recent of which was adopted in early 2010. Government of Kuwait (2009).
6. With a brief exception during the Iraqi invasion in 1990/1 as a result of the halting of all industrial activity in the country.
7. The 42 per cent figure does not take into account those in full-time education, for which we do not have data. Approximately one quarter of 25–29 year olds and 30–34 year olds have university or post-graduate education. Assuming that a quarter of 15–24 year olds are in education and removing them from the total population implies a participation rate of 46 per cent, still a low figure.
8. World Bank, *World Development Indicators 2009.*
9. See the AHDR's gender-related development index, *Arab Human Development Report* (2009) Table 25, p. 253.
10. Criticism concerns mainly the mismatch between the skills of Kuwaiti graduates with the needs of the economy (Al-Sabah 1997: 58; Crystal 1992: 62). While much has been done by the government to encourage more students to study science subjects and to undertake vocational training, a report produced by MBRF and UNDP/RBAS (2009: 105–31) argued that many problems remain (see also the section on the labour market below).
11. Ministry of Finance (2008/9).
12. The last time an Amiri grant was paid out to all nationals was in the fiscal year of 2006/7. The grant was worth KD200 per citizen, or US$690 (NBK 2006: 25; IMF 2009: 20).
13. There are no Kuwaitis that fall in the first income group.
14. From an economic point of view the correct cost to use is the opportunity cost, but this is not always followed.
15. One further argument for subsidies sometimes given by policy-makers is that they reduce inflation. This argument is not, however, valid in general. A distinction has to be made between the price *level* and the rate of inflation. A subsidy lowers a given price and thereby probably lowers the overall price level, so removing a subsidy will result in a one-off rise in the price level. However, in the absence of other pressures, this implies only a one-off rise in inflation: once the subsidy has gone and the average price has risen there will be no continuing inflation. But though the price level has risen, the country has saved the money it was spending on the subsidy, and overall the country is better off. So if the price level has risen by 1 per cent then nominal income will have risen by more than 1 per cent. Thus this inflation-based argument for subsidies is spurious.
16. In the fiscal year 2008/9, wages and salaries rose in absolute terms but were down to 16.6 per cent of total expenditure; However, this is due to an extraordinary increase in the government's spending on miscellaneous expenditure and transfers. See also Table 8.1.
17. This distortion would occur if employers find it cheaper to employ Kuwaitis, which would be the case if the wage gap between Kuwaitis and non-Kuwaitis were smaller than the total subsidy to employing Kuwaitis.
18. Reiterated throughout Kuwait's development plans, e.g. Government of Kuwait (2009: 5).

19. Only foreign companies owned more than 50 per cent by non-nationals pay a corporate income tax, which is in any case negligible and is discussed below; GCC nationals are treated as Kuwaiti nationals following GCC agreements.
20. Kuwait's foreign investment programme is kept off-budget and its total value is thus unknown.
21. For more details, see the longer working paper version of this chapter (El-Katiri et al. 2011).
22. Going back to 2000, no national Gini coefficient this low is reported in the United Nations University's *World Income Inequality Database* (WIID) available at http://www.wider.unu.edu/wiid (accessed 11 August 2011).
23. See the longer working paper version of this chapter for details on these estimates (El-Katiri et al. 2011).

References

Al-Sabah, Y.S.F. (1980) *The Oil Economy of Kuwait*. London: Kegan Paul International.

Al-Yahya, Mohammed Abdulrahman (1993) *Kuwait. Fall and Rebirth*. London: Kegan Paul International.

Anand, Sudhir and Segal, Paul (2008) 'What do we know about global income inequality?', *Journal of Economic Literature*, 46(1): 57–94.

Arab Union of Producers, Transporters and Distributors of Electricity (2009), *Statistical Report 2009*.

Baumol, William J. (1990) 'Entrepreneurship: productive, unproductive, and destructive', *Journal of Political Economy*, 98(5): 893–921.

Beblawi, Hazem (1987) 'The rentier state in the Arab world', in Hazem Beblawi and Giacomo Luciani (eds), *The Rentier State*. London: Croom Helm, pp. 49–62.

BP (2010) *Statistical Review of World Energy*, June, online at: http://www.bp.com/productlanding.do?categoryId=6929&contentId=7044622 (accessed 5 February 2011).

Cornia, Giovanni. A. and Stewart, Frances (1993) 'Two errors of targeting', *Journal of International Development*, 5(5): 459–96.

Crystal, Jill (1992) *Kuwait: The Transformation of an Oil State*, Westview Profiles: Nations of the Contemporary Middle East. Boulder, CO and Oxford: Westview.

Crystal, Jill (1995) *Oil and Politics in the Gulf: Rulers and Merchants in Kuwait and Qatar*, Cambridge Middle East Library. Cambridge: Cambridge University Press.

Datt, G. (1998) *Computational Tools for Poverty Measurement and Analysis*, International Food Policy Research Institute, Discussion Paper No. 50.

De Moor, A. and Calamai, P. (1997) *Subsidizing Unsustainable Development*. San Jose, Costa Rica: Earth Council and the Institute for Research on Public Expenditure.

Deaton, Angus (2005) 'Measuring poverty in a growing world (or measuring growth in a poor world)', *Review of Economics and Statistics*, 87(1): 1–19.

Devarajan, Shanta, Le, Tuan M. and Raballand, Gael (2010) *Increasing Public Expenditure Efficiency in Oil-rich Economies: A Proposal*. Paper presented at the Centre for the Study of African Economies Annual Conference, 2010.

Eifert, B., Gelb, A. and Tallroth, N.B. (2003) 'Managing oil wealth', *Finance and Development*, 40(1).

El-Katiri, L., Fattouh, B. and Segal, P. (2011) *Anatomy of an Oil-Based Welfare State: Rent Distribution in Kuwait*, Kuwait Programme on Development, Governance and Globalisation in the Gulf States, London School of Economics, January.

Fasano, U. and Rishi, G. (2004) *Emerging Strains in GCC Labor Markets*, IMF Working Paper No. WP/04/71.

Girgis, Maurice (1984) *Industrial Progress in Small Oil-Exporting Countries: The Prospect for Kuwait*, Westview Special Studies. Boulder, CO and Harlow: Westview and Longman.

Government of Kuwait (2009) *General Framework Proposal for Kuwait's Five-Year Development Plan 2009/10–2013/14* (in Arabic).

Government of Kuwait (2010) PIFSS website, online at: http://www.pifss.gov.kw/ (accessed 11 August 2011).

Government of Kuwait, *Annual Statistical Abstract*, various issues.

IBRD (1965) *The Economic Development of Kuwait*. Baltimore, MD: Johns Hopkins University Press.

IEA (2005) *World Energy Outlook*, 2005 edition.

IMF (2009) *Kuwait Article IV Consultation 2009*, online at: http://www.imf.org/external/pubs/ft/scr/2009/cr09152.pdf (accessed 11 August 2011).

Ismael, J.S. (1993) *Kuwait: Dependency and Class in a Rentier State*. Gainesville, FL: University Press of Florida.

Karl, Terry L. (1997) *The Paradox of Plenty: Oil Booms and Petro-States*. Berkeley, CA: University of California Press.

Khalaf, S. and Hammoud, H. (1988) 'The emergence of the oil welfare state: the case of Kuwait', *Dialectical Anthropology*, 12: 343–57.

Khouja, M.W. and Sadler, P.G. (1979) *The Economy of Kuwait: Development and Role in International Finance*. London: Macmillan.

Krueger, A.O. (1974) 'The political economy of the rent-seeking society', *American Economic Review*, 64(3): 291–303.

Luciani, Giacomo (1987) 'Allocation vs. production states: a theoretical framework', in Hazem Beblawi and Giacomo Luciani (eds), *The Rentier State*. London: Croom Helm, pp. 63–82.

Mahdavy, Hussein (1970) 'The patterns and problems of economic development in rentier states: the case of Iran', in M.A. Cook (ed.), *Studies in Economic History of the Middle East*. London: Oxford University Press, pp. 428–67.

Ministry of Electricity and Water (2006) *Statistical Year Book 2006*.

Ministry of Finance of Kuwait (2008/9) *Al-hisab al-khatami lil-idarah al-maliayyah lil-dawlah 'an al-sanah al-maliyyah 2008/2009*.

Ministry of Finance of Kuwait (2010) *Taqrir al-maliayyah al-shahri li hisabat al-idarah al maliyyah lil-dawlah*, January.

Ministry of Finance of Kuwait, various statistics, online at: http://www.mof.gov.kw (accessed 11 August 2011).

Mohammed bin Rashid Al Maktoum Foundation and UNDP/RBAS, *Arab Knowledge Report 2009*, online at: http://www.mbrfoundation.ae/English/pages/AKR 2009.aspx (accessed 11 August 2011).

Murphy K.M., Shleifer, A. and Vishny, R.W. (1993) 'Why is rent-seeking so costly to growth?', *American Economic Review*, 83(2): 409–14.

NBK (2006) *Kuwait Economic and Financial Review*, October, online at: http://www.kuwait.nbk.com/InvestmentAndBrokerage/ResearchandReports/EconomicReviews_en_gb.aspx (accessed 11 August 2011).

NBK (2010) *Doing Business in Kuwait*, January, online at: http://www.kuwait.nbk.com/investmentandbrokerage/researchandreports/doingbusinessinkuwait_en_gb.aspx (accessed 11 August 2011).

NBK, *Annual Report*, various issues, online at: http://kuwait.nbk.com/investmentand

brokerage/researchandreports/annualreports_en_gb.aspx (accessed 11 August 2011).

OECD (2008a) *Employment in Government in the Perspective of the Production Costs of Goods and Services in the Public Domain*, Public Employment and Management Working Party, online at: http://www.olis.oecd.org/olis/2008doc.nsf/LinkTo/NT00000A16/$FILE/JT03239319.PDF (accessed 11 August 2011).

OECD (2008b) *Growing Unequal? Income Distribution and Poverty in OECD countries.* OECD.

Ross, M.L. (2004) 'Does taxation lead to representation?', *British Journal of Political Science*, 34: 229–49.

Segal, Paul (2011) 'Resource rents, redistribution, and halving global poverty: the resource dividend', *World Development*, forthcoming.

UNCTAD (2009) *World Investment Report 2009*, online at: http://www.unctad.org/en/docs/wir2009_en.pdf (accessed 11 August 2011).

UNDP (2006) *Arab Human Development Report 2005*, online at: http://www.arab-hdr.org/ (accessed 11 August 2011).

UNDP (2009) *Arab Human Development Report 2009*, online at: http://www.arab-hdr.org/ (accessed 11 August 2011).

UNESCO (2008) *Statistical Yearbook 2008*, online at: http://www.uis.unesco.org/ev.php?ID=2867_201&ID2=DO.TOPIC (accessed 11 August 2011).

Wessel, R.H. (1967) 'A note on economic rent', *American Economic Review*, 57 (5): 1221–6.

World Bank (2005) *A Water Sector Assessment Report on the Countries of the Cooperation Council of the Arab States of the Gulf*, online at: http://siteresources.worldbank.org/INTMNAREGTOPWATRES/Overview/20577193/GCCWaterSectorReport- -Englishversion.pdf (accessed 11 August 2011).

World Bank (2009) *World Development Indicators 2009.*

World Bank/IFC (2010) *Doing Business 2010: Kuwait.* Washington, DC, available online at: http://www.doingbusiness.org/Documents/CountryProfiles/KWT.pdf (accessed 11 August 2011).

Various issues of:
  Arab Times Kuwait
  Businessweek
  Financial Times
  MEES
  The National
  Wall Street Journal

9

VOLATILITY, DIVERSIFICATION AND DEVELOPMENT IN THE GULF COOPERATION COUNCIL COUNTRIES

Miklós Koren and Silvana Tenreyro[1]

Introduction

Confronting the economic and security challenges posed by an unstable regional environment, the governments of Bahrain, Kuwait, Oman, Qatar, Saudi Arabia, and the United Arab Emirates agreed in 1981 to form the Gulf Cooperation Council (GCC). Initially a common trade bloc, the GCC launched a common market on January 1, 2008, and plans to establish a common currency, the *Khaleeji*.

The economic history of these six countries has been powerfully shaped by the discovery of oil fields, which started in Bahrain in the early 1930s, Saudi Arabia and Kuwait in the late 1930s, and Qatar, Oman, and the United Arab Emirates in the 1940s and 1950s. While initially the oil fields were exploited by British companies, by the early 1970s all six countries had gained independence and were in full control of the fields and means of production, as well as being active members (except for Bahrain and Oman) of the Organization of Petroleum Exporting Countries (OPEC). Oil had by then become the dominant sector in these economies.

The steep rises in oil prices caused by the 1973 Arab oil embargo and the 1979 Iranian revolution, and the dramatic six-year-long decline in prices caused by the oil glut that followed, led to increased concern for the insurmountable volatility brought about by the economies' heavy reliance on oil. These developments were to a large extent the motivation for one of the central objectives of the 1981 Unified Economic Agreement between the Countries of the Gulf Cooperation Council, which seeks to "coordinate industrial activities, formulate policies and mechanisms which will lead to industrial development and the diversification of their products on an integrated basis" (Article 12).

In this chapter, we seek to study whether and to what extent the objectives of industrial development and diversification envisioned in the formation of the GCC have materialized.[2]

The second component relates to aggregate country-specific shocks. This component captures aggregate shocks that affect all sectors in the economy, reflecting, for example, policy, institutional, or political changes, as well as technological shocks that are common to all sectors.

The third component relates to the covariance between country-specific and sector-specific shocks; in particular, changes in fiscal or monetary policy instruments in some countries might be a response to shocks experienced by different sectors. This component would be negative, and hence reduce aggregate volatility, for example, if macro-economic policies are countercyclical, that is, they are aimed at neutralizing or mitigating the effect of economic cycles. In the context of GCC countries, this would entail reducing government spending or tightening credit during downturns or periods of relatively low demand for oil and gas. As we show in this chapter, in most GCC countries this component is instead positive and large, contributing to aggregate volatility. We argue that this is largely due to the lack of actively countercyclical monetary policy (due to the choice of a fixed exchange-rate regime) and a generally pro-cyclical government spending pattern.

We put the results into context by comparing the countries' patterns of volatility with those observed in other countries at the same level of development, as well as with those observed in other resource-rich economies.

The chapter is organized as follows. The following section describes the evolution of growth rates, volatility, and the shares of different sectors in the six GCC economies from 1970 to 2006. The next section studies the sources of economic volatility and compares the performance of GCC countries vis-à-vis countries at the same level of development or rich in natural resources. The final section offers concluding remarks.

Economic growth, volatility and diversification

The economic performance of GCC countries has been anything but uniform, as illustrated in Figure 9.1.[3] The Figure depicts the average yearly growth rate of per capita GDP (left bars) and the level of volatility, measured as the standard deviation of annual growth rates (right bars), by decade, from 1970 through 2006, for all countries in the GCC.[4] Measured as such, volatility captures deviations, both up and down, from the average growth rate of the decade. These deviations are what we refer to as "shocks." The 1970s witnessed large growth rates in the United Arab Emirates (12 percent), Saudi Arabia (5.7 percent), Oman (5.5 percent), and Bahrain (3 percent), together with negative growth rates in Kuwait and Qatar. The common denominator for the period was the extremely high volatility faced by all six countries. The 1980s opened a grim chapter of negative growth rates for all countries (except Oman), with losses ranging from 3.6 percent per year in Kuwait to 6.5 percent per year in Saudi Arabia, and continually high levels of volatility.

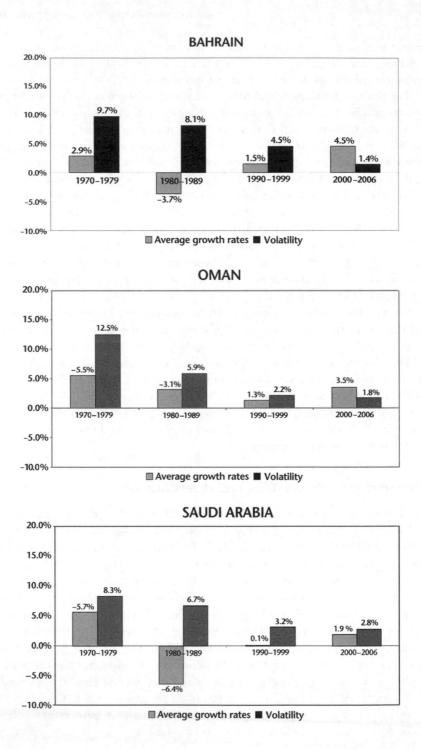

FIGURE 9.1   Average yearly growth rates and volatility, by country (1970–2006)

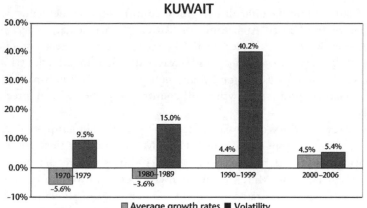

KUWAIT

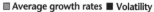

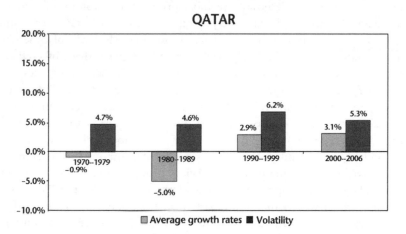

QATAR

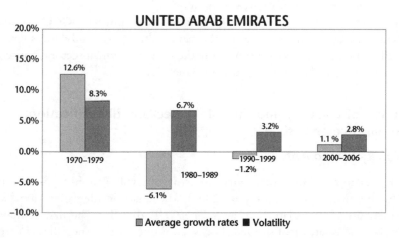

UNITED ARAB EMIRATES

FIGURE 9.1 continued

In the 1990s, despite the difficult start, most countries posted net gains, with the exception of the United Arab Emirates. Kuwait, in particular, experienced an average growth rate over the decade of 4.4 per cent, after two decades of negative growth. Volatility during the decade was still high in all countries, with Kuwait's being dramatically high by any metric. The early 2000s paint a totally different picture: positive growth in all countries together with unprecedented stability.

The lower volatility of the later period does not seem simply the result of positive contagion from the so called "Great Moderation," or the long period of low volatility enjoyed by most developed countries before the onset of the current financial crisis. More fundamental changes seem to have taken place in GCC countries, as illustrated in Figure 9.2. The figure shows the shares of different sectors in total GDP from 1970 through 2006 for all six GCC countries. As Figure 9.2 shows, the most prominent sector in all subplots is Mining and Utilities, reflecting the preponderance of oil in GCC economies.[5] The prevalence of oil, however, has been decreasing. Most notably, the United Arab Emirates have seen a steady decline in Mining as a share of GDP, from above 70 percent in the 1970s to around 30 percent in the 2000s, despite the sharp increase in oil prices in recent years. "Other activities," comprising financial intermediation, real estate, public administration, education, health, and other services, have gained ground during this period to reach above 20 percent of the Emirates' GDP by the end of the period. Other GCC countries have undergone a similar, though less steep, structural transformation. The earliest diversifier is Bahrain, where services grouped under "Other activities" had already reached roughly 50 percent of the economy in the 1980s. Manufacturing, which was virtually nonexistent at the beginning of the 1970s, has also increased significantly as a share of GDP in all countries, accounting for about 10 percent or more of GCC economies.

In spite of the progress over the past decades, however, GCC economies continue to be highly volatile. In the next section, we study the sources of volatility and, in particular, we measure the extent to which sectoral concentration accounts for the observed outcome volatility.

Sources of volatility and the role of sectoral diversification: a comparative analysis

Volatility components

In this section we study the sources of economic volatility in GCC countries. Following Koren and Tenreyro (2007), the analysis identifies three main components of the volatility of aggregate GDP growth.[6] The first component relates to the volatility of sectoral shocks: an economy that specializes in sectors that exhibit high intrinsic volatility will tend to experience higher aggregate volatility. Two different elements play a role: one is the degree of sectoral

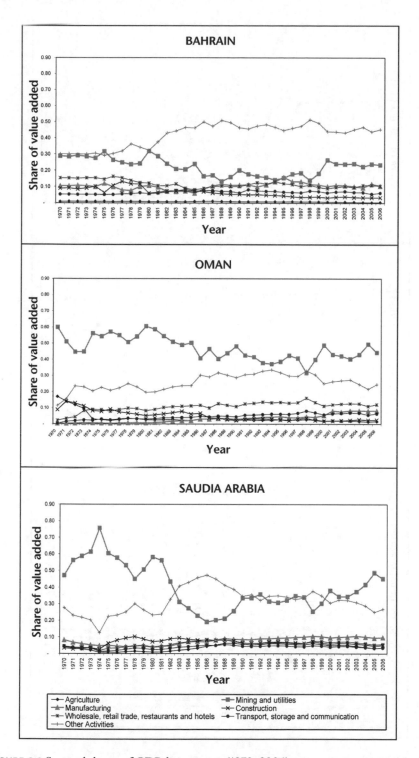

FIGURE 9.2 Sectoral shares of GDP, by country (1970–2006)

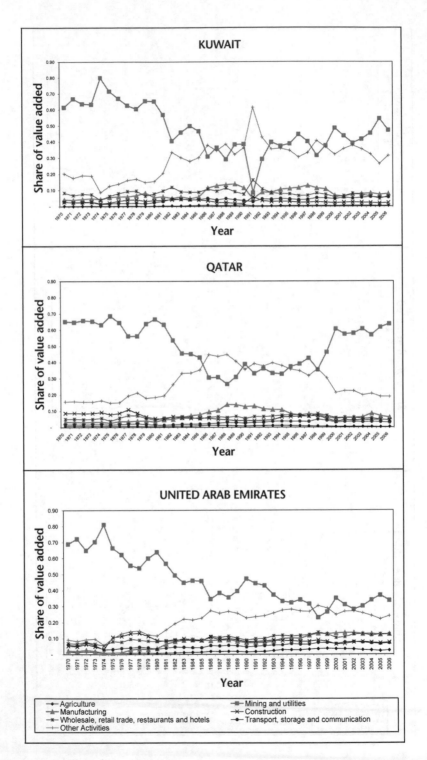

FIGURE 9.2 continued

concentration (how concentrated or diversified the economy is in terms of the number and relative sizes of the sectors) and the other is the volatility of the different sectors. In GCC economies, traditionally, the two elements have played in the same direction: the economies have been highly concentrated in one, very volatile sector.

The second component relates to aggregate country-specific shocks that are common to all sectors in the economy. This component aims at capturing the volatility due to macro-economic policy or political instability. In our study, it will also capture the volatility induced by the 1991 Gulf War. It may also capture other aggregate shocks, such as technological developments that affect all sectors in the economy.

The third component of volatility relates to the covariance between country-specific and sector-specific shock. Concretely, changes in fiscal or monetary policy in some countries might be deliberate responses to shocks experienced by particular sectors. This component will be negative, for example, if macro-economic policies are countercyclical, that is they are aimed at mitigating or neutralizing the effect of economic cycles; in the context of the GCC economy, a countercyclical policy would imply reducing government spending or tightening credit during periods of relatively weak demand for oil. We show later that this component tends to be positive in most countries, largely reflecting the lack of actively countercyclical policies.

This breakdown of volatility is important because it allows us to assess the extent to which volatility in GCC countries is due to high exposure to the oil sector as opposed to country-specific shocks, more likely to be caused by domestic macro-economic policy; in other words, aggregate volatility might result from possibly inadequate domestic policies.

Formally, as in Koren and Tenreyro (2007), the variance of GDP growth, $Var(y)$, can be decomposed as (see Appendix B: technical supplement):

$$Var(y) = \text{Sectoral Variance} + \text{Country Variance} + \text{Sector}-\text{Country Covariance}$$

where the sectoral-variance component can be further decomposed into the variance due to global shocks, that is shocks that affect all countries in the world in the same fashion, and the variance due to idiosyncratic (or country-specific) sectoral shocks, which affect different countries in different ways.

$$\text{Sectoral Variance} = \text{Global Sectoral Variance} + \text{Idiosyncratic Sectoral Variance}$$

In the case of GCC countries, we expect both the idiosyncratic sectoral variance (mostly generated by the oil sector) and the country-specific variance (mostly due to policy and political instability, including the 1991 Gulf War) to account for a large part of the economies' volatility. In words, the method used for the volatility decomposition can be summarized as follows. We first compute for each country (c), sector (s) and year (t), a measure of "shock," denoted y_{cst}. This is calculated as the deviation of the growth rate of a given sector in a given country from the average growth rate over the period. We measure sector-specific shocks (λ_{st}) as the average of y_{cst} over all countries for a given sector.[7] Put differently, a sector-specific shock is the average shock affecting a given sector in all countries. Country-specific shocks are then identified as the average shock in a given country, after subtracting the sector-specific shock.[8] In other words, a country-specific shock is the average shock affecting all sectors in a given country. The residual is the country and sector-specific shock, ε_{js}.[9] Once the three different shocks (λ_{st}, μ_{jt}, ε_{jst}) are identified, we compute variances and covariances as detailed in Appendix B.

To carry out the sectoral decomposition, we use data on GDP in constant 2000 US dollars from the United Nations (UN) Statistical database from 1970 through 2006. The countries in the analysis are listed in Appendix A. Before proceeding, it should be said upfront that one limitation in studying the productive structure of GCC economies is the paucity of organized information on the subject, especially for the early period. The UN database is the only source available with comparable data across GCC countries. We are hence unavoidably exposed to inaccuracies due to measurement error by the source. The estimation procedure yields a decomposition of volatility into different sources for each country and year. Figures 9.3 through 9.8 plot the decomposition for the six GCC countries in 1975, 1985, 1995, and 2005.

Figure 9.3 shows the volatility decomposition for Bahrain, which is surprisingly stable over the thirty-year period we analyze. The most important source of volatility in Bahrain is the aggregate country-specific variance, the component that is common to all sectors in the economy. This accounts for more than 60 percent of overall volatility. The second biggest component is the idiosyncratic sectoral variance, which accounts for almost 30 percent of volatility. The covariance term and the global sectoral variance component account for the remainder 10 percent.

Figure 9.4 shows the volatility decomposition in Kuwait. As the plot shows, in the 1970s the idiosyncratic sectoral variance – mostly dominated by shocks to the oil sector – was the biggest source of volatility, accounting for more than 50 percent of overall volatility. Country-specific volatility in the decade accounted for about 45 percent of aggregate volatility, while the other two components were jointly below 5 percent. The picture changes in the 1980s and particularly the 1990s, when the idiosyncratic sectoral variance becomes less important, explaining about 35 and 30 percent of overall volatility, respectively. Country-specific volatility became the dominant source of volatility reaching 70 percent in the 1990s.

This pattern only slightly reverted in the 2000s, with the idiosyncratic sectoral-volatility component accounting for 40 percent and the country-volatility component accounting for 57 percent of overall volatility. As the picture shows, global shocks play a relatively small role in the Kuwaiti economy.

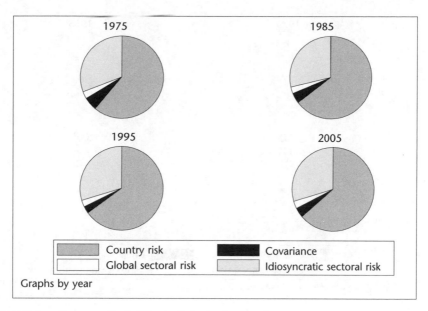

FIGURE 9.3   Sources of volatility in Bahrain, by decade

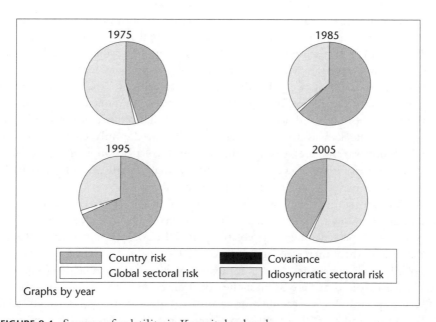

FIGURE 9.4   Sources of volatility in Kuwait, by decade

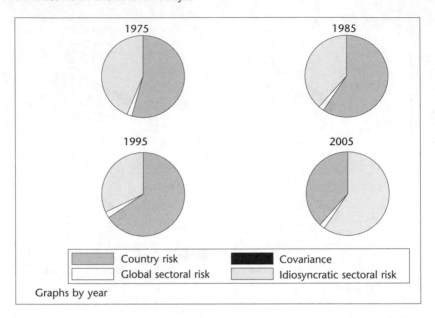

FIGURE 9.5 Sources of volatility in Oman, by decade

The volatility decomposition for Oman, depicted in Figure 9.5 shows a similar pattern. In the 1970s, the idiosyncratic component accounted for about 45 percent of the variance, while the country-specific component accounted for about 57 percent. The role of idiosyncratic sectoral shocks decreased over the 1980s and 1990s, reaching just a third of the overall volatility in the 1990s. The 2000s saw a reversal, with the idiosyncratic component climbing back to 42 percent of the variance. The time-series evolution of the country-specific component is the mirror image of the idiosyncratic component, increasing over the 1980s and 1990s and decreasing in the 2000s. The covariance of sectoral and aggregate shocks was actually negative in Oman (the only GCC country for which this was the case), contributing to lower volatility (not shown in the pie chart); its magnitude, however, was relatively small. Finally, the global volatility component played virtually no role in the economy.

Qatar's volatility decomposition is portrayed in Figure 9.6. As was the case in Kuwait and Oman, the idiosyncratic component in Qatar was high in the 1970s, reaching 55 percent of overall volatility. It fell to 35 percent in the 1980s and 1990s and then increased again in the 2000s to about half of the overall volatility. The opposite trend is followed by the country-specific component. Unlike in the other economies, the covariance between macroeconomic and sector-specific shocks accounts for a non-negligible share of the overall volatility, in the order of 10 percent throughout most of the period, suggesting that more could be done in terms of enacting countercyclical fiscal or monetary policies in the economy. Finally, global sectoral shocks account for roughly 3 percent of volatility, with no significant changes over time.

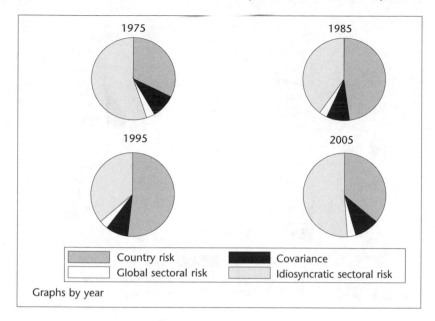

FIGURE 9.6   Sources of volatility in Qatar, by decade

The pattern of decrease in idiosyncratic sectoral volatility from the 1970s to the 1980s and 1990s and the reversal in the 2000s is intensified in Saudi Arabia (see Figure 9.7). The idiosyncratic component accounted for 72 percent of overall volatility in the 1970s; 35 and 45 percent in the 1980s and 1990s, respectively; and 63 percent in the 2000s. Country volatility, in turn, moved from 20 percent in the 1970s peaking at 50 percent in the 1990s, falling to 29 percent in the 2000s. The covariance between aggregate and sectoral shocks was high in the 1980s and 1990s, at just below 10 percent of overall volatility, and smaller in the 1970s and 2000s.

The volatility decomposition for the United Arab Emirates is shown in Figure 9.8. Differently from the other GCC economies, the idiosyncratic component fell steadily over time in the Emirates, going from 45 percent in the 1970s to about 20 percent in the 2000s. The country-specific component increased accordingly from 50 percent to 70 percent during the period. The covariance term as well as the global sectoral-volatility component accounted for a small share of overall volatility during the period.

The general message from these pictures is that the idiosyncratic component of volatility, which is to a large extent unavoidable in a resource-rich economy, is of the same order of magnitude as the country-specific component, which is to a large extent a reflection of aggregate domestic policy. Equally important, the covariance between aggregate shocks and sectoral shocks is positive in most countries. This suggests that there is scope for improvement in terms of domestic policies. Specifically, more aggressively countercyclical monetary and fiscal

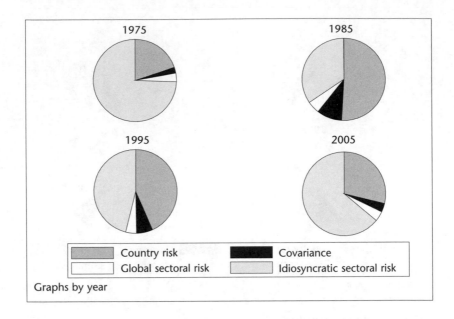

FIGURE 9.7 Sources of volatility in Saudi Arabia, by decade

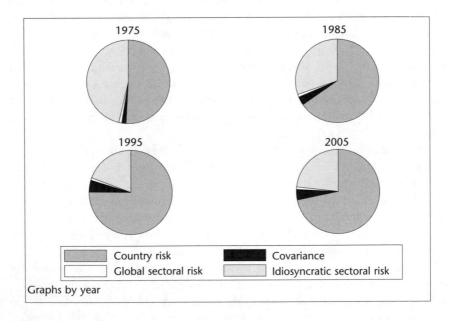

FIGURE 9.8 Sources of volatility in United Arab Emirates, by decade

policy should help attenuate the fluctuations in output caused by the inherently volatile nature of the oil sector. With regard to monetary policy, however, most GCC countries have maintained a fairly passive stance. In particular, most currencies of GCC countries have been formally pegged to the SDR (special drawing rights), except for the Omani rial, which has been pegged to the dollar since the 1970s, and the Kuwaiti dinar, which has been pegged to an undisclosed basket of currencies. De facto, however, most countries have been pegged to the US dollar for the last three decades, with the peg becoming official in the early 2000s. Pegging the exchange rate under free movement of capital implies that GCC countries have relinquished monetary policy autonomy and the scope for actively counteracting shocks is hence limited. (Only Kuwait and Oman have used direct instruments − ceilings on certain types of credit − in order to use monetary policy more actively.)

With regard to fiscal spending, GCC countries have failed to undertake countercyclical policies (Fasano and Wang 2002), though the extent of procyclicality in spending is hard to gauge, partly because of the lack of clear and comparable fiscal concepts, methods, and data across GCC countries. Fasano and Wang (2002) argue that most GCC countries have followed highly procyclical spending policies (that is increasing government spending in times of oil booms and decreasing it in downturns).

Volatility patterns in perspective: comparative analysis of volatility patterns vis-à-vis other countries

In this section, we study the evolution of the different components of volatility over time for the six GCC countries. We compare their performance with that of countries at the same level of development, measured by the level of GDP per capita in the year analysed. We also compare their performance with countries that are also rich in oil, which we call our control group.

To build the control group, we sorted countries by the share of petroleum, petroleum products, and gas in their exports in 2000. We selected the top 25 countries. Out of these 25, we formed a control group according to the following two criteria: (1) the country is not in the Gulf region; (2) the country exports more than $4 billion worth of oil or gas. This resulted in the following countries: Control group: natural-resource-rich exporters not in the Gulf:

1. Algeria
2. Canada
3. Colombia
4. Indonesia
5. Nigeria
6. Netherlands
7. Norway

In what follows, we graphically show the performance of each component of volatility in 1975, 1985, 1995, and 2005, plotted against the level of real GDP per capita in the corresponding country and year. Data on real PPP-adjusted GDP per capita come from the World Bank's World Development Indicators.[10] We highlight in the plots both the "treatment group," that is, the group of six GCC countries, and the "control group," listed above. The list of countries and the conventional alphabetic code abbreviations are displayed in Appendix A.

Sectoral volatility

Figure 9.9 shows the plot of the (natural logarithm of) the sectoral volatility component (the aggregate of both global and idiosyncratic volatility) against the (log of) level of development in 1975. The fitted line is the result of a linear regression.[11]

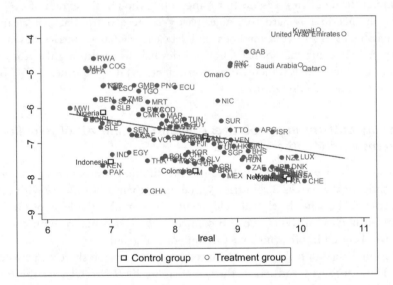

FIGURE 9.9 Sectoral volatility (global and idiosyncratic) component and development (1975) (all countries)

As the plot shows, sectoral volatility tends to fall quite markedly with the level of development. Strikingly, all six GCC countries stand out as the biggest outliers in the plot, meaning that their levels of sectoral volatility are significantly above those in countries at similar levels of development. Interestingly, they also stand out in 1975 when compared to other resource-rich countries. The latter systematically fall on or below the predicted regression line for the whole sample, showing that natural resource endowments do not necessarily imply high volatility.[12]

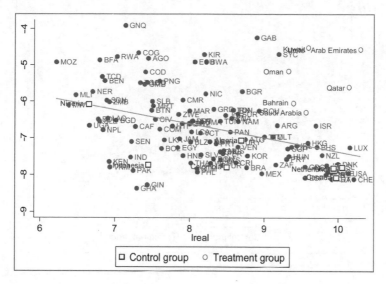

FIGURE 9.10 Sectoral volatility (global and idiosyncratic) component and development (1985) (all countries)

Figure 9.10 shows the relation between the (log of) sectoral volatility and the (log of) level of development in 1985. As before, the relationship is strongly negative and hence we should expect relatively richer countries to display lower levels of sectoral volatility. GCC countries are, as before, remarkable outliers in the regression. Compared with the levels a decade earlier, however, some progress can already be appreciated: while still outliers, the GCC countries are relatively closer to the prediction line, with Saudi Arabia particularly close to it. The figure clearly shows where resource-rich countries stand in the sectoral-volatility-development line. GCC countries are overwhelmingly more volatile than other resource-rich economies outside the Persian Gulf, with Kuwait and the United Arab Emirates at the high end of the group.

Figures 9.11 and 9.12 show the relation between (logged) sectoral volatility and (logged) GDP per capita in 1995 and 2005, respectively. The overall relation continues to be significantly negative. The most salient change from previous decades is the decline in sectoral volatility of GCC countries. While still above the prediction line, the countries appear to be much closer to countries at their same level of development.[13]

In comparison with other resource-rich countries, significant progress can be appreciated as well, as now two out of the seven control-group countries are above the fitted line. While still above the levels typical of other countries rich in natural resources, the convergence is evident.

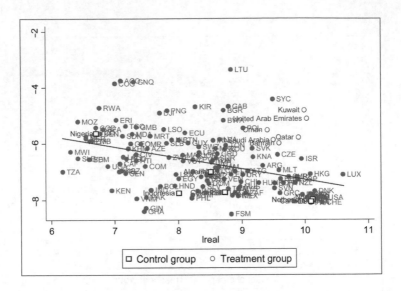

FIGURE 9.11 Sectoral volatility (global and idiosyncratic) component and development (1995) (all countries)

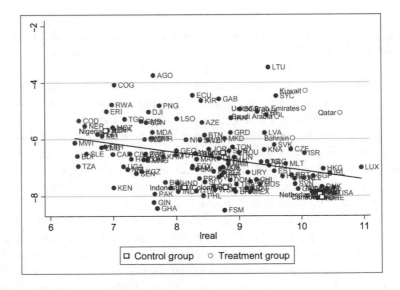

FIGURE 9.12 Sectoral volatility (global and idiosyncratic) component and development (2005) (all countries)

Covariance of sector-specific and country-specific shocks

Figure 9.13 shows the covariance of sector-specific and country-specific shocks in 1975 for all countries, plotted against the (log of) real GDP per capita in that year. The scatter plot, together with the regression line, shows that there is no systematic relation between the two. All GCC countries, however, with the exception of Oman, appear to have above-average covariance. This suggests, as argued earlier, that there is no systematic countercyclical response of policies to shocks. More concretely, monetary and fiscal policies have failed at being sufficiently countercyclical (that is, they have not been expansionary in recessionary times – or in times in which oil prices are low); this lack of countercyclicality can explain why most countries feature negative values for the covariance. When compared to other resource-rich economies, GCC countries also perform rather poorly, again, with the exception of Oman, which shows a negative covariance. The picture proves resilient to the passage of time. In 1985, there is a change in rankings, with the United Arab Emirates becoming the country with the highest covariance in the group and in the world. This is shown in Figure 9.14, which shows the plot of the covariance against the (logged) level of development in 1985. Oman is systematically the country with the lowest (most negative) covariance among the resource-rich control group.

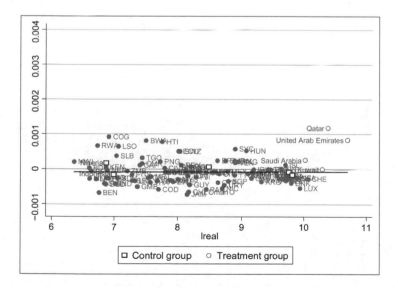

FIGURE 9.13 Covariance of sectoral and country-specific volatility and development (1975) (all countries)

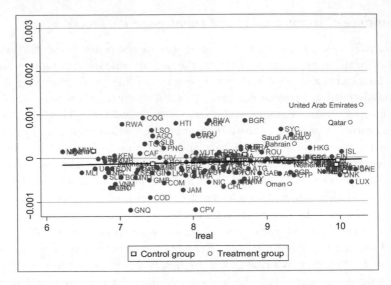

FIGURE 9.14 Covariance of sectoral and country-specific volatility and development (1985) (all countries)

Figures 9.15 and 9.16 show the covariance component of volatility in 1995 and 2005, plotted as before against the level of development. The conclusion from these diagrams is that no significant progress has been made in terms of lowering the level of the covariance over time, whether in absolute terms or relative to other countries at the same level of development or endowment with natural resources.

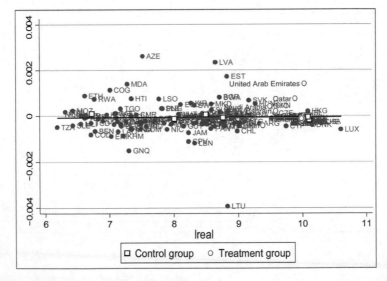

FIGURE 9.15 Covariance of sectoral and country-specific volatility and development (1995) (all countries)

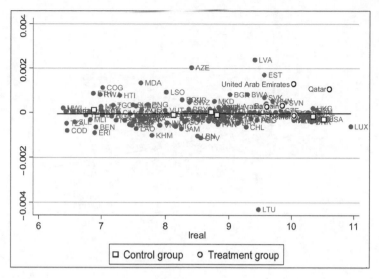

FIGURE 9.16 Covariance of sectoral and country-specific volatility and development (2005) (all countries)

As argued before, this is perhaps one of the determinants of volatility that policy-makers could more effectively influence through more aggressive counterbalancing policies.

Country-specific volatility

The last component of volatility, country-specific volatility, is studied in Figure 9.17. (As explained in Appendix B, by construction, the country-specific volatility component is invariant over time.) The figure shows the (log of) country-specific volatility against the (logged) real GDP per capita in 1995. (The picture does not change substantially when volatility is plotted against GDP per capita in other years.)

As before, the regression line shows the fitted values from a regression of (log) country volatility on real GDP per capita. The relation is significantly negative, that is countries at a lower level of development tend to experience higher country-specific volatility. The figure also shows that GCC countries tend to be outliers when compared to the reference groups, showing higher country volatility than countries at the same level of development or countries that are also rich in natural resources.

Saudi Arabia is the best performer, being just above the level predicted for countries at the same level of development. The United Arab Emirates and Kuwait are the countries that show the highest level of country volatility.

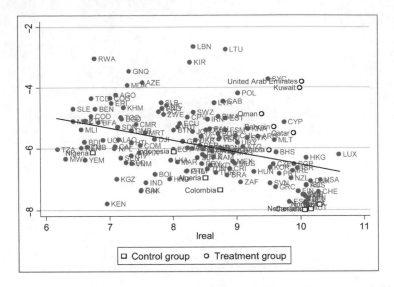

FIGURE 9.17 Country-specific volatility component (1970–2006) and development (1995) (all countries)

Concluding remarks

In part due to their strong dependence on oil, GCC economies are intrinsically more volatile than other economies at the same level of development. Startling progress has been achieved, however, since the 1970s, with volatility falling in most GCC countries by a factor of four or more by 2005. The fall in volatility is mostly due to two factors. The first is the rise of the service economy (comprising, among others, financial intermediation, tourism, and real estate), which is inherently less volatile than the oil sector and has led to higher levels of sectoral diversification. The second is the general decline in volatility in world markets since the 1980s, a period that economists have called the "Great Moderation." The current Great Credit Crisis, however, has interrupted this trend.

Our comparative analysis of the sources of volatility suggests that despite the progress achieved, there is still scope for improvement. First, other resource-rich economies facing the same challenges (and shocks) as GCC countries tend to systematically display lower levels of volatility.

Second, and perhaps more relevant, the high levels of country-specific volatility and the positive covariance between sectoral shocks and country-specific shocks suggest that macroeconomic policy could be improved to further mitigate volatility. Concretely, it seems that more aggressively countercyclical fiscal and monetary policies could be put in place in GCC economies to lower the macroeconomic impact of oil shocks. With regard to monetary policy, most GCC countries have maintained a fairly passive stance. In particular, most currencies of GCC countries have been de facto pegged to the US dollar for the last three decades, with the peg becoming official in the early 2000s. (Officially, most were pegged to the SDR, except for the Omani rial, which has been pegged to the dollar since the 1970s, and the Kuwaiti dinar, which has been pegged to an undisclosed basket of currencies, but de facto, the currencies have mostly followed the dollar.) Pegging the exchange rate in a context of free movement of capital implies that GCC countries have relinquished monetary policy autonomy. The scope for actively counteracting shocks through credit policy is hence limited. (Only Kuwait and Oman have used direct instruments – ceilings on certain types of credit – in order to use monetary policy more actively.)

With regard to fiscal spending, GCC countries have failed to undertake countercyclical policies (i.e., cutting government spending during booms and increasing spending in downturns); on the contrary, fiscal policy in most GCC countries has been highly procyclical (Fasano and Wang 2002), contributing to higher volatility.

In sum, the overall balance for GCC countries over the past four decades is positive. Significant progress has been made in terms of increasing stability in the region. There is, however, scope for further gains, as the experience from other resource-rich economies shows, and more countercyclical policies appear to be a promising route. Last, but not least, the current global financial crisis has also underscored financial sector vulnerabilities that need to be addressed (on this GCC countries are by no means unique) – diversification alone is not enough, as it does not shield countries from aggregate shocks. Dubai is perhaps the best example in point: its efforts to diversify and develop other sectors (real estate, tourism, finance) have led to significant improvements in performance and living standards, along with lower dependence on oil. However, it also opened the door to other sources of shocks (e.g., financial and real estate bubbles) that led to sharp disruptions in the economy when the global credit crunch caused substantial falls in real estate and stock markets. We leave for future work the new challenges underscored by the global crisis.

Appendix A: list of countries

Country name	Code	Country name	Code
Afghanistan	AFG	Congo	COD
Albania	ALB	Costa Rica	CRI
Algeria	DZA	Cote d'Ivoire	CIV
Andorra	AND	Cuba	CUB
Angola	AGO	Cyprus	CYP
Antigua and Barbuda	ATG	Czech Republic	CZE
Argentina	ARG	Democratic People's Rep. of	
Armenia	ARM	Korea	PRK
Aruba	ABW	Democratic Republic of the	
Australia	AUS	Congo	COG
Austria	AUT	Denmark	DNK
Azerbaijan	AZE	Djibouti	DJI
Bahamas	BHS	Dominica	DMA
Bahrain	BHR	Dominican Republic	DOM
Bangladesh	BGD	Ecuador	ECU
Barbados	BRB	Egypt	EGY
Belarus	BLR	El Salvador	SLV
Belgium	BEL	Equatorial Guinea	GNQ
Belize	BLZ	Eritrea	ERI
Benin	BEN	Estonia	EST
Bermuda	BMU	Ethiopia	ETH
Bhutan	BTN	Fiji	FJI
Bolivia	BOL	Finland	FIN
Bosnia and Herzegovina	BIH	France	FRA
Botswana	BWA	French Polynesia	PYF
Brazil	BRA	Gabon	GAB
Brunei Darussalam	BRN	Gambia	GMB
Bulgaria	BGR	Georgia	GEO
Burkina Faso	BFA	Germany	DEU
Burundi	BDI	Ghana	GHA
Cambodia	KHM	Greece	GRC
Cameroon	CMR	Greenland	GRL
Canada	CAN	Grenada	GRD
Cape Verde	CPV	Guatemala	GTM
Cayman Islands	CYM	Guinea	GIN
Central African Republic	CAF	Guinea-Bissau	GNB
Chad	TCD	Guyana	GUY
Chile	CHL	Haiti	HTI
China	CHN	Honduras	HND
Colombia	COL	Hong Kong SAR of China	HKG
Comoros	COM	Hungary	HUN

Country name	Code	Country name	Code
Iceland	ISL	Mozambique	MOZ
India	IND	Myanmar	MMR
Indonesia	IDN	Namibia	NAM
Iran (Islamic Republic of)	IRN	Nepal	NPL
Iraq	IRQ	Netherlands	NLD
Ireland	IRL	Netherlands Antilles	ANT
Israel	ISR	New Caledonia	NCL
Italy	ITA	New Zealand	NZL
Jamaica	JAM	Nicaragua	NIC
Japan	JPN	Niger	NER
Jordan	JOR	Nigeria	NGA
Kazakhstan	KAZ	Norway	NOR
Kenya	KEN	Oman	OMN
Kiribati	KIR	Pakistan	PAK
Kuwait	KWT	Palau	PLW
Kyrgyzstan	KGZ	Panama	PAN
Lao People's Democratic		Papua New Guinea	PNG
Republic	LAO	Paraguay	PRY
Latvia	LVA	Peru	PER
Lebanon	LBN	Philippines	PHL
Lesotho	LSO	Poland	POL
Liberia	LBR	Portugal	PRT
Libyan Arab Jamahiriya	LBY	Puerto Rico	PRI
Liechtenstein	LIE	Qatar	QAT
Lithuania	LTU	Republic of Korea	KOR
Luxembourg	LUX	Republic of Moldova	MDA
Macao SAR of China	MAC	Romania	ROU
Madagascar	MDG	Russian Federation	RUS
Malawi	MWI	Rwanda	RWA
Malaysia	MYS	Saint Kitts and Nevis	KNA
Maldives	MDV	Saint Lucia	LCA
Mali	MLI	Saint Vincent and the	
Malta	MLT	Grenadines	VCT
Marshall Islands	MHL	Samoa	WSM
Mauritania	MRT	San Marino	SMR
Mauritius	MUS	São Tomé and Príncipe	STP
Mexico	MEX	Saudi Arabia	SAU
Micronesia (Federated States		Senegal	SEN
of)	FSM	Serbia	SRB
Monaco	MCO	Seychelles	SYC
Mongolia	MNG	Sierra Leone	SLE
Montenegro	MNE	Singapore	SGP
Morocco	MAR	Slovakia	SVK

Country name	Code	Country name	Code
Slovenia	SVN	Tunisia	TUN
Solomon Islands	SLB	Turkey	TUR
Somalia	SOM	Turkmenistan	TKM
South Africa	ZAF	Uganda	UGA
Spain	ESP	Ukraine	UKR
Sri Lanka	LKA	United Arab Emirates	ARE
Sudan	SDN	United Kingdom	GBR
Suriname	SUR	United Republic of	
Swaziland	SWZ	Tanzania: Mainland	TZA
Sweden	SWE	United States	USA
Switzerland	CHE	Uruguay	URY
Syrian Arab Republic	SYR	Uzbekistan	UZB
TFYR of Macedonia	MKD	Vanuatu	VUT
Tajikistan	TJK	Venezuela	VEN
Thailand	THA	Vietnam	VNM
Timor-Leste	TLS	Yemen	YEM
Togo	TGO	Zambia	ZMB
Tonga	TON	Zimbabwe	ZWE
Trinidad and Tobago	TTO		

Appendix B: Technical supplement

Two main ideas underlie the discussion over the determinants of the volatility of GDP growth. The first emphasizes the role of the sectoral composition of the economy as the main determinant of volatility: a high degree of specialization or specialization in high-volatility sectors translates into high aggregate volatility. The second idea points to domestic macroeconomic volatility, possibly related to policy mismanagement or political instability, among other country-specific factors.

The emphasis on sectoral composition motivates us to first break down the value added of a country into the sum of the value added of different sectors, each of which has a potentially different level of intrinsic volatility. Innovations in the growth rate of GDP in country j, ($j=1, \ldots, J$) denoted by q_j, can then be expressed as the weighted sum of the innovations in the growth rates of value-added in every sector, y_{js}, with $s=1, \ldots, S$:

$$q_j = \Sigma \alpha_{js} \, y_{js},$$

where the weights, α_{js}, denote the share of output in sector s of country j. The object of our study is the variance of q_j, $Var(q_j)$, and its components.

To separate the role of domestic aggregate volatility[14] from that of the sectoral composition of the economy, we can further breakdown innovations to a sector's growth rate, y_{js}, into three disturbances:

$$y_{js} = \lambda_s + \mu_j + \varepsilon_{js}.$$

(9.1)

The first disturbance (λ_s) is specific to a sector, but common to all countries. This includes, for example, a shock to the price of a major input in production, such as steel, which may affect the productivity of sectors that are steel-intensive. More generally, technology- and price-shocks that affect a sector or group of sectors across countries in the same way will fall in this category.

The second disturbance (μ_j) is specific to a country, but common to all sectors within a country. So, for example, a monetary tightening in country j might deteriorate the productivity of all sectors in country j, because all need some amount of liquidity to produce.

The third disturbance (ε_{js}) captures the shocks that are specific to a sector and country. In the previous example, if some sectors are more sensitive to the liquidity squeeze and have a deeper fall in productivity, the difference with respect to the average will be reflected in ε_{js}. Similarly, if some global shocks have different impact on sectoral productivity in different countries, the differential impact will be captured by ε_{js}. Finally, any disturbance specific to both a country and sector will be reflected in ε_{js}. Oil shocks, which affect countries in different ways, depending on whether they are net exporters or importers, will tend to fall in this category. This is why, as the analysis will show, this term will be particularly high in GCC economies.

Of course all three disturbances can potentially be correlated with each other. For example, λ_s and μ_j will tend to be correlated if in some countries macro-economic policies are more responsive to global sectoral shocks, or, alternatively, if a country is highly influential in a particular sector, in which case an aggregate shock in that country may affect that sector in other countries. Moreover, as pointed out above, certain sectors may be more responsive to country-specific shocks (implying that ε_{js} and μ_j could be correlated) or sectoral productivity in certain countries may be affected differently by global sectoral shocks (implying that ε_{js} and λ_s could be correlated).

Expression (9.1) provides a convenient way of partitioning the data. Written as such, it is simply an accounting identity, since $\mathring{a}_{js}$ picks up everything not accounted for by the sector- or country-specific shocks, and since we do not place any restriction on the way the three disturbances covary.

In what follows, we explain how to decompose the variance of q_j into the corresponding variances and covariances of these different disturbances.

It is convenient to rewrite innovations to growth of GDP in matrix notation. Denoting by $\mathbf{y}_j$ the vector of sectoral innovations y_{js} and by $\mathbf{a}_j$ the vector of sectoral shares α_{js}, our object of interest, $\text{Var}(q_j)$, can be written as:

$$\text{Var}(q_j) = \mathbf{a'}_j \, E(\mathbf{y}_j \, \mathbf{y'}_j) \, \mathbf{a}_j$$

(9.2)

Thus, in order to decompose $\text{Var}(q_{js})$, we need to decompose the variance-covariance matrix of the innovations to sectoral growth rates, $E(\mathbf{y}_j \, \mathbf{y}'_j)$. Simple matrix algebra shows that the variance-covariance matrix of country j's sectoral shocks can be written as:

$$E(\mathbf{y}_j \, \mathbf{y}'_j) = \Omega_\lambda + \Omega_{\varepsilon j} + \omega_{\mu j}^2 \mathbf{1}\mathbf{1}' + (\Omega_{\lambda\mu j} \, \mathbf{1}' + \mathbf{1} \, \Omega_{\lambda\mu j}) + \Gamma_j$$

where:

$$
\begin{aligned}
\Omega_\lambda &= E(\lambda\lambda') \\
\Omega_{\varepsilon j} &= \text{diag}(\sigma_{j1} \ldots \sigma_{jS}^2) \\
\omega_{\mu j} &= E(\mu_j) \\
\Omega_{\lambda\mu j} &= E(\lambda\mu_j)
\end{aligned}
$$

where $\mathbf{1}$ denotes the $S \times 1$ vector of ones, and λ and μ denote the vectors of sectoral shocks (λ_s) and country shocks (μ_j), respectively. The matrix Ω_λ is the variance-covariance of sector-specific global shocks; $\Omega_{\varepsilon j}$ is the matrix collecting the variances of the sector- and country-specific residuals $\varepsilon_{\varepsilon j}$, $\sigma_{js}^2 = E(\varepsilon_{\varepsilon j}^2)$; $\omega_{\varepsilon j}^2$ is the variance of country-specific shocks; $\Omega_{\lambda\mu j}$ is the covariance between country-specific and global sectoral shocks; and finally, the matrix Γ_j collects the remaining components of $E(\mathbf{y}_j \, \mathbf{y}'_j)$, that is the covariances between the residuals and the sectoral and country-specific shocks, and the covariance among residuals.

It turns out that the term Γ_j plays a quantitatively negligible role in accounting for aggregate volatility. In anticipation of that result, the exposition that follows ignores this last component. More specifically, we will maintain the working hypothesis that the residual shocks are idiosyncratic (uncorrelated with each other and with the sector- and country-specific shocks), and hence Γ_j is null. This implies that we can write the variance-covariance matrix as:

$$E(\mathbf{y}_j \, \mathbf{y}'_j) = \Omega_\lambda + \Omega_{\varepsilon j} + \omega_{\mu j}^2 \mathbf{1}\mathbf{1}' + (\Omega_{\lambda\mu j} \, \mathbf{1}' + \mathbf{1} \, \Omega_{\lambda\mu j})$$

$$(9.3)$$

Plugging (9.3) into (9.2), aggregate volatility can be written as:

$$\text{Var}(q_j) = \mathbf{a}'_j \, E(\mathbf{y}_j \, \mathbf{y}'_j) \, \mathbf{a}_j = \mathbf{a}'_j \, \Omega_\lambda \mathbf{a}_j + \mathbf{a}'_j \, \Omega_{\varepsilon j} \mathbf{a}_j + \omega_{\varepsilon j}^3 + 2 \, \mathbf{a}'_j \, \Omega_{\lambda\mu j}.$$

$$(9.4)$$

This formulation clearly shows that production in country j is more volatile:

1. If the country specializes in volatile sectors, that is sectors exposed to large and frequent shocks. This is reflected in the first two terms:
    -   the first, $\mathbf{a}'_j \, \Omega_\lambda \mathbf{a}_j$, relates to global sectoral shocks – this term is large when sectors exposed to big and frequent global shocks account for a large share of the country's GDP;

- the second term, $\mathbf{a'_j}\,\Omega_{\varepsilon j}\mathbf{a_j}$, relates to idiosyncratic sectoral shocks – this term is large when sectors with high idiosyncratic volatility, σ_{js}^2, account for a large share of GDP.
2. If country risk ($\omega_{\mu j}^2$) is big, that is the country is more volatile if aggregate domestic shocks are larger and more frequent.
3. If specialization is tilted towards sectors whose shocks are positively correlated with country-specific shocks ($\mathbf{a'_j}\Omega_{\lambda\mu j}$ is big). This term will tend to be small, for example, if policy innovations are negatively correlated with the shocks to sectors that have a large share in country j's GDP.

Thus the aggregate volatility of the economy can be decomposed as the sum of components with fundamentally different meanings.

In order to quantify the various components of volatility in equation (9.4), we need to estimate the variance–covariance matrices Ω_λ, $\Omega_{\varepsilon j}$, $\omega_{\mu j}^2$ and $\Omega_{\lambda\mu j}$. Our general strategy is to use data across countries, sectors, and time to back out estimates of the sectoral shocks, λ_s, and the country shocks, μ_j. We then compute the sample variances and covariances of the estimated shocks and treat them as estimates of the corresponding population moments.

Innovations to growth in value-added in country j and sector s, y_{jst}, are computed as the deviation of the growth rate from the average (growth rate) of country j and sector s over time.

We measure global sector-specific shocks as the cross-country average of y_{jst} in each of the sectors. Country-specific shocks are then identified as the within-country average of y_{jst}, using only the portion not explained by sector-specific shocks. The residual is then the difference between y_{jst} and the two shocks. Formally:

$$\lambda^e_{st} \equiv (1/J) \times \Sigma_{jst}$$
$$\mu^e_{jt} \equiv (1/S) \times \Sigma\,(y_{jst} - \lambda^e_{st})$$
$$\varepsilon^e_{jst} \equiv y_{jst} - \lambda^e_{st} - \mu^e_{jt}$$

where superscript "e" stands for "predicted."

Note that we normalize shocks so that $\Sigma\,\mu^e_{jt} = 0$, that is country shocks are expressed as relative to world shocks.

An equivalent way to formalize this is to frame the analysis as a set of cross-sectional regressions of y_{jst} on country and sector dummies. More specifically, the formulas for λ^e_{st}, μ^e_{jt}, and ε^e_{jst} given above will be the result of running a regression, for each time t, of y_{jst}, on a set of sector-specific and country-specific dummies (see Koren and Tenreyro 2007). Estimates of the matrices Ω_λ, $\Omega_{\varepsilon j}$, $\omega_{\mu j}$, and $\Omega_{\lambda\mu j}$ are then computed using the estimated shocks. In particular, $\Omega^e_\lambda = (1/T) \times \Sigma\lambda^e_t\,\lambda^e_t{}'$ is the estimated variance-covariance of global-sectoral shocks; $\omega^e_{\mu j} = (1/T) \times \Sigma\mu^e_{jt}{}^2$ is the estimated variance of country j-specific shocks; $\Omega^e_{\lambda\mu j} = (1/T) \times \Sigma\lambda^e_t\,\mu^e_{jt}$ is the estimate of the covariance between sectoral shocks and country j shocks; and $\sigma^e_{js}{}^2 = (1/T) \times \Sigma\varepsilon^e_{jst}{}^2$, with s=1, ..., S as the estimated variances of the sectoral idiosyncratic shocks.

Given the estimates of the variance-covariance matrix of factors, we use data on sectoral GDP shares, α_{jst}, to compute the various measures of risk exposure:

$$
\begin{aligned}
\text{GSECT}_{jt} &= \mathbf{a'}_{jt}\,\Omega^e_\lambda \mathbf{a}_{jt} \\
\text{ISECT}_{jt} &= \mathbf{a'}_{jt}\,\Omega^e_{\varepsilon j} \mathbf{a}_{jt} \\
\text{CNT}_j &= \omega^e_{\mu j}{}^2 \\
\text{COV}_{jt} &= 2\,\mathbf{a'}_{jt}\,\Omega^e_{\lambda\mu j}
\end{aligned}
$$

where GSECT_{jt} is the part of the volatility of country j at time t due to global sectoral shocks that are common to all countries (Global Sectoral Risk); ISECT_{jt} is the part of volatility due to sectoral shocks idiosyncratic to country j (Idiosyncratic Sectoral Risk); CNT_j is the part of volatility due to country shocks, which, by construction, does not depend on time (Country-Specific Risk); and COV_{jt} is the covariance of global sectoral shocks with the jth country shock at time t (Covariance of Sector and Country-specific Risk). Total volatility can hence be expressed as the sum of these four components.

Notes

1. The authors would like to thank Francesco Caselli for useful discussions and two anonymous referees for thoughtful comments.
2. For theories linking risk, diversification, and development, see Acemoglu and Zilibotti (1997), Greenwood and Jovanovic (1990), Kraay and Ventura (2007), Obstfeld (1994), and Saint-Paul (1992). For theories of sectoral transformation, see Caselli and Coleman (2000) and the references therein.
3. All subplots share the same scale, except for Kuwait's, since the high volatility of the 1990s, caused mainly by the war, is exceedingly large.
4. The raw data come from the United Nations (UN) Statistical database from 1970 through 2006.
5. Mining and quarrying is mostly oil, while utilities include electricity, gas, and water supply. Unfortunately, the source (United Nations Statistics) does not disaggregate the data further.
6. For alternative or complementary empirical studies see Forni and Reichlin (1996), Brooks and del Negro (2004), del Negro (2003), Kose et al. (2003), Imbs and Wacziarg (2000), Imbs (2007), Lehman and Modest (1985), Ramey and Ramey (1995), Stockman (1988).
7. In formula, this is $\lambda_{st} = (1/C)\Sigma^C_{i=1}\, y_{cst}$, where C denotes the number of countries.
8. In formula, this is $\mu_{jt} = (1/S)\Sigma^S_{i=1}\, y_{cst} - \lambda_{st}$, where S is the number of sectors.
9. In formula $\varepsilon_{jst} = y_{cst}, - \lambda_{st} - \mu_{jt}$.
10. Data for Bahrain in 1975 and for Oman in 2005 are not available from this source.
11. We aggregate both sources of sectoral risk for ease of exposition.
12. Note that the prediction line in these and the following graphs are obtained from a regression that uses the whole sample.
13. Oman is not displayed in the figures for 2005, since data on real GDP per capita is not available from WDI for that year.
14. The terms risk and volatility are used interchangeably.

References

Acemoglu, Daron and Zilibotti, Fabrizio (1997) "Was Prometheus unbound by chance? risk, diversification, and growth," *Journal of Political Economy*, 709–51.

Brooks, Robin and del Negro, Marco (2004) *A Latent Factor Model with Global, Country and Industry Shocks for International Stock Returns*, Working Paper 2002–23, Federal Reserve Bank of Atlanta.

Caselli, Francesco and Coleman, Wilbur John (2000) "The U.S. structural transformation and regional convergence: a reinterpretation," *Journal of Political Economy*, 109(3): 584–616.

Del Negro, M. (2002) "Asymmetric shocks among U.S. states," *Journal of International Economics*, 56: 273–97.

Fasano, Ugo and Wang, Qiang (2002) *Testing Relationship between Government Spending and Revenue: Evidence from GCC Countries*, IMF Working Paper 02/201, International Monetary Fund.

Forni, Mario and Reichlin, Lucrezia (1996) "Dynamic common factors in large cross sections," *Empirical Economics*, 21: 27–42.

Greenwood, J. and Jovanovic, B. (1990) "Financial development, growth, and the distribution of income," *Journal of Political Economy*, 98(5): 1076–107.

Heston, Alan, Summers, Robert, and Aten, Bettina (2002) *Penn World Table Version 6.1*, Center for International Comparisons at the University of Pennsylvania (CICUP).

Imbs, Jean (2007) "Growth and volatility," *Journal of Monetary Economics*, 54(7): 1848–62.

Imbs, Jean and Wacziarg, Romain (2003) "Stages of diversification," *American Economic Review*, 93: 63–86.

Koren, Miklos and Tenreyro, Silvana (2007) "Volatility and development," *Quarterly Journal of Economics*, 122(1): 243–87.

Kose, Ayhan, Otrok, Christopher, and Whiteman, Charles H. (2003) "International business cycles: world, region, and country-specific factors," *American Economic Review*, 93: 1216–39.

Kraay, Aart and Ventura, Jaume (2007) "Comparative advantage and the cross-section of business cycles," *Journal of European Economic Association*, 5(6).

Lehmann, Bruce N. and Modest, David M. (1985) *The Empirical Foundations of Arbitrage Pricing Theory I: The Empirical Tests*, NBER Working Paper 1725.

Obstfeld, Maurice (1994) "Risk taking, global diversification, and growth," *American Economic Review*, 84(5): 1310–29.

Ramey, Garey and Ramey, Valerie (1995) "Cross-country evidence on the link between volatility and growth," *American Economic Review*, 85: 1138–51.

Saint-Paul, Gilles (1992) "Technological choice, financial markets and economic development," *European Economic Review*, 36: 763–81.

Stockman, Alan C. (1988) "Sectoral and national aggregate disturbances to industrial output in seven European countries," *Journal of Monetary Economics*, 21: 387–409.

10

SOVEREIGN WEALTH FUNDS IN THE GULF – AN ASSESSMENT

Gawdat Bahgat

From the early 2000s to mid-2008 oil prices witnessed an unprecedented surge, reaching a peak of $147.00 per barrel in July 2008, before collapsing by the end of the year and later stabilizing around $80.00 by early 2010. Most oil exporting countries, particularly the Gulf Cooperation Council (GCC) states (Bahrain, Kuwait, Oman, Qatar, Saudi Arabia, and the United Arab Emirates – UAE) continue to be heavily dependent on oil revenues as their main source of income. Thus the rise in oil prices provided crude exporters with a massive accumulation of wealth. The relative small size of their economies and the concern about fueling inflation meant that their ability to absorb these oil revenues domestically was, and still is, limited. Thus a large proportion of these revenues had to be invested abroad. A number of sovereign wealth funds (SWFs) were founded to initiate and manage these investments. It is important to point out that other fast-growing economies, particularly China and Singapore among others, have witnessed a similar development, accumulated massive current account surpluses, and created their own SWFs. The focus of this paper is on the oil funds created by the GCC states.

This is not the first time a set of SWFs has been created. A similar wave had occurred in the 1970s following the jump in oil and gas prices. The newly established funds, however, have substantially expanded the number and size of SWFs. The overall volume of assets under management by SWFs is still relatively small in comparison with total global financial assets. However, these assets are significant relative to hedge funds or private equity (Santiso 2008: 2). Furthermore, their assets are projected to substantially increase over the next few years. Deutsche Bank predicts that SWF holdings will rise from $3.6 trillion in 2008 to $10 trillion by 2015 (Deutsche Bank 2008: 6) and JP Morgan researchers make a similar prediction, stating that SWFs' assets are likely to double from 2009 to 2015 (JP Morgan 2009: 4). In short, one important element in the changing global economy is the increasing prominence of SWFs from a wide range of home countries.

This increasing prominence of SWFs and the emergence of oil exporting countries as major creditors to the world, and to industrialized countries in particular, have highlighted two fundamental changes in the international financial system. First, the progressive running of large current account surpluses in oil exporting countries had been in parallel to current account deficits built by major industrial countries in Europe and the United States. Indeed, it can be argued that without the contribution of oil funds in bailing out major international financial institutions, the global recession would have been deeper and would have lasted longer. In short, oil exporting countries have increasingly resumed a prominent role as major creditors. Second, these oil funds are owned by their home governments and are largely controlled by the state. This framework is at variance with the traditional private-sector, market-oriented approach, dominant in most Western countries (Truman 2008: 3).

The rapid expansion of petrodollar investments has fueled anxiety regarding these new dynamics in the global financial system. Principally, most countries welcome foreign investments. However, when the money is owned and controlled by foreign governments, suspicion arises. Policy-makers in receiving markets are concerned about possible political objectives behind these SWF investments. Following their capital injections into European and US banks that suffered big losses from the sub-prime mortgage crisis, oil funds have attracted heightened attention from policy-makers, national legislatures and the media in the United States and several European countries. Meanwhile, these capital injections have been welcomed by the International Monetary Fund (IMF) and others because they have helped to stabilize markets.

This heightened attention and the lack of consensus on the role of SWFs underscore the fact that the structure, objectives, and investment strategies of SWFs in general and those in the Gulf region in particular are poorly under-stood. This study seeks to contribute to the growing systematic academic research of oil funds. In the next section I discuss the different definitions of the concept and highlight the points of differences and similarities between them. This will be followed by an analysis of the pros and cons of opening the door for foreign investments, including from the Middle East. The attempts to regulate foreign investment, including those made by oil countries, will be discussed, as well as Arab policy-makers' responses.

Definition of sovereign wealth funds

Sovereign wealth funds have been around for more than half a century. The proliferation of SWFs since the early 2000s, however, has stimulated academic and political curiosity to define what SWFs are and how to distinguish them from other investment vehicles. Analysts at the IMF see SWFs as government-owned funds, set up for a variety of macro-economic purposes. They are commonly funded by the transfer of foreign exchange assets that are invested long term overseas. They allow for a greater portfolio diversification and focus more on return than traditionally is the case for central bank-managed reserve assets (Allen and Caruana 2008: 4).

The United States government's definition focuses on the degree of risk-tolerance: SWF managers typically have a higher risk tolerance and higher expected return than traditional official reserve managers (US Department of Treasury 2007: 1). The European Commission's definition concentrates on the source of funding – the distinguishing feature of SWFs from other investment vehicles is that they are state-funded (European Commission 2008: 4).

These definitions suggest a number of common characters of SWFs. First, the underlying characteristic of SWFs that distinguishes them from other investment vehicles is that they involve a dramatic increase in the role of governments in the ownership and management of international assets. Second, SWFs are commonly established out of balance of payments surpluses. In the case of oil exporting countries, high oil prices for a prolonged period of time provide such surpluses. Third, there is a general preference to place SWFs' assets abroad, mainly to allay fears about appreciation of the domestic currency. Fourth, SWF holdings do not include foreign currency reserve assets held by monetary authorities for the traditional balance of payments or monetary policy purposes; operations of state-owned enterprises in the traditional sense; government employee pension funds; or assets managed for the benefit of individuals.

Fifth, typically, SWFs have a diversified investment strategy, with a higher level of risk accepted in search of higher returns. Sixth, the various objectives of SWFs imply different investment horizons and risk/return trade-offs, which lead to different approaches in managing these funds. SWFs usually pursue multiple objectives. Seventh, generally SWFs can be divided into two categories based on the source of their assets. Commodity funds receive most of their holdings from exporting one or a few commodities that are largely owned by the government (e.g., oil funds). Non-commodity SWFs are usually established through transfers of assets from official foreign exchange reserves (e.g., some Asian SWFs such as China's and Singapore's). The goal of such transfers is to pursue higher returns. Eighth, two broad types of SWFs can be identified based on their main objectives: (1) stabilization funds, where the primary objective is to insulate the economy against commodity price swings; and (2) savings funds for future generations which aim to share wealth with upcoming generations.

To sum up, SWFs are a heterogeneous group. They take many forms, pursue different strategies, and establish a variety of legal, institutional, and governance structures.

Investment portfolios

SWFs from the Gulf region employ a wide range of investment strategies that seek to strike a balance between safe assets and high returns. Given these broad objectives, Gulf SWFs have allocated their holdings in a variety of investment vehicles, ranging from conservative (relatively safe with low returns) vehicles such as debt and equity securities to riskier investments with potential for higher returns such as private equity, real estate, and hedge funds. By their nature,

SWFs are expected to invest in more diversified portfolios and riskier assets than traditional reserve holdings.

The older Gulf SWFs such as the Kuwait Investment Authority (KIA), the Abu Dhabi Investment Authority (ADIA), and Oman's State General Reserve Fund tend to be cautious, discreet, and conservative investors. Meanwhile, the "younger" funds (those founded since the early 2000s) tend to be more aggressive investors, reflecting the financial confidence of high oil prices during most of the decade. Many of them have pursued attractive opportunities in all sectors all over the world. Some of these newly created funds borrowed to invest in high-profile assets instead of relying on their own capital accumulations. The collapse of oil prices in mid-2008, and the end of the era of cheap and easy credit, have underscored the shortfalls of such a strategy.

The investment portfolios of the Gulf SWFs are not different from their counterparts in other countries. According to researchers at the Organization for Economic Cooperation and Development (OECD), SWFs invest on average 38 percent in the financial sector, 14 percent in the communication and transportation sectors, and 6 percent in the energy sector. Other sectors, with allocations below 5 percent each, are consumer durables and non-durables, utilities, and technology services (Avendano and Santiso 2009: 20).

Investments by Gulf SWFs have established similar portfolios, with even more concentration on the financial and energy sectors. Other sectors include real estate, industrial, aerospace, healthcare, and transportation. A close examination of the Gulf SWFs' portfolios shows that they have disproportionately favored financial companies, particularly since the early 2000s. At least two factors contributed to this concentration. First, large banks continued to be regarded as having substantial growth and profitability potential in the medium and long term. Second, investing in the US and European financial institutions has improved SWFs' image. Shortly before the eruption of the sub-prime crisis and broad economic recession, many American and European policy-makers and media outlets were suspicious of SWFs' motives and goals.

Another large and growing target of SWF investments is the nascent market for Islamic finance, or investment products that comply with Islamic law (Sharia). From profit-sharing accounts and crude products, Islamic finance spans derivatives, bonds, fund management, credit cards, and car loans – all of which often use complex structures to circumvent the Islamic ban on interest.

To sum up, SWF portfolios typically involve more diversified asset allocations than traditional reserve holdings, with considerable stakes in equities and a wide geographical dispersion.

Historically, Gulf SWFs favored investments in Western markets. Traditionally, European and American capital markets offer the widest selection of investments and a high level of liquidity, and are thus able to absorb the large volumes institutional investors typically seek to allocate. Within the OECD, most SWF investments have gone to just two countries, the United States and the United Kingdom. Gulf SWFs make more cross-border investments in US-headquartered companies than in any other country. These heavy Gulf investments in the United States simultaneously reflect and cement the strategic relations between the two sides.

Meanwhile, SWF investments in the UK have their roots in the establishment of the Kuwait Investment Office in London in the early 1950s. Since then, the ups and downs of the British economy have not deterred Gulf SWF investments from coming to London. These strong financial ties are driven by two fundamental dynamics. First, long-standing political and economic relations have served as the glue in strengthening the partnership between Britain and the Gulf states. Second, London enjoys special characteristics which make it a leading global financial services hub, attracting businesses and traders not only from the Gulf region, but from all over the world. These include a legacy of internationalism, a tradition of economic opening and stability, and a broad and liquid market.

Despite these strong financial ties to Western markets, Gulf SWFs have shown great interest in investing in emerging markets in Asia, particularly China, Hong Kong, India, Indonesia, Malaysia, Singapore, Taiwan, and Thailand. The underlying reason for investing in Asian markets is their miraculous economic performance over the last few decades. This astonishing performance means that SWF investments in Asia can earn a much higher profit rate than in OECD countries.

Finally, the global economic recession of the late 2000s prompted Gulf SWFs to invest a large proportion of their assets in their own home countries and the broad Middle East. Gulf states, like the rest of the world, could not escape the severe economic and financial crisis. They called on their SWFs to help address challenges such as low financial liquidity, high unemployment, and economic systems that have stagnated overall. They also sought to play a role in helping overcome the economic crisis in the broad Middle East.

The debate for and against sovereign wealth funds

The large and growing size of SWFs has created an intense controversy in recipient countries, particularly the United States and Europe. The management of their assets has become a major focus of national and international economic and financial policy. Some Western policy-makers and media outlets have expressed concern about SWFs' role in their countries. These concerns focus on at least five overlapping main issues.

1. The capacity of the economy to absorb foreign resources efficiently. SWF investments can lead to equity price bubbles and the related decline in demand for Treasury bonds. The long-term impact of high oil prices and large petrodollar investments might be fueling inflationary pressure and increasing the volatility of financial markets.

2. SWF investments can trigger defensive reactions from the recipient countries. Such reactions can provoke a wave of investment protectionism, which may undermine globalization and harm the global economy.
3. The fact that SWF assets are not private money and are largely owned and managed by their home governments raises concerns about the expanding role of governments in the economic systems and the broad international markets.
4. SWF investments might not be driven by purely commercial interests. Rather, they might seek to obtain technology and expertise that would serve the strategic goals of their home countries. In short, they might have a political agenda that is not necessarily in line with the national interests of recipient countries.
5. Generally, there is little public information about Gulf SWFs' assets, liabilities, or investment strategies. This lack of transparency has fueled suspicion regarding their management practices and strategic goals.

The limited number of cases and problems with data complicate a comprehensive evaluation of the operations of Gulf SWFs and their overall performance and the adequacy of Western concerns. In recent years, domestic and international pressure has intensified on SWFs to improve their governance and accountability practices. In response there have been some small but significant improvements. Since the late 2000s, several Gulf SWFs have introduced changes to comply with international financial norms and the IMF guidelines. SWFs from Bahrain, Kuwait, and the United Arab Emirates have published information on their assets and established websites to inform the public of their management practices and financial goals.

On the other side, proponents of SWFs argue that these investment funds have already proven themselves crucial to economic prosperity, in both their home and recipient countries, to the stability of the international financial system. They call for the elimination of restrictions on foreign investments and, instead, the provision of more incentives to facilitate and encourage cross-border movement of capital. Their argument is based on five pillars:

1. Extracting and selling oil amounts to running down capital. Preventing or imposing strict restrictions on investments by SWFs from oil exporting countries would make it harder for them to diversify their economies and to maximize their profit. Under such a scenario, it would make economic sense to keep oil underground. This would lead to shortage of oil supplies and higher prices, which would harm the interests of oil consuming countries and add pressure on the international financial system.
2. SWFs tend to have long-term horizons, with no commercial liabilities that they are obligated to pay out on and no external investors able to withdraw capital at short notice. These characteristics enable them to withstand market pressures in times of crises, and dampen volatility, and serve as a stabilizing force.

3. SWFs are a way to help recycle petrodollar surpluses internationally. As the economic recession of the late 2000s had demonstrated, Gulf SWFs were able to inject badly needed capital into several American and European financial institutions.
4. SWFs should be seen as a win–win equation. They provide new sources of liquidity to recipient countries and help to spread technology and know-how among their home countries. As a result, SWFs help all parties to adjust to imbalances.
5. In addition to these financial benefits, SWFs have significant strategic implications. SWF investments bind all people together and reinforce bonds of mutual dependence among countries, thereby increasing the costs of international conflict. They mean that SWF home and recipient countries develop direct stakes in the economic prosperity and political stability of each other.

In sum, SWFs represent a large and rapidly growing stock of government-controlled assets invested more aggressively than traditional reserves. Attention to SWFs is inevitable given that their rise clearly has implications for the international financial system. They bring benefits to the system, but also raise potential concerns.

Attempts to regulate sovereign wealth funds

Cross-border investments are generally seen as a contributor to global prosperity. However, some policy-makers in the United States and Europe worry about the potential implications of letting state-controlled funds acquire stakes in powerful companies and critical economic and strategic sectors. Consequently, many Western leaders have called on SWFs to be more open, and demanded the imposition of restrictions on their investments.

At the peak of the global recession (2008–9), hostility towards SWFs lessened considerably as several Gulf SWFs (and their Asian counterparts) participated in bailing out major financial institutions in the United States and Europe. It is uncertain whether the hostility and suspicion will wane or will be reactivated when the global economy rebounds. Rather, what is clear is that SWFs will remain controversial, arousing concerns for governments around the world. Within this context, the United States, the European Union, the OECD, and the International Monetary Fund (IMF) have sought to articulate new policies to strike a balance between protecting sensitive sectors and industries on national security grounds and ensuring a free flow of capital through transparent and stable rules.

United States

Generally, the United States welcomes all kinds of foreign investments including those from SWFs. Washington has long been open and receptive toward foreign investments as has been demonstrated by several US administrations in various statutory frameworks, policy measures, and international agreements. In the last half century, the United States has entered into several treaties with other countries and international organizations that acknowledge its commitment to openness to foreign investment and free-market principles.

The Department of Treasury collects data on foreign portfolio investment in the United States through surveys of US financial institutions and others. These surveys collect data on ownership of US assets by foreign residents and foreign official institutions. The data are used to provide aggregate information to the public on foreign portfolio investments. SWF investment holdings are included in the foreign investment data collected by the Treasury, but cannot be specifically identified because of data collection limitations and restraints on revealing the identity of reporting persons and investors.

Since the sub-prime crisis of 2008–9 it has become more difficult to finance the US deficit. In contrast to the stock market boom of the 1990s and the post-2001 real-estate bonanza, foreign private investors have become reluctant to enter the market. Instead, financing mainly relies on inflows from central banks and SWFs. In 2008, nearly half of all US Treasuries were owned by foreigners and, according to Federal Reserve Chairman Ben Bernanke, about a third of recent emergency funding for Western financial institutions has come from Asian and Arab SWFs (Woertz 2008). Despite a rise in political sensitivity and a growing suspicion in SWFs' investments, the United States has continued to attract the bulk of these investments.

Foreign investments – governmental or non-governmental – in the US financial or non-financial institutions are likely to continue their historical rise. The two sides (SWF holders and the US market) need each other. The challenge facing the United States is how to find the right balance between making herself safe and attractive to SWFs, and simultaneously maintain her open market-based regime in which private sector actors are the dominant players. The challenge facing SWFs is how to address and mitigate growing private and public political suspicion in their operations. For several decades, SWFs and the United States have engaged in multi-dimensional and multi-billion dollar investments. This complicated partnership is likely to further grow in the foreseeable future. The economic and financial well-being of the United States is in the best interest of SWFs. Meanwhile, the continuing rise of SWFs is good for the US market.

European Union

The EU's stance on SWFs shares some similarities and differences with that of the United States. The commitment to openness to investments and free movement of capital has been a long-standing principle of the EU. Joaquín Almunia, European Commissioner for Economic and Monetary Policy, asserts that the EU Member States are well aware that investment and openness "are the elements that drive our economy forward and without them we cannot advance" (Almunia 2008).

With regard to SWFs, what worries European leaders is not only that governments are taking a leading role in allocating huge financial resources, but also that many of these governments do not adhere to the democratic and free-market principles that drive European societies and vision for the international system. (Barysch et al. 2009: 5). Despite these fundamental differences, the EU leaders acknowledge the positive role SWFs have played. As José Manuel Barroso, the European Commission's President, asserts, SWFs are "not a big bad wolf at the door. They have injected liquidity and helped stabilize financial markets" (Barber 2008). This acknowledgment aside, European leaders have sought to articulate a common EU stance on the rise of SWFs. In early 2008 the European Commission adopted a communication that was later endorsed by the EU heads of state and government during a meeting of the European Council. In essence, the EU has been calling on SWFs to commit to good governance practices, adequate accountability, and a sufficient level of transparency.

Thus, instead of seeking to regulate SWFs, the European approach relies heavily on constructive dialogue and a cooperative effort between recipient countries on one side, and SWFs and their sponsor countries on the other. Accordingly, there are few, if any, high-profile cases of an EU government blocking an SWF investment. Usually, recipient countries and investors try to avoid public controversies.

The global economic recession of the late 2000s has introduced new dynamics in the EU's perception of SWFs. On the one hand, in an environment where capital is extremely scarce, SWF investments are considered an important component of the European efforts to overcome the financial crisis and initiate and consolidate economic recovery. On the other hand, the collapse in market valuations has raised concern that foreign investors, including SWFs, may acquire significant stocks in major European companies at very low prices. Thus a number of political leaders and some media outlets have raised the alarm against SWF investments. The French President Nicolas Sarkozy argued that falling share prices meant that big industries were in imminent danger of being taken over by non-European investors. "I don't want European citizens to wake up in several months and find European companies belonging to non-European capital, which bought them at the share price's lowest point" (Charter 2008). The French president called on EU Member States to launch national sovereign wealth funds to take stakes in key industries to stop them from falling into foreign hands. Similarly, the Italian government set up a national interests committee to establish rules about SWF investments. Foreign Minister Franco Frattini called for imposing a five percent stake ceiling on foreign investment in any individual Italian company (Dinmore 2008).

Organization for Economic Cooperation and Development

The fact that the United States and several EU Member States are also members of the OECD means that the latter's stance on SWF investments is similar to those of Washington and Brussels. Angel Gurría, the OECD Secretary-General, asserts that the organization's findings "show that these funds (SWFs) bring benefits to home and host countries" (Gurría 2008). A recent OECD Ministerial Council Meeting concluded that protectionist barriers to foreign investment would hamper growth. Far from being a threat to OECD financial systems, SWFs could be "allies in the struggle to stimulate development and support donors as development finance partners" (OECD 2008a).

Like the United States and the European Union, the OECD has repeatedly issued statements confirming its adherence to an open-door investment policy and accommodating foreign capital from all sources, including those owned by governments. Most OECD Member States have developed guidelines aimed at striking a balance between welcoming SWF investments and protecting their own economic interests and national security. For example, in late 2007 Canada issued guidelines under which the authority in Ottawa examines the corporate governance and reporting structure of non-Canadian investors. This examination includes whether the non-Canadian companies follow Canadian standards of corporate governance (including commitments to transparency and disclosure, independent members of the board of directors, independent audit committees, and equitable treatment of shareholders) and Canadian laws and practices (OECD 2009). Similarly, Australia indicated that foreign government-controlled investors are examined in the same way as proposed investments by private investors, but noted that its screening regime applies to all proposed direct investment by foreign government-controlled companies. In February 2008, Australia issued "Principles Guiding Consideration of Foreign Government Related Investment in Australia" in order to enhance the transparency of its review procedure (Treasurer of the Commonwealth of Australia 2008).

In addition to these guidelines developed by individual OECD Member States to attract SWF investments without jeopardizing their national security and strategic interests, the organization reached a consensus on a number of rules and regulations to pursue a similar balance. The key OECD investment rules are the OECD Code of Liberalization of Capital Movements, adopted in 1961 (OECD 2010a), and the OECD Declaration on International Investment and Multinational Enterprises of 1976, as revised in 2000 (OECD 2010b). These include procedures for notification and multilateral surveillance under the broad oversight of the OECD's governing Council to ensure their observance. The two documents are regularly updated by decisions of the OECD Council. They serve as a reference manual to the obligations of Member States to the degree of liberalization achieved by each one in regard to capital movements.

In 2006, the OECD launched the Freedom of Investment (FOI) process under the auspices of the OECD Investment Committee, which for decades has been in charge of discussing all issues related to foreign investment. The FOI provides a unique multilateral forum for investment policy. It includes a process of peer surveillance to ensure that international commitments to openness are respected (OECD 2008b) The goal is to help OECD member and non-member governments to preserve and expand an open environment for international investment, while also safeguarding essential security interests. In the late 2000s, participants in the FOI process agreed on a set of guidelines to contribute to confidence-building between SWFs and host countries and facilitate the free movement of foreign capital.

International Monetary Fund

Recognizing the growing importance of SWFs and the role of the IMF in monitoring the health of its member countries' economies and the global financial system, the IMF's ministerial guidance body – the International Monetary and Financial Committee – called on the Fund to engage in a dialogue with countries to arrive at a voluntary set of best practices in the management of SWFs. The IMF has developed similar guidelines in the past, particularly in the areas of fiscal transparency and foreign exchange reserves management. In response, representatives of SWFs met at the IMF Headquarters in Washington DC in late April 2008. The meeting facilitated a useful exchange of views among the SWFs, recipient countries, representatives from OPEC, and the European Commission. An International Working Group of SWFs (IWG) was formally established by the meeting to reach a consensus on a set of principles that properly reflects the SWF investment practices and objectives.

The IWG was co-chaired by Hamad al-Suwaidi, Undersecretary of the Abu Dhabi Department of Finance and a Director of the Abu Dhabi Investment Authority (ADIA), and Jaime Caruana, Counselor and Director of the IMF's Monetary and Capital Markets Department (IWG 2008a). The IWG was comprised of representatives from 26 IMF member countries. It held meetings in Washington, DC (30 April–1 May), Singapore (9–10 July), and Santiago (1–2 September), all in 2008. In their third meeting these representatives reached an agreement on the Generally Accepted Principles and Practices for Sovereign Wealth Funds (GAPP), also known as the Santiago Principles. This voluntary framework aims to guide the appropriate governance and accountability arrangements, as well as the conduct of appropriate investment practices by SWFs.

The IWG's work was guided by four main objectives: (1) to help maintain a stable global financial system and free flow of capital and investment; (2) to comply with all applicable regulatory and disclosure requirements in the countries where they invest; (3) to invest on the basis of economic and financial risk and return-related considerations; and (4) to have in place a transparent governance structure that provides for adequate risk management and accountability (IWG 2008b).

The work of the IWG and the publication of GAPP should be seen as important steps in establishing and consolidating a dialogue and understanding between SWFs and recipient countries. Other steps in this direction include the founding of the International Forum of SWFs and the issuing of the Kuwait Declaration. In April 2009, SWF representatives who participated in the IWG and endorsed the Santiago Principles met in Kuwait City. The meeting was hosted by the Kuwait Investment Authority (KIA). They agreed to establish the Forum as a permanent organization. The purpose is to meet, exchange views on issues of common interest, and facilitate an understanding of the Santiago Principles and SWF activities.

Gulf sovereign wealth funds

The Gulf Cooperation Council (GCC) was established in 1981 by Bahrain, Kuwait, Oman, Qatar, Saudi Arabia, and the United Arab Emirates to enhance their economic and financial integration. Its total population – including expatriates – is estimated at 38 million, with a GDP of $1.1 trillion in 2008. The six GCC countries possess 40 percent of the world's proven oil reserves and provide 23 percent of world production. The figures for natural gas are 25 percent proven reserves and 24 percent of global production (British Petroleum 2010: 6, 22). Their spare oil production capacity accounts for the bulk of the world's total. All these figures illustrate the leading role the region plays in global energy markets. On the other hand, despite persistent efforts to diversify their economies and reduce their heavy dependency on hydrocarbon resources, the GCC states are still deeply dependent on oil revenues. Oil accounts for about 50 percent of the region's GDP and 80 percent of fiscal and export revenues (Khamis and Senhadji 2010: 1).

The GCC states are home to some of the largest and oldest SWFs, with estimated assets between $600 billion and $1 trillion at the end of 2008 (Friedman and Meakin 2009: 65). The main impetus for the growth of these SWFs came from high oil prices up to 2008. Thus, through most of the 2000s, the GCC states became the largest source of net global capital flows in the world, rivaling China as a "new financial superpower" (*Economist* 2008: 2).

Countries such as the GCC states that rely on oil and other non-renewable resources for a substantial share of their revenue face two key problems: the revenue stream is uncertain and volatile, and the supply of the resource is exhaustible. Stated differently, government revenue derived from the exploitation of non-renewable resources differs from other revenue in that it partly represents a depletion of wealth. This suggests that some of this wealth should be saved – both to help stabilize the financial market and for inter-generational equity (Davis et al. 2001: 4). These two objectives, stabilization and saving, are further reinforced by the fact that most oil-producing countries cannot absorb the amount of wealth they are generating.

The combination of all these factors was the main drive for the creation and growth of a large number of SWFs in the Gulf region. Indeed, each jump in oil and gas prices has increased the number and size of SWFs in the region. Thus it is not a coincidence that the majority of Gulf SWFs were founded in the 2000s, when oil prices started their inexorable climb to their peak of July 2008, reflecting the confidence of a Gulf flooded with cash. Little wonder the region represents the highest concentration of SWF assets worldwide. In 2008, analysts at the Deutsche Bank estimated assets under management by Gulf SWFs at $1.6 trillion, representing 46 percent of total SWF assets worldwide (Deutsche Bank 2008: 4). Other analysts raise the share to 60 percent (Friedman and Meakin 2009: 6). This disparity is due to the fact that most SWFs in the Gulf and elsewhere do not publish official figures of their assets.

The availability of substantial financial resources proved crucial to both the ability of the Gulf SWFs to play a significant role in overcoming the global financial crisis of the late 2000s in their own home countries, and in continuing their investments, albeit at a much lower level, in troubled Western banks and corporations. According to one source, the market value of the Gulf's foreign portfolio fell by an estimated $350 billion over the course of 2008 (Setser 2009: 1). Another source estimated that the Gulf SWFs lost on average between 20 and 25 percent of the value of their known equity portfolios (Barbary and Chin 2009: 4). The IMF estimates that the GCC states' combined current account surplus fell to $53 billion in 2009, after having risen more than tenfold in the previous decade to $362 billion in 2008 (IMF 2010: 1). Thus, as the global financial crisis deepened, the demand for oil, and consequently the prices, declined. As a result, the stock and real-estate markets plunged, and external funding for the financial and corporate sectors tightened. Despite these huge losses, Gulf SWFs have managed to maintain their financial leverage. This relative success is due to the execution of comprehensive economic strategies prior to the global financial crisis. The GCC states grew on average by a robust 5.75 percent a year between 2005 and 2008 (IMF 2009: 6). They launched huge investment projects to pursue economic diversification and human capital development through investments in oil and gas and infrastructure, as well as in petrochemicals, tourism, financial services, and education. In addition they saved and invested a significant portion of their oil revenues.

This strong economic base has enabled the GCC states to address the severe global financial crisis from a relatively better stance than most other countries. Governments used their strong international reserve positions to maintain high spending and introduce exceptional financial measures. Saudi Arabia adopted a $400 billion public investment package (equivalent to 110 percent of its annual GDP, the largest fiscal stimulus package relative to GDP among the G20 for 2009–10) to be implemented over five years. The increased spending on social sectors and infrastructure in 2009 cushioned the downturn. Countercyclical fiscal policy in the UAE also played a key role in avoiding a major disruption in economic activity. Abu Dhabi's support of Dubai during the debt crisis limited contagion to the rest of the economy and the banking system not only in the UAE, but in the rest of the Gulf region. In Qatar, the government's preemptive intervention in the banking sector was equivalent to 6.6 percent of GDP, mainly in the form of equity injections and asset purchases by the Qatar Investment Authority (QIA). The Kuwaiti authorities' response to the financial crisis was complicated by prolonged negotiations between the government and the parliament. In early 2010 the parliament approved a four-year $105 billion spending package (95 percent of GDP). The Omani and Bahraini authorities introduced liquidity and prudential measures that helped mitigate the adverse effects of the crisis, particularly on the banking system (Institute of International Finance 2010: 5).

In short, the GCC authorities' response to the global financial crisis focused on restoring liquidity by providing capital injections into the banking system, supplemented by deposits from government institutions. To shore up investor confidence, Kuwait, Saudi Arabia, and the UAE provided guarantees for deposits at commercial banks and asked SWFs to support domestic asset prices and to provide capital injections for banks. SWF resources in Bahrain, Kuwait, Oman, and Qatar were used to set up funds investing in local equity markets. Furthermore, the KIA and QIA bought domestic bank shares to help boost bank capitalization and confidence. Thus the experience of the late 2000s demonstrates that in times of financial stress, SWF domestic investments may temporarily deviate from pure profit maximization to support broader macro-economic and financial stabilization objectives.

The role Gulf SWFs played in addressing and mitigating the impact of the global financial crisis in their home countries was crucial. On the other hand, with regard to foreign markets, on the whole, the Gulf SWFs weathered the financial storm fairly well, outperforming their Asian counterparts in some cases. Generally, older funds with large and diversified portfolios were somewhat protected from critical damage, while younger funds that pursued aggressive investment strategies fared much worse. For example, after buying stocks in Western banks at the height of the global financial crisis, the KIA sold a large portion of its stakes in Citigroup, and ADIA and QIA did the same with their portions of the British bank Barclays plc. The three Gulf SWFs made huge profits in these transactions.

The experience of the last several years has contributed to the formulation of the Gulf SWF response to the criticism and reservations expressed by some Western policy-makers and media outlets. Indeed, as their profile has risen in recent years, Gulf SWFs were ill-prepared to counter the negative coverage they received in some European countries and the United States. Officials from the Gulf SWFs have repeatedly argued that their record shows that their investment decisions are driven exclusively by economic and financial interests, and that they do not have any political agenda. They rightly challenge politicians in the United States and Europe to name a single Gulf investment that was made for political rather than commercial reasons (Khalaf 2008).

Gulf investors accept the need for increased scrutiny from recipient countries when the investments have potential national security implications, so long as the process is clear, fair, and timely. In return, they call for a reciprocal responsibility, meaning that the entire world community (SWF home and recipient countries) has a shared interest in ensuring that financial markets remain open, that investors (private or government) playing by the rules are not discriminated against, and that the regulatory process remain transparent and predictable (Al-Otaiba 2008).

Gulf investors also argue that Western suspicions of their SWFs are grossly inflated. The efforts to regulate SWF investment operations are unjustified given that there are no similar guidelines for private-equity or hedge funds, and therefore it is unfair to single out SWFs. They assert that SWFs tend to be passive rather than active investors. On average, a SWF takes less than 5 percent of the shares outstanding in a company, not a controlling stake. With such a small share, SWFs can hardly be viewed as possessing control over companies (Avendano and Santiso 2009: 12). Furthermore, the majority of the Gulf SWFs use external managers, partly to fill the skill gap and partly due to their relative shortage of indigenous professional financial experts.

Two conclusions can be drawn from this discussion of the Gulf SWFs. First, while the GCC states' short-term economic outlook is clouded by the global economic slowdown and by the credit crisis in Dubai, the region's medium-term outlook seems broadly positive. This projection is based on the substantial investments in both economic and human infrastructures. All over the region, new cities have been built, economic projects and financial centers have opened, and new schools and universities have been established. In short, it can be argued that the Gulf governments have managed their massive petrodollars in the 2000s better and wiser than they did in the 1970s (following the jump in oil prices). Not surprisingly, analysts at the McKinsey Global Institute conclude that petrodollar investors are "poised for future growth in almost any scenario. Their foreign assets will reach nearly $9 trillion by 2013 in our base case, and more than $13 trillion if the economy recovers more quickly" (Roxburgh et al. 2009: 12).

Second, it is true that the GCC states have amassed immense financial reserves and accordingly have managed to weather the global economic crisis much better than many other regions, and that their outlook in the medium and long term looks promising. But their prosperity is still largely linked to oil prices. The efforts to diversify the region's economies away from oil and create other sources of national income have achieved only a modest success.

Conclusion

The global financial crisis in the late 2000s and the constructive role Gulf SWFs have played in the efforts to overcome the challenges and provide liquidity have partly reduced the intensity surrounding SWFs. It is uncertain what direction the controversy might take in coming years. Will skeptics in the United States and Europe accept these government-controlled investment vehicles? Or will they seek more regulations? The experience of the last several years suggests a few lessons. First, the financial muscle and leverage that Gulf SWFs might have in coming years will largely depend on future oil prices and the scale of their domestic spending. The higher the price and the lower domestic spending, the more assets they have to invest overseas.

Second, while some information on Gulf SWF assets, strategies, management, and governance is available, there is no uniform public disclosure. As the experiences of KIA and ADIA suggest, a number of SWFs have come to accept the need for transparency and accountability in recent years. This acceptance might be driven by pressure from domestic public opinion or the desire to adhere to the Santiago Principles. Still, there is much to be desired.

Third, both SWF host and recipient countries share a mutual interest in maintaining an open international investment climate in which all participants have confidence. A sensible management of oil-producing countries' petroleum wealth in well-functioning financial markets is in everyone's interest.

Fourth, the record of Gulf SWFs − and indeed most SWFs − demonstrates that they are generally passive investors with no desire to impact company decisions by actively using their voting rights, purchasing controlling shares, replacing old management, or any other means. Furthermore, there is no evidence that these SWF investments are motivated and driven by political objectives. Like other investors, Gulf SWFs seek to maximize their profit.

Finally, in the last several years there have been many political and academic arguments put forth regarding the potential positive and negative effects of SWFs on global financial markets. Despite the hyperventilation surrounding SWFs, a close examination suggests these funds are not threatening to the established financial system. Rather, the evidence suggests that they can be, and have been, a stabilizing force.

References

Al-Otaiba, Yousef (2008) "Our sovereign wealth plans," *Wall Street Journal*, 19 March.

Allen, Mark and Caruana, Jaime (2008) *Sovereign Wealth Funds − A Work Agenda*. Washington, DC: International Monetary Fund.

Almunia, Joaquín (2008) "The EU Response to the Rise of Sovereign Wealth Funds," available at: http://europa.eu/rapid/pressReleasesAction.do?reference=SPEECH/08/165&format=pdf&aged=1&language=EN&GuiLanguage=en (accessed 2 April 2008).

Avendano, Rolando and Santiso, Javier (2009) "Are SWFs' Investments Politically Biased? A Comparison with Mutual Funds," OECD, available at: http://www.oecd.org/dataoecd/43/0/44301172.pdf (accessed 13 May 2010).

Barbary, Victoria and Chin, Edward (2009) "Testing Time: Sovereign Wealth Funds in the Middle East and North Africa and the Global Financial Crisis," available at: http://www.monitor.com/portals/0/MonitorContent/imported/MonitorUnited States/Articles/PDFs/Monitor_testing_time_SWF_MENA_May_2009.pdf (accessed 11 May 2010).

Barber, Tony (2008) "Brussels pushes wealth funds to sign code," *Financial Times*, 27 February.

Barysch, Katinka, Tilford, Simon, and Whyte, Philip (2009) "State, Money and Rules: An EU Policy for Sovereign Investments," Center for European Reform, available at: http://www.cer.org.uk (accessed 17 January 2009).

British Petroleum (2010) *BP Statistical Review of World Energy*. London: BP.

Charter, David (2008) "Sarkozy calls for halt to foreign ownership," *The Times*, 21 October.

Davis, Jeffrey, Ossowski, Rolando, Daniel, James and Barnett, Steven (2001) *Stabilization and Savings Funds for Non-renewable Resource: Experienceand Fiscal Policy Implications*. Washington, DC: International Monetary Fund.

Dinmore, Guy (2008) "Italy set to curb sovereign wealth funds," *Financial Times*, 21 October.

Economist (2008) "Asset-backed insecurity," 389(8564), 27 January.

Deutsche Bank (2008) *Sovereign Wealth Funds and Foreign Investment Policies – An Update*, available at: http://www.dbresearch.com/PROD/DBR_Internet_EN-PROD/PROD0000000000232851.pdf (accessed 8 May 2010).

European Commission (2008) "A Common European Approach to SWFs," available at: http://ec.europa.eu/internal_market/finances/docs/sovereign_en.pdf (accessed 9 May 2010).

Friedman, Tim and Meakin, Sam (2009) *The 2009 Preqin Sovereign Wealth Fund Review*. London: Preqin.

Gurría, Angel (2008) "Sovereign Wealth Funds and Recipient Country Policies," available at: http://www.oecd.org/dataoecd/34/9/40408735.pdf (accessed 4 April 2008).

Institute of International Finance (2010) "GCC Regional Overview," available at: http://www.iif.com/press/press+146.php (accessed 17 May 2010).

International Monetary Fund (2009) *Regional Economic Outlook: The Middle East and Central Asia*. Washington, DC: IMF.

International Monetary Fund (2010) *Regional Economic Outlook: The Middle East and Central Asia*. Washington, DC: IMF.

International Working Group (2008a) "International Working Group of Sovereign Wealth Funds Meets in Singapore; Continues to Make Progress on Drafting Set of Principles and Practices," available at: http://www.iwg-swf.org/pr.htm (accessed 23 July 2008).

International Working Group (2008b) "Sovereign Wealth Funds Generally Accepted Principles and Practices 'Santiago Principles,'" available at: http://www.iwg-swf.org/pubs/eng/Santiagoprinciples.pdf (accessed 30 October 2008).

JP Morgan (2009) "Sovereign Wealth Funds: A Bottom-up Primer," available at: http://www.econ/puc-rio.br/mgarcia/Seminario/textos_preliminares/SWF22May09.pdf (accessed 22 May 2009).

Khalaf, Roula (2008) "Transparency is in everyone's interest," *Financial Times*, 19 May.

Khamis, May and Senhadji, Abdelhak (2010) "Learning from the past," *Finance and Development*, 47(1): 1–4.

Organization for Economic Cooperation and Development (2008a) "Ministers Adopt Declaration on Sovereign Wealth Funds," available at: http://www.oecd.org/document print/0,3455,en_2649_34887_40790173_1_1_1_1,00.html (accessed 19 November 2008).

Organization for Economic Cooperation and Development (2008b) "Sovereign Wealth Funds and Recipient Countries – Working Together to Maintain and Expand Freedom of Investment," available at: http://www.oecd.org/dataoecd/0/23/41456730.pdf (accessed 11 October 2008).

Organization for Economic Cooperation and Development (2009) "Foreign Government-Controlled Investors and Recipient Country Investment Policies: A Scoping Paper," available at: http://www.oecd.org/dataoecd/1/21/42022469.pdf (accessed 21 January 2009).

Organization for Economic Cooperation and Development (2010a) "OECD Codes of Liberalization of Capital Movements and of Current Invisible Operations," available at: http://www.OECD.org/daf/investment/codes (accessed 28 May 2010).

Organization for Economic Cooperation and Development (2010b) "OECD Declaration and Decisions on International Investment and Multinational Enterprises," available at: http://www.OECD.org/daf/investment/declaration (accessed 28 May 2010).

Roxburgh, Charles, Lund, Susan, Lippert, Matt, White, Olivia, and Zhao, Yue (2009) *The New Power Brokers: How Oil, Asia, Hedge Funds, and Private Equity Are Faring in the Financial Crisis.* San Francisco: McKinsey Global Institute.

Santiso, Javier (2008) *Sovereign Development Funds*, OECD Policy Insights No. 58, available at: http://www.oecd.org/dataoecd/17/57/40040692.pdf (accessed 8 May 2010).

Setser, Brad (2009) "How Badly Were the Gulf's Sovereign Funds Hurt by the 2008 Crisis?" Council on Foreign Relations, available at: http://blogs.cfr.org/setser/category/sovereign-wealth-funds (accessed 17 January 2009).

Treasurer of the Commonwealth of Australia (2008) "Government Improves Transparency of Foreign Investment Screening Process," available at: http://www.Treasurer.gov.au/DisplayDocs.aspx?pageID=003&doc=../content/pressreleases/2008/009.htm&min=wms (accessed 28 May 2010).

Truman, Edwin M. (2008) "A Blueprint for SWF Best Practices," Peterson Institute, available at: http://www.iie.com/publications/pb/pb08-3.pdf, p. 3 (accessed 8 May 2010).

United States Department of Treasury (2007) "Semiannual Report on International Economic and Exchange Rate Policies," available at: http://www.UStreas.gov/offices/international-affairs/economic-exchange-rates/pdf/2007_appendix-3.pdf (accessed 9 May 2010).

Woertz, Eckart (2008) "GCC needs the dollar and the U.S. needs the funding," *Financial Times*, 29 May.

11

ENERGY AND SUSTAINABILITY POLICIES IN THE GULF STATES

Steffen Hertog and Giacomo Luciani

Per capita oil and gas consumption and, by implication, CO_2 emissions in the GCC countries are uniquely high. This chapter will argue that under current global market conditions, fossil fuel conservation is a rational strategy for the Gulf monarchies. In electricity production in particular, there are large-scale opportunities for introducing non-carbon energy sources. Gulf industrial and upstream structures also offer strong opportunities for carbon capture and storage (or 'sequestration').

The Gulf regimes' commitment to sustainable energy policies appears increasingly serious, reflecting their ambition to be taken seriously as international actors. Much of the policies currently under way can be pursued on a project basis, building on technocratic enclaves under the direct patronage of rulers. These are more likely to be successful than broader regulatory policies aimed at changing consumer and business behaviour in general. There is considerable potential to build up local technology clusters, but spillover into society and business at large is likely to remain limited.

The chapter will develop this argument in two parts, the first expounding the economic rationale for specific types of sustainable energy policies, the second analysing the institutional embedding of these policies.[1]

The rationale for sustainable energy in the Gulf

As the Gulf is expected to be the incremental supplier of oil and gas for the entire world for decades to come, the simplistic assumption is frequently made that the region enjoys an abundant supply of cheap energy. This, however, is not the case and, indeed, the Gulf countries face their own 'energy crisis', which will become more and more apparent in the years and decades to come. The Gulf energy crisis is the consequence of rapidly growing domestic demand for energy and, specifically, for electric power.

In discussing the sustainability of the GCC energy systems we should clearly distinguish between the consumption of liquid fuels and that of electricity. Consumption of liquid fuels has grown very rapidly in all GCC countries, thanks to low, politically motivated domestic prices. The high level of consumption constitutes a problem, to the extent that some of the GCC countries are forced to be net importers of refined products. There is no economic logic in selling petroleum products domestically at prices way below what the same can fetch on the international market, and even the national oil companies complain about this practice. However, the political logic is very strong, and the probability that prices might be significantly realigned is low (see below). Besides containing consumption through higher prices, there is little the GCC countries can do to improve sustainability of liquid fuel supply. There is certainly no reasonable alternative to producing liquid fuels from oil in these countries: biomass is obviously a non-starter.

Electricity is different, because alternative means for producing electricity that make sense in the region are available. Both renewable sources – meaning primarily solar and to some extent wind – and nuclear energy are valid options. Coal, too, has been considered, but would not help in the direction of reducing greenhouse gas (GHG) emissions.

The latter is increasingly recognised as a problem. The GCC countries have per capita emissions of carbon dioxide (CO_2) that are among the highest on the planet (Fgure 11.1). This is, of course, partly due to the tiny population of some of them, but the energy intensity of economic life in the Gulf is an undeniable feature.

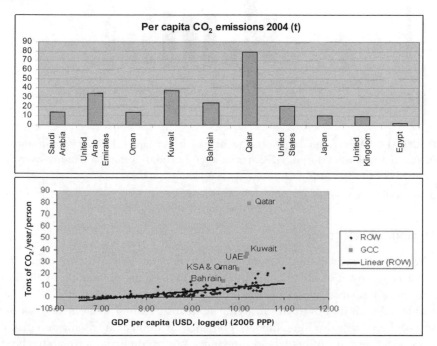

FIGURE 11.1 GCC CO_2 emissions relative to GDP (2004) (based on UNDP and World Bank data)

The discussion in this chapter concentrates on electricity as the most critical area for the future of the Gulf countries' energy sustainability. We begin by exploring causes of the current 'electricity crisis' of the GCC countries and then consider the prospects and rationale for reliance on carbon capture and sequestration (CCS), for rational use of energy and for the use of alternative sources of power generation, notably solar, wind and nuclear.

Causes of growth in electricity demand

Economic growth is always accompanied by growth in energy demand, but the elasticity may vary greatly; the Gulf countries have experienced high rates of per capita growth in electricity consumption, resulting in high absolute consumption levels (Figures 11.2 and 11.3). The rapid growth in energy demand may be attributed to three main concomitant causes.

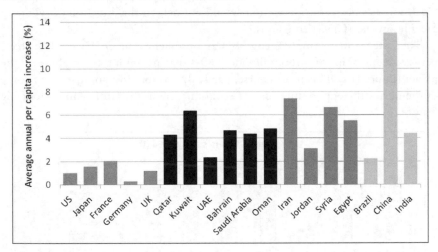

FIGURE 11.2 Average annual percentage increase in per capita electricity consumption of selected major developed, GCC, regional and major developing nations, over the period 1990–2003

Source: Al-Ibrahim (2009).

Demographic changes

The first and most important cause is the rapid increase in the numbers and purchasing power of the urban population. The national population in all Gulf countries has been increasing rapidly by rich-country standards. This has combined with improvements in living standards, leading to an increase in the size of the average dwelling, universal reliance on ambient air conditioning, and very widespread use of household appliances. While population growth has been slowing down, consumption patterns of nationals and expatriates could still expand for many years to come.

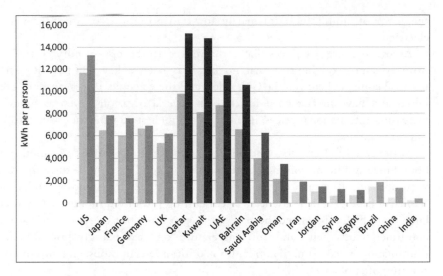

FIGURE 11.3 Per capita electricity consumption of selected major developed, GCC, regional, and major developing nations for 1990 and 2003 (lighter, left-hand bars, are for 1990; darker, right-hand bars, are for 2003)

Source: Al-Ibrahim (2009).

Industrialisation

The second important cause is the process of economic diversification and the concentration on energy-intensive industries, for which the GCC has been emerging as a regional and, increasingly, global hub.

Here one should distinguish industries that use oil and/or natural gas as feedstock (petroleum refining, petrochemicals) and industries that use the same as sources of heat (again, petroleum refining and petrochemicals, but also cement, iron and steel, building materials, glass, etc.). Although some of the latter activities are important consumers of electricity in addition to heat, they also offer the opportunity of recovering waste heat on a much larger scale than is done already, and use the same to produce electricity more efficiently. Combined heat and power (CHP) offers significant potential for the improved efficiency of energy use. Water desalination is already now normally combined with power generation.

But the industrialisation process has also led to the growth of industries that specifically require electricity rather than other forms of energy – notably aluminium smelting.

Low prices

The third fundamental determinant of energy consumption is price. The cost of energy to industry as well as to the final consumer has been kept low, whether in the form of liquid fuels (primarily for transportation) or in the form of electricity.

Access to energy at prices that are unrelated to the opportunity cost of the primary source on international markets has been a key component of the political compact between the Gulf rulers and their people. Prices have not been raised and have in fact been lowered on several occasions, even at times of increasing international prices, in order to compensate for the increasing cost of imported goods.

In the case of electricity, which is the main form of energy consumption in households and in the commercial sector, the wasteful pattern of consumption is very obvious. It is also deeply rooted, in the sense that building codes and standards have paid little attention to containing power requirements. On top of large and badly insulated homes, the region is characterised by wasteful consumer habits, with ambient temperature kept exceedingly low, abundant illumination based primarily on traditional incandescent bulbs, and unrestrained running of appliances.

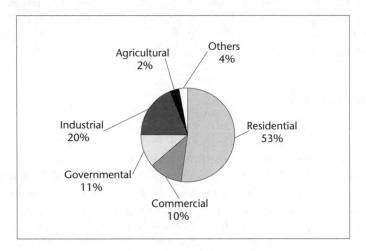

FIGURE 11.4 Saudi electricity consumption by sector (JICA 2008)

Source: Electricity 2006, MOWE.

Households constitute by far the most important component of electricity demand, accounting for 53 per cent of total consumption in Saudi Arabia (Figure 11.4).

Encouraging them to change their electricity consumption pattern is much more difficult than pursuing a more rational use of energy in industry, and it is especially difficult if the price lever cannot be used. Emphasis will therefore probably be on increasing electricity production rather than reining in consumption and, if anything, savings efforts will be focused on industry rather than the residential sector (Figure 11.5).

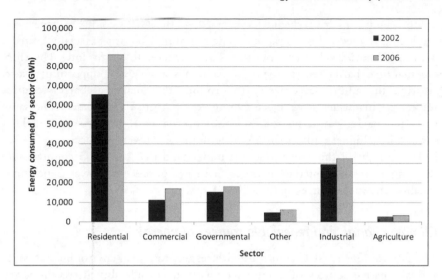

FIGURE 11.5 Growth of energy consumption by sector in Saudi Arabia (2002 and 2006)
Source: Al-Ibrahim (2009).

Investment requirements and the choice of primary source

According to APICORP[2] in the period 2011–15 the GCC will need to add 48 GW to its 2009 capacity of close to 88 GW, for a total investment requirement of 53 billion US dollars, or more than 10 billion per year.

Such near doubling in barely seven years represents a challenge not just from the point of view of finance, but also from the point of view of project management and procurement. Power plants utilising primarily gas as fuel – in so-called combined cycles or in simple gas turbines – are the easiest and cheapest to build, making them an obvious choice. As gas is much more expensive to transport than oil, netback returns on exported liquefied natural gas (LNG) are many times lower than for oil. It is rational for the GCC countries – as indeed for all oil producers – to devote gas to domestic uses and maximise the share of oil production which is available for export, a policy pursued by most countries.

However, gas is in short supply in most GCC countries. The only country that enjoys an absolute abundance of gas is Qatar, and it has declared a moratorium on new projects at least until 2012. The pressure to burn crude oil in local power plants is increasing.

In the past the GCC countries enjoyed excess production capacity for oil and gas. One could therefore argue with reason that the cost of producing one marginal barrel to be burned in a power plant was close to nil. It was, therefore, logical and justified to provide fuel to power plants at very low cost, allowing for the generation of very cheap electricity.

But conditions have changed. Since 2004, the GCC countries have been producing at a level close to capacity. The recent global crisis has again created a margin of unutilised capacity, but this is not expected to last for long. Therefore the marginal barrel sent to a power plant has a very real opportunity cost: creating the additional capacity to produce that marginal barrel requires substantial investment in projects whose cost has greatly increased. The same marginal barrel could be sold on the international markets and yield a substantially higher return than if sold to domestic power producers.

In the light of the above, one can understand that the GCC countries are showing increasing interest in other primary sources for power generation, notably renewable sources and nuclear energy.

Climate change and renewable sources of energy

The position of the GCC countries with respect to global environmental issues and alternative sources of energy has evolved considerably in recent years. Throughout the 1990s, when global demand was still short of global production capacity, and some of the latter had to be shut down, calls to contain emissions and the use of fossil fuel were viewed as a ruse by the industrial countries to undermine the future of OPEC. Today this is no longer the case; a genuine appreciation of the danger and the disastrous potential consequences of climate change, coupled with the wish not to increase much further oil production and investment in additional capacity, have opened the door for a substantial change in the rhetoric. All GCC member countries signed and ratified the Kyoto Protocol in 2005 or 2006.

In recent times the Saudi Minister of Petroleum and Mineral Resources, Ali Al-Naimi, has repeatedly spoken in favour of alternative sources of energy, and of Saudi Arabia as a future solar power research hub and potential exporter of electricity. He has also shown himself enthusiastic about the potential of energy efficiency research, new fuels, and carbon capture technologies.

Solar and other alternative energy sources figure prominently in the research agenda of such Saudi institutions as the King Abdulaziz City for Science and Technology and the King Abdullah University for Science and Technology, while national oil champion Saudi Aramco is interested in carbon capture and sequestration.

In 2006, Abu Dhabi launched the Masdar Initiative, presented as 'a bold and historic decision to embrace renewable and sustainable energy technologies'. Masdar has initiated the Masdar City project, which intends to create a carbon emissions-free community (see below). Other GCC countries have also initiated smaller renewable energy projects in recent years.

Renewable sources of energy

The Gulf countries enjoy a clear advantage for the development of one key renewable source of energy: solar. The average annual solar radiation falling on the Arabian Peninsula is about 2200 kWh (th)/m^2, and the vast expanses of uninhabited land offer potential for building large facilities. The region enjoys 40 per cent more sun than Spain.

Interest in solar energy has existed for decades. In Saudi Arabia the King Abdulaziz City for Science and Technology (KACST) has engaged in solar energy research since its establishment in 1977, and has initiated several new international partnerships in the last three years.

In Abu Dhabi, research in the field of solar energy is again led by Masdar. It has invested in several large ventures to produce photovoltaic panels, has provided capital for several plants based on photovoltaic technology and is pursuing research in thermal solar energy based on concentrators (mirrors) of various shapes.

Smaller solar energy initiatives are pursued in the rest of the GCC.[3] However, costs are still high and even the scale of the largest projects in Abu Dhabi is smaller than that of large conventional power plants. Actual progress in the direction of implementing major solar energy projects will be conditional on further decreases in the cost of equipment. The Gulf countries are pragmatically leveraging their financial resources to engage in international scientific cooperation and 'import' the best available technology. Their approach is very long term, hoping their geographic advantages will allow solar to break even in the Gulf earlier than elsewhere.

Nuclear energy

The other possible means by which the GCC countries could diversify power generation away from exclusive dependence on oil and gas – and relatively faster than through solar technology – is nuclear energy. The mid-term potential for significant diversification based on renewable sources is insufficient to solve the sustainability issue for the GCC countries – indeed, the same is true at the global level. A nuclear energy component is therefore probably a necessary ingredient to achieve sustainability.

In the international context, the GCC countries happen to be very favourably positioned to develop quickly a nuclear power generation component while at the same time actively pursuing the adoption of CCS technologies to contain their carbon emissions.

For most countries, the main drawback of nuclear energy is the high initial investment requirement. In most cases, utilities are short of investment funds and must rely heavily on debt or other outside financing. The GCC countries, by contrast, have large liquid balances which might grow further in the mid-term.

The GCC countries will obviously continue to engage in international investment, but it is already clear that this strategy has risks and limitations. This means that the opportunity discount rate for GCC official investment is very low or even negative. Rational behaviour in these conditions would tend to favour domestic investment – where risks are much reduced – and capital-intensive projects. Nuclear power plants conform to the desired profile very well, as they cater to an essential need and are especially competitive if the cost of capital is low.

In fact, the development of nuclear energy should be viewed not purely from the point of view of rational financial placement, but also from the point of view of the strategy for longer-term economic and political sustainability. The long-term survival of the GCC countries requires a sustainable source of energy: this is true of all countries, but even more so of countries whose climate complicates human residence and working conditions. Water desalination requirements are the most obvious aspect of vulnerability and potential non-sustainability of the Gulf economies. If water desalination were to become insufficient or interrupted, living conditions in most GCC metropolises would quickly become unbearable. Finding a reliable and sustainable solution for water desalination is therefore an essential aspect of GCC security and sustainability.

At the same time nuclear energy may also be developed to become complementary to fossil fuel production and optimal resource utilisation. Nuclear energy may progressively substitute for fossil fuels in all stationary uses requiring heat, including for enhancing oil recovery (steam injection), in petroleum refining and in the production of petrochemicals. In this way, the use of scarce fossil fuels can increasingly be concentrated where they are not substitutable or are substitutable only with greater difficulty – that is in transportation and as petrochemical feedstock.

It should be noted that the GCC countries, unlike many other emerging countries, have consistently built their development model on strong global integration and reliance on external sources of technology, know-how and manpower. They never had the ambition of technological autonomy that other large developing countries harboured, instead focusing on managing the absorption of foreign technology and manpower.

This approach has been spectacularly successful in many areas, and is especially important in judging the prospects for nuclear energy development. In essence, it is certain that nuclear energy know-how will be imported lock, stock and barrel: this includes copying all required national and international legislation and regulation, including reliance on foreign experts for their implementation.

Along these lines, the GCC countries have initiated close cooperation with the International Atomic Energy Agency (IAEA) in Vienna. This is the main dimension of the collective GCC nuclear initiative, while at the bilateral level several cooperation agreements with other governments have been signed.

It is unfortunate that the Gulf countries' interest in nuclear energy is frequently interpreted as little more than a cover for – sooner or later – establishing a military capability. In reality, the GCC interest in nuclear energy also has the potential of offering to the region and the world a model of civilian nuclear development which is accompanied by guarantees of non-proliferation.

The rational use of energy

Technocrats in the ministries and companies in charge of electricity supply are well aware of the issue of energy wastage, but implementing the rationalisation of consumption requires the convergence of a very large number of independent decision-makers and necessarily becomes political.

We mentioned at the outset that residential consumption is the main component of total electricity demand. Individual consumers respond primarily to prices, which range from zero for nationals in Qatar to levels that are believed to make a difference for the consumer in Saudi Arabia, but are in any case well below international norms.

Initiatives are under way to introduce green labelling and to encourage consumers to buy more energy-efficient products. Saudi Arabia has introduced labels to distinguish more efficient equipment (Figure 11.6 reproduces a label used for washing machines), and it is possible that the more affluent and environmentally conscious consumers may respond to such information. However, the vast majority of the Saudi population is not in a position to engage in such luxury and will simply go for the cheapest product that does the job.

FIGURE 11.6 Saudi washing machine label

In this respect, the issue of the rational use of energy is an important indicator, as it is one of the many manifestations of the inevitable trade-off between quality and price in development strategy. Improving energy efficiency requires a modification of building codes to encourage greater insulation and higher quality of dwellings, inevitably increasing the cost of housing. If the increase in cost were also to encourage a decrease in the standard size of homes, the energy benefit might be further increased. As we shall argue below, this probably runs counter to the ingrained preferences of the vast majority of the public.

Carbon capture and sequestration

Against the background of large capital resources and a tradition of large-scale project investment, it should be noted that the Gulf oil producers are also favourably positioned to make systematic use of carbon capture and sequestration: important carbon emission sources in their territories are concentrated (oil refineries, petrochemical, steel and cement plants, power generation, often concentrated in 'industrial cities'). At the same time, CO_2 injection can be used as an enhanced oil recovery method in oil and gas fields, in turn liberating more associated gas for other uses. They have much to gain out of international schemes promoting CCS, for example through a form of revamped or extended Clean Development Mechanism.

CCS has emerged as a necessary component of any global strategy aiming at reducing global emissions and stabilising the CO_2 content in the atmosphere. CCS costs depend on the technology to separate the CO_2 (the capture) and on the availability of adequate geological formations for sequestration. The latter may be close to or distant from the point of emission, and the cost of gathering CO_2 from several scattered sources and transporting it to the sequestration site adds to the total.

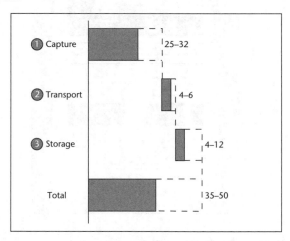

FIGURE 11.7 Total cost of early commercial project – € per ton of CO_2 abated

Source: McKinsey (2008).

The main cost component is the capture stage (Figure 11.7). Retrofitting an existing power plant that was not conceived with CO_2 capture in mind is more expensive than building a new plant equipped for CO_2 capture. The main cost of capture in a new plant is the investment cost and the loss in efficiency.

In the presence of determined global policies to reduce GHG emissions, the GCC countries' position towards early adoption could be very favourable. In the Gulf countries, where significant new capacity is being built in power generation as well as in other energy-intensive and carbon-emitting industries, it would moreover be easier to implement carbon capture before burning the fossil fuel. This in essence entails separating the hydrogen from the carbon in a process called reformation, and then burning hydrogen, a process that only generates steam.

For the time being, only one CCS project is planned in the Arabian Peninsula, located in Abu Dhabi: the Hydrogen Power Abu Dhabi (HPAD) venture launched by Masdar and HydrogenEnergy10. It is expected that 1.7 million tonnes of CO_2 per year will be injected. This project could be the first industrial-scale installation of an integrated hydrogen power and CCS system. It will take natural gas from the grid and convert it to hydrogen and CO_2, using pre-combustion separation technology. The project requires a total capital investment (excluding CO_2 transportation and storage) of about US$2 billion.[4]

In Saudi Arabia, the King Abdullah University of Science and Technology (KAUST) is planning to invest funds in research into carbon capture in partnership with international universities.[5] Qatar has negotiated a partnership with London's Imperial College that involves Qatar Petroleum, the Qatar Science and Technology Park and Shell in a ten-year, $70 million research project on new CO_2 storage technologies that can be applied in Qatar. In November 2007, Gulf OPEC members have collectively pledged $750 million to fund research on clean technologies, focusing especially on carbon capture and storage in order to fight global warming.

Concluding remarks

The GCC electricity crisis is one of the major development challenges to which the region needs to respond in the coming decades, and is a fundamental dimension of the search for sustainability of the GCC economies. The GCC countries will need to reduce their reliance on fossil fuels and are aggressively exploring the potential of renewable sources, primarily solar, as well as nuclear energy. By increasing their reliance on these alternatives, they may well persist in the pattern of economic diversification based on the expansion of energy-intensive industrial transformations. Their relative specialisation in these industries may be supported by their favourable position for engaging in CO_2 capture and sequestration. In a scenario of global consensus towards reducing GHG emissions and stabilising CO_2 in the atmosphere, the GCC countries may emerge as significant providers of energy-intensive products to the rest of the world.

Today, the bulk of electricity is consumed in the residential rather than the industrial sector. Curbing the wasteful private habits of energy consumption is a clear technocratic priority but may represent more of a political challenge for the GCC countries. It should be viewed in the broader context of the need for the political leadership to find a new point of equilibrium in the trade-off between quality and cost, in which greater priority might be given to the former, even if to the detriment of short-term competitiveness and growth.

The political and institutional context

Although many technological and managerial intricacies still need to be sorted out, the broad economic rationale for pursuing sustainability policies in the GCC is clear. The new initiatives have been announced so rapidly and in such close succession, however, that further considerations must have been driving Gulf leaders. The following section of the chapter addresses the political motivations and the institutional framing of the new sustainability policies, and assesses their organisational and regulatory feasibility against this background.

The 'branding' of GCC states as technology leaders

One significant impetus for many of the recent high-profile project announcements in the Gulf has arguably been to recast the image of the GCC states on the international stage. Rhetoric and the scale of undertakings reflect a desire to 'brand' the Gulf monarchies as global leaders in new technology sectors and, more broadly, as responsible members of the international community. This would be difficult to deduce from energy-related policies alone, but there are ambitious projects in other policy fields – cultural endowments and museums, universities, internationally oriented charities and so on – which have recently been promoted in a very similar fashion. The motley ensemble of initiatives has one clear common denominator: the ambition to be taken seriously on the international stage.

Qatar and Abu Dhabi in particular – two late developers even by Gulf standards – are trying to style themselves as technological and cultural leaders. Abu Dhabi campaigned vigorously to attract the headquarters of the newly established International Renewable Energy Agency (IRENA) to Masdar City, and saw its bid accepted in June 2009 – a first sign that its international ambitions are being taken seriously.

GCC states' appropriation of the sustainability discourse as well as their integration into international regimes will bring them closer to Western powers, and nuclear cooperation in particular also provides an element of insurance in that it increases the West's stake in protecting local partner regimes. It seems no coincidence that Abu Dhabi has been deepening nuclear and military cooperation with France at the same time.

The large fiscal surpluses since 2003 have given the young ruling elites especially of the smaller GCC countries large-scale autonomy for institutional and technological experiments, and have awoken new ambitions of international leadership. Players with small populations like Abu Dhabi and Qatar retain considerable resources for new ventures. Large, state-supported projects are by and large fiscally protected, and with the project finance market having unfrozen after the recent crisis, state-owned companies are forging ahead.

It should be pointed out that the ambition to diversify into sustainable energy can build on a stronger competitive advantage and institutional track record than many of the other 'branding' policies mentioned above: the new technology sectors will dovetail with existing industrial structures in the Gulf, and in many cases will be managed by large public organisations with deep experience in project management. Moreover, some of the largest enterprises in the Gulf, both private and public, have managed to establish themselves as regional and even global exporters of specialised services, such as telecoms, logistics or upstream energy. It is conceivable that a similar structure could be built up in sustainable energy technologies.

The institutional setting: who is in charge?

It is the institutional structures in which new projects will be embedded to which we now turn. The first thing that needs to be pointed out is that most of the successful large state enterprises in the Gulf are under the direct patronage of the ruling elite, and hence are shielded from much of the political interference and rent-seeking that happens in other sectors.

Ever since the first oil boom, GCC rulers have tended to delegate complex policy tasks in high-priority sectors to selected technocratic clients who enjoyed special access to them and could cut through much of the sluggish national bureaucracy. On this basis, the Gulf has witnessed a successful pattern of project-based and sector-specific development since the 1970s, be it the roll-out of national infrastructures in the 1970s and 1980s, the regulation of fledgling financial sectors in Bahrain or Saudi Arabia, or the creation of a competitive heavy industry sector in Saudi Arabia and, to a lesser extent, Qatar and Abu Dhabi. GCC elites have been very effective at using international expertise in the process.[6]

With the new boom, a new window of opportunity for institutional engineering and the creation of 'pockets of efficiency' has opened. Many, but not all, of the recently announced sustainability policies will be implemented on a project basis that is quite similar to the large projects that the existing enclaves of efficiency have been operating during the last decades. Technocrats tend to have long planning horizons, even more so in the electricity sector than in the upstream oil sector.

Once established, islands of efficiency have been quite stable in the GCC. Together with the GCC's above-mentioned openness to foreign technical assistance, the institutional setting seems to be highly amenable to large-scale sustainable energy projects with long planning horizons, be they nuclear, solar or CCS.

Conditions for the emergence of islands of efficiency in the past

In the past, a number of conditions had to be fulfilled for pockets of efficiency to emerge:

- significant increments of state income over time allowing for institutional experimentation;
- regime autonomy from societal demands so that institutional decisions are made by a limited set of elite actors; and
- a non-populist development ideology that does not systematically subject economic and managerial decisions to distributional and nation-building considerations.

All the GCC states bar Kuwait – but very few other oil states – fulfilled these conditions during the oil boom from the early 1970s to the mid-1980s. It is in this period that most of the Gulf's impressive modern institutions were created. Even during lean times, however, existing islands of efficiency have continued to operate swiftly and coherently, increasing our confidence in the stable long-term management of new sustainable energy projects.

By contrast, the quality and coherence of the national bureaucracy at large has generally been limited, at least relative to other wealthy countries. Regulatory penetration of society, and the economy at large, has been partial at best, and non-project, non-enclave spending policies – public employment, pricing of public services and so on – have often followed political rather than economic rationales. This, as we shall see, limits the scope for more diffuse sustainability policies aimed at regulating social behaviour.

Sustainability policies as a new phase of enclave-oriented development?

The current fiscal surpluses have opened a new window of opportunity for institutional experiments. For the first time in twenty years, governments have returned to large-scale project spending (Figure 11.8).

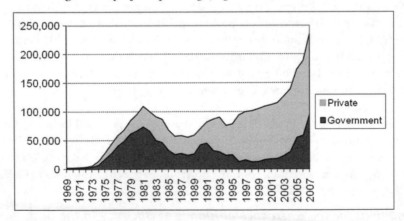

FIGURE 11.8 Saudi gross fixed capital formation (million SR)

Source: Saudi Arabian Monetary Agency.

At the same time, they have embarked on the creation of new state-owned enterprises and sectoral regulators, recruiting a new generation of young technocrats and importing high-quality foreign manpower and expertise on a scale last seen in the early 1980s. But there are important differences between countries, both in terms of institutional conditions and the specific nature of sustainable energy projects, which warrant a country-by-country discussion.

Institutional outlook, country by country

Abu Dhabi

The rulers of Abu Dhabi enjoy very high regime autonomy, thanks to large fiscal surpluses and a small local population that is easily bought off without demanding a say in national-level policy issues. Abu Dhabi is one of the Gulf countries with the fewest accoutrements of formal democracy and a high level of institutional stability. After the death of long-term ruler Shaikh Zayed in 2004, a new generation of leaders has avidly embarked on project-based modernisation.

The publicly owned Mubadala Development Company, set up in 2002, is the main promoter of Abu Dhabi's sustainability-related projects through its fully-owned subsidiary Abu Dhabi Future Energy Company or 'Masdar' (Arabic for 'source'), founded in 2006 (see above for its specific technology projects). The CEO of Mubadala, Khaldoon al Mubarak, is also the chairman of the Executive Affairs Authority of Abu Dhabi, serving the Abu Dhabi Executive Council, which is in turn chaired by Crown Prince Mohammed bin Zayed. The two leading figures in Masdar are Ahmed Ali Al Sayegh (chairman) and Sultan Al Jaber (CEO).

The Mubadala/Masdar leaders are long-term technocratic clients of Mohammed bin Zayed from the energy sector and have been selected for managerial prowess. Drawing on his existing pool of elite technocrats, the Crown Prince aims at building up another cluster of excellence. Mubarak in particular enjoys close access to him, and Masdar will be managed largely autonomously from the rest of Abu Dhabi's government. It appears well suited for managing capital-intensive, long-term projects.

Masdar's flagship project, Masdar City, is in fact also an enclave in geographical terms and will function completely differently and separately from the rest of the emirate. A city of 6.5 sq km, it is supposed to become a 'carbon-free' home to 90,000 people, focused on investment, research and development in sustainable energy.

Mubadala and Masdar have entered an untested field but their managerial structures are based on patterns that have been successful before. It is a typical enclave project, administered by trusted technocratic lieutenants with established track records and special access to the leadership, and who have proven their capacity in the management of national oil and electricity sectors.

Dubai

Historically, neighbouring Dubai has taken the lead over Abu Dhabi in terms of sectoral innovation and high-profile projects. Its leadership has been daring and highly autonomous from local society when it came to strategic project decisions. It does not, however, have the wherewithal seriously to engage in the GCC-wide competition for large-scale, sustainability-focused projects as it simply lacks the fiscal resources – especially after the recent economic crash which has made it dependent on Abu Dhabi.

Dubai could create an environment for smaller, private sector service companies catering to the environmental technology sector at large, in particular if domestic energy regulations in the GCC get stricter. It has itself recently made attempts to regulate business and consumer behaviour, for example by introducing LEED (Leadership in Energy and Environmental Design) building standards. Dubai's free-wheeling business environment has in the past not been very amenable to forceful regulatory intervention, however.

Saudi Arabia

Saudi Arabia is the prime candidate in the GCC to take technology leadership on the basis of resources and scale. It is the country whose bureaucracy at large scores worst by most accounts, and the government has been struggling to effectively regulate local business and consumer behaviour. The kingdom, however, is also a player with significant fiscal depth and, perhaps more importantly, the most impressive islands of efficiency, in the energy sector in particular. When it comes to the use of incremental oil surpluses, its leadership is autonomous from most interest groups which are weakly organised.

The most impressive of the Saudi institutions is Saudi Aramco, probably the most efficient and technologically autonomous national oil company in any OPEC country (Marcel 2006). It has managed to preserve the managerial structures of its foreign-owned predecessor Aramco, which was taken over by the Saudi government in 1980, and commands impressive in-house expertise and research capacities. It is largely autonomous from the rest of the state in both managerial and infrastructural terms. Its senior management enjoys good access to the leadership and oil minister Ali Al-Naimi, himself an Aramco man. Its planning horizons are long and its managerial ranks are stable and shielded from political intervention.

As mentioned above, Aramco has declared its interest in sustainable energy technology in recent years, including carbon capture, clean fuels and combustion engines, and solar energy. It has already started several research projects in this regard and is probably the Gulf player that can bring not only much capital but also the most expertise to international joint ventures. Aramco has recently been entrusted with managing the new, above-mentioned King Abdullah University of Science and Technology (KAUST) in the Western Province, endowed by the king with US$10 billion. KAUST stands a good chance of emerging as an Aramco-style island of meritocracy and could make Saudi Arabia the research and development leader on sustainable energy in the Gulf. Due to its size, Saudi Arabia has a much stronger national technocratic workforce than Abu Dhabi.

The Saudi electricity sector is regulated by a recently created body that has been spun off from the Ministry of Industry and Electricity, the Electricity and Cogeneration Regulation Authority. In its short history, it has managed to oversee the start-up of a number of successful private water and power projects with international involvement. It could also emerge as an effective regulator of the alternative energy sector.

Nuclear research in Saudi Arabia was until recently managed by the King Abdulaziz City for Sciences and Technology (KACST), which suffered more from budget cuts in the 1980s than Aramco or SABIC. In May 2010, however, the Saudi government announced a new technocratic enclave initiative, the King Abdullah City for Atomic and Renewable Energy, which is likely to be endowed with significant resources and managerial autonomy, setting the stage for a domestic nuclear industry.

Qatar

Qatar is another country enjoying both significant surpluses and large regime autonomy. It has a shorter history of technocratic enclave-building, but its leadership is willing to take risks and keen to augment its international profile. It is the first Gulf country to have created a dedicated Ministry of Environment, in June 2008, and it is trying to make research into sustainable energy part of its international brand.

In May 2007, Qatar Petroleum registered the first Gulf-based clean development mechanism project, an oilfield gas recovery and utilisation venture operated by Maersk Qatar Oil that will prevent flaring of natural gas at the Al-Shaheen field. In November 2008, a QIA-sponsored £250 million Qatari-British fund was created, dedicated to clean energy technologies and research. Again, international cooperation is encouraged and projects are outward-oriented.

Qatar's leadership clearly has the ambition of putting the country on the map as a technology leader. Its layer of national technocrats is very thin, however, and it is not clear whether Qatar Petroleum can operate on the same scale as Aramco or even ADNOC in Abu Dhabi.

Oman

Oman is another country with a largely autonomous leadership and also a reasonably well-functioning bureaucracy but its fiscal resources are limited. It will not lead in world-scale projects. It could operate in a number of niches, however; it has some experience with desalination driven by photovoltaic power. Its Electricity Regulation Authority has proposed an ambitious 750 MW solar plant project.

Kuwait and Bahrain

The one country which would have most of the resources required for large-scale sustainable energy projects but which has not seen any significant developments is Kuwait. The main reason for its sluggishness – like in many other economic policy fields – is primarily its parliament, which severely compromises the political autonomy of the leadership. Various groups in parliament have spent much energy on arranging free give-aways to the national population and on stalling any large, new state-financed projects. Parliament occasionally teams up with well-organised public sector unions in preventing bureaucratic streamlining and the creation of independent, efficient bodies.

In Bahrain, the government is somewhat more autonomous but still under much pressure to disburse funds to the population due to a very polarized and politically mobilised political scene. It is the one other Gulf country with a parliament that has at least some influence. Due to its dwindling oil resources, it is under stronger fiscal constraints. Neither Kuwait nor Bahrain will emerge as sustainable energy leaders in the region.

Institutional context: summary

In sum, political autonomy and the scale of rents are the main constraints on sustainability projects in the Gulf. These two factors influence both the scale of projects under way and their future prospects. The main players on the big projects thus far have been special para-statal bodies and state-owned enterprises outside the regular state apparatus, with direct links to the leadership as driving agents. Most of the projects have been outward-oriented, following the GCC's tradition of relative economic openness and technological cooperation with international partners.

Sustainable energy projects are driven by a small number of ambitious elite actors in a top-down fashion, with little resonance thus far in local society. While they are unlikely to have much impact on local consumers, they can also be managed more coherently and autonomously than policies in most other rentier states, thanks to long planning horizons and technocratic autonomy.

Enclaves and projects vs consumer regulation

Not all sustainability policies are project-based, however. Some are regulatory in nature: they cannot be administered on a project basis but require different types of state capacities. Influencing local consumption behaviour in particular requires more regulatory power and interaction with local business and society.

Given the levels of per capita energy consumption in the Gulf, this is not a marginal issue.

The jury is still out on the LEED initiative in Dubai and on Istidama, a comparable building standard initiative in Abu Dhabi. Several governments have either introduced or enhanced slab tariff systems, which charge higher rates for higher levels of household water and electricity consumption. GCC governments have also been working on energy-saving product and process standards and harsher sanctions for pollution. In many cases, however, they have to rely on rather weak ministries of commerce and industry or environmental regulators with a short and patchy track record.

Some consumer-related infrastructure can be managed on a project basis – for example, district cooling, which considerably lowers electricity use compared with conventional air conditioners. Similarly, public transport systems in larger conurbations, such as the Dubai Metro, can be managed on a project basis by specialised bodies.

Apart from these large-scale, infrastructure-related initiatives, however, influencing domestic consumption patterns will be difficult. Past attempts at broader-based regulation in terms of national taxation systems, enforcement of intellectual property rights, information-gathering through censuses and business surveys, residency registration or even just the enforcement of traffic rules have proven difficult and have met considerable resistance.

It has been much easier historically to build up efficient technocratic enclaves than to build up broad-based regulatory powers vis-à-vis societies which have been most of all distributional clients of the states. In some ways, one appears to be the result of the other: by clientelising and 'buying off' large chunks of society, regimes could create political space for autonomous technocratic institution-building in other fields. But the co-optation of society has come at a cost that is both fiscal and regulatory.

The GCC states' rentier nature makes price changes for utilities and petrol politically difficult. Reduced prices have traditionally been perceived as part of the ruling bargain and attempts to increase them have been repeatedly reversed. In a time when the governments are flush with cash but many nationals are struggling to adapt to rising prices and the socio-economic dislocations of the boom, significant increases in electricity or water tariffs appear unlikely. Only in April 2006, King Abdullah of Saudi Arabia significantly decreased domestic petroleum prices in Saudi Arabia to allow the population to partake in the boom and ease the strains of inflation (Figure 11.9). Recent revisions of electricity tariffs spared residential consumers.

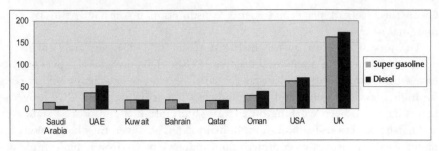

FIGURE 11.9 Fuel prices (2006) (US$ cent/litre; source: GTZ)

Source: GTZ (at time of citation – as of 2011 part of CIZ – Deutsche Gesellschaft für Internationale Zusamm-enarbeit).

Such problems are less relevant for sheikhdoms with a small national population such as Abu Dhabi and Qatar. The larger population and more diffuse business activities of Saudi Arabia, by contrast, make local consumption patterns more important for both the country's ecological footprints.

Sustainability initiatives hence are likely to have limited impact on the outlook of local society and business. As far as regulatory change having an impact on consumer behaviour, most of the sustainable technology in consumer durables, housing, etc. will continue to be imported, with the partial exception only of building materials. Similarly, the spillover from new research units and universities to business and society at large is likely to be limited, as most of their output will not find local takers outside the large joint ventures and state-owned enterprises mentioned above.

Conclusion and outlook

In many ways, the current boom is giving back to GCC states the economic and developmental leadership they had to some degree lost after the 1980s. Sustainable energy is one of the niches in which the Gulf countries could attain real competitive advantage, based on a sound rationale of local energy conservation and use of its geo-economic position.

Prospects for a wide-reaching adoption of sustainability standards in society and the private sector are dim, but prospects for enclave-based, project-focused initiatives are much better. This is due to the favourable institutional and fiscal environment in at least three of the GCC states, and due to the substantial interest of nuclear power companies as well as international energy companies in partnering with national oil companies and host governments. Significant parts of local elites seem seriously committed to establishing the Gulf as an exporter of technology and of carbon certificates.

Many technological and economic questions are still to be answered – but if solar energy and CCS are feasible under the geological and geographical conditions of the Gulf, they are likely to be implemented successfully.

Notes

1. A fuller, if less up to date version of this research has been published as an LSE Kuwait Program working paper – see http://www.lse.ac.uk/collections/LSEKP/energyandsustainability.htm (accessed 11 August 2011).
2. APICORP Research (2010) *Economic Commentary*, 5(10–11).
3. For a detailed analysis of these initiatives see EPU-NTUA (2009).
4. Hydrogen Energy, available at: http://www.hydrogenenergy.com (accessed 11 August 2011).
5. Cornell University, available at: http://www.research.cornell.edu/VPR/KAUST-Cornell/index.html (accessed 11 August 2011).
6. This argument is developed at much greater length in Hertog (2010).

References

Al-Ibrahim, A. (2009) *Energy Efficiency Activities in the Kingdom of Saudi Arabia*. Presentation to the GRC/EPU-NTUA/CEPS workshop on 'Enhancing the EU-GCC Relations within a New Climate Regime: Prospects and Opportunities for Cooperation', Brussels, 26 February.

EPU-NTUA (2009) 'Background Paper to the Workshop on Enhancing the EU-GCC Relations within a New Climate Regime: Prospects and Opportunities for Cooperation', Brussels, unpublished report.

Hertog, S. (2010) *Princes, Brokers, Bureaucrats: Oil and State in Saudi Arabia*. Ithaca, NY: Cornell University Press.

JICA (2008) 'The Master Plan Study for Energy Conservation in the Power Sector in the Kingdom of Saudi Arabia', draft final report.

McKinsey & Co. (2008) *Carbon Capture and Storage: Assessing the Economics*. McKinsey Climate Change Initiative.

Marcel, V. (2006) *Oil Titans: National Oil Companies in the Middle East*. Washington, DC: Chatham House and Brookings Institution.

PART 3

Internationalisation of the Gulf

Security and foreign policy

12

SECURITY AND STRATEGIC TRENDS IN THE MIDDLE EAST

Anoushiravan Ehteshami

Introduction

The Middle East continues to be one of the most volatile and dynamic regions of the world. Beyond the dramatic impact of developments after 9/11 on the region's security, the Middle East has in recent years acquired a further strategic edge as demand for its hydrocarbon resources has soared. The substantial growth in this demand has followed the rapid globalisation of China and India, and sustained growth in the other pivotal regional economies (such as Brazil, South Africa and the East Asia tigers). Despite the dramatic downturn in the global economy following the 2008/9 financial crisis demand for hydrocarbons rebounded very rapidly, enabling the most resilient oil states (such as Saudi Arabia, Kuwait, Libya, the UAE, Qatar) to bounce back. The global financial crisis left its mark on many Middle East economies, but it also provided some with the opportunity to accumulate Western assets at bargain prices, and indeed also brought unexpected prominence for Saudi Arabia. The Kingdom became the first Middle Eastern country to join the high table of global power, as its membership of the G20 community of states also confirmed its position as the region's leading economy.

Regional volatility though has continued to contribute to the worsening of the security dynamics of the Middle East, and (state-led and non-state-driven) violence and rapid re-militarisation of the region since the end of the 1990s have deepened the sense of insecurity across the area (Ehteshami 2006). Not surprising then that defence and wider security expenditures in the Middle East and North Africa continue to stay above global averages, capturing around 5 per cent of the region's GDP in 2008, nearly double the global average of 2.56 per cent. Saudi Arabia ($38.2 billion), Israel ($14.8 billion), the UAE ($13.7 billion), Iran ($9.6 billion), Kuwait ($6.8 billion), Algeria ($5.1 billion) and Egypt ($4.6 billion) account for some 80 per cent of the region's defence expenditure. And in the UAE, Kuwait, Qatar, Israel, Saudi Arabia and Oman defence expenditure is above $1,200 per capita (IISS 2010). Six of the world's top ten weapons importers in 2008 were in the Middle East, with Saudi Arabia and the UAE leading the field by a significant margin.

Moreover, new security problems have emerged to add more complexity to an already unstable environment. One of the region's major players, Iran, has striven in a concerted effort since the early 2000s to make significant advances in the development of its indigenous nuclear power programme, which has placed it in the eye of the security storm threatening to engulf the Middle East. Iran's extensive nuclear programme, which came to light in 2002, emerged at the height of the Iraq security crisis, merely added to the dynamics of insecurity gripping the region. Iran's nuclear programme, moreover, compounded regional insecurity at the inter-state level as at the same time Tehran increasingly was finding itself ever closer to the heartland of the Arab region. Simultaneously, geopolitical developments on Iran's western border in neighbouring Iraq magnified Iran's new regional role and increased the sense of fear gripping the Arab region. Iraq, formerly the 'eastern gateway of the Arab world' with a pre-eminent role in Arab politics, saw its influence and geopolitical weight shrink after regime change in 2003, and the ensuing imbalance of power between these neighbours transformed the power dynamics of the Persian Gulf sub-region in the first instance and the Middle East more broadly as the Sunni dominance of Iraq ended with the defeat of the Baath regime in that country (Wehrey et al. 2010).

In the longer term, problems associated with demography (and a growing 'youth bulge'), unemployment and underemployment, uneven distribution of limited resources, environmental degradation and limited access to natural and strategic resources such as water and food, and the vulnerability of the Middle Eastern countries to the post-oil order (either through reduced demand for their oil or due to the depletion of their oil production capacity) will become increasingly important to the mapping of the Middle East's security and strategic trends. For now, however, this overview draws on the broader macro-level trends, as it sets about analysing the security and strategic environment of the Middle East.

A restructured regional power balance

The Middle East's power relations have been fluid for well over half a century, as exemplified by the failure of the Baghdad Pact to put in place a sustainable Middle East regional security structure capable of containing the fragmentation of the region or to prevent its penetration by the Soviet Union. The Soviets, as we know, entered the region through the side door while the Baghdad Pact was still embryonic, and in the aftermath of Egypt's Free Officers coup in 1952 proceeded to establish a series of regional relationships with some of the core Arab states – namely Egypt, Iraq, Syria and South Yemen (and also with Algeria, Libya and the Sudan). The 'Arab cold war' between the pro-Western and populist–nationalist regimes which ensued provided the main strategic backdrop to the region's landscape until the early 1970s and the rise of the Arab oil monarchies. The Arab cold war as a strategic fault-line of the region was only diluted at the end of the 1973 Arab–Israeli war as Arab poles slowly converged, but it did not disappear fully. Indeed, it was only superseded by the geopolitical reality of the withdrawal of the British forces 'east of Suez', which threw into confusion the West's principal security structure in the region and opened the first deep chasm in the security dynamics of the Persian Gulf sub-region.

The pace of change dramatically increased, moreover, in the aftermath of the 1979 Iranian revolution and the Camp David Egypt–Israel peace agreement. The polarisation and rapid fragmentation of the Arab region began anew as the Arab states divided again between a club of Camp David rejectionists and the West's allies who censured Egypt but did not join the rejectionist camp led by Syria and Iraq. But despite the centrifugal impact of Egypt's unilateral peace with Israel, it was Iraq's policies and actions which did most damage to the integrity of the Arab order in the 1980s and 1990s. It did so twice within ten years and in succession. The first was in 1980 when it invaded Iran: the unnecessary war which followed lasted for eight years sapping Arab political, diplomatic and financial energies. The end of the war in 1988 was followed by Iraq's occupation and annexation of Kuwait in August 1990. The latter act caused the most damage to an already fragile Arab order, for this was the first act of blatant aggression against another Arab state. It thus intensified fragmentation and deepened the tendency for uneven distribution of power in the region.

The pattern of fragmentation had indeed been established by Egypt's unilateral peace treaty with Israel in 1979, after having led a number of Arab military campaigns against the Jewish state since 1948. Iraq's two wars with two of its immediate neighbours exacerbated the fragmentation and the occupation of a fellow Arab neighbour in 1990 added to the Arab region's rapid polarisation. With Iraq thus weakened and under international sanctions between 1990 and 2003 other players grew in prominence. Israel, Iran, Egypt and Syria (in different ways and to different degrees) all gained from the demise of Iraq as a powerful military force in the area. But it was not until after the early twenty-first century that new power lines were firmly drawn. It is in fact arguable that with the fall of Baghdad in early April 2003 a new and totally different power dynamics has appeared in the region, giving birth to a new 'Middle East cold war' which has pitted non-Arab Iran against a coalition of pro-Western Arab states and also Israel. Observers have characterized the new cold war thus:

> On one side of this divide are those states willing to work in various forms of strategic partnership with the United States, with an implied acceptance of American hegemony over the region. This camp includes Israel, those Arab states that have made peace with Israel (Egypt and Jordan), and other so-called moderate Arab states (e.g., Saudi Arabia and the rest of the Gulf Cooperation Council). On the other side of this divide are those Middle Eastern states and non-state actors that are unwilling to legitimize American (and, some in this camp would say, Israeli) hegemony over the region. The Islamic Republic of Iran has emerged in recent years

as the *de facto* leader of this camp, which also includes Syria and prominent non-state actors such as HAMAS and Hizballah.

(Leverett and Leverett 2009)

Although power may be more diffuse today than it was in the 1960s and 1970s, with some smaller countries exercising a greater role than before, nevertheless the tendency for the key actors to shape the region's strategic map has never been more evident. It is this new dynamic which is of increasing importance.

Of equal importance is the role and nature of the major regional players as each competes for a greater regional role. Iran and Israel can be said to be the prominent actors today in terms of having a clear mission in their role conception and in possession of the necessary drive to achieve their objectives. These states are accompanied by Saudi Arabia, Turkey, Syria and to a significantly lesser extent Egypt. Each of the three Arab actors has definable roles, but at the same time they have to adjust to a new dynamic between them. While in the 1990s one could see the beginnings of a tripartite relationship emerging between these three Arab states, since 2003 it has been the rise of Saudi Arabia's influence against Syria's and Egypt's weakened position that is extraordinarily significant. Syria and Egypt remain critical players in the Arab–Israeli theatre, of course, and the former's role is also important in the context of the conflict in Iraq. But the ways in which Saudi Arabia has emerged with a clear voice and presence across the Middle East theatres – the Gulf, the Arab–Israeli arena, east Africa and the Red Sea, Afghanistan and Pakistan – is strategically significant. It is tempting to view its position as that of 'first among equals' in the Arab order, which in turn has raised its prominence in the conflict borderlands of the region. Although the Kingdom's population base, military strength, problems of religious militancy at home and exposure to oil price fluctuations continue to make it vulnerable, its huge oil wealth and steady capital accumulation, coupled with its successful global diplomacy (joining the G-20 and forging links with China, India, the European Union, Turkey, and of course keeping its traditional US ties strong after a blip in 2001/2) highlight its ambition of trying to manage the many, often competing, Arab agendas. Thus, with regard to Lebanon, Palestine and Palestinian groups, the wider Arab–Israeli peace process, Gulf Arab responses to Iraq's transformation and Iran's strategic challenge, Riyadh's diplomatic presence has become a real force to reckon with. The Kingdom is now perceived as a real regional player, a proactive and sure-footed Arab power of the twenty-first century.

A further significance of this new reality is to be found in Saudi Arabia's prominence in the Gulf sub-region's delicate power relations. The growth of the Gulf sub-region (or Gulf security sub-complex) is in itself a feature of the further sub-regionalisation of the Arab world (Buzan and Waever 2003). This sub-region, however, is not an entirely Arab one, placing the Gulf Cooperation Council countries and also Iran and Iraq as direct players, and Afghanistan, Pakistan and Yemen as extended members of the sub-region. Pakistan and

Yemen in particular represent serious security challenges for the sub-region and affect Gulf politics in a direct way. Both Pakistan and Yemen are weak centrally, and, in both, radical transnational Islamist groups are taking root.

Indeed, as the deteriorating security situation in Yemen in 2009 demonstrated, the new unstable strategic environment has lowered the threshold for confrontation between the key regional actors. During the escalation of the al-Houthi tribal-confessional rebellion in Yemen, Saudi Arabia and Iran were compelled to intervene. Riyadh mobilised its substantial military power and used its armed forces in anger for the first time since their deployment for the liberation of Kuwait in 1991 as it rushed to secure its border with Yemen and to shore up the Yemeni government. Iran on the other hand proceeded to provide political, financial and moral support for the Shia al-Houthis in what it characterised as a direct attack on the minority Shia communities of Yemen. Such incidents can easily darken relations between the region's competing powers while also easily eroding the stability of the GCC group of states on whose oil and financial reserves so much of the international system relies.

An additional associated danger is such ailing states as Yemen or Pakistan becoming host to the returning insurgents from the war in Iraq. Iraq itself, of course, is another interesting challenge, for its demise as a prominent Arab state could undermine efforts to stabilise the Middle East region after US disengagement post-2011. Yet the success of its alternative (and inclusive and transparent) political format – alternative that is to its neighbouring Arab countries and also to Iran – can pose a different challenge: that of legitimacy.

Iran, on the other hand, poses a potent state-level challenge to the status quo as it grows into an independent regional power not beholden to others. As an independent regional power it is often assumed that it can absorb external pressures placed upon it, though of course this conventional wisdom remains to be tested. For the United States, Iran has remained an adversary and is said to be a 'grave threat' were it to acquire a nuclear weapons capability, according to President Obama. For the Arab states, Iran is a 'challenge' that should be dealt with collectively, according to Saudi Foreign Minister Prince Saud Al-Faisal.[1] From the Israeli perspective, Iran poses a grave existential threat. A nuclear-armed Iran would drastically shift the regional balance of power in Tehran's favour, fuel a new and deadly regional arms race and thus leave Israel more vulnerable as Israel's Arab neighbours scramble to develop their own nuclear deterrence. Israel's nuclear monopoly would thus end in a cascade of proliferation that would spread from Tehran's acquisition of a nuclear weapons capability. Iran then poses a direct and an indirect challenge to Israel's regional supremacy.

New power relationships have ensued, therefore, following regime change in Iraq and as a consequence of direct military intervention in the region. Not only have relationships become more securitised, but they are also sharper edged and confrontational. The fragmentation of the Arab world has also encouraged the emergence of different kinds of poles in the region, ensuring a greater presence for the three non-Arab regional players of Iran, Israel and Turkey.

Economic interdependence and the strategic significance of hydrocarbons

Both directly and indirectly, oil exports have provided the backbone of the region's economies since the 1960s. But it was in the 1970s that oil income became the driver of the Middle East's political economy. Multi-digit increases in oil income from 1973 onwards provided the new engine for growth in the region. To put this in perspective, OPEC members' value of exports increased from $17.3 billion in 1970 to $41.3 billion in 1973. It rose to $149.2 billion four years later and on the eve of the Iran–Iraq war in 1980 jumped to $292.6 billion. Saudi Arabia's income increased from a modest $2.4 billion in 1970 to $101.6 billion just ten years later, for instance, and that of Kuwait, Qatar and the UAE combined rose from $2.4 billion in 1970 to $48 billion (OPEC). These were staggering sums for these young states to manage, and as they grappled to utilise their new found wealth for productive purposes they began weaving a complex set of interdependencies with their neighbours and also the wider international system which survive to this day.

Oil income, thus, was established as the dominant driver of change, and global dependence on oil secured the central place of hydrocarbons in the world's relationship with the Middle East and North Africa (MENA) oil states. A strategic relationship was established between the two, and the intricate interdependencies which emerged have tied the economic fortunes of the Middle East oil states to the stability of the international system – and vice versa. Regionally, too, through remittances, aid, development assistance and investment, other countries have become dependent on the health and also the strategic priorities of a small number of capital-surplus oil states.

Nothing since the end of the Cold War has changed these relationships. To underline the importance of this, Ali bin Ibrahim al-Naimi (Saudi Arabia's Minister of Petroleum and Mineral Resources) noted in May 2010 that 'We do enjoy great international importance considering the oil and gas reserves we own. In 2008, the Arab region accounted for about 58% of the total global oil reserves and 30% of natural gas reserves.'[2] Not surprisingly, in the aftermath of the Iraq war, oil geopolitics again occupied the centre stage of international politics.

As was the case in the 1970s, developments post-2003 proved to be a bounty for the Middle East oil states. As oil prices rose from a low of $28 per barrel in September 2003 to the spot market price of over $150 per barrel in July 2008 so did their income.[3] Egypt, Sudan, Syria and even Yemen were all beneficiaries, as indeed have been Algeria and Libya, the traditional oil states of North Africa. But in practical terms, it has been the GCC states which have enjoyed a spectacular windfall. In the boom years the Middle East's total income from oil exports had risen to a staggering $2.4 trillion, with the Gulf states' share of this bounty standing at close to $2 trillion. In excess of $600 billion of these sums have been invested abroad, thus directly greasing the wheels of the international economy. Indeed, in 2009, the GCC's gross foreign assets stood at $1.47 trillion, over 100 per cent of their GDP, and in 2010 their current account surplus was around $120 billion. The region's fiscal revenues from oil and gas thus will exceed $5.6 trillion cumulatively during 2008–13 if prices hold firm above $70 per barrel. Capital transfer of such magnitude has generated three strategic realities. First, the GCC countries have now emerged as major regional investors in their own right, ploughing petrodollars into other Middle Eastern economies (Burke and Bazoobandi 2010). From Morocco to Pakistan, GCC private and state investors are now significant players, providing badly needed job opportunities and extra sources for financing overstretched budgets. As a consequence, the stake of the regional host countries in the stability of the Gulf oil monarchies has also increased.

Second, the rapid injection of petrodollars has facilitated the growth of the GCC states' sovereign wealth funds as an effective arm of their 'soft power'. According to one estimate, the Gulf Arab sovereign wealth funds hold well over $1 trillion in cash and assets (Behrendt 2008). Since September 2008 we have seen these countries flex their financial muscles in the international system through sovereign wealth funds (SWFs). They have emerged as key providers of badly needed cash for Western banks and finance houses. With these SWFs has come influence and with that has also come the recognition that these countries' stability is an essential plank in today's integrated economic networks. Their stability and economic and political health is now of paramount importance to the well-being of the international system.

Thirdly, as noted earlier, high oil prices and rising Asian demand have led to the emergence of new strategic partnerships across Asia. The boom also deepened their emerging energy and economic partnerships with other Asian countries (Malony 2009). Japan, South Korea and Taiwan (Asia's main Gulf oil importers of the 1970s and 1980s) have been joined this century by China, India, Malaysia, Thailand and others. China and India ('Chindia') have indeed become large oil importers in their own right in a relatively short period of time, consuming over 11 million barrels of oil per day in 2009, and as a consequence becoming increasingly dependent on Gulf oil supplies. These energy-driven partnerships also have a sharp geopolitical dimension to them, increasing the vulnerability of Asian oil consumers to the stability of the Gulf sub-region and that of its largest oil states in particular. In this new environment, Iran, Iraq, Kuwait, Saudi Arabia, Qatar (for LNG) and the UAE (Abu Dhabi in particular) are all developing strong partnerships with a whole host of Asian countries. The pattern for Iran in particular is a gradual 'easternisation' of its orientation, and for the others growing partnerships with Asian countries alongside, and even in preference to, their traditional Western alliances.

With petrodollar success in international terms have come some serious pressures too: rising inflation, demands for higher wages and state subsidies for basic consumables, pressures on the routine business of government machinery, bottlenecks in supply chains, citizen resentment of rising expatriate labour forces, rising expectations, and a growing reliance on oil income and therefore further rentier pressures. These are all dangers to the stability of the oil states. But the 2008/9 credit crunch exposed other weaknesses in a number of MENA quarters.

Dubai and Iran in particular found themselves badly exposed to the winds of change – but for very different reasons. Dubai was badly exposed to the credit crunch because of the developmental model it adopted (Davidson 2008). Pursuing a high-risk strategy of attracting international capital and relying on international borrowing for real estate, tourism and financial services investment, when the downturn hit Dubai was unable to find shelter from global pressures. Losing its way, capital, skilled workers and its reputation, Dubai has since had to scale back its ambitions for creating a new non-oil city-state in the Arab world, and has only managed to keep its head above the waterline thanks to the largesse of the oil rich sheikhdom of Abu Dhabi. The Dubai boom and bust has not been good for the petrodollar economies of the Middle East and Dubai's fragile state has posed a reputational challenge, if nothing else, to the robustness of the GCC economies. Going forward, the balance seems to have shifted back in favour of oil-based activities.

Iran, on the other hand, has found itself less exposed to financial swings, largely because of its economic isolation. But due to Iran's dependence on oil exports for foreign exchange accumulation and for national income generation, international oil price fluctuations have had a direct impact on the country. Iran badly needs high oil prices in order to be able to cushion its weak economy and also to weather the series of sanctions ranged against it. Its budgetary deficit is restricting the government's ability to pursue its populist policies and inflation is crippling what remains of its industrial base and financial sector. Reliance on high oil prices for the pursuit of its adventurist foreign and domestic policies also left it badly exposed to internal pressures, particularly as the administration of President Ahmadinejad has tried to mitigate the impact of the opposition Green Movement on society and the political life of the Islamic Republic. Oil prices have become even more important in Iran's macro-level policy-making circles in the aftermath of its widely disputed electoral outcome in June 2009. Today, the ruling establishment is vulnerable to external forces, and exposed at home to internal pressure, so oil plays a central role in the political economy of its grossly state-dominated system.

Though petro-politics is not a new phenomenon, nevertheless the changed nature of petro-politics today has made this phenomenon a fundamental strategic trend to observe. As we follow the adjustments being made at system level to the role of hydrocarbons in the international economy it is hard to see a perceptible reduction in the impact of oil (output and prices) on the stability of normal flow of international trade and investments. In terms of their traditional role as the modern world's essential sources of energy, hydrocarbons are likely to remain significant for the foreseeable future. Indeed, the rise of Asian economies in the slipstream of globalisation will ensure a high-level role for the traditional oil states and their global strategic importance. Furthermore, in terms of the financial resources generated by a relatively small group of states in the Middle East, they are increasingly important players in the region itself. The concentration then of so much in a highly dynamic and potentially unstable part of the world is unlikely to diminish in strategic importance in the near future, and as oil and geopolitics continue their dance of death to the edge so shall regional and international actors helplessly follow.

Identity politics

Identity politics has arguably occupied a greater role in Middle East regional affairs than elsewhere and as elites increased their efforts to deepen territorial nationalism the tensions between the state-sanctioned and community-driven identities became more visible, and also more confrontational. This has been so largely because of the role that ethnicity plays in this region and in the states' construction of national myths. As Binder notes:

> Perhaps more than anywhere in the world, ethnic competition in the Middle East has encouraged the assertion of extreme claims to primordiality stretching back to biblical and pre-biblical times. Prophetic truth, divine promises, holy covenants, and miraculous signs are commingled with images of tribal nomads led by noble patriarchs and heroic warriors.
>
> *(Binder 1999: 18)*

Cultural pressures of globalisation, moreover, have exposed the contradictions between vertical state and horizontal sub-state identities, feeding the challenges being posed to the state-dominant discourses. As ethnicity and confessional affiliations have tended to draw the broad outlines of 'national' identities, so it is that within these realms the identity faultlines can be found, and where new regional battlelines are being drawn. Indeed, since the end of the Cold War the Middle East has experienced a real hike in ethnic and confessional tensions as transnational identities – nationalisms – have also bubbled to the surface of intra-regional debates. Such tensions are not new, of course, and in North Africa, Egypt, Lebanon, Iran, Iraq, Afghanistan, Pakistan, Sudan and Turkey they have been more the norm than exception. Sadly, while intra-Islamic violence is not a new phenomenon, having scarred Islam since the emergence of the four Caliphs in the seventh century, the potential for intra-state confessional tensions degenerating into inter-state conflict is a new and dangerous development. In recent years, and particularly since the fall of Baghdad in April 2003, confessional tensions and sectarianism have acquired a much sharper edge. Of prime importance in this context has been the growing tension between the Shia and Sunni communities of the Middle East (Louër 2008). Olivier Roy has characterised this latest geopolitical development as a 'trauma' in Arab politics, as significant in scale as the end of the Ottoman empire in 1918, and the establishment of the state of Israel in 1948 (Roy 2007). The transformation of Iraq into a largely Shia-dominated country, and Tehran's increasingly strident presence in the Arab region, are arguably the root causes of this renewed hostility. Essentially, Iran's Sunni communities (concentrated in Kurdistan, Khouzestan and Baluchestan provinces) feel besieged and deprived in this Shia-majority country, and Sunni Arab states feel under pressure domestically from their own Shias feeling more empowered by developments in Iraq and Lebanon. Added to the inter-state problems are the tensions between these two Muslim communities within various Middle East countries – in Bahrain, Iran, Iraq, Lebanon, Saudi Arabia and Yemen, a sense of discrimination and injustice has already manifested itself in protest or violence, and the spectre of the so-called 'Shia crescent' (coined by King Abdullah II of Jordan in 2004) is arguably haunting the Sunni-majority Arab states. The Sunni sect of Islam may have a numerical majority globally (only 10 per cent of the world's 1.5 billion Muslims are Shia), but it is in the Middle East that the Shia minority has its strongest presence, so for a number of Arab countries the new partnership between Tehran and Baghdad is inevitably being viewed through a geopolitical prism in which the Shia are seen to be on the march (Blanche 2010).

As noted already, the geopolitical fallout from the 2009 conflict in Yemen is also being perceived in these terms. Thus internal ethnic and confessional tensions have the real potential to play themselves out regionally, and as they do, to also intensify the vocabulary of inter-confessional rivalries. Such tensions and the perceptions of Sunni–Shia rivalries add inter-societal to the perceived inter-state threats associated with Shia empowerment. Indeed, it is arguable that, at the regional level, developments in Yemen have

> the potential to emerge as an all-out proxy campaign between Shiite Iran and Sunni Saudi Arabia. The Iranians likely view the al-Houthi rebels as a potential proxy – just like Hizbullah and Hamas – through which to exert influence in the region. Having a proxy right on the doorstep of Saudi Arabia – an arch-rival of Iran – would provide it with leverage in future regional and international negotiations. Saudi Arabia, thus, would like to see the elimination of the al-Houthi rebels. Further, Saudi Arabia has no interest in seeing the al-Houthi rebellion spark a similar movement amongst the Kingdom's small Shiite population (Shiites make up between five and fifteen percent of Saudi Arabia's population).
>
> *(Harnisch 2009)*

Then there is the Kurdish nationalist movement which periodically affects the domestic politics of Iran, Iraq, Syria and Turkey. Kurdish tensions have led to violence in northern Iraq and eastern Turkey on numerous occasions in recent years, and such ethnic tensions, combined with confessional confrontations, continue to beset the region. As inter-state struggles continue in this rather 'anarchic' region so the states continue to find it difficult to find constructive and cooperative ways of minimising the dangers in ethnic/confessional tensions. The key to achieving this lies in Iraq, but a more positive outcome is also dependent on the wider regional dynamics and the policies of Tehran and Washington in particular.

Political violence and terrorism

In addition to ethno-confessional violence and tensions, al-Qaeda, its affiliates and the Taliban continue to disrupt the flow of political relations across the region. The result is continuing insecurity and a heavy-handed state response, which combined inevitably weakens the resolve of the elites to open up their public spaces to open political interaction. The crushing presence of terrorism is usefully captured by the 2008 report from the US National Counterterrorism Center. It calculates that of the 11,770 terror attacks recorded in that year, some 4,600 (40 per cent of the total) occurred in the Middle East, accounting for 35 per cent of global terror casualties (National Counterterrorism Center 2009). As many as 75 per cent of the high casualty attacks in that year occurred in the Middle East–South Asian security zone, and since 2004 25 countries have suffered 'high-fatality attacks' perpetrated by Sunni extremists. As we have seen in Iraq such attacks are not only highly traumatic, they also help keep the sense of personal vulnerability at the forefront. While al-Qaeda's overall influence can be argued to be on the wane in Iraq after 2007, its presence in Afghanistan, Pakistan, Yemen, Somalia and even Lebanon has been growing. In Afghanistan, Pakistan and Yemen in particular, it has been working closely with local tribes and radical Islamist groups to develop its domestic presence, and also to use these territories as launching pads for further terror attacks.

Al-Qaeda thus remains a thorn in the side of many Arab states, in particular in Saudi Arabia, and also a source of threat to the Shias of the Muslim world. So, al-Qaeda remains a serious challenger to regional stability and a pressure point on Gulf societies in particular. As the case of Iraq demonstrates, the potential for a rise in inter-confessional Shia–Sunni violence, instigated by al-Qaeda attacks on Shias, remains a destabilising influence in the region.

Beyond this, the absence of peace in Palestine continues to breed violence and, indeed, fuel it. The Arab–Israeli conflict remains a catalyst for violence in the region, but what is increasingly clear is that absence of peace is raising tensions between Israel and pro-Western regimes (and also Turkey) as well as the potential for violent confrontation with the non-state Arab actors. The potential for conflict between Israel and its non-state adversaries (namely Hamas, Islamic Jihad and Hezbollah) remains high. In strategic terms, Iranian arming of Hezbollah does pose a new kind of terror threat to the stability of the Levant, and the irony is that Israel's success in 'regulating' the conflict at the state level between its neighbours has, in fact, encouraged the perpetration of violence at the sub-state level. This is a new strategic crisis which is set to deepen with the worsening of rivalries between Iran, as Hezbollah's premier supporter, and Israel.

Weapons of mass destruction

Weapons of mass destruction (WMDs) have found their own place as a critical strategic factor (Karsh et al. 1993) in the Middle East. Such weapons have been present in this region since the 1960s, when chemical agents were present in the wars in Yemen and also deployed in the 1967 six-day war. But since the 1970s, WMDs have acquired much more significance with Israel's development of nuclear weapons and acquisition of advanced delivery systems, and Iraq's efforts in the 1980s to follow Israel's lead (Bhatia 1988; Ehteshami 1989). Today, while Iraq's WMD programme has been extinguished, Israel's has grown in sophistication, but its monopoly of nuclear know-how has been challenged by other players, notably Pakistan and Iran (Russell 2005). A clear distinction still needs to be drawn, however, between the Israeli and Pakistani nuclear programmes – which are unashamedly military – and Iran's, which is largely driven by its civilian sector and remains (largely) under the IAEA inspections regime. For Israel, however, Iran's programme is a direct high-level security challenge, and for the Arab states it is a sign of Iran's drive for regional domination, if not hegemony.

From the GCC states' perspective the situation has been deteriorating rather rapidly:

> the GCC's concern about the true nature and development of the Iranian nuclear program has deepened with the surfacing of new information and statements [in 2009]. Different sources have indicated that Iran is moving fast and unhindered towards the objective of acquiring military nuclear capability. During an interview with a leading Arab newspaper, French Foreign Minister Bernard Kouchner pointed out that reliable sources show that Iran has set up a new site (apart from the known Natanz site) to accommodate thousands of additional centrifuges to speed up the process of uranium enrichment. This statement, coupled with the assessment of US Joint Chiefs of Staff Chairman Admiral Mike Mullen, that new evidence points to Iran having enough enriched uranium to make a nuclear weapon, has justifiably generated uneasiness and cause for further concern about Iran's intentions and the recent progress of its nuclear program. At the same time, the satellite launch by Iran in February this year indicates that Tehran is improving the capability of its ballistic missiles development program. It also strengthens Iranian military capabilities as the missiles could be used in the long term to carry nuclear warheads.
>
> *(Stracke 2009)*

The sets of concerns, spelled out in terms of the complexity and secret dimension of the programme itself and Iran's ballistic missile advances, have compelled senior GCC figures, such as the UAE's Foreign Minister, Sheikh

Abdullah bin Zayed al-Nahyan, to raise the subject of Iran to the top of their diplomatic exchanges.[4] This is to be expected, given the fear that revolutionary Iran has engendered in its Arab neighbours. Under Ahmadinejad's bellicose tone, fear of Iran's nuclear strength has been magnified, particularly as Iran's extensive ballistic missile programme (including the deployment of solid-fuel long-range missiles and satellite launch vehicles) has become inseparable from its nuclear programme. The view that Iran's nuclear ambitions are unlikely to go unchecked and that the international community is impotent to deal with this threat has the potential to fuel a new WMD arms race in the region (Cordesman and Seitz 2009). In the last analysis, therefore, Iran's advances in the nuclear field have provided a new watermark in the changing strategic map of the Middle East. The resolution of the problem remains an international priority and so long as the West and its allies remain committed to containing Iran, then the potential for another war in the region also remains (Khan 2010).

Ballistic missiles and ballistic missile defence

Ballistic missiles (BMs) have littered the Middle East theatres of war for a generation, having established themselves as tools of conflict with Egypt's deployment of Soviet-supplied SCUD surface-to-surface missiles (SSMs) in the 1973 war as an offensive weapon and also to deter Israel from bombing Cairo. Israel followed suit, and had by 1974 developed its own missile force. But it was in the course of the Iran–Iraq war that ballistic missiles established themselves as offensive weapons with the potential to change the theatre of conflict. The two sides used SSMs as a terror weapon and in their 'war of the cities' in 1988 they committed some 240 SSMs to battle, against urban centres. Since then, missiles have been deployed by Iraq (1991), in Yemen (1994) and in the Hezbollah–Israel confrontation in 2006. Thus we have today a ballistic missile architecture shaped by war and sustained by inter-state and sub-state confrontation. Iran, Israel, Egypt and Syria lead the region, with a handful of other countries (Libya, Saudi Arabia, the UAE and Yemen) keeping a basic BM infrastructure in place. Intense regional insecurity, which anticipates the arrival of more conflicts, has ensured that Israel and some of the wealthier Middle East states think about ballistic missile defence (BMD) as a key component of their military structures. But it is in Iran and Israel, the region's cold warriors, that a sophisticated and expansive indigenous ballistic missile defence industry has developed to serve the state's broader strategic ambitions – and also facilitate their hostile posture towards one another. They both now deploy a large array of missile systems, covering ranges from 100 km to over 1,500 km, and are capable of attacking targets well beyond their immediate environment.[5] What is more, with Hezbollah reportedly receiving SCUD missiles from Syria in 2010, a new and more dangerous threshold in the balance of terror between Israel and the so-called 'forces of resistance', sustained by the Iranian–Syrian alliance, may have been established.

Missiles today are more accurate, their numbers are growing and their warheads are getting bigger, making them more central to the regional balance of power with every new development (Russell 2002: 485).[6] Such missiles have been developed and deployed for a variety of reasons, chief among which are: to project power, to compensate for the lack of strategic depth, to deter, to compensate for modest defence budgets, to deploy for fast payload delivery, to use psychologically (to scare and to intimidate), to use as a surprise weapon and to use as an 'indefensible' weapon. BMs then can qualitatively change the battlefield, and the key strategic consequence of their deployment is in the ways in which such weapons alter the nature of security calculations of regional states. As countries like Iran and Israel develop advanced BMs capable of delivering heavy payloads to far away targets very fast, so we can expect other states to respond to this new source of threat. In the absence of any regional arms control regimes or mechanisms for confidence-building, other countries will expand their own BMs to deter attack, and many will aim to adopt sophisticated and expensive BMD shields (such as the US Patriot system and the joint US–Israel Arrow system) as compensation. The exercise of the latter option, which has been pursued by the US's closest allies, has meant that adversaries (Iran and perhaps Syria to a lesser extent, for the sake of argument) may be encouraged to think about effective deterrence against a pre-emptive strike on their territories, which can only mean one thing: to deter attack they will have to have in place a credible and overt option of a strike capability at US and Western targets in and outside of the Middle East (Senn 2009). Intensification of BM deployment then has emerged as a serious international security challenge to contend with.

Conclusions

As we have seen, the region's international relations remain complex and unpredictable. This is arguably so because 'the Middle East regional system is not a single undifferentiated arena but rather a complex of partly distinct but overlapping and interrelated sectors' (Noble 2008: 101). There are, as such, too many moving parts to this regional system and, in strategic terms, interdependence ensures the transfer of instability across state borders and into the national corridors of power. In the last analysis, then, what we see is that while the Middle East regional system has a dynamic life of its own, the segmented globalisation and partial international integration of the region has resulted in the Middle East being exposed to pressure from the great powers. Since 2001, moreover, the regional balance of power has been moving away from the great Arab powers and congregating around the non-Arab regional states. It is in this context that we can begin to talk of a new regional cold war undermining efforts to restore stability to the Middle East. The policies of the Arab states will of course feed into the balance of forces taking shape, and their role in determining the overall strategic make-up of the region remains significant. Their ability to bandwagon in order to block the hegemonic drive of their adversaries should also not be underestimated. But the reality is that they cannot shape the region's destiny themselves, despite the extraordinary soft power being accumulated by the Arab oil monarchies.

Within the Arab region itself power has been shifting – the role of Saudi Arabia has grown among the big three, and some smaller players, with their considerable financial muscle and also US support, have grown in significance. The Gulf countries of Qatar, the UAE and to a lesser extent Kuwait have raised their diplomatic game and are now able to project influence. These countries are said to be emerging as new influential actors in their own right in the Middle East arena, affecting regional politics in ways that do not always meet with the interests of the major regional actors.

Internationally, the Middle East remains a highly dynamic and also penetrated region, in which external powers have proven unable to regulate its politics and yet have little option but to interact with its powerful and influential state actors and non-state forces. The US has little option but to confront the manifestly revisionist tendencies of the 'resistance front'. This dialectic has dramatically influenced the United States' relations with the region, and since 9/11 has made this relationship more tense and on the whole more confrontational. External intervention is partly driven by the knowledge that this region has a significant place in the international security framework and in the globalised and rather fragile international political economy. Decisions of the Middle East actors, therefore, are highly significant in international terms. Without being fully globalised economically, this region is nevertheless well placed to spread its instabilities across the planet. It is the region's concrete realities therefore which have influenced the behaviour of the United States as the dominant power in the Middle East. Indeed, while President Obama expressed a direct interest in 2009 in reaching out to Iran and Syria, working towards peace in Palestine, reducing America's military presence in Iraq and generally mending bridges with the Muslim world, it is important to note that for strategic reasons there is also some clear continuity with the previous administration's posture. Indeed, a sceptic might argue that the US's priorities have remained hostage to the same mindset that drove President Bush's policies. Interestingly, the absolute security of Israel seems to have been linked to the containment of Iran, directly affecting the Obama Administration's agendas with such global actors as China and Russia (Solomon 2009).[7] Isolating Iran, through a new bridge-building exercise with Syria and a reshaping of the Levant's politics has been viewed through the same prism, as indeed have the efforts to reignite the peace process.

But that is not the end of the story, for while the Middle East's permeability makes it vulnerable to outside forces, the same process also facilitates regional instabilities being exported. In this context, the relationship represents the classic model of strategic interdependence. Interdependence, furthermore, is not only a function of the Middle East's relations with the outside world; it also regulates inter-state relations within it. Inter-state relations in turn remain in flux as the regional actors continue to look for mechanisms which could enable them to cope with the rise of a new kind of regional multi-polarity. Insecurity and dynamism are thus combined.

Readers familiar with Arab political history of the turbulent Arab cold war of the 1950s and 1960s will read this and probably exclaim, 'so what else is new!'

Notes

1. *Khaleej Times*, 4 March 2009.
2. *Gulf Times*, 10 May 2010.
3. Between 1998 and 2002 the average price of oil was $23 per barrel.
4. For example, the conversation between senior US and Arab diplomats on the margins of the 'Palestine Summit' in Sharm El-Sheikh in March 2009 was above all about Iran. See Solomon (2009).
5. 'Thread: emerging ballistic missile threat from the Middle East, and South Asia', *Yaleglobal Forums*, 28 April 2009.
6. Russell captures one of the chief attractions of BMs as follows: 'combat aircraft, which can fly at more than 1,000 kilometers per hour, reach targets 900 kilometers away in about an hour, while ballistic missiles can reach them in about six minutes' (Russell 2002: 485).
7. Jay Solomon, 'U.S. engages Russia, Syria to isolate Iran', *Wall Street Journal*, 4 March 2009.

References

Behrendt, Sven (2008) *When Money Talks: Arab Sovereign Wealth Funds in the Global Public Policy Discourse*, Carnegie Papers No. 12. Beirut: Carnegie Middle East Center.

Bhatia, Shyam (1988) *Nuclear Rivals in the Middle East*. London: Routledge.

Binder, Leonard (1999) 'International dimensions of ethnic conflict in the Middle East', in Leonard Binder (ed.), *Ethnic Conflict and International Politics in the Middle East*. Gainesville, FL: University Press of Florida, pp. 1–40.

Blanche, Ed (2010) 'Iran tightens its grip on the "new" Iraq', *Middle East*, May, pp. 13–17.

Burke, Edward and Bazoobandi, Sara (2010) *The Gulf Takes Charge in the MENA Region*. Madrid: FRIDE.

Buzan, Barry and Waever, Ole (2003) *Regions and Powers: The Structure of International Security*. Cambridge: Cambridge University Press.

Cordesman, Anthony H. and Seitz, Adam C. (2009) *Iranian Weapons of Mass Destruction: The Birth of a Regional Arms Race?* Santa Barbara, CA: Praeger.

Davidson, Christopher (2008) *Dubai: The Vulnerability of Success*. London: Hurst.

Ehteshami, Anoushiravan (1989) *Nuclearisation of the Middle East*. London: Brassey's.

Ehteshami, Anoushiravan (2006) 'The Middle East and security strategy', in Roland Dannreuther and John Peterson (eds), *Security Strategy and Transatlantic Relations*. New York: Routledge, pp. 78–96.

Ehteshami, Anoushiravan (2007) *Globalization and Geopolitics in the Middle East: Old Games, New Rules*. London: Routledge.

Harnisch, Chris (2009) *A Critical War in a Fragile Country: Yemen's Battle with the Shiite al-Houthi Rebels*, American Enterprise Institute, 31 August.

International Institute for Strategic Studies (2010) *The Military Balance 2010*. London: Routledge.

Karsh, Efraim, Navias, Martin S. and Sabin, Philip (1993) (eds) *Non-Conventional Weapons Proliferation in the Middle East: Tackling the Spread of Nuclear, Chemical, and Biological Capabilities*. Oxford: Clarendon Press.

Khan, Saira (2010) *Iran and Nuclear Weapons: Protracted Conflict and Proliferation*. London: Routledge.

Leverett, Flint and Leverett, Hillary Mann (2009) *The Race for Iran: Will America's Arab Allies Strike their own Deal with Iran?* New America Foundation, 21 December.

Louër, Laurence (2008) *Transnational Shia Politics: Religious and Political Networks in the Gulf*. London: Hurst.

Malony, Suzanne (2009) 'The Gulf's renewed oil wealth: getting it right this time?', *Survival*, 50(6): 129–50.

National Counterterrorism Center (2009) *2008 Report on Terrorism*. Washington, DC: Office of the Director of National Intelligence.

Noble, Paul (2008) 'From Arab system to Middle Eastern system? Regional pressures and constraints', in Bahgat Korany and Ali E. Hilal Dessouki (eds), *The Foreign Policies of Arab States: The Challenge of Globalization*. Cairo: Cairo University Press, pp. 67–165.

OPEC (various years) *OPEC Annual Statistical Bulletin*. Vienna: OPEC Secretariat.

Roy, Olivier (2007) *The Politics of Chaos in the Middle East*. London: Hurst.

Russell, Richard L. (2002) 'Swords and shields: ballistic missiles and defenses in the Middle East and South Asia', *Orbis*, Summer, pp. 483–98.

Russell, Richard L. (2005) *Weapons Proliferation and War in the Greater Middle East: Strategic Contest*. London: Routledge.

Senn, Martin (2009) 'The arms-dynamic peacemaker: ballistic-missile defense in the Middle East', *Middle East Policy*, 16(4): 55–67.

Solomon, Jay (2009) 'U.S. engages Russia, Syria to isolate Iran', *Wall Street Journal*, 4 March.

Stracke, Nicole (2009) 'GCC and the challenge of US–Iran negotiations', *GRC Analysis*, 5 March.

Wehrey, Frederic, Dassa Kaye, Dalia, Watkins, Jessica, Martini, Jeffrey and Guffey, Robert A. (2010) *The Middle East After the Iraq War*. Santa Monica, CA: Rand Corporation.

13

THE CHALLENGE OF TRANSITION

Gulf security in the twenty-first century

Kristian Ulrichsen

This chapter examines the evolution of 'Gulf security' in response to a range of existing and emergent threats and challenges. It argues that the rise of primarily non-military sources of potential insecurity is profoundly reshaping the security paradigm in the Gulf states in the medium and longer term. This is inextricably bound up with the broader impact of the processes of globalisation on their political economy, which itself is undergoing a systemic transformation toward post-oil redistributive forms of governance. Regional concepts of security need to be re-conceptualised as part of a holistic approach that locates the drivers of change within the rapidly globalising international environment and interlinks them with socio-political and economic dimensions. It must also acknowledge that security is composed both of material and ideational considerations and is as much a social construct as a survival mechanism in a world of threats and balances.

An opening section argues that concepts of security need to be re-conceptualised toward a multi-level and holistic security approach. This distinguishes between the idea of security as a social construct and as a material threat. The focus then shifts to the contextual parameters within which this reformulation of Gulf security will evolve over coming years and decades. It locates the drivers of change within the broader processes of globalisation and internationalisation that are rebalancing the Gulf states within the global order. The third section examines the broadening and deepening of regional security agendas by disaggregating the emerging and longer-term challenges into three major clusters. These are non-traditional and non-military issues which contain the potential to strike at the heart of the social contract and redistributive mechanisms that tie states and societies together. The fourth section examines the downward trajectories and threat multipliers in Yemen and describes the interlinking of these non-traditional challenges in a systemic and multi-dimensional crisis of governance and legitimacy. The final section assesses the prospects for a new approach to security based upon the concept of human security.

An integrated approach to security

Reformulating concepts of security to adopt a deeper and broader agenda encompassing non-military challenges builds upon the cognitive shift in thinking about global security. This has accelerated since the 1990s during an era of accelerating complexity of global interconnections and transnational flows of people, capital and ideas (Dillon 2005: 3). New threats to national and international security have emerged from transnational terrorism, cross-border criminal networks and flows, and global issues such as climate change. Increasingly, these bypass the state and erode Cold War-era demarcations between the domestic and foreign-policy spheres of policy (Kaldor 2007: 32). Simultaneously, the concept of 'security' has been redefined away from a mere focus on relations between states and a narrow ambit of military security (Clarke 2005: 20).

Taken together, these trends necessitate a more nuanced approach predicated as much on meeting the human security of populations as well as the national security of states. This is important as comparative political science demonstrates that states in transition are vulnerable to sub-state contestation and outbreaks of political violence. Integral to this expanded agenda is its theoretical underpinnings in a constructivist approach to security that investigates how issues become securitised and why, in whose name, and for whom. This examines the motivations and objectives that guide states and societies in constructing local and regional security agendas (Krause 1996: 325). It studies the role of norms as social constructs in determining approaches to questions of power and security (Price 2008: 53). Constructivist approaches ascribe value to the location and distribution of nodes of power within society as well as the relationships between knowledge, power and interests.

Analysing 'how people act' also addresses one of the central deficiencies of the broader international relations literature, namely a neglect of the human dimension in contemporary world politics. Delineating the role of local agents is particularly important in deciding which issues come to dominate security agendas in the GCC states. This is because the conduct of foreign and security affairs in these oil monarchies is restricted to a tightly drawn circle of senior members of the ruling family. In common with many other developing countries' experience, 'regime security' in the Gulf states is frequently conflated with 'national security' and this informs regimes' notions of the hitherto successful strategies of survival needed to achieve this (Kechichian 2008: 240). Consequently, our understanding of the dynamics of policy formulation is enhanced by taking into consideration the factors that inform regimes' perceptions of their internal security matrix and how this might interact with their volatile external sphere of policy-making.

Contextual parameters framing the evolution of Gulf security

Accelerating processes of globalisation and increasing complexity of global interconnections form the backdrop to this reformulation of security. Issues such as transnational flows and networks and global issues such as climate change link old problems in new ways and create new challenges that permeate friable state structures and controls. These broader global linkages are mirrored by the revolution in information and communication technologies. Rapid technological advances in wireless mobile devices equipped with cameras erode boundaries over the control of the flow of information and make it virtually impossible for officials to suppress public discussion of sensitive or proscribed issues. These have fundamentally reshaped the linkages between the internal and external aspects of security and created new spaces in which to mobilise, organise and channel societal demands for representation and participation (Murphy 2008: 183).

This steady erosion of regimes' control over the flow of information to individuals and groups within their borders directly links their domestic stability to external sources of insecurity that no longer can be isolated or contained within national boundaries. Processes of globalisation have enmeshed the Gulf states within a wider interconnected region with multiple ideational and latent physical threats to security. The ease of communication and travel means that the rise of transnational terrorism in Afghanistan and Pakistan poses a direct threat to the GCC states through the recruitment of personnel and flows of illicit funding in both directions. This internationalisation of the Gulf is also apparent in its emergence as the centre of gravity in West Asia by virtue of its energy reserves and financial resources. With the Gulf region's share of global oil and natural gas production projected to rise from 28 per cent (including Iraqi and Iranian output) in 2000 to 33 per cent in 2020, and with most of that increase going to Asian markets, its strategic significance will only grow in coming decades. China alone accounted for nearly 40 per cent of the increase in global oil consumption between 2004 and 2007, and is projected to account for another 40 per cent of the increase in world demand for oil through 2030 (Simpfendorfer 2009: 30-2).

This introduces a major new dynamic into the regional security matrix as it raises the stakes for a greater number of external actors and contributes to the shifting of the geopolitics of oil. In addition, although European Union member states have steadily diversified their sources of supply to reduce their share from Saudi Arabia and the GCC, their two largest suppliers (Russia and Norway) will deplete far sooner, and hence may lead to a renewed focus on supplies from the Gulf States (Aarts et al. 2008: 140). Although individual countries such as Qatar have negotiated long-term bilateral energy deals that tie their interests to regional stability, the internationalisation of the Gulf does carry risks. Chief among them is the potential for the current cooperative regional environment to become more conflicted if, in spite of thickening interdependencies and energy dialogues, access to regional energy resources becomes sharpened in the future.

Issues of energy interdependence and security of access to resources thus give external actors an interest in regional security structures. International reactions to the burgeoning incidence of piracy in the Gulf of Aden that accelerated sharply from 2008 may prove a harbinger of future policy trends. The European Union launched its first-ever naval mission (Operation Atalanta) in November 2008 in response to more than 100 acts of piracy against international shipping, including the seizure of the fully laden Saudi supertanker *Sirius Star*. It has a mandate to protect deliveries of food aid by the World Food Programme to Somalia, as well as other vulnerable vessels transiting the Gulf of Aden, within the framework of the European Security and Defence Policy. Significantly, many other countries, including China, India, Russia and Iran, also deployed their own warships to protect energy security interests in the Gulf of Aden (Kraska and Wilson 2009: 76).

The emergence of new and 'non-traditional' challenges to security

Three major longer-term challenges to security and stability in the Gulf constitute non-conventional and non-military threats whose full consequences will unfold over a period of decades rather than years. They are intricately connected to the transformational changes to the political economies in all of the Arabian Peninsula states as they move toward post-rentier structures of governance and reformulate the social contract hitherto based on the redistribution of oil rents. This section describes the interaction of these shifts in political economy with the complex and rapidly shifting socio-political environment at its various local, regional and global levels.

Demographic shifts and structural imbalances

The first cluster of non-traditional and longer-term challenges to societal security and stability centre on demographic shifts and structural imbalances within Gulf polities. The monarchies of the Arabian Peninsula have experienced four decades of exceptionally rapid demographic growth that is only now beginning to slow. A youth bulge will continue to work its way through the population structure for decades to come. These trends resulted in the population of the Arabian Peninsula increasing from 8 million in 1950 to 58 million in 2007, with a projected rise to 124 million in 2050 (Drysdale 2010: 124). A further breakdown of this figure reveals even more remarkable trends, most notably the near-doubling of the Qatari population from 800,000 in 2006 to 1.5 million by the end of 2007, and an unexpected announcement of a 41 per cent jump in the population of Bahrain in the same year (Richer 2008: 3).

The combination of rapid population growth with inadequate employment opportunities represents a major long-term challenge to internal cohesion in the

GCC. This dilemma is not unique to the region and is common to the wider Arab and developing world as a whole, although its impact in the GCC states is compounded by stratified labour markets and rentier mentalities that have created imbalanced and dual labour market systems that are unique in the contemporary world (Winckler 2009: 60). Signs of socio-economic strain have already emerged in all the GCC states and Yemen. They may be expected to have a particularly destabilising effect on successive generations of citizens under the age of 40, who take for granted the redistribution of wealth and provision of public goods and lack any point of comparison with the hardships experienced by their elders (Longva 2004: 134).

Rising disparities of income and wealth provide a visible indicator of the growing inequalities within GCC societies. A case in point is Saudi Arabia, where the level of income per capita more than halved, from $16,650 in 1980 to $7,239 in 2000, while the level of oil exports per capita declined more steeply throughout the GCC from an average of $15,000 in 1980 to $6,000 in 2000 (Dresch 2005: 16). These divergent trajectories are potentially destabilising because in many cases they follow fissures within society. They may overlay sectarian divisions, as in Bahrain or Saudi Arabia where absolute and relative rates of poverty are interlinked with the politics of uneven development, or they may exist between citizens and expatriates. Both faultlines reveal considerable tensions and societal pressures that may become systemic if they are not addressed in a comprehensive and sustainable manner. Elsewhere, and particularly in the United Arab Emirates but throughout the GCC states more generally, the presence of large numbers of migrant labourers with no civil or political rights and few economic and human rights constitutes another potent source of human insecurity.

As of 2002–3, expatriate labourers provided the majority of the labour force in each of the six GCC states, ranging from 60 per cent in Saudi Arabia and Bahrain to 65.7 per cent in Oman, 80 per cent in Kuwait, 89.5 per cent in Qatar and 90 per cent in the UAE (Winckler 2009: 69). These communities survive on low margins of disposable income and have a heightened vulnerability to food or resource insecurity. Moreover, the absolute and relative size of the expatriate population means that regimes are faced with a dilemma should their marginalised and disenfranchised labour migrants ever make a claim for civil or political rights in the future. Already, significant (by GCC standards) labour unrest has occurred in Dubai, Bahrain and Kuwait in 2007–8. The unrest coincided with the beginning of the global financial and economic crisis, and rising inflationary and cost-of-living pressures (Hardy 2008).

In November 2007, a study conducted by the McKinsey consultancy group laid bare the scale of the regional challenge posed by mounting unemployment. The report estimated that, contrary to official claims of much lower rates, real unemployment in Bahrain, Oman and Saudi Arabia exceeded 15 per cent, and that the figure rose to 35 per cent for those aged between 16 and 24. It also found that the saturated public sector was no longer able to guarantee employment to citizens entering the job market. Furthermore, it identified severe deficiencies in local education systems that meant that most entrants into GCC labour markets lacked the requisite qualifications to enter the private sector. The situation is bleaker still in Yemen, where overall unemployment rates are between 35 and 40 per cent amid the continuing reluctance of GCC states to admit unskilled or semi-skilled Yemeni labour migrants in place of workers from non-Muslim, Asian countries (Boucek 2009: 11).

With such a large proportion of GCC populations under the age of 16 and about to enter the labour market, the issue of unemployment is both urgent, and inseparable from the role and quality of educational attainment and the misalignment between local standards of education and labour market require-ments (Donn and Al-Manthri 2010: 56). These connected challenges risk marginalising an entire generation of young people who lack the requisite skill sets and language abilities to compete with cheaper sources of expatriate labour. Officials and policy-makers are not unaware of this looming crunch, particu-larly in Kuwait where it is interlinked with political frustration with the slow pace of reform, but also in Bahrain and Oman, where resource depletion is more imminent and Yemen and Saudi Arabia which confront demographic challenges that do not exist in the more lightly populated smaller Gulf States.

Their awareness of the potential problems formed the cornerstone of the ambitious projects of economic diversification launched in each GCC state during the 2000s. Beginning in the mid-1990s, a plethora of national 'visions' and plans set out targets and objectives for diversifying GCC economies and expanding the productive base. Although Oman and Bahrain were early movers in diversification, their efforts have since been surpassed in order of magnitude by Qatar, Saudi Arabia and the United Arab Emirates. Qatar's utilisation of its natural gas reserves provides an illustration of the geo-strategic dimension of economic diversification. The supply of liquefied natural gas (LNG) to leading industrialised and emerging countries, including the United States, the United Kingdom, South Korea, Japan and China, thickens the web of interdependences with powerful external actors with a direct stake in Qatari stability and security (Wright 2008: 12–13).

Resource security and patterns of distribution

This second cluster of security issues examines the long-term strategic dimen-sions of ensuring security of access to sufficient food, water and energy supplies. These are critical to meeting the challenges of rapid economic and demographic growth described above. Officials in the GCC states have taken innovative steps to meet the requirements of food security in particular, but water supplies and power generation capabilities remain a challenge. These leave the Gulf states vulnerable to the contestation of resources if scarcities interact with the politics of uneven development. Competition over dwindling natural resources can accent-uate traditional and emerging tensions between individuals and communities both within societies and between states, if perceptions of unequal access or exploitation arise.

The dilemma facing the Gulf states is that attempts to attain food security by promoting agricultural productivity have paradoxically made the problem worse. These policies have neither been successful in increasing food self-sufficiency and reducing reliance on imported foodstuffs, nor sustainable in their careful managing of scarce water resources. Agriculture accounted for a mere 6.5 per cent of GDP in Saudi Arabia and a total of 1.6 per cent throughout the GCC, but nearly 60 per cent of total water consumption usage in 2000. This far outstripped industrial and domestic usage and represented an unsustainable utilisation of resources in what was already one of the most arid regions in the world. In 2006 Kuwait ranked as the most water-scarce country in the world, and three other GCC states featured in the top ten, with the United Arab Emirates third, Qatar fifth and Saudi Arabia eighth (Raouf 2009: 22).

Belated recognition of the intertwined problems of water and food security led Saudi Arabia to announce in February 2008 that it would cease producing grain by 2016. Officials attributed this abrupt reversal in food policy to the impact of climate change, drought and the depletion of fossil water. All of Saudi Arabia's wheat depended on central pivot irrigation that drew its water from fossil reserves. The drawdown of these reserves clashed with Saudi industrialisation plans and rapid population growth, both of which significantly increased the demand for scarce water supplies. This contributed to the policy shift away from three decades of state-sponsored agricultural development programmes. Unsustainable agricultural production has therefore resulted in over-exploitation of fossil water reserves and the depletion of underground aquifers throughout the Arabian Peninsula.

Water insecurity is part of a broader trend throughout the Middle East, although the rapidity of population growth and industrial development underway in the Gulf states exacerbated its effects. The full extent of the regional problem became clear in November 2008 in a report issued by the Islamic Development Bank. This found that average annual water availability per capita in the Middle East had declined by two-thirds since 1960, and is projected to halve again by 2050 to leave the entire region acutely water-scarce (IsDB 2008). Moreover, the mining of fossil water from deep transboundary aquifers provides another potentially potent cross-border flashpoint in the Arabian Peninsula. Beginning in the 1990s, Saudi Arabian over-exploitation of its aquifers for agricultural use began to reduce the water availability and agricultural potential in Bahrain and Qatar (Berman and Wihbey 1999). These trends contain the seeds of future political tension and an emerging conflict over transboundary water resources on the peninsula, particularly as cooperation between GCC member states on utilising and managing joint aquifers has been negligible (Raouf 2009: 3).

Energy security operates at two interconnected levels. Internally, privileged access to resources through policies of widespread subsidisation constitute powerful centripetal mechanisms and pillars of regime legitimation. Externally, governments' ability to provide these resouces to their citizenry is intimately bound up with (and vulnerable to disruption to) the constant and unimpeded flow of revenues from hydrocarbon exports. This, in turn, feeds into a third dimension, which is the energy security requirements of the oil-consuming nations that purchase their oil and gas from the Gulf region. The dimensions are interlinked as any disruption to one heightens the vulnerability of the other. This was evidenced in the Arabian Peninsula when Al-Qaeda specifically targeted the core of regime legitimacy in Saudi Arabia through its attack on the kingdom's oil-processing facilities at Abqaiq in February 2006.

Power generation and energy availability represent a further example of resource insecurity. Both approached peak capacity during the second oil boom as the accelerating pace of regional development and mega-projects placed existing facilities under severe strain. High (and increasing) reliance on energy-intensive desalination plants for water supplies compounded the problem, as the proportion of desalinated water reached 99 per cent of total demand in Qatar, 96.5 per cent in Kuwait, 92 per cent in Bahrain and 85 per cent in the United Arab Emirates in 2005. In Bahrain alone, energy consumption doubled between 2006 and 2008 and demand for energy was forecast to grow a further 65 per cent to 2014. All of the Gulf states, with the sole exception of Qatar, face current and future shortages in power generation caused by high population growth, over-demand and under-pricing (Hertog and Luciani 2009: 5–6). This complicates strategies to promote sustainable development as it challenges embedded notions of subsidised consumption that inform perceptions of the social contract.

Gas consumption in Saudi Arabia, Qatar, Kuwait and the United Arab Emirates surged by 50 per cent between 2002 and 2008 yet barely kept pace with competing demands from electricity generation, water desalination and energy-intensive industrialisation into petrochemicals and aluminium. These reflect the interconnections between economic diversification, security of access to resources and environmental degradation. In particular, water desalination plants are energy-intensive, environmentally harmful and central to the political economy of subsidisation in the GCC. So, too, are cheap electricity prices, which (as with the price of water) neither reflect global norms nor encourage sustainable consumption. Yet government-led policy initiatives focused on diversifying the sources of energy rather than addressing patterns of unsustainable consumption. Emphasis on supply-side expansion has enabled them to avoid taking politically sensitive demand-side changes that would tamper with the social contract in its current format (Krane 2010: 1).

The steps being taken by governments to attain food, water and energy security are important in themselves. Nevertheless, a more intractable problem facing several GCC states and Yemen comes from the interaction of dwindling levels of resources with the persistence or sharpening of unequal patterns of distribution. In numerous comparative instances elsewhere, the concentration of resources in one particular or privileged grouping while scarcities exist else-where has been a demonstrated source of sub-national — and occasionally cross-border — conflict (Homer-Dixon 2004: 265–6). This occurred in the Arabian Peninsula in Saudi Arabia in 1979, in Bahrain between 1994 and 1999 and in Yemen since the 1990s. These examples emphasise the ties that interlink the trajectories of resource depletion and demographic growth with the choices of political and societal actors and the persistence of patterns of unequal access to and distribution of increasingly-scarce resources.

Any breakdown of social cohesion would jeopardise the web of social relationships that bind together the many different communities and groups within the highly stratified Gulf polities. Alternatively, the implementation of inclusive counter-measures to promote and strengthen internal cohesion will increase the likelihood of a consensual and non-violent transition toward post-oil political economies. For this reason, leaderships, particularly in the richer GCC states, have invested large amounts of time and money in attaining food and energy security and attempting to delay the moment when the carrying capacity of their rapidly expanding populations exceeds the boundaries of economic, social and environmental sustainability. Yet these represent short-term initiatives to boost supply rather than the politically more difficult yet long-term more sustainable measures to regulate demand through the introduc-tion of market pricing or progressive dismantling of subsidy regimes.

Climate and environmental security

Internal tensions and faultlines also weaken states' capacities to absorb and overcome external shocks, such as the danger of abrupt or irreversible changes arising from environmental degradation or climate change. Particularly in the low-lying coastal zones of the Arabian Peninsula, the direct and indirect impact of long-term climate change could profoundly affect long-established patterns of human settlement and urbanisation. Furthermore, these pressures have already placed the fragile ecosystem of the Peninsula under great stress and reduced its resilience to any exogenous shock. The interaction of these environ-mental scarcities and stresses with systems of perceived or actual inequalities in access to dwindling resources thus represents a potent future threat to internal stability in a climate-stressed world (Homer-Dixon 2004: 269).

There is, nevertheless, a growing disjuncture between international and Gulf-centric discourses on the environmental and security dimensions of climate change. Interlocking power circles and interest networks play a critical role in determining how perceptions of climate change in the Gulf states feed through to policy formulation. These are dominated by policy-makers' concern for the stability and continuity of the revenues from oil exports. Processes of energy-intensive industrialisation and prestigious mega-projects that dominate the economic landscape of the GCC have contributed to among the highest levels of per-capita energy consumption and carbon emissions in the world (Luomi

2010: 2). Nevertheless, climate change and environmental degradation are global issues, the effects of which will accelerate over the course of the twenty-first century and present a serious and enduring threat to human (as well as state) security. Their effects will be transboundary and cannot be resolved without a comprehensive and multilateral approach. This marks them out as bell-wethers of the profound shift in global politics in which problems and responses transcend national borders and rigid distinctions between domestic and international policy.

Recent research into their security implications has positioned climate change in the nexus between conflict and resource scarcity outlined in the previous section. Nick Mabey argued that if it is not slowed, climate change will become a primary (and proximate) driver of conflict and destabilising flows of environmental refugees or migrants within and between states (Mabey 2008: 5–7). Moving toward an assessment of the likely implications in the Middle East, Oli Brown and Alec Crawford of the International Institute for Strategic Development examined the security challenges of climate change in the Levant. They agreed that climate change is likely to aggravate existing tensions and constitute one (of numerous) drivers of future conflict over issues such as access to scarce resources, food insecurity and the changing availability of water resources. The indirect impact of climate change was thus particularly important in the conflict-afflicted region of the Middle East, where numerous actual and latent tensions and inter- and intra-state faultlines abound (Brown and Crawford 2009: 2–3).

Climate security has therefore embedded itself in global security discourse. It straddles a dangerous intersection between development, governance and sources of conflict. However, its position on the fuzzy margins between domestic and global politics complicates strategies to address it. While human-induced climate change already poses a hard security threat in certain manifestations and locations, its full effects will become apparent over decades rather than months and years. These will require concerted and multilateral solutions that tackle both its environmental and security aspects. Yet the disappointing outcome of the December 2009 United Nations Climate Change Conference in Copenhagen demonstrated the difficulties inherent in reaching even a global consensus, let alone agreement, on climate change. It also highlighted the paradoxical disjuncture between the growing urgency of global challenges and the continuing inability to arrive at global solutions to these interconnected problems (Held 2007: 199).

In the Gulf region, climate change and environmental degradation present multi-dimensional threats to internal and regional security. These range from rising sea levels to the impact on already fragile ecosystems and more highly contested access to food and water resources, alongside a potential shift toward a de-carbonised world economy that might depress global demand for Gulf oil. In all of these instances, climate change can act as a stressor that exacerbates existing tensions and creates new drivers of conflict within and between societies. The anthropogenic causes of human-induced climate change are manifold and encompass political, economic, socio-cultural and demographic factors. These include population growth, demographic shifts, economic and technological development, cultural values and belief systems, and governance and institutional structures. Underlying all of these, and interlinking them, is the incompatibility of current models of economic growth with sustainable development (Raouf 2008: 15).

These trends skew institutional structures and political willpower against substantive reformulation of these patterns of unsustainable growth. What is lacking is a coherent sense of the emerging interrelationships between climate and security. Only in Oman has widespread awareness of sustainable development and climate change mitigation entered policy-making discourse at a high level, with the formation of a dedicated Ministry of Environment and Climate Affairs in 2007. This is unsurprising in a regional context lacking even an internal consensus on the environmental aspects of climate change. This was evidenced in successive rounds of international climate change negotiations leading up to the 2009 Copenhagen Summit. With the notable exception of Oman, GCC states earned a reputation for obstructionist tactics focusing on the (negative in their perception) economic implications of a climate-changed world rather than the environmental impacts of climate change itself (Depledge 2008: 20).

The Gulf states are nevertheless highly exposed to the effects of climate change and environmental degradation on already stressed ecosystems and patterns of habitation. The UK Meteorological Office Hadley Centre warned that a predicted long-term rise in temperature of 3.2 degrees Celsius to 2070, coupled with increasing water stress and salinity and further degradation of soil quality, will negatively affect crop yields and make the region still more reliant on imported foodstuffs (Hadley Centre 2009: 2–4). Meanwhile, the interaction of rising temperatures with falling precipitation will intensify still further the competition for already scarce resources of food and water, and open them up for potential contestation in times of hardship. More than 90 per cent of the limited arable land on the Peninsula already suffers from overgrazing and land degradation, leading to further desertification of the already limited regions of non-desert (Launay 2006: 43).

This creeping desertification is matched by an increasing salinity of depleting fossil water reserves. Saltwater intrusion into groundwater has resulted in massive increases in salinity levels in Qatar in particular, and is directly attributable to unsustainable overexploitation of underground aquifers. Coastal patterns of settlement and development in the GCC states also render them especially vulnerable to changes in sea levels arising from climate change. In 2007, the *Fourth Assessment Report of the Intergovernmental Panel on Climate Change* predicted sea level rises of anything between 18 and 59 centimetres by 2100. Moreover, it predicted with very high confidence that 'Many millions more people are projected to be flooded every year due to sea-level rise by the 2080s', and added that 'The unavoidability of sea-level rise, even in the longer term, frequently conflicts with present-day human development patterns and trends' (IPCC 2007: 317).

Changing patterns of temperature, precipitation and sea levels represent the tangible effects of climate change that have already started to occur in the Gulf, as elsewhere. These trends, to a high probability, are expected to accelerate over the course of the twenty-first century and constitute an increasingly direct challenge to security and stability. Although current awareness is low through-out the GCC, the tangible manifestations of climate change do at least hold the potential to be targeted by adaptive counter-measures to mitigate some of their effects. Rather more difficult to predict is the intangible impact of the processes of climate change over the medium and longer term. The variable lies in the interaction of internal and external stressors that may arise with political, economic and socio-cultural behaviour. These will play out over the coming years and decades and their effects cannot be predicted with any certainty.

Here, the issue of combating and mitigating climate change becomes bound up with the maintenance of the social contract in its current redistributive guise. This presents policy-makers with difficult and potentially painful choices. The paradox facing officials is that while the advocacy of adaptive measures or changes to unsustainable patterns of living carries its own risks, the long-term consequences of inaction are likely to be much higher. This will be magnified still further if they become intertwined with depleting oil reserves and states' declining ability to redistribute wealth toward their societies in times of comparative economic hardship. Here, the unpalatable factor facing Gulf policy-makers is that they will eventually face this shift toward a post-oil era at some point in coming decades, although this will occur at different speeds in each country. The common denominator is that the predicted acceleration of climate change represents an exogenous stressor during a time of vulnerable transition.

The case of Yemen

This final section examines the interlinking of multiple sources of insecurity and causes of state weakness in Yemen. Collectively, they amount to a crisis of governance and regressive political implosion that constitutes the single most dangerous short-term challenge to the security and stability of the Arabian Peninsula. Furthermore, they raise a number of comparative worries for the GCC states to consider as they gradually move toward the delicate task of disentangling the layers of patronage and rent-seeking networks inherent in moves to a post-oil political economy.

Yemen faces a combination of underlying challenges, each of which, on its own, would be profoundly destabilising. These include a military rebellion in the northern province of Sa'dah that has flared intermittently with six rounds of fighting since 2004, a growing southern secessionist movement that challenges the post-1990 reunification settlement, as well as the reconstitution of Al-Qaeda in the Arabian Peninsula following the merger of its Yemeni and Saudi wings in January 2009. Underlying all of these hard threats to security is the imminent depletion of oil and water reserves, and the erosion of regime legitimacy and state capacity to govern effectively or even fairly. Across the Gulf of Aden, state collapse in Somalia has facilitated destabilising flows of men, money and material between Somalia and Yemen. This has injected the multiple drivers of conflict and insecurity in the Horn of Africa into the Gulf's regional security equation. The result is a failing political economy and fragmenting society on the south-western flank of the Arabian Peninsula that can no longer be contained within Yemen itself.

The example of Yemen demonstrates how intractable can be the reformulation of governance and the basis of state–society relations in periods of rapid and profound transition. It also highlights the tensions between the reconstruction of failing institutions and the reconstitution of social relations when these begin to break down under the strain of internal and external stresses and a rejection of central authority or legitimacy. Empowering the capacity and reach of an already contested governing structure may sharpen the centrifugal forces fragmenting state–society relations within Yemen and further weaken what little social cohesion currently exists. For all of these reasons, Yemen provides a prescient case study of how rapid socio-economic transitions may overwhelm fragile state capacity and intersect with eroding political legitimacy to produce a 'perfect storm' of a systemic crisis of governance and breakdown of legitimate political authority (Hill 2010: 11).

The intertwined problems of imminent resource depletion, environmental degradation and the reformulation of regime legitimacy during a period of profound political and economic transition demonstrate the interlocking challenges to security described in this chapter. All of these issues will, in some combination, also face the GCC states over the course of the twenty-first century. Yemen's downward spiral demonstrates how each can exacerbate the other and lead to a transition that is marked more by violence than consensus. It is this security dilemma that cuts to the heart of the Gulf states' socio-political and economic trajectories over the course of the twenty-first century. Consequently, the crisis of governance in Yemen provides a worrying bell-wether of the difficult changes that confront its neighbours on the Arabian Peninsula as they too embark on the processes of rapid transition during periods of declining resources and burgeoning socio-economic challenges.

The case study of Yemen shows how the fragmentation of social relationships and the contestation of political authority accelerates the decline of regime legitimacy and increases the risk of state failure or, at least, protracted state weakness. While it is undoubtedly the case that the GCC states possess greater material resources than Yemen to buttress this shift, their dependence on oil has both been longer lasting and more deeply rooted. In addition, short-term avoidance of the difficult decisions inherent in rolling back redistributive and subsidisation mechanisms and embedding sustainable post-oil structures of governance will make these harder to achieve over the medium to longer term. Yet the fundamental paradox facing policy-makers in the Gulf states is that they are reliant on precisely these mechanisms for their legitimacy and the continuance of the social contract for short-term internal security and stability.

Transitioning toward a post-oil era in all GCC states will therefore involve painful socio-political decisions and the dismantling of decades of rent-seeking patterns of behaviour. The contestation of governmental authority by different groups in southern and northern Yemen illustrates how existing socio-economic discontent and regional marginalisation can fracture and fragment societal cohesion. Moreover, the violent contestation of power in Yemen provides a visible example of how troubled the eventual transition may become. Gulf officials' uneasy awareness of their own looming transition may be a contributing factor to their reluctance to engage too publicly or closely with Yemen's ills. Yet this inconvenient truth clashes with the ambitious developmental models that have been embraced so firmly in the GCC.

A new approach to Gulf security?

The concept of human security has gained considerable traction since the 1990s to describe a new, people-centred notion that focuses on the security of individuals and communities rather than of states. Regional debates on security in the Gulf, as well as the broader Arab Middle East, have increasingly begun to anchor new approaches in this discourse. This emerging conceptual awareness could form an important element of a comprehensive approach to tackling the difficult underlying causes of the socio-economic challenges facing the transition to a post-oil political economy in the Gulf. Alternatively, ruling elites in the GCC may instead view their advocacy of human security as part of a strategy to update regime security and legitimacy, resulting in a 'half-way' house of stalled reforms that do not substantively shift the regional security architecture or paradigm. This is the turning-point that policy-makers and regional stakeholders in the Gulf will need to address in the years and decades to come.

In recent years, debates among groups and organisations in the GCC and the wider Middle East have begun to recognise the value of human security as a foundation-stone for constructing a new security paradigm. In November 2008, the Arab Women's Organisation, an intergovernmental body led by Arab First Ladies or their representatives, themed its biennial conference around women and human security. The delegates devoted the event, which took place in Abu Dhabi, to formulating a human security strategy that embraces women as equal participants and contributors. They cast this in developmental terms, arguing that the interconnected crises afflicting the Middle East 'require the total mobilisation of a nation's resources and capabilities, particularly the fuller participation of women in our societies ... it is a national, regional and global necessity' (*Gulf Times* 2008).

The Arab Women's Organisation's top-down approach was followed by a decidedly more bottom-up advocacy of human security in the fifth Arab Human Development report. This was entitled *Challenges to Human Security in the Arab Countries* and was published by the UNDP in July 2009. Its focus on the symbiosis of human development and human security marked the logical culmination of the four previous Arab Human Development Reports, which identified the lag in key indices of human development, governance and the political, economic and social empowerment in the Arab world. The report adopted its own definition of human security as 'the liberation of human beings from those intense, extensive, prolonged, and comprehensive threats to which their lives are vulnerable' (AHDR 2009: 17–18).

The developments and high-profile advocacy of the concept of human security described above are promising. Nevertheless, they raise a number of problematic considerations, not the least of which is the presence in the GCC states of large numbers of non-citizen labourers with few civil, political, economic or human rights. With this in mind, any top-down conception of a human security approach may be expected to differ substantially from the essence of the notion of a genuinely people-centred, bottom-up strategy to securing individual freedoms and rights. It remains to be seen how serious is the regional discourse on human security and whether or not it develops into a substantive redefinition of security in the GCC states. This notwithstanding, the idea of human security has become more visible and entered policy-making debates in recent years, and it does offer the intellectual building-blocks for a new vision on security should it develop a momentum of its own that takes it beyond the smothering embrace of the elite.

Intertwined with the rising awareness of human security are increasing references to issues of gender security. Alongside the United Arab Emirates, Oman and Qatar have led the way in publicising women's rights and placing women in visible positions of political and economic leadership. Prominent royals such as Sheikha Mozah of Qatar have assumed a leading role in educational and cultural development through initiatives such as the Qatar Foundation for Education, Science and Community Development and the Arab Democracy Foundation, in addition to becoming more assertive in entering the policy-making arena. In Oman, Sultan Qaboos appointed 14 women to the 70-strong State Council (*Majlis ad-Dawla*) in 2007, as part of a strategy designed to change public perceptions of the role of women in society, to create role models for future generations, and to extend his endorsement of the entry of women into public life (Valeri 2009: 169). Similarly high-profile appointments in Bahrain included the first Arab woman to lead the UN General Assembly and first judicial appointment to the Higher Civil Court, both in 2006, and the first female Ambassador to the United States, in 2008. Meanwhile in Kuwait, the historic election of four female members of the National Assembly in May 2009 reflected popular levels of frustration with the 'old guard' of Kuwaiti politicians and a desire for a new and more responsible approach to politics in the state.

As with human security, the prioritisation of gender security provides an opportunity for policy-makers to work toward an inclusive and empowering agenda that strengthens internal social cohesion. If this is allowed to take place, it can contribute both to human and national security by addressing the latent faultlines and internal fissures that might otherwise be vulnerable to manipulation by external variables or stresses. Such an approach would also lessen the likelihood of political violence and social conflict accompanying the transition to post-oil forms of governance and political economy, as states in transition have historically been more susceptible than others to contestation and challenge. Much initially depends on the attitude of the ruling families as agents of change, as the nature of reform processes in the Gulf are initially top-down and state-controlled, at least in their early stages. Their actions will determine whether fledgling reforms or discursive shifts develop into a substantive commitment to the values of people-centred security without discrimination between individuals and communities, including those with interests distinct from those of the ruling elite.

The future evolution of Gulf security will be framed by the need to find sustainable balances – between competing visions of the national and regional security architecture, between incremental changes to governing and economic structures and the deeper systemic problems that undermine long-term solutions, and between rising demands for, and falling supplies of, natural resources. At its core lies the balance between state and society and the reformulation of the social contract and frameworks of governing institutions to ensure as orderly a transition into the post-oil era as possible. In this regard, the management of dwindling oil reserves in Bahrain, Oman and Yemen will provide a barometer of the longer-term prospects for internal security and external stability in the Arabian Peninsula.

References

Aarts, P. Meertens, R. and van Duijne, J. (2008) 'Kingdom with borders: the political economy of Saudi–European relations', in M. Al-Rasheed (ed.), *Kingdom without Borders: Saudi Arabia's Political, Religious and Media Frontiers*. London: Hurst.

AHDR (2010) *Arab Human Development Report 2009: Challenges to Human Security in the Arab Countries*. New York: UNDP.

Berman, I. and Wihbey, P. M. (1999) 'The new water politics of the Middle East', *Strategic Review*, available at: http://www.iasps.org/strategic/water.htm (accessed 11 August 2011).

Boucek, C. (2009) *Yemen: Avoiding a Downward Spiral*, Carnegie Middle East Program Paper No. 102, Washington, DC.

Brown, O. and Crawford, A. (2009) *Rising Temperatures, Rising Tensions: Climate Change and the Risk of Violent Conflict in the Middle East*. Winnipeg: International Institute for Sustainable Development.

Clarke, M. (2005) 'Rethinking security and power', in D. Held and D. Mepham (eds), *Progressive Foreign Policy: New Directions for the UK*. Cambridge: Polity Press, pp. 18–35.

Depledge, J. (2008) 'Striving for no: Saudi Arabia in the climate change regime', *Global Environmental Politics*, 8(4): 9–35.

Dillon, M. (2005) 'Global security in the 21st century: circulation, complexity and contingency', in C. Browning and P. Cornish (eds), *The Globalization of Security*, ISP/NSC Briefing Paper 05/02, Chatham House, pp. 2–3.

Donn, G. and Al-Manthri, Y. (2010) *Globalisation and Higher Education in the Arab Gulf States*. Oxford: Symposium Books.

Dresch, P. (2005) 'Societies, identities and global issues', in P. Dresch and J. Piscatori (eds), *Monarchies and Nations: Globalization and Identity in the Arab States of the Gulf*. London: I. B. Tauris, pp. 1–33.

Drysdale, A. (2010) 'Population dynamics and birth spacing in Oman', *International Journal of Middle East Studies*, 42(1): 123–44.

Gulf Times (2008) 'Sheikha Fatima's efforts in women's cause hailed', 13 November.

Hadley Centre (2009) *Climate Change Middle East: Met Office Report*. Met Office Hadley Centre.

Hardy, R. (2008) 'Migrants demand labour rights in Gulf', *BBC News*, 27 February.

Held, D. (2007) 'Multilateralism and global governance: accountability and effectiveness', in D. Held and D. Mepham (eds), *Progressive Foreign Policy: New Directions for the UK*. Cambridge: Polity Press.

Hertog, S. and Luciani, G. (2009) *Energy and Sustainability Policies in the GCC*, Kuwait Programme Working Paper No. 6. London: LSE.

Hill, G. (2010) *Yemen: Fear of Failure*, Chatham House Briefing Paper. London: Chatham House.

Homer-Dixon, T. (2004) 'Environmental scarcities and violent conflict: evidence from cases', in M. E. Brown, O. R. Cote, S. M. Lynn-Jones and S. E. Miller (eds), *New Global Dangers: Changing Dimensions of International Security*. Cambridge, MA: MIT Press, pp. 265–300.

IPCC (2007) *Impacts, Adaptation and Vulnerability*, Working Group II Fourth Assessment Report. Intergovernmental Panel on Climate Change.

IsDB (2008) *IDB and UNSGAB Team Up to Support Water Sector in Arab Countries*, press release, 23 November, available at: http://www.isdb.org (accessed 11 August 2011).

Kaldor, M. (2007) *New and Old Wars: Organized Violence In a Global Era*, 2nd edn. Stanford, CA: Stanford University Press.

Kechichian, J. A. (2008) *Power and Succession in Arab Monarchies: A Reference Guide*. Boulder, CO: Lynne Rienner.

Krane, J. (2010) *Energy Conservation Options for GCC Governments*, Dubai School of Government Policy Brief, Dubai.

Kraska, J. and Wilson, B. (2009) 'The co-operative strategy and the pirates of the Gulf of Aden', *RUSI Journal*, 154(2): 74–81.

Krause, K. (1996) 'Insecurity and state formation in the global military order: the Middle Eastern case', *European Journal of International Relations*, 2(3): 319–54.

Launay, F. (2006) *Environmental Situational Awareness for the GCC Countries*. Dubai: Gulf Research Centre.

Longva, A. N. (2004) 'Neither autocracy nor democracy but ethnocracy: citizens, expatriates and the socio-political in Kuwait', in P. Dresch and J. Piscatori (eds), *Monarchies and Nations: Globalization and Identity in the Arab States of the Gulf*. London: I. B. Tauris, pp. 114–35.

Luomi, M. (2010) 'Abu Dhabi's alternative-energy initiatives: seizing climate-change opportunities', *Middle East Policy*, 16(4): 102–17.

Mabey, N. (2008) *Delivering Climate Security: International Security Responses to a Climate*

Changed World, RUSI Whitehall Paper Series No. 69. London: Royal United Services Institute.

Murphy, E. (2008) 'ICT and the Gulf Arab states: a force for democracy?', in A. Ehteshami and S. Wright (eds), *Reform in the Middle East Oil Monarchies*. Reading: Ithaca Press, pp. 181–216.

Price, R. M. (2008) *Moral Limit and Possibility in World Politics*. Cambridge: Cambridge University Press.

Raouf, M. A. (2008) *Climate Change Threats, Opportunities, and the GCC Countries*, Middle East Institute Policy Brief No.12. Washington, DC: Middle East Institute.

Raouf, M. A. (2009) *Water Issues in the Gulf: Time for Action*, Middle East Institute Policy Brief No. 22. Washington, DC: Middle East Institute.

Richer, R. (2008) *Conservation in Qatar: Impacts of Increasing Industrialization*, Center for International and Regional Studies Occasional Paper No. 1. Doha: CIRS.

Simpfendorfer, B. (2009) *The New Silk Road: How a Rising Arab World is Turning Away from the West and Rediscovering China*. Basingstoke: Palgrave Macmillan.

Valeri, M. (2009) *Oman: Politics and Society in the Qaboos State*. London: Hurst.

Winckler, O. (2009) 'Labor and liberalization: the decline of the GCC rentier system', in Joshua Teitelbaum (ed.), *Political Liberalization in the Persian Gulf*. London: Hurst.

Wright, S. (2008) *Fixing the Kingdom: Political Evolution and Socio-Economic Challenges in Bahrain*, Center for International and Regional Studies Occasional Paper No. 3. Doha: CIRS.

14

FOREIGN POLICIES WITH INTERNATIONAL REACH

The case of Qatar

Steven Wright

Introduction

Qatar has a unique importance on an international level in that despite its small size, it possesses the third largest reserves of natural gas, and has emerged as the leading global producer and exporter of liquefied natural gas (LNG) and gas to liquid fuels (GTL). This has allowed it to attain a role considerably beyond its geopolitical position. With Qatari gas now being exported to Europe, South Asia and North America, it has tied itself in with energy security calculations which brings with it a significant presence within the international system. Qatar's foreign policy is therefore of importance not only as a case study in the foreign affairs of a GCC member country, but more specifically in the international relations of the Gulf, given the manner in which it is engaging on a multi-regional level which is not the case with all of the GCC member states.

From the early 1990s, Qatar's foreign policy has been regarded as one based on pragmatism, in that it has not followed the traditional rules or expectations. Qatar's independent, or more accurately autonomous, foreign policy has complicated interpretations and the general wisdom on foreign policy-making within the Gulf. Qatar has broken with important common positions its neighboring Arab states have taken on issues ranging from establishing trade links and engaging in dialogue with Israel to successful summit-style diplomacy on Lebanon and also through its engagement with Iran. Its relations with Saudi Arabia until 2007 were unsettling for the GCC and itself a useful case study on inter-Gulf relations. Al Jazeera too has become a byword for controversy: not just among Qatar's regional neighbors, but on a truly global level. Indeed, analysts found it difficult to reconcile Qatar's strategic partnership with the United States through the hosting of a vast US military presence against the independently minded coverage of Al Jazeera, which the Bush administration saw as contradicting a changed US foreign policy stance with the onset of the global War on Terror (Gaddis 2005: 2).

The purpose of this chapter therefore is to identify the strategic pillars on which Qatari foreign policy can be historically conceptualized and to understand how this can be understood within a domestic, regional and international context. It will seek to offer observations on how Qatar has adopted an innovative foreign policy that underlines the generational changes taking place within the region. Qatar is therefore an excellent study not only in how it is becoming more integrated with other countries on a regional level, but also that it is becoming interconnected within the international state system through its vast energy supplies. In order to achieve this, the following section will therefore seek to offer observations on the historical context and development of Qatar's international relations.

Historical context of Qatari international relations

For Qatar, its geopolitical location has naturally been a key factor that has shaped its foreign policy agenda towards security and is an appropriate area to begin any discussion on Qatari foreign relations. In comparison to Iran and Saudi Arabia, which are regional superpowers, Qatar's geographical size and population stand in marked contrast. India, too, has been a geopolitical center which has significantly shaped the external relations of Qatar (and indeed the Gulf region): from 1916 Qatar was given the status of a British-protected state up to 1971, and during this period it was informally part of the British Indian Empire until 1947 (Onley 2007: 11–60). Qatar's security from seaward attack was guaranteed, as was sovereignty over its domestic affairs, yet, in return, Britain was allowed the control over its foreign policy. In the contemporary era, the United States has taken on a similar yet unstated security guarantor role since it relocated its forces from the Prince Sultan airbase in Saudi Arabia to Qatar in 2001, yet Qatar has retained autonomy in its foreign affairs despite this relationship. Given Qatar's size and its geopolitical perceptions of threat, it has been motivated to seek a countervailing protective alliance or security umbrella in order to have more autonomy of action and thus is the gateway for Qatar fulfilling its aspirations as an independent foreign policy actor (Nonneman 2005: 6–18).

As discussed above, within the Gulf, it is Saudi Arabia which has played the most decisive geopolitical role in foreign policy formation of the small sheikhdoms. In the pre-modern era, for Qatar and the other smaller GCC member states, Saudi Arabia has historically been an aspiring hegemonic power which brought with it natural challenges and perceived threats. Notable examples of this occurred in 1835 and 1851 as Emir Faisal bin Turki Al Saud saw the Qatari peninsula as being one of his dominions. In the context of the challenges posed by Saudi Arabia, the Al Khalifa of Bahrain and to a lesser extend the Al Nahyan of Abu Dhabi, a closer relationship was forged between the Al Thani and the Ottomans in 1871, and the British in 1916, in order to achieve externally backed security and provide for a continuity of tribal rule. This followed the historic tribal system of overlapping alliances and security guarantees, so cultivating relationships with other powers would have been an obvious way to safeguard tribal autonomy over the Qatari peninsula from the al Saud. It is worth recognizing that Sheikh Jassim bin Mohammed Al Thani pioneered the strategy in the Gulf of playing international powers off against each other as a means of maximizing security and avoiding "mono-dependence." Indeed, this approach was later notably copied by Sheikh Mubarak bin Sabah Al Sabah of Kuwait (known as Sheikh Mubarak the Great). As with Qatar, such strategy came to define Kuwait's foreign relations for some time.

Within the context of the First World War, an opportunity presented itself whereby Qatari and British interests coalesced: Britain's desire for a greater controlling influence within the Gulf was compatible with the Qatari objective of achieving security. This ultimately led to the signing of a special 'protectorate' treaty with Britain in 1916.[1] Its significance was that the provisions of the treaty afforded Qatar, and the other sheikhdoms who signed similar treaties, the security they badly needed to survive as fledgling states against the geopolitical weight of Saudi Arabia in particular. This relationship was long-lasting and continued until the protectorate relationship ended with the withdrawal of the British from the region in 1971. Even though the protectorate relationship placed Qatar within a pax Britannica security umbrella, the perception of threat from Saudi Arabia was significant enough to prompt repeated requests from the Qatari ruler, Sheikh Abdulla bin Jassim Al Thani, for a greater guarantee of protection from Saudi Arabia. The potential threat was acknowledged by Britain and a provision for Qatari sovereignty and security was included in the Anglo-Saudi agreement of 1927 (the Treaty of Jeddah). It called for peaceful relations to be maintained between Saudi Arabia and Qatar, in addition to the other Gulf sheikdoms. Nevertheless, despite the treaties of 1916 and 1927, Qatar faced an ongoing battle for a greater degree of autonomy from these geopolitical pressures, which placed limitations on its autonomy of action.

On a collective level, the GCC states have historically had geopolitical concerns with Iran. Iran is a country that has special geopolitical importance within the Gulf region by virtue of its size. Its regional foreign policy is representative of this privileged geopolitical position and the fears and pre-judices about Iran, which are common among the Arab Gulf monarchies, predate the Islamic revolution. Indeed, under the rule of Shah Abbas I during the sixteenth century, Iran came to be understood as a geopolitical and cultural heavyweight which had clear-cut regional aspirations for dominance. Yet Iran markedly differs from the Gulf Arab states given that it is comprised of the minority Shia sect within Islam. Such cultural, linguistic, religious, and identity differences have all played a key role in defining GCC–Iran relations.

Qatar's relations with post-revolutionary Iran have, however, differed from the other GCC states, and are an interesting case study in themselves. Qatar has enjoyed a more tempered relationship given the shared strategic asset of the vast North Field/South Pars natural gas field (the largest non-associated field in the world). Qatar and Iran's mutual economic interests in the field have developed progressively, based on this shared resource, especially since the mid-1980s, when Qatar took the strategic decision to view its economic future as resting on the reserves held within the field. Given Qatar's own strategic economic interests, its relations with Iran are grounded by this calculation and thus make Doha more willing to engage pragmatically with Tehran than its fellow GCC partners.

Qatar has also historically had to contend with perceived geopolitical challenges from Bahrain, which had used intermittent tribal relationships as an attempt to extend their authority from Bahrain to the Qatari peninsula. Indeed, the Al Khalifa and Al Jalahma branches of the Al Utub tribe had in fact migrated from Kuwait in 1766 to the Zubara area on the Qatari peninsula, and established a fort in Al Murair on the outskirts of Zubara. While there is no evidence that the Al Khalifa ever exercised authority over the people of Zubara, over time they were to become wealthy pearl merchants in the community. In 1786 they formed part of a coalition of tribes that ousted the Persian Governor of Bahrain, given his repeated attacks on Zubara town. The Al Khalifa then relocated from their fort in Al Murair in 1786 and became the rulers of Bahrain after a struggle for power against competing tribes. Yet, in this pre-modern-state system, authority was exercised through traditional tribally based patterns of governance, and thus the European concept of sovereignty is not a suitable guide. Indeed, a ruling tribe's domain should not necessarily be understood through the ability to exercise exclusive control, but rather through the possession of territory stemming from the loyalty of particular tribal roaming or habited areas (Joffe 1994: 78–93). Therefore relations in the pre-modern era with Bahrain can be historically conceptualized through the intermittent efforts by Al Khalifa to craft relationships with certain tribes and so extend their reach after they became the rulers of Bahrain.

In 1867, there was an outbreak of war with the Al Khalifa of Bahrain which ultimately led to the sack of eastern towns in Qatar by a united force from Bahrain and Abu Dhabi. In the wake of this breach of the maritime peace by Bahrain, Britain's relationship with the Al Thani was initially forged through Sheikh Mohammed bin Thani having signed with Britain a maritime treaty on preventing piracy in 1868. The maritime agreement in 1868 was not a protectorate treaty, but was significant in that it signaled Britain's formal recognition of Sheikh Mohamed Al Thani as the paramount Sheikh of the Qatari peninsula. However, by 1871, the Ottomans established a military presence on the Qatari peninsula, and Sheikh Jassim bin Mohammed Al Thani crafted a relationship with the Ottomans, in addition to the British, which effectively insulated the Qatari peninsula from the geopolitical challenges from the Al Khalifa, and also from the Saudi state. The trend of Qatar pragmatically using a foreign power as a guarantor of its security had thus emerged, and this is a strategy which continues to the contemporary era with the logic of allowing a United States military presence.

However, in the context of the First World War, which saw the Ottomans withdraw from the peninsula, Britain was to sign a treaty of protection with Sheikh Abdullah bin Jassim Al Thani in 1916. With the Ottomans having departed, a closer security relationship with Britain thus made strategic sense for the Al Thani. When Qatar signed a treaty with Britain in 1916 to become a protected state, it achieved a formal external security arrangement which allowed for a degree of regime security and autonomy in its domestic affairs, though leaving its foreign relations and security to the British. Britain's announcement in January 1968 that it would be ending its protection of the Gulf region by the end of 1971 meant that the security umbrella the emirate enjoyed came to an abrupt end. Qatar entered into negotiations with Bahrain and the Trucial States for the formation of a union, but this ultimately proved an unsuccessful vision. While Britain still had strategic and other commercial interests in Qatar, the type of arrangement which afforded Qatar autonomy and security from an external power was clearly missing. Qatar's relations with the United States at this time were still in their infancy and Washington did not even establish an embassy in Qatar until 1973.

The reality of Qatar's geopolitical situation in the initial years after independence translated to it opting that it was in its interests to "bandwagon" under the Saudi Arabian sphere of influence.[2] In other words, Saudi Arabia replaced Britain as Qatar's external security guarantor, but given Saudi Arabia is its neighbor, it meant that an obviously different dynamic existed to the relationship that had been enjoyed with the British. Therefore the situation was such that Qatar and the other Gulf Arab states faced increased pressures on their ability to exercise full autonomy in their foreign relations, but used Saudi Arabia to extend their international reach on common issues of concern. However, it was with the Iranian revolution in 1979 that Qatar, along with the other Gulf Arab states, coalesced behind their shared understanding of external and intra-state security from Tehran's Islamic theocracy. Qatar predictably formed part of the collective security voice of the GCC based on its own national interest. This was particularly so given Iran's apparent willingness to interfere in the domestic affairs of the Gulf states, as was evidenced by the Iranian-backed coup attempt in Bahrain in 1981.

With the ensuing Iran–Iraq war commencing in 1980, and the threats posed by Iran to regional oil supply routes, it is understandable that on the basis of national interest Qatar's foreign policies largely endorsed the collective GCC response. Closer relations with Saudi Arabia were thus part of this pragmatic strategy, yet it is important to recognize that autonomy and regime security remained the cornerstone of the objectives of Qatar's decision-making elite.

The new generational outlook: an autonomous international role

In the years following full independence in 1971, decision-making and policy formation under the Emir, Sheikh Khalifa bin Hamad Al Thani, can be characterized as largely centralized and patrimonial in character.[3] It was the changes to the decision-making structures, toward a more diffuse system with a greater degree of autonomy, which were to sow the seeds for the domestic structural pluralism of later years that would impact on the character of Qatar's future foreign policy and overall economic development strategies. In some respects, this was a product of the absence of competing interest groups that were sufficiently influential, but it also was a product of the idiosyncratic nature of the leader who chose to centralize decision-making. This was especially so in that, after 1972, Qatar was not only going through a transitional period, given the withdrawal of the British, but also a change in leadership from the first Emir, Sheikh Ahmed bin Ali Al Thani, which had taken place a year after independence. Such centralization in the domestic political sphere thus catered to a more personalized foreign policy. Yet, even though a centralized decision-making structure could be initially observed in Qatar, governmental changes and the ceding of autonomy in decision-making to other actors resulted in the concentration of power gradually evolving away from this structure. In Qatar's case, the main reasons for this shift can be understood through a political economy perspective, as will be discussed later. This evolving structure is a significant issue, as it largely explains the changed character Qatar's foreign policy took in the context of the Iran—Iraq war. The expanding roles of the then Crown Prince, Sheikh Hamad bin Khalifa Al Thani, serves as a good illustration of how Qatar's political system was becoming more decentralized as part of its development path. Importantly he was of a younger generation, and as a graduate of the Sandhurst military college, he had an education which offered him a more rounded international exposure. In addition to being Crown Prince, Sheikh Hamad was also Minister of Defense and Commander-in-Chief of the armed forces, and by May 1989, he had assumed a more autonomous role within the government as Chairman of the Higher Council for Planning, a position of key importance in state-building. This was all part of a trend which emerged from the late 1980s which saw the Emir cede more autonomy to the Crown Prince for the day-to-day running of the government. Significantly, this occurred within the context of the global slump in oil prices and Qatar running a budget deficit. A small budget deficit was first detected in 1985, but this became more acute and lasted from 1986 until 2000 when Qatar's economy eventually returned to surplus fiscal years.[4] Such an economic context was probably instrumental behind the Emir granting more autonomy to the Crown Prince as he was increasingly made responsible for achieving overall economic development and state-building.

With Sheikh Hamad playing an increasingly instrumental role in Qatar's government policies, a palatable change in foreign policy, in tandem with the reformed domestic policies, began to emerge after the ending of first the Iran—Iraq War and then the liberation of Kuwait by coalition forces in 1991. Given the manner in which Qatar's foreign policy had been crafted on pragmatism, and based on an interpretation of the national interest, we can clearly observe that the regional geopolitical context had changed the rules of the game in the Qatari–Saudi relationship. These changes were the beginnings of a more autonomous foreign policy, conducted largely out of Qatar's own perception of the national interest, and done so with little regard to the geopolitical pressures it was under. Here it is instructive that, as mentioned earlier, in 1991 Qatar opted to submit its territorial disputes with Bahrain to the International Court of Justice rather than resolve the issue through mediation with Saudi Arabia. In some respects this can be understood as a reflection of Sheikh Hamad's new independent approach to Qatari foreign policy, which placed emphasis on the international rule of law and the role of the United Nations. Indeed, Bahrain did not initially recognize the jurisdiction of the court over the dispute, and preferred to resolve the issue through mediation by Saudi Arabia which had agreed to take on this role. Qatar's willingness to exercise autonomy vis-à-vis the pressure it was under from Saudi Arabia to resolve this issue multilaterally within the GCC is particularly telling, as it is consistent with the altered domestic decision-making context in Qatar. The new context, which had steadily been emerging, was grounded in the ambitious vision of Sheikh Hamad, which steadfastly sought an independent country that prioritized the conduct of its foreign relations through objective international legal frameworks.

With Sheikh Hamad bin Khalifa Al Thani subsequently taking power in June 1995, Qatar's international relations can be understood as having entered into a more pronounced reflection of the new dynamism and autonomous character that had begun earlier within its domestic politics. By February 1996, there was a counter-coup attempt made, reportedly at the behest of the former Emir.[5] This underlines the geopolitical threats Qatar was facing, and served to underline that security was best achieved through adopting a multifaceted foreign policy matrix geared toward overcoming these tangible threats.

What is also of great significance is the extent to which the new Emir, Sheikh Hamad bin Khalifa Al Thani, set about reconstituting the very character of Qatar's political, economic and social system. The manner in which he did this would also see Qatar's foreign relations gradually evolve along with it, largely because of greater autonomy at the agency level. At this stage, however, it is important to fully appreciate the wide-ranging nature of reforms that were implemented from this fresh generational change (Bahry 1999: 118–27). A good example of the formal manifestation of Qatar's new foreign policy agenda under Sheikh Hamad bin Khalifa Al Thani was enshrined in the 2004 constitution, where Article 7 stated:

> The foreign policy of the State is based on the principle of strengthening international peace and security by means of encouraging peaceful resolution of international disputes; and shall support the right of peoples to self-determination; and shall not interfere in the domestic affairs of states; and shall cooperate with peace-loving nations.[6]

Qatar's constitution thus envisaged it having a proactive global role by the inclusion of the objective of "encouraging peaceful resolution of international disputes." In many respects, this was a reflection of the generationally influenced outlook of the new Emir, Sheikh Hamad bin Khalifa Al Thani. Nevertheless, since the late 1980s, when Sheikh Hamad began to play a more decisive role in foreign policy, a pattern is identifiable whereby the strategic objective was for Qatar to have autonomy of action in order to fulfill an independent foreign policy. Such a foreign policy was guided by the generational and personal outlook of the Emir, who wanted Qatar to have international recognition and a positive global role in the world. This was to be achieved through the leverage Qatar can demand through its natural gas card, while also working to support international law and the United Nations. In some respects, with Qatar and the other smaller GCC states having been in the shadow of Saudi Arabia, whose international role was based on its position as the leading oil supplier, so too did Qatar see the potential to play an equally important role, given its capacity as the leading global producer and exporter of natural gas products. A key strategy Qatar adopted in order to achieve this was to fulfill its security needs through entering into a security cooperation agreement with the United States.

As indicated earlier, relations with the United States were slow in developing as an embassy was only opened in Doha in 1973, with a resident ambassador from 1974. Indeed, it was not until over two decades later that a strategic partnership with Doha was to emerge. Although Qatar participated in the 1991 coalition to liberate Kuwait from Iraq, the regional presence of the United States was concentrated at the Prince Sultan airbase south of Riyadh. Qatar signed a defense cooperation agreement with the United States in 1992 which allowed for the prepositioning of defense equipment and access to military facilities and joint military exercises, but it was not until Sheikh Hamad took power in 1995 that the foundations were set for a changed foreign policy strategy of seeking a long-term hard-security arrangement to offset the geopolitical threats that were being faced.

In 1996 work commenced on the construction of an airbase facility in Al Udaid, which was widely reported as costing Qatar over US$1 billion. The decision to devote the financing to the construction of the Al Udaid airbase underlines a strategic decision that was made to entice the positioning of a significant portion of US forces away from Saudi Arabia's Prince Sultan airbase facility in order to provide security for Qatar. Yet given the deteriorated relationship with its neighbors following the change of leadership in 1995, the decision to lay the foundations for entering into a security arrangement with the United States was obviously based on practical considerations. In several respects, a parallel could be drawn with the calculations made by the Qatari leadership in 1916, where they entered into a special treaty relationship which afforded protection under the British security umbrella. Policies to support this strategic objective of developing ties with the United States included the opening of an Israeli trade office in Doha in May 1996: a clear break with the long-standing collective position of the GCC. On a contextual level, the invitation to US universities to relocate to Qatar's Education City further enhanced bilateral relations. Even the establishment of Al Jazeera as a beacon of free press in the Middle East region proved to be a welcome policy by Western countries until the onset of the War on Terror in 2001. During this period of strategic consolidation, Qatar–US relations were further reinforced by the successful diplomacy undertaken by the Prime Minister and Foreign Minister, Sheikh Hamad bin Jassim Al Thani.

While the Al Udaid airbase is owned and run by the Qatari armed forces, it was only in the aftermath of the terrorist attacks of 9/11 in the United States, and the onset of the War on Terror grand strategic context, that the Al Udaid facility took on a greater importance. The United States' relations with Saudi Arabia were under intense scrutiny after the attacks, given that the majority of the hijackers and bin Laden himself were of Saudi origin. The redeployment of US forces from Prince Sultan airbase to Al Udaid also saw the facility become the location for the Headquarters of US Central Command, and the willingness of Qatar to facilitate the United States military was in marked contrast to the situation in Saudi Arabia. Overall, for Qatar the positioning of US forces on its territory was a strategic accomplishment, as it now enjoyed the protection of the US security umbrella against the geopolitical threats it had been susceptible to since the British military withdrawal from the Gulf in 1971. It was, however, in the context of the decision of the ICJ in March 2001 on the territorial dispute Qatar had with Bahrain that a similar agreement was finalized with Saudi Arabia on its border with Qatar.[7] The indications of a potential new phase of cooperation were thus beginning to take shape; yet this was thwarted by the actions of Al Jazeera, whose autonomy created a serious diplomatic incident in September 2002 between the two countries, and resulted in the withdrawal of Saudi Arabia's Ambassador to Doha. Ultimately, relations were restored and the rapprochement with Saudi Arabia was not only linked to the context of Qatar's altered security situation, but also to the diffusion of intra-state insecurity stemming from the former Emir, Sheikh Khalifa bin Hamad. Their differences were resolved by direct diplomacy to an extent that, by 14 October 2004, Sheikh Khalifa bin Hamad was permitted to return to Qatar to attend the funeral of his wife. With Sheikh Khalifa being granted the title "Emir-al-Ab" (Emir Father), and being granted full state honors upon arrival, a public reconciliation had been achieved.

It was, however, at a summit in Jeddah in September 2007 between Sheikh Hamad and King Abdullah that the main outstanding differences that had complicated the bilateral relationship since the mid-1980s, but particularly so since 1995, were resolved. The Jeddah summit was thus a historic turning point in the Qatari–Saudi relationship, and the deal was followed by King Abdullah's visit to Doha for the GCC summit in December 2007, and Crown Prince Sultan bin Abdulaziz al Saud's subsequent visit in March 2008, which underscored the renewal of the bilateral relations.

Overall, relations with Saudi Arabia and the United States demonstrates how Qatar sought to achieve security, firstly through entering into a hard-security arrangement with the United States, and then using this platform to normalize its relations with Saudi Arabia. Given Qatar's geopolitical neighborhood, it is reasonable to see such a strategy as having made strategic sense, and is a largely successful foreign policy in this regard. Nevertheless, since the onset of the War on Terror, Qatar's relationship with the United States has been hampered by Al Jazeera, and thus paints a paradoxical picture given these shared strategic interests. Al Jazeera's coverage of the invasion of Iraq, and its willingness to air the full audio or video broadcasts of Al Qaeda's leadership, was to the Bush administration a highly provocative act in the context of the War on Terror while to Qatar it was evidence of even-handed reporting. Qatar's unwillingness to curtail Al Jazeera's broadcasts brought international notoriety for the country and for the channel itself. This underlines that Qatar sees Al Jazeera as an attempt at soft power: it seeks to set the news agenda based on free speech, and therefore to exert influence internationally. Nevertheless, although such a hard-security relationship and dynamics with external powers have been key for Qatar achieving its objectives of increased autonomy and security, it is important at this stage to recognize that Qatar has also seemingly adopted a supplemental strategy of security diversification (or managed multi-dependence) in order to further enhance and maintain its grand strategic pillars. The following sections therefore show how Al Jazeera emerged, and how Qatar has benefited from it, and then move on to a discussion of the role of energy resources and conflict resolution as a means of enhancing its international profile.

The Al Jazeera factor

Al Jazeera has proved to be as controversial as it was revolutionary to the region's media, and it has had a profound influence on Qatar's foreign relations and international image. State censorship was abolished in October 1995, a few months after Sheikh Hamad became Emir. The Ministry of Information and Culture was subsequently abolished in 1998. Yet Sheikh Hamad had indicated as early as August 1994 that he was in favor of the establishment of an independent news channel, and by February to March 1995, while he was still Crown Prince, preparations were made for the foundation of the channel (Bahry 2001: 88–99). His generational outlook was clearly more progressive, and such commitments to freedom of speech and expression struck a chord with many in the West, who sought liberalization in the Middle Eastern region. Al Jazeera was formally established by an Emiri decree in February 1996 and began its transmissions in November 1996. Initially, Al Jazeera only broadcast for six hours per day from the Arabsat satellite and it was only in January 1999 that a 24-hour broadcast was achieved.[8] The sister channel, Al Jazeera English, was launched in November 2006.

With Qatar's censorship laws being repealed in 1995, Al Jazeera was granted editorial independence, and thus can be understood as having autonomy. It is important to recognize that the autonomous application of freedom of speech and editorial independence to this agency gives journalists a carte blanche to focus on issues considered the most newsworthy for its regional audience: in several respects, it is reasonable to conclude that this would increase the type of journalism which has so often proved unpalatable to several governments, particularly those in the region. This is especially so, given Al Jazeera's penchant for investigative journalism and unhindered debates, and so is quite different from having an underhanded editorial agenda. Yet Al Jazeera has suffered from criticisms that it seldom covers domestic issues within the Qatari state, and therefore is evidence of bias. In part, of course, this depends on the available international newsworthiness of domestic events within Qatar as Al Jazeera is after all a global news media broadcaster. However, a notable issue which Al Jazeera provided critical coverage on in Qatar was the plight of the foreign laborers in a documentary entitled *Blood, Sweat and Tears*, which was broadcast in 2007. While this broadcast was telling, it is the exception which raises the issue of the extent to whether Qatari domestic affairs are simply not seen as news-worthy, or whether an editorial self-censorship is practised. While this unre-solved issue is a clear area for future scholarship and research, what can be concluded is that Al Jazeera has ushered in a new era of free (or freer) speech to the region.

The allowance of free speech is clearly a progressive liberalization, but it is also something of a double-edged sword. On the one hand it resulted in regional recriminations against Doha by neighboring states, and on the other it was an innovative method of showing the country's commitment to liberalism and forward-thinking. Indeed, the control over the dominant media player in the Middle East, coupled with its reputation for unfettered broadcasting, can prove to be a powerful political weapon in shaping domestic attitudes within the societies of Middle Eastern states. Such unfettered broadcasting is a powerful tool, and this has been underlined by the establishment, in 2003, of Al Arabiya, which is a Dubai-based satellite news broadcaster. It is largely owned by Lebanon's Hariri group, with investors from Saudi Arabia and the other Gulf states, and so is a direct competitor to Al Jazeera. This, in itself, underlines the shifting boundaries between domestic and external spheres that Qatar has brought to the Gulf region. Such developments are significant to the relation-ship between the rulers and the people, yet it should be remembered that there is a difference between an informed and an empowered citizenry: Al Jazeera and Al Arabiya can therefore be conceptualized as the means by which states are not only balancing external and internal pressures, but also the new way in which it is creating an informed regional citizenry and blurring the boundaries of the regional and domestic spheres.

Al Jazeera's regional accessibility, and willingness to broadcast controversial themes about neighboring countries, have helped it develop a reputation for investigative journalism and uninhibited live debates. These have allowed it to become one of the most widely watched satellite news channels in the world.

While Al Jazeera only had a limited air-time until 1997, by 1998 many regarded it as the most influential media outlet in the region, and it had a widely accepted impact on competing media outlets throughout the Middle East. With its large audience and reputation, in addition to its editorial willingness to court controversy by allowing guests free speech, the channel had a clear impact on Qatari foreign relations. Qatar had thus developed an effective agency which, based on the principal of freedom of speech and editorial independence, allowed it to have a commitment to "universal ideals" that supported its wider efforts to enter into a hard-security arrangement with the United States in order to best achieve the goals of autonomy and security. Yet, as Al Jazeera seeks to set the news agenda and therefore exert influence internationally, it is Qatar's attempt at soft power. While there are tangible benefits to providing autonomy to such an agency, it also presents the very real challenge of not necessarily allowing for integration with Qatari diplomacy, or for objectives with regard to both regional countries and to the United States: it thus presents a paradoxical picture which can hamper foreign policy outcomes.

Energy and security diversification

The discovery by Shell Oil in 1971 of the North Field, which is the world's largest natural gas field at around 6,000 sq km, has given Qatar a unique position in regional and international natural gas markets. Qatar possesses the third largest reserves of natural gas after Russia and Iran, yet the development of its natural gas potential from the mid-1980s has allowed it to become the leading exporter of liquefied natural gas (LNG), and Qatar is poised to become the leading exporter of the more environmentally friendly gas to liquid fuels (GTL). With global energy consumption showing an increasing demand for LNG and GTL fuels, the ability of Qatar to play a major role in key countries' and regions' energy security mix is clear.

Qatar's energy policy appears to be dictated by the fundamentals of supply and demand, with energy contracts going to the market where the highest price or volumes can be achieved.[9] By providing a significant proportion of foreign countries' energy needs, Qatar is creating "stakeholders" in its own stability and security. While this does not necessarily translate to the hard-security guarantee that it enjoys with the United States, it is catering for profile-building, influence and stronger diplomatic ties with key countries that enhances its indirect security. In other words, although energy policy may not necessarily be fully integrated with Qatar's foreign policy, it indirectly offers Qatar what can be considered as supplemental security diversification. Therefore it is justified to provide an overview of how Qatar's energy sector is indirectly enhancing the mainstream foreign policy.

The manner in which Qatar is exploiting its energy "trump card" explains not only its future political economy, but more pertinently the manner in which an additional level of security diversification is taking place at the agency level.

Qatar's energy policy, with regard to its foreign policy drivers, can be conceptualized on both the regional and the international level. On the regional level, projected rising demand for natural gas resulted in GCC discussions as early as the 1980s for a regional gas grid. Regional demand was rising at above world average rates, not only because of domestic demand for gas-fired power stations, but also because of the need for increasing levels of gas for reinjection into the oil fields. While there was consideration of an extended gas pipeline out of the GCC from Qatar to Israel, Pakistan and India, for a variety of political, technical, and economic reason these proposals were shelved. Ultimately this gave way to a regionally located grid linking Qatar with Kuwait, Oman, and the UAE, but given the context of Qatari–Saudi relations, Riyadh voiced opposition to the construction of a pipeline that was to go through its territorial waters. It therefore became unfeasible to include Kuwait in any such project. In the wake of this, the Dolphin Project emerged which was more limited in scope, as it would only link Qatar with the UAE and Oman. Therefore, in foreign policy terms, Qatar's energy supply relationship with Oman and the UAE, which came on stream in 2008, allowed for enhanced regional relationships for Qatar based on mutual interests with these two countries.

On the international level, however, the major importers of Qatar's LNG in 2008 were South Korea, Japan and India. However, by 2012, other leading importers of Qatar's LNG will include the United Kingdom and the USA, but this may prove to be delayed, given the global economic downturn that began in late 2008. Interestingly, Qatar has been able to take advantage of the energy security needs of European countries, as its supply relationship with Europe indicates that, given the geopolitical need to diversify their natural gas imports away from Russia, Italy, Belgium, Spain, and France will see Qatar's LNG constituting an increasingly important proportion of their energy imports. Qatar should, by 2012, provide in the region of 20 per cent of Europe's natural gas imports. As with the regional implications of Qatar's supply of natural gas to the UAE and Oman, the indirect byproduct of Qatar's significant global supply relationships has translated into the country taking on an increased importance for the global community. This translates to a form of indirect security diversification, which builds on the hard-security arrangement that Qatar has with the United States. Yet, with energy contracts being signed on economic criteria, the energy policy can be considered as operating with a degree of autonomy at the agency level. The key issue for Qatari energy policy, and how it links in with the overarching foreign policy objectives, appears to be whether a pan-GCC gas grid, or indeed an extension of the Dolphin pipeline, will be able to deliver similar profit margins as compared to those that can be obtained by exporting it as a commodity to markets beyond the region. The indirect effects of such calculations translate into Qatar having a higher level of importance in energy security either on a regional or an international level, which caters for influence and indirect security diversification through the creation of energy stakeholders.

Conflict resolution and security diversification

The manner in which Qatar has sought to enhance its national security has allowed for a greater degree of autonomy in foreign policy, especially since the hard-security relationship with the United States was formalized. Although the achievement of security allows for autonomy of action, Qatar's dynamic role in regional conflict resolution and mediation poses the interesting question of its underlying motives, given that these are not obviously related to the drivers of achieving autonomy and security, as outlined above. Is it merely the clearest expression of an autonomous Qatari foreign policy behavior, or does it have a particular purpose, such as profile-building? Qatar has become engaged in backchannel diplomacy and high profile conflict resolution in Lebanon, Yemen, Sudan, Libya, and Iraq, among other cases. The high-profile Doha-brokered agreement between the contesting parties in Lebanon in 2008 is particularly worthy of note, with parties being flown to Doha, showing Qatar's willingness to engage in high-profile summit-style diplomacy.

The evolution of Qatar's role in conflict resolution is a relatively recent development and has become apparent largely after the security situation was formalized with the United States. While a hard-security arrangement has allowed Qatar autonomy of action, and thus allowed for such diplomacy to take place, it is also largely explainable from a political economy perspective. As discussed earlier, Qatar suffered from budget deficits from the mid-1980s until 2000. This is an important explanatory factor, as surplus wealth has allowed the country to engage in mediation, and also use "dollar-diplomacy" as a foreign policy tool. This method was notably employed by Qatar in order to broker the Doha agreement on Lebanon in 2008. Further motivating factors behind such involvement in conflict diplomacy are the idiosyncratic motivations towards such causes by Qatar's elite decision-makers. It is clear that the Emir, Sheikh Hamad bin Khalifa Al Thani, has aspirations for Qatar to be not only a key regional actor, but also a prominent player on the international stage (as shown in the constitution), and he has also shown a great personal commitment towards the cause of the Palestinians, among others. The regional leadership role Qatar wished to take over the Israeli–Gaza conflict in January 2009 is a clear example of the deep commitment felt towards the Palestinian cause by elite decision-makers. Qatar's engagement with and support of such causes is a clear expression of its autonomy: the challenge in Qatari diplomacy is therefore to balance the expression of autonomy against its cooperative relationship with the United States.

Concluding observations

Qatar's foreign policy provides a useful case study on how foreign policy-making within the Gulf monarchies is changing and, in the case of Qatar, becoming much more internationally orientated and involved in diplomacy outside the Gulf region. Among the GCC, Qatar is often hailed as the exception to the rule of the traditional "hedging" nature of Gulf-styled diplomacy. It is true that Kuwait has shown an increased tendency to feel unobligated to support common-GCC or even pan-Arab initiatives, as has been the case in Qatar. Nevertheless, Doha's approach to foreign relations shows marked differences to its neighbors, in that it actively seeks global diplomatic roles and international status through upholding its mantra of having a truly independent policy. This has been carried out with little regard to whether it has offended neighboring countries, which is a clear departure from the norm of traditional diplomacy within the GCC.

Qatar is clearly a small state with huge ambitions, as evidenced by its role in conflict resolution. The origins of this desire appear to be idiosyncratic in that generational change in 1995 brought with it a new global outlook and an ambition to achieve recognition through profile-building. Qatar underlines the potency of generational change on policies and outlooks; given the hereditary structure of government, and the manner in which decisions are typically formulated by a small number of elites, it is understandable that when succession of a leader takes place, a new agenda will be initiated which can markedly differ from that of its predecessor.

The lessons Qatar teaches us for the increasingly globalized Gulf region is that the old rules of the game do not necessarily apply; yet this is very different from suggesting that this is part of a wider transformation in GCC foreign policy-making. Indeed, Qatar's radical new behavior in its foreign policy is actually largely explainable by factors which are specific to Qatar. Its political economy may fit the rentier model, but its role as the leading supplier of natural gas products on a global basis brings with it a different dynamic than in any of the Gulf states. This capacity allows Qatar a genuine policy of security diversification which moves beyond the post-Cold War scenario of security being guaranteed by the United States, and is consistent with the historical trend of the Gulf Sheikdoms seeking an external power that can cater for their regime and dynastic security interests. Qatar's approach is one of "diversified security" through the utilization an overlapping global security matrix, which is premised on foreign powers having a vested interest in Qatar's security. This goes far beyond the traditional situation of quid pro quo, which a mere hosting of a military presence brings with it. For Qatar, as it continues its security diversification strategy, it is building capacity for itself to have the confidence to exercise autonomy and continue its independently orientated diplomacy.

Notes

1. The Anglo-Qatar Treaty of 1916 was signed on 3 November 1916 but was not ratified by the British until 23 March 1918.
2. Such was the character of the relationship that existed between the two countries given the altered geopolitical context since 1971, an example of strong bilateral ties

can be highlighted by the situation after the assassination of Saudi Arabia's King Faisal bin Abdul-Aziz al Saud in March 1975 and the death of King Khalid bin Abdul-Aziz al Saud in 1982, as Qatar observed a 40-day mourning period for both monarchs.

3. The decision-making structure is after all of key importance to understanding how cohesive or non-integrated a foreign policy manifests itself in developing countries (Korany 2008).

4. According to Qatar's Planning Council, Qatar had an uninterrupted budget deficit trend from 1985 to 2000 with the exception of the fiscal year 1990–1 where a budget surplus was achieved.

5. "Life sentences for Qatari coup plotters," *BBC News Online* (1996).

6. Permanent Constitution of the State of Qatar, 2004, Article 7.

7. This was based on the conclusions of a joint technical committee which came to an agreement over the border in 1999, but given the outstanding Bahrain–Qatar dispute at the ICJ, the formal signing of this agreement was delayed until March 2001.

8. Transmission was increased to eight hours in January 1997 and then subsequently to 12. With a change to a C-band transponder in November 1997, an 18-hour transmission was implemented.

9. Personal interview, Doha, December 2007.

References

Aitchison, C. U. (1987) *Treaties and Engagements Relating to Arabia and the Persian Gulf.* Gerards Cross: Archive Editions.

Al-Arayed, J. S. (2003) *A Line in the Sea: The Qatar vs. Bahrain Border Dispute in the World Court.* Berkeley, CA: North Atlantic Books.

Bahry, L. Y. (1999) "Elections in Qatar: a window of democracy opens in the Gulf," *Middle East Policy*, 6(2): 118–27.

Bahry, L. Y. (2001) "The new Arab media phenomenon: Qatar's Al-Jazeera," *Middle East Policy*, 8(2): 88–99.

Buzan, B. and Little, R. (2000) *International Systems in World History: Remaking the Study of International Relations.* Oxford: Oxford University Press.

Cole, D. P. (1975) *Nomads of the Nomads: The Al-Murrah Bedouin of the Empty Quarter.* Chicago: Aldine.

David, S. (1991) "Explaining third world alignment," *World Politics*, 43(2): 233–56.

Gaddis, J. L. (2005) "Grand strategy in the second term," *Foreign Affairs*, 84(1): 2.

Gause, F. G. (2002) "The foreign policy of Saudi Arabia," in R. Hinnebusch and A. Ehteshami (eds), *The Foreign Policies of Middle Eastern States.* London: Lynne Rienner, pp. 193–4.

Hinnebusch, R. (2002) "Introduction: the analytical framework," in R. Hinnebusch and A. Ehteshami (eds), *The Foreign Policies of Middle Eastern States.* London: Lynne Rienner, p. 1.

Joffe, G. (1994) "Concepts of sovereignty in the Gulf region," in R. Schofield (ed.), *Territorial Foundations of the Gulf States.* New York: St. Martin's Press, pp. 78–93.

Kechichian, J. A. (2008) *Power and Succession in Arab Monarchies: A Reference Guide.* London: Lynne Rienner, pp. 201–2.

Korany, B. and Dessouki, A. E. H. (2008) *The Foreign Policies of Arab States: The Challenge of Globalization.* Cairo: American University of Cairo Press.

Lorimer, J. G. (1986) *Gazetteer of the Persian Gulf, Oman and Central Arabia.* Gerrards Cross: Archive Editions, pp. 1505–35.

Nonneman, G. (2005) "Analysing the foreign policies of the Middle East and North Africa: a conceptual framework," in G. Nonneman (ed.), *Analyzing Middle East Foreign Policies and the Relationship with Europe.* London: Routledge, pp. 6–18.

Onley, J. (2007) *The Arabian Frontier of the British Raj: Merchants, Rulers, and the British in the Nineteenth-Century Gulf.* Oxford: Oxford University Press, pp. 11–60.

Palgrave, W. G. (1865) *Narrative of a Year's Journey through Central and Eastern Arabia (1862–63).* London: Macmillan.

Peterson, J. E. (2006) "Qatar and the world: branding of a micro-state," *Middle East Journal*, 60(4): 732–48.

Tuson, P. (1991) *Records of Qatar: Primary Documents 1820–1960.* Slough: Archive Editions.

Wright, S. (2008) *Fixing the Kingdom: Political Evolution and Socio-Economic Challenges in Bahrain,* Center for International and Regional Studies Occasional Paper No. 3. Doha: CIRS.

Zahlan, R. S. (1979) *The Creation of Qatar.* London: Routledge, p. 19.

Government Publications

State of Qatar (1971) *Census of 1971.* Doha: Qatar Ministry of Information.

Newspaper and Media Sources

Qatar

Gulf Times
Qatar News Agency
The Peninsula
Al Jazeera.net

UK

BBC News Online

15

TRENDS IN GULF STATE ASSISTANCE TO CRISIS-AFFECTED CONTEXTS

Sultan Barakat and Steven A. Zyck

Introduction

The past decade has witnessed the resurgence of official development assistance (ODA) from the Gulf states. Bilateral aid contributions from the Kingdom of Saudi Arabia (KSA), Kuwait and the United Arab Emirates (UAE) have leapt from slightly more than US$400 million in 1999 to nearly US$6 billion a decade later. In doing so, the Arab Gulf is beginning to reclaim its position, which it had gradually given up throughout the 1980s and 1990s, as a major humanitarian and development financier. Consider for instance that, in 1978, the KSA, Kuwait and the UAE contributed funds equivalent to 40.3 per cent of that provided by the then 18 'traditional' donors comprising the Development Assistance Committee (DAC) of the Organisation for Economic Cooperation and Development (OECD). Furthermore, in 1980, ODA provided by the KSA was over three times the value of aid given globally by the United Kingdom (Porter 1986: 46).[1] However, the following two decades saw a significant decline in Gulf state financing in both relative and real terms, whereas contributions from the DAC continued to grow (Haldane 1990). By 1999, KSA, Kuwait and the UAE – three of the most significant Gulf state donor countries – were providing barely half a per cent of the world's humanitarian and development assistance (see Figure 15.1).

Conflict-affected contexts in the Middle East have received a significant proportion of aid from the likes of KSA, Kuwait, the UAE and others, such as Qatar. It is thus necessary not only to understand how much the Gulf states have provided but also how they have provided it – through what mechanisms, to what implementing partners, for what types of programmes and with what effect. This chapter aims to move beyond the speculative analysis of Gulf states' humanitarian motives, which has preoccupied much of the earlier research into the question of Gulf state donorship (see Alesina and Dollar 2000; Villanger 2007). These previous studies have tended to sidestep the technical dimensions of Gulf state donorship addressed in this chapter given the dearth of quality data which was, and is, available. The Gulf states publicly report only a portion of the aid they provide and, given that aid is provided through a range of state

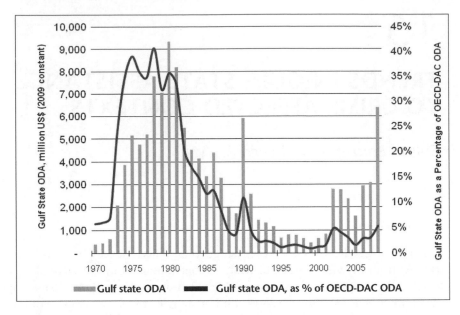

FIGURE 15.1   OECD–DAC and Gulf state ODA (1970–2008)

Source: OECD 'Stats', Query Wizard on International Development Statistics, at: http://stats.oecd.org/qwids/.

institutions within individual Gulf countries, may not themselves have a clear picture of their net ODA. While the authors draw upon data reported by the Gulf states to the OECD and the UN's Financial Tracking Service (FTS), the lack of comprehensive, credible and organised data, as has previously been noted (UNESCWA 2007; Hamid 2009), poses an immense challenge for research into Arab donorship.[2] As such, this chapter should be read as a best-possible analysis of available data. Research which moves beyond the contours of Gulf state aid and which examines its internal variations and nuances will require far greater transparency on the part of the Gulf states, an issue which continues to receive attention from DAC member countries and Arab multilateral institutions, particularly the Arab Fund for Economic and Social Development (AFESD), but which has seen little progress in recent years (Al-Hamad and Deutscher 2009).

Gulf state donorship: a review

Before progressing further, it is important to understand the diverse landscape of Gulf institutions engaged in providing humanitarian and development assistance. As in DAC member countries, ODA from the Gulf has been channelled through an array of bilateral and multilateral channels. The only Gulf states with formal, fully governmental donor agencies are Kuwait, the UAE and the KSA (Neumayer 2003b, 2004). The oldest of these institutions is the Kuwait Fund for Arab Economic Development (KFAED), founded shortly following Kuwait's independence in 1961, and it is widely considered as the most innovative of Gulf state donor institutions (Porter 1986: 45). The UAE followed Kuwait and founded the Abu Dhabi Fund for Arab Economic Development in 1971, since renamed the Abu Dhabi Fund for Development (ADFD). The Saudi Fund for Development (SFD) was then established in 1974 (El Mallakh 1982). These three agencies, or funds, have been joined by a number of quasi-non-governmental and *ad hoc* donor institutions which, while formally private, disburse assistance from and in the name of the state. While much of foreign assistance from Qatar, for instance, is provided via direct financial transfers, Qatari officials suggest that the non-governmental Qatar Foundation appears poised to take on a similar role as that played by specialised donor agencies in the other Gulf states. Even in the absence of a recognisable governmental organ overseeing ODA, Qatar, after KSA, Kuwait and South Korea, was the fourth largest non-DAC donor in 2003 and the twenty-fifth most significant overall (Cotterrell and Harmer 2005: 17).

Following the founding of these bilateral institutions, multilateral aid agencies started to emerge. In 1974, multilateral institutions were established in rapid succession. Kuwait, as with bilateral donor institutions, instigated this development when it began hosting the Arab Fund for Economic and Social Development (AFESD) in 1974 (Nonneman 1988). The Islamic Development Bank (IsDB) was founded in 1975 and has been referred to as an institution designed to promote Islamic solidarity (Porter 1986; Meenais 1989). The IsDB has promoted Sharia-compliant finance more than other Arab multilateral donor institutions (Wilson 2009).[3] In 1976, the UAE followed suit when it established the Arab Monetary Fund (AMF) in Abu Dhabi (Hallwood and Sinclair 1981). Although the AFESD, IsDB and AMF concentrated on general development cooperation throughout the region, with a focus upon concessional loans and guarantees, other relatively more specialised, or geographically focused, multilateral bodies developed later (Van den Boogaerde 1991). These included the Arab Bank for Economic Development in Africa (BADEA), founded in 1974, which solely assists those countries which are members of the Organisation of African Unity (OAU) but not of the Arab League (BADEA 1974). The only multilateral institution not to focus upon loans and other forms of development financing has been the Arab Gulf Programme for the United Nations Development Organisation (AGFUND). AGFUND was founded at the recommendation of the KSA's Prince Talal Bin Abdul Aziz Al Saud in 1980 and primarily allows Arab countries to support UN activities, through an Arab-owned channel, rather than supporting a stand-alone agency. A final multilateral institution frequently associated with the Gulf states is the OPEC Fund for International Development (OFID). Including all member countries of the Organisation of Petroleum Exporting Countries (OPEC), it primarily provides loans to highly indebted poor countries (HIPCs) with a smaller focus upon grants and post-emergency assistance (Benamara and Ifeagwu 1987).

Multilateral Gulf state institutions, despite their number and variety, have traditionally proved far less financially significant than the bilateral donor agencies, particularly with regard to the sort of grant-funded assistance which is most common in conflict-affected contexts. While heavily utilised in the years following their establishment, multilateral agencies have frequently fallen out of fashion as the Gulf states have turned to forms of assistance for which each government received direct credit in recipients' eyes (Cotterrell and Harmer 2005: 12). Multilateral sources have comprised an average of only between 3 and 5 per cent of the Gulf states' total assistance to developing countries and, as such, are only a minor focus of this chapter. The remainder of this chapter will focus upon bilateral Gulf state agencies in the KSA, Kuwait, the UAE and Qatar.

Origins of Gulf state donorship

Humanitarian and development assistance from the Arab Gulf emerges from the Islamic principle of charity, or *zakat*, which requires contributions to the poor and vulnerable by those who have the means to do so (Anwar 1995; Benthall and Bellion-Jourdan 2003; ICG 2003; Weiss 2002). Before institutionalised, international donorship emerged, *zakat* funds existed, and still do, for primarily domestic causes in many Islamic countries (Benthall and Bellion-Jourdan 2003). The Gulf states' foray into government-sponsored aid activities developed during, and in the aftermath of, the 1967 Arab–Israeli War. Countries bordering Israel–Palestine absorbed the largest numbers of Palestinian refugees and became known as the 'frontline states' – this included Jordan, Lebanon, Syria and, until 1979, Egypt. These countries were the primary targets of regional aid and consequently received more than half of all Gulf state assistance from the late 1960s to the late 1970s (Porter 1986: 44). At that time, and into the present, assistance from Arab countries primarily served a dual political and humanitarian role in signalling opposition to the state of Israel and succouring those adversely affected by Israeli policies (Mertz and Mertz 1983; Simmons 1981). Such a sentiment was emphasised during an interview with Mohammad Shtayeh, Palestinian Minister of Public Works and Housing, who noted in 2009 that 'the Arab states are completely motivated in our case by helping the people of Palestine'.

Other motives beyond altruism and the Palestinian cause encouraged aid from the Gulf. Hunter (1984) notes that ODA from oil-rich Gulf states often financed balance-of-payments deficits for poor countries in order to mitigate the impact of high oil prices. For instance, during the 1970s, the IsDB primarily financed the importation of oil from the Gulf by Islamic countries that were suffering as a result of price shocks. Others have suggested that Arab aid should primarily be viewed as a form of public diplomacy aimed at winning the 'hearts and minds' of citizens in recipient nations (Harmer and Cotterrell 2005; Melissen 2005). With much the same rationale, the authors (Barakat and Zyck 2010: 29) have previously posited that Gulf states' generosity comprises a form of 'diplomatic defence mechanism' which protects them from blame for their close relationships with Israel's chief ally (i.e. the United States), for their unwillingness to militarily oppose Israel and for their possession of a disproportionate share of the region's wealth. Yet it is Western experts that have led the assignment of strategic rather than humanitarian motives (Neumayer 2004: 285). Individuals from within the Gulf states and Islamic countries, including those interviewed by the authors, have more often subscribed to those explanations, particularly *zakat* and Palestinian solidarity, which centre upon religious solidarity and a genuine concern for human well-being (Humaidan 1984; Ibrahim and Sherif 2009).

While such controversies over the motives of Arab donors exist and flourish, it is important to recognise that they are frequently based on limited and primarily anecdotal evidence. Neumayer (2003a) has provided the sole econometric analysis to date in his examination of the period between 1974 and 1997. This study differentiated between those factors that rendered a country more likely to receive Gulf state assistance and those which determined the likely level of assistance to be received. It was found that a country is more likely to receive support from Gulf states if they are 'poor, Arab, [and] Sub-Saharan African' or if they vote similarly to the KSA in the UN General Assembly (Neumayer 2003a: 141). Such countries are also likely to receive greater levels of assistance. For example, an Arab country would receive 22 times more bilateral aid from Gulf states (bilaterally) and approximately six times more from Arab multilateral institutions (Neumayer 2003a: 142–3). Recipient countries' poverty levels were found to be significant in gaining access to Gulf state aid – with poor countries more likely to receive aid – but did not have an impact on the amounts provided by the Gulf states (i.e. poorer countries would not necessarily receive aid proportional to their need). This dynamic is further examined by Nonneman (1988), who highlights that donor countries belonging to OPEC, of which the Gulf states were the most significant, provided 26 per cent of their aid to middle income countries in 1975 but that this amount rose to 76 per cent by 1981. DAC member countries, on the other hand, provided only half as much to countries in this category and concentrated their assistance primarily upon low-income and least-developed countries (LICs/LDCs). These figures, although they do not convey motive, at least suggest that Gulf states (and other OPEC members) have in the past preferred to focus assistance upon countries which were trade partners, or major oil importers, or which seemed to have the potential to become so (Heintz and Pollin 2008).

Gulf states' aid allocation is influenced by such factors; however, the total amount of aid on offer was determined primarily by two key factors: oil prices and the occurrence of crises with economic or diplomatic ramifications for the Gulf (UNESCWA 2007). In particular, the Arab–Israeli conflict is responsible for many of the peaks which appear in the timeline of Gulf state assistance (see Figure 15.2). The phenomenal increase in Gulf state assistance from the early to mid-1970s to the early 1980s, however, is more likely to do with the 429 per cent increase in the price of crude oil during this time period (see Figure 15.2) than with any regional political dynamics. Indeed, the same can be seen in 2008, the most recent year for which data is available; crude oil prices which were 120 per cent higher than the average for the period examined (1970–2008) brought about aid levels which were more than twice the norm. As is evident in Figure 15.2, a close relationship existed between the price of Gulf states' donorship and their oil-derived income.

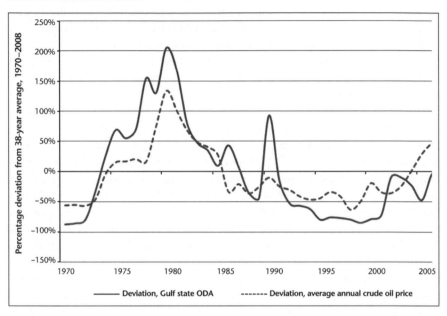

FIGURE 15.2 Deviation of Gulf state ODA and crude oil price from 39-year average (1970–2008)

Sources: OECD 'Stats', Query Wizard on International Development Statistics, http://stats.oecd.org/qwids/; oil prices were calculated from monthly data from the International Monetary Fund, http://www.imf.org.

Gulf state donorship: by the numbers

The use and impact of these fluctuating aid levels remains poorly understood, thus leading the authors to question not only how much has been provided and why but also how it is has been provided, to whom, for what types of programmes and to what effect. Conflict and fragility were particularly highlighted as a useful frame of analysis given the presence of numerous so-called 'fragile states' in proximity to the Gulf and given the international community's increasing recognition that donor behaviour has a major impact upon conflict dynamics and state legitimacy (Barakat 2009; Ghani et al. 2006; Schiavo-Campo 2003). For instance, a donor channelling large sums of money for post-crisis reconstruction or development around – rather than through – the state may weaken the capacities and credibility of governing institutions, or donors' selection of implementing partners or contractors may be seen as favouring one ethnic, political or regional grouping over another. In other words, the stakes for donors (and recipients) are far higher in fragile and conflict-affected contexts, thus rendering donors' methods in these environments an important subject of enquiry. Furthermore, a recent meeting of Arab multilateral and bilateral donor agencies – the so-called 'Coordination Group Institutions' – recently cited '[r]ehabilitation and reconstruction in situations of fragility (e.g. Afghanistan; Yemen)' as one of their key 'areas of collaboration' (Al-Hamad and Deutscher 2009: 3).

In considering what conflict-affected countries to include in the analysis of available quantitative information, the authors focused strictly upon conflict-affected or post-conflict contexts in which the Gulf states have expressed a particular interest and where they have either pledged or disbursed a significant amount of aid. According to these criteria, the following contexts were identified: Bosnia-Herzegovina, Afghanistan, Iraq, Lebanon, the Palestinian Territories and Yemen. According to the UN's Financial Tracking Service (FTS), which monitors assistance to crisis-affected contexts, these six contexts received a *recorded* US$1.34 billion bilaterally from the Gulf states between 1999, when the FTS began operating, and June 2009 (Table 15.1).[4] Far more assistance was certainly provided by the Gulf states to these contexts during this time period but was not recorded with the UN. The KSA provided over two-thirds of the recorded support, with relatively smaller contributions from UAE, Kuwait and Qatar. The question, as previously stated, however, is not only how much they provided but also, or perhaps more importantly, how they provided it. The following subsections address the Gulf states' preferred modalities, partners and sectors.

TABLE 15.1 Gulf states' bilateral assistance to selected conflict-affected contexts,* (1999–2009)

Donor country	Total amount (US$ million)	Proportion of total %
KSA	926.59	69.30
UAE	207.17	15.49
Kuwait	167.99	12.56
Qatar	35.31	2.64
Total	1,337.06	100.00

*These contexts are Bosnia, Afghanistan, Iraq, Lebanon, Yemen and the Palestinian Territories.

Source: UNOCHA, Financial Tracking Service, as of 1 July 2009.

Modalities

According to the available data, Gulf states employ a range of common modalities, though their assistance is distributed among them in a unique

manner relative to the 'traditional' and predominantly Western donors comprising the DAC. While DAC donors have customarily utilised the direct implementation of development projects and programmes via international NGOs
and, increasingly, private contractors, the Gulf states provide nearly half of their
assistance to recipient government institutions in fragile and conflict-affected
contexts bilaterally (see Table 15.2). The remaining assistance is channelled via
the Red Cross and Red Crescent Societies and through the United Nations,
particularly the UN Relief and Works Agency (UNRWA) for Palestinian
refugees (see UNRWA 2009, 2010).

TABLE 15.2 Modalities of Gulf state assistance to selected conflict-affected contexts
(1999–2009)

Recipient category	Proportion of Total %
Bilateral, government-to-government	46.77
Red Cross and Red Crescent Societies	14.11
United Nations agencies	13.43
Other recipient/not specified	25.69

*These contexts are Bosnia, Afghanistan, Iraq, Lebanon, Yemen and the Palestinian Territories.

Source: UNOCHA, Financial Tracking Service, as of 1 July 2009.

Gulf states' selection of aid modalities belies several underlying interests and
values. First, these countries have preferred to act as donors in basic terms; by
providing funds to governments or implementing agencies and then stepping
back. Many DAC donors establish large foreign offices or have direct involvement with technical aspects of projects, whereas the Gulf states have traditionally focused operations around their headquarters. As such, they have tended to
near-universally front-load project management with extensive pre-approval
assessments but little post-approval follow up. To provide just one example from
the early days of formalised Arab donorship, in the 1970s, the Kuwait Fund was
working with less than 35 staff despite the fact that by 1978 it had approved 124
loans to 45 countries totalling more than $1.6 billion (Lawton 1979). Second,
there is a desire to engage with implementing partners that are viewed as
relatively neutral and overtly concerned with humanitarian well-being. By
relying upon Red Crescent societies and UNRWA, which are among the most
trusted institutions in at least the Middle East, there is a keenness to engage with
partners that do not have 'political' agendas such as modifying gender relations,
instituting new patterns of governance or advocating in favour of democracy
and human rights. Finally, the emphasis on direct government-to-government
aid comprises, albeit implicitly, an argument in favour of recipient states'
sovereignty. Providing funds to the states rather than around them fosters the
legitimacy of those states and respects their role as the overseer of activities in
their territory (Barakat 2009). In contrast, the OECD (2008) survey on

implementation of the Paris Declaration shows that only 22 per cent of ODA from DAC member countries is provided in the form of bilateral budgetary assistance. Given the OECD's campaign to double donors' levels of budgetary support – to the level currently achieved by the Gulf states – it appears that Gulf state donor institutions are currently far ahead of their primarily Western counterparts.

Programmatic preferences

As with modalities, the Gulf states' programmatic preferences are different from, but often complementary to, those of DAC donor countries. Activities that are largely devoid of political significance, such as infrastructure, economic development, basic education and humanitarian assistance, traditionally make up the greatest part of Gulf states' activities.

Furthermore, the vast majority of aid from the Gulf states in the countries included in this study has historically supported basic, life-saving and life-sustaining relief interventions. Smaller amounts were recorded for immediate post-crisis recovery, and sustainable, long-term development-oriented activities were given limited support according to the FTS. While the limited level of recorded support for reconstruction and sustainable development is likely exaggerated by donors' tendency to use the FTS primarily in mid- and immediate post-crisis contexts, a number of stakeholders interviewed by the authors noted that the Gulf states do tend to focus upon 'quick interventions' while foregoing 'long-term planning'. In accordance with the Gulf states' preference for relief assistance, they commonly provided in-kind assistance such as food, clothing, vehicles and construction materials rather than technical assistance or training. Indeed, technical assistance, which is a common feature of Western and DAC aid programmes, comprised less than one per cent of the total value in the FTS of Gulf state aid to the conflict- and fragility-affected contexts included within this study. The central difference between Gulf state and Western donor programming has often been characterised as 'hardware' versus 'software', whereby the former often prefer to build and equip hospitals, for instance, while the latter train the staff and contribute to healthcare policies (Al-Hamad and Deutscher 2009: 2). Clearly this is an oversimplification; however, both Western and Gulf state aid officials interviewed by the authors identified with such a comparison. Interviewees were unanimous in noting that such a division of labour was beneficial in a number of ways as long as it was accompanied by adequate technical coordination (which it rarely has been).

Case studies: Gulf state donors in conflict-affected contexts

Such modalities, partners and programmatic preferences can be seen in a number of high-profile instances of Gulf state engagement in fragile and conflict-affected contexts such as post-1995 Bosnia-Herzegovina, post-9/11

Afghanistan and Lebanon following the 2006 war with Israel. Short case studies of each of these international interventions and the role of the Gulf states within them are included below.[5]

Bosnia-Herzegovina

In the early-to-mid 1990s, the attention of Arab countries was drawn to the conflict in Bosnia-Herzegovina. This was largely due to the perception that it constituted a religious war aimed at the destruction of an Islamic population (Champion 1998). While populations from the Middle East mobilised to fight on behalf of their fellow Muslims in the Balkans during the war, governments in the Gulf did not formally intervene until after the 1995 Dayton Peace Agreement (DPA), which brought an end of the conflict (Hedges 1995). By 1997, Islamic countries had pledged just under US$160 million for Bosnia's reconstruction; the KSA provided half (US$50 million), with Kuwait (US$21.15 million) and Qatar (US$5 million) also pledging significant amounts (GAO 1997). Turkey provided the majority of the remainder, apt given its historical and cultural links to Bosnia and Bosnian Muslims, and Brunei and Malaysia also pledged funds (ibid.). The KSA, Kuwait and the UAE, according to OECD databases, ultimately provided US$191.18 million to Bosnia within the decade following the signing of the DPA, which constituted 2.41 per cent of the total given by international donors during that time period.[6] However, official figures may only capture a small portion of Gulf state assistance as media reports indicate that the KSA provided more than US$600 million for Bosnia after the war for food, energy and electricity (Whitmore 2002).[7]

A significant proportion of Saudi support was dedicated to the resurrection of mosques damaged or destroyed during the conflict (Schwartz 2000).[8] However, Saudi designs determined the rehabilitation and reconstruction of the mosques and this conflicted with the traditional Ottoman architecture of the country's mosques (Peuraca 2003). According to the Zurich-based International Relations and Security Network (ISN 2009b), these mosques were 'run by the Saudis entirely, with no involvement by the local Bosnian Islamic community'. Consequently, a portion of the Bosniak community criticised Saudi assistance for being culturally insensitive. These reconstruction efforts were further criticised for being intimidating to Croat and Serb populations who were already fearful of the rise of Islamic fundamentalism within the region given the role played by foreign Islamic fighters during the war in Bosnia (ibid.). Further assistance was provided for building schools and education, which provided an opportunity for Wahhabi religious teachings. Female students were required to cover their heads in these schools, a largely uncommon practice among Bosnian Muslims and which remains relatively uncommon today (ICG 2001). At times such demands were perceived to be a breach of Bosniak culture, and polls show that 70 per cent of Bosnian Muslims opposed Wahhabi influence upon Bosnia (ISN 2009b). In essence, the Gulf's intervention in the Balkans appears to have been only partly 'humanitarian' in nature (Whitmore 2002). Indeed, principles such as conflict sensitivity – which were then only beginning to coalesce in Western donor countries – had not yet developed among the Gulf states and today are still only just beginning to enter Saudi, Kuwaiti, Emirati and Qatari donor discourses.

Post-9/11 Afghanistan

A somewhat similar approach, though with far less funding, was witnessed half a decade later in Afghanistan. While many Arab countries in the Gulf, the KSA perhaps chief among them, had long supported the mujahideen, and later the Taliban, Gulf states' humanitarian involvement in Afghanistan was not institutionalised until after the US-led invasion in 2001. The KSA co-chaired the January 2002 donor conference on the reconstruction of Afghanistan held in Tokyo and representatives from Kuwait, Qatar and the UAE were also in attendance. This demonstrated that Gulf state donor institutions were considered key partners in the country's recovery and development (Ministry of Foreign Affairs of Japan 2002). At that conference, the KSA made the sixth largest pledge, in annual terms, when it commited US$220 million over three years, or US$73.33 million per year (UNOCHA 2002). The UAE pledged US$36 million across an unspecified time period, an amount which was increased to US$50 million later in the year. Although Kuwait did not pledge funds at the Tokyo conference, it did later commit US$30 million to Afghanistan's reconstruction (ibid.).

At the Tokyo conference, the Saudi and UAE pledges accounted for 5.69 per cent of all pledges made. Hamid Karzai, then Afghanistan's interim leader, recognised the potential role the Gulf states could play in his country's reconstruction. Karzai then travelled to Abu Dhabi, a month after the donor conference, to reopen the Afghan embassy in the UAE. On this trip, he noted that the Gulf states would, and should, give 'more, more, more aid to Afghanistan, because they are Muslims, they are our neighbours, and they are rich' (Afghan News Centre 2002). Despite this, many have noted that the Gulf states played a relatively small role in the recovery process in Afghanistan. Lakhdar Brahimi, who served as the Special Representative of the UN Secretary General in Afghanistan, noted that the Gulf states played a 'very marginal' role in the reconstruction, a sentiment which is supported by the financial data available. Pledged funds largely failed to materialise, which some attribute to the Afghan government's reliance upon the West and inadequate courtship of the Arab Gulf states. The KSA, Kuwait and the UAE, according to the OECD, provided Afghanistan with a total of US$68.19 million from 2001 to 2007, which equated to approximately one-quarter of the pledged amount. As of 2008, the Gulf states' bilateral contributions to Afghanistan's reconstruction amounted to less than one quarter of one per cent of the total.[9]

Afghan government officials interviewed by the authors noted that 'the amount from Gulf states is far too little, bearing in mind that we are a Muslim country in crisis'. They, as well as Lakhdar Brahimi, stated that amounts of aid from the Gulf were given unrecorded – both governmental and private – but this aid had overwhelmingly funded religious education, Islamic 'clubs' and madrassas rather than genuinely humanitarian priorities such as safe drinking water. One official stated, 'I think we received around US$250 million from the Saudis for building a religious group. But really does Afghanistan need a religious group when it doesn't have food and water?' Gulf states' interventions in conflict-affected countries had once again been rooted in the donor countries' religious and ideological agendas rather than in more genuine concern for poverty alleviation.

Post-July war Lebanon

Not all instances of Gulf state donorship were as overtly religious in nature as those in Bosnia and Afghanistan. The Gulf states were to find themselves far more 'successful' in many respects when addressing conflict-affected countries within 'their' own region and where they had been delivering assistance amid conflict for decades, such as in Lebanon. Indeed, Lebanon provides, perhaps, the only example of fulfilled contributions from the Gulf states (Barakat and Zyck 2008). More than 1,100 civilians were killed and 100,000 dwellings damaged or destroyed during the 'July War' in 2006 between Israel and Hezbollah. There was significant damage to infrastructure, and Gulf state donors, determined to intervene, did so in a manner not seen since the Second Intifada in the Palestinian Territories. US$600 million was provided by the KSA, and US$315 million of this was targeted at housing rehabilitation (Table 15.3). According to the authors' interviews, the Kuwait Fund allocated US$300 million in total, which included US$115 million for housing compensation. Although Qatar did not provide records of its assistance publicly or to the Lebanese authorities, it is estimated to have contributed at least US$150 million.[10] Other Middle Eastern and Islamic countries, including aid recipients such as Iraq, Jordan, Indonesia and Yemen, provided a further US$42 million according to representatives of the Lebanese High Relief Commission.

TABLE 15.3 Housing-Related Contributions from Gulf states to post-July War Lebanon

Donor	Amount (US$ millions)[*]
Qatar	149.98
KSA	315.00
Kuwait	115.00
Other non-OECD-DAC donors	42.00
Total	621.98

[*]These values reflect the amounts provided at the time of disbursements, primarily between late 2006 and mid-2007.

Source: Barakat and Zyck (2008).

The July 2006 war in Lebanon was condemned as an act of Israeli aggression (or overreaction) throughout the Gulf states and elsewhere. This led to wide-scale involvement of Islamic donors (Pascual and Indyk 2006). The predominantly Sunni Gulf states were impelled to view contributions as a public diplomacy battle orientated around winning hearts and minds, following the assumption – which proved accurate – that Shia Iran would play a major role in rebuilding the South and in doing so would strengthen its foothold there (Hamieh and Mac Ginty 2009). This strategy can clearly be seen in Qatar's focus of funds in the southern Shia stronghold of Bint Jbeil, which some estimates put at over a quarter of a billion dollars (Putz 2007).[11]

Unlike the prominent pledges made to Afghanistan by Gulf state donors at international donor conferences, their involvement in Lebanon was far more discreet. There was surprisingly little publicity for Gulf state contributions, and few outside of the country were aware of the scale of assistance provided by the Gulf. However, Lebanon may represent the first instance of an externally financed post-crisis recovery process which was driven primarily by non-DAC member countries. The Gulf states' engagement, however, merits greater attention not only given its size but also given the varied and at times innovative means of injecting assistance which the KSA, Kuwait and Qatar employed. According to representatives of the Saudi Popular Committee for Lebanese Relief, the KSA transferred funds to the Lebanese government for disbursement to those affected by the war. Ownership and responsibility, including financial oversight, was delegated to the Lebanese authorities, and little follow-up was requested. In a different approach Qatar provided funds directly to individual families without involving Lebanese government personnel or institutions (Barakat and Zyck 2008). Finally, and more interestingly, Kuwait provided the Lebanese government with cheques made out to each head of household that the Kuwait Fund intended to provide with housing compensation. Lebanese government personnel then distributed these cheques so allowing the state to play a visible role without the opportunity for it to misappropriate any of the contributed funds. If Saudi assistance can be understood as most 'owned' by the Lebanese state and Qatari aid as least 'owned', Kuwait steered a middle ground which balanced apparent government ownership with accountability.

The amount of money received by households, the level of recipient satisfaction and the reputations of the donor countries were all majorly affected by these different means of delivering assistance. For instance, records from the Lebanese High Relief Commission – which was financed primarily by the KSA – indicate that the Lebanese government provided an average of US$8,200 to 35,611 households; yet nearly 500 recipients surveyed during a study led by the authors (Barakat and Zyck 2008) report having received slightly more than a third of that amount (US$2,757.69).[12] The use of the difference, which amounts to nearly US$5,500 per household, remains unknown although many report that it was more than likely lost to corruption. Recipients of KSA funds were, thus, disappointed with assistance while beneficiaries of Qatari and Kuwaiti aid

– which government officials did not have the ability to misappropriate – were pleased with the amounts received and the processes involved. This example demonstrates that the amounts provided by the Gulf states to conflict-affected environments may be understood as only one (albeit important) aspect of their donorship activities. Methods of delivery and the design of assistance packages may prove equally, if not far more, important in many cases.

Conclusion: innovations and future directions

The case of Lebanon is perhaps a telling example when examining Gulf state aid. More than anything else, it suggests the degree to which Gulf states' interventions in conflict-affected contexts are highly varied and reflective of each country's agenda. The KSA and the UAE in many respects remain archetypal Gulf state donors with their large volumes and limited amount of attention to the use of their assistance. Funds are provided in order to signal their willingness to share their wealth rather than with much regard for the recipients (Barakat and Zyck 2010). Qatar, which has notably been seeking a role as a regional mediator (see ISN 2009a), provided assistance in the most visible manner possible in order to ensure that recipients were aware of who had aided them. Finally, Kuwait, the first Gulf state to develop a donor agency, remained the most innovative and the most closely concerned with the technical dimensions of its interventions in Lebanon. However, despite these stereotypes of Gulf state donorship, their approaches are nuanced, highly varied, at times innovative and worthy of replication by DAC members. Despite many experts' and policymakers' distrust of their motives and agendas, they embody a range of innovations and missteps, which are addressed below, alongside a series of options for their future development and for their relationship with the broader international development and donor communities.

Innovations

The Gulf states have proved innovative in a number of critical areas, at times by reverting to models long ago dropped by DAC donors with their increasing sets of conditionalities and bureaucratic processes. In Lebanon as well as in the Palestinian Territories, the Gulf states' focus upon cash compensation for losses suffered during conflict demonstrates a high degree of responsiveness and flexibility while fostering private-sector development. Furthermore, the Gulf states' aversion to invasive models of intervention, which attempt to change social relations or undermine customary sources of authority, may also be interpreted as a form of respect for cultural autonomy which contrasts with the external socio-political agendas frequently emphasised by Western donors. DAC member countries, which have consistently fallen short of UN-established aid targets of 0.7 per cent of GDP, should replicate the notable amount of aid committed and disbursed by the Gulf states.

Perhaps most notably, the Gulf states have led the way in financing public institutions rather than international and non-governmental implementing agencies in fragile and conflict-affected environments. The decision to do so is not merely an administrative preference but reflects the understanding these donors have of the central importance government leadership has in reconstruction. The large proportion of Gulf state aid flowing into the coffers of conflict-affected states, almost exclusively without formal earmarks or conditionalities, also represents a clear argument in support of state sovereignty. This is a concept which has been under threat from DAC donors, multilateral agencies and NGOs who have tended to bypass, ignore and, at times, marginalise the state when providing assistance.

Future strategies and options

Although the Gulf states have introduced innovative means of aid delivery, there remains room for Gulf state donorship to improve and, in select cases, learn lessons from DAC members. They may wish to consider a fuller form of engagement which involves not only funding states in conflict-affected environments but that also aims to ensure that government institutions have the capabilities and systems in place to manage this aid effectively. This may include paying greater attention to the development of institutions, not just providing financial support. In each of the case study countries noted above, aid from the Gulf would have been far more effective if it was accompanied by guidance on how to manage it effectively. Doing so will require a partial move away from purely financial or in-kind aid packages and greater reliance upon technical assistance, which currently comprises less than one-tenth of one per cent of Gulf state assistance to the conflict-affected contexts included within this study. Such assistance may be provided in the form of international advisers or, alternatively, extensive capacity-building activities perhaps orientated around elite civil service training centres which could and perhaps should be established within or at least with support from the Gulf states (WANA Forum 2009: 19).

Steps could also be taken to ensure that Gulf state aid to conflict-affected environments has the greatest impact possible. In particular, Arab donors may develop systems and processes to prevent the sorts of misappropriation which the authors (Barakat and Zyck 2008) found to have affected the KSA's and the UAE's assistance to the housing sector in Lebanon in the aftermath of the 2006 July War. Especially given the Gulf states' religious affinity with conflict-affected countries in the WANA region, they may be able to approach increased financial accountability in a manner which represents recipients' responsibility under Islam to ensure that not a penny intended for vulnerable populations is lost to inefficiency or corruption, rather than in the technocratic manner imposed by select DAC donors and international financial institutions (IFIs). However, it appears somewhat unlikely that Gulf state aid will be used to better effect unless they are willing to establish meaningful presences in conflict-affected environments, a step which would also aid in the development of lasting partnerships with recipient institutions as well as with DAC donors.

The Gulf states would also be wise to pay increased attention to results-orientated accountability and the rigorous measurement of the impact of their activities. It will be fundamental for the Gulf states to understand what their funds have supported and what effect this aid has had on the well-being of recipients and, more generally, on polities and economies of conflict-affected contexts. However, measuring impact should not strictly focus upon technical outcomes and impacts but also upon conflict vulnerability and the potential for renewed conflict or entrenched fragility.

While greater accountability would be useful, it should not be permitted to significantly reduce the speed with which the Gulf states have been able to respond to crises in places such as Lebanon in 2006 or the Gaza Strip following the war with Israel in late 2008 and early 2009. In fact, donor institutions from the Gulf may benefit from greater differentiation – in terms of conceptualisation and financial modalities – between humanitarian relief and longer-term reconstruction and development. Humanitarian relief currently comprises a large proportion of Gulf state aid and can be delivered in a manner aligned with the principles of *zakat*. These funds come with few 'strings' pertaining to recipient reporting and accountability and can be injected quickly, thus ensuring that the funds are not overburdened by delays or bureaucratic procedures. Longer-term funding mechanisms which support reconstruction in conflict-affected contexts or sustainable development may be treated differently and, indeed, may be housed within distinctive institutions or sections of the Gulf states' aid agencies. These funds may be accompanied by more stringent procedures such as needs assessments, baseline studies and impact assessments and may require further measures related to financial accountability from recipients.

Finally, Gulf states may wish to consider establishing better coordination mechanisms between themselves and DAC members. Past performance on coordination and harmonisation between DAC and non-DAC donors has been notoriously weak, and the Gulf states are no exception. Furthermore, the Arab Gulf states have often found themselves operating in parallel with Western donors despite a spate of meetings organised by the OECD and others (including Japan, the United Kingdom, Germany and the World Bank) to promote greater coordination. At the highest levels, such dialogues – which are inherently diplomatic rather than technical processes – have had to overcome their inherent suggestion of Western superiority (i.e. that the Gulf states must learn to behave more like their DAC peers). Within conflict-affected countries, the authors' interviews suggest that more parochial matters, ranging from the selection of locations for coordination meetings to aid actors' concern with their own security, have inhibited coordination on the ground (see Barakat and Zyck 2008, 2010). Yet the absence of improved harmonisation at the highest levels and coordination in the field has resulted in overlap, duplication and the loss of potential synergies between Gulf states and DAC priorities. Further progress in this key area must remain a priority, and, indeed, it may best be achieved if harmonisation is framed as a technical rather than a political process, and if it begins with the recognition that the Western donors of the DAC have a great deal to learn from their peer institutions within the Gulf.

Notes

1. See OECD, 'Stats' Query Wizard for International Development Statistics, at: http://stats.oecd.org/qwids/ (accessed 11 August 2011).
2. The OECD's donor database keeps detailed information upon both DAC and non-DAC member countries and is considered the most credible source. However, donor data for the Gulf states is amalgamated under the heading of 'Arab States' – inclusive of the KSA, Kuwait and the UAE – and cannot be disaggregated by country. The OECD's additional databases, particularly the Creditor Reporting System (CRS), do not provide data on non-DAC donors. The UN's Financial Tracking Service, which is operated by the UN Office for the Coordination of Humanitarian Assistance (OCHA), provides an alternative source with donor-specific data and accompanying details in many cases. However, it is primarily used for recording mid-crisis or post-crisis relief activities and may not capture a large proportion of assistance for post-conflict reconstruction and development.
3. See http://www.isdb.org/irj/portal/anonymous (accessed 11 August 2011).
4. UNOCHA, Financial Tracking Service, at: http://ocha.unog.ch/fts/ (accessed 1 July 2009).
5. These contexts were selected given the availability of data regarding the Gulf states' interventions there and the relatively noteworthy part played by the states. Arab engagement with Palestine has been too broad and lengthy to summarize here, and their assistance to post-2003 Iraq has been too insignificant to be instructive. Yemen appears to be an up and coming arena for Gulf states' development assistance, though little recorded aid has yet been provided there for 'mid-conflict' relief or 'post-conflict' reconstruction.
6. See OECD, 'Stats' Query Wizard for International Development Statistics, at: http://stats.oecd.org/qwids/ (accessed 11 August 2011).
7. However, it appears likely that only a portion of these, such as the previously indicated US$30 million, were from SFD or other official governmental channels as opposed to private contributions.
8. According to Champion (1998), Saudi funds paid initially for the following mosque and infrastructure projects: the restoration of 115 mosques, the furnishing of 330 mosques, the construction of mosques in Tuzla and Sarajevo, the construction of Saudi and Islamic cultural centres in Mostar, Bihac and Sarajevo, the restoration of schools, the reconstruction of 600 homes and the construction of 159 kilometres of railway.
9. See OECD, 'Stats' Query Wizard for International Development Statistics, at: http://stats.oecd.org/qwids/ (accessed 11 August 2011).
10. This estimate was provided by the Lebanese High Relief Commission. The authors' own calculations dispute this figure, however, and indicate that the total amount provided by Qatar may have been closer to US$300 million.
11. Iran also reportedly contributed funds for southern Lebanon's reconstruction via

Hezbollah and a Hezbollah-affiliated NGO, Jihad al-Bina'a. While figures were never publicly disclosed, the authors (Barakat and Zyck 2008) estimate that Iranian contributions equalled between US$600 million and US$900 million for temporary shelter, rental housing and furniture alone.

12. The levels of housing damage experienced by the total, the government/KSA-assisted population and the survey sample were similar.

References

Afghan News Centre (2002) 'Karzai, seeking Gulf aid, reopens embassy in the Emirates', 12 February, at: http://www.afghanistannewscenter.com (accessed 11 August 2011).

Al-Hamad, Abdlatif and Deutscher, Eckhard (2009) *Chair's Report: Joint Meeting of Coordination Group Institutions and the OECD Development Assistance Committee*. Kuwait City: Arab Fund for Economic and Social Development.

Alesina, Alberto and Dollar, David (2000) 'Who gives foreign aid to whom and why?', *Journal of Economic Growth*, 5(1): 33–63.

Anwar, Muhammad (1995) 'Financing socioeconomic development with zakat funds', *IIUM Journal of Economics and Management*, 4(2): 15–32.

BADEA (1974) *General Agreement Establishing the Arab Bank for Economic Development in Africa*. Khartoum: Arab Bank for Economic Development in Africa.

Barakat, Sultan (2009) 'The failed promise of multi-donor trust funds: aid financing as an impediment to effective state-building in post-conflict environments', *Policy Studies*, 30(2): 107–26.

Barakat, Sultan and Zyck, Steven A. (2008) *Housing Compensation and Disaster Preparedness in the Aftermath of the July 2006 War in South Lebanon*. Beirut and York: Norwegian Refugee Council and the Post-war Reconstruction and Development Unit, University of York.

Barakat, Sultan and Zyck, Steven A. (2010) *Gulf State Assistance to Conflict-Affected Environments*. London: Centre for the Study of Global Governance, London School of Economics.

Benamara, Abdelkader and Ifeagwu, Sam (1987) *OPEC Aid and the Challenge of Development*. Vienna: OPEC Fund for International Development.

Benthall, Jonathan and Bellion-Jourdan, Jerome (2003) *The Charitable Crescent – Politics of Aid in the Muslim World*. London: I.B. Tauris.

Champion, Daryl (1998) *Saudi Arabia and the Genocide of Muslims in Bosnia-Hercegovina*, at: http://www.darah.org.sa (accessed 11 August 2011).

Coordination Group Secretariat (2008) 'Coordination Secretariat of the Arab National and Regional Developmental Institutions, the Islamic Development Bank, and the OPEC Fund for International Development', Arab Fund for Economic and Social Development, at: http://www.arabfund.org/Default.aspx?pageId=472 (accessed 9 December 2010).

Cotterrell, Lin and Harmer, Adele (2005) *Aid Donorship in the Gulf States*. London: Overseas Development Institute, Humanitarian Policy Group.

El Mallakh, Rageai (1982) *Saudi Arabia: Rush to Development*. London: Croom Helm.

GAO (1997) *Bosnia Peace Operation: Progress Toward Achieving the Dayton Agreement's Goals*. Washington, DC: General Accountability Office.

Ghani, Ashraf, Carnahan, Michael and Lockhart, Claire (2006) *Stability, State-Building and Development Assistance: An Outside Perspective*. Princeton, NJ: Princeton Project on National Security.

Haldane, John T. (1990) 'Arab aid drops sharply', *Washington Report on Middle East Affairs*. Washington, DC: American Educational Trust

Hallwood, Paul and Sinclair, Stuart (1981) *Oil, Debt and Development: OPEC in the Third World*. London: Allen & Unwin.

Hamid, Habiba (2009) *Overseas Development Assistance from the UAE: Structuring Donor Relations in the Context of the Arab League's Fragile States*. Dubai: Dubai School of Government.

Hamieh, Christine Sylva and Mac Ginty, Roger (2009) 'A very political reconstruction: governance and reconstruction in Lebanon after the 2006 war', *Disasters*, 34(S1): S103–S123.

Harmer, Adele and Cotterrell, Lin (2005) *Diversity in Donorship: The Changing Landscape of Official and Humanitarian Aid*. London: Overseas Development Institute, Humanitarian Policy Group.

Hedges, Chris (1995) 'Foreign Islamic fighters in Bosnia pose a threat for G.I.s', *New York Times*, 3 December.

Heintz, James and Pollin, Robert (2008) *Targeting Employment Expansion, Economic Growth and Development in Sub-Saharan Africa: Outlines of an Alternative Economic Programme for the Region*. Addis Ababa: United Nations Economic Commission for Africa.

Humaidan, Saleh H. (1984) 'The activities of the Saudi Fund for Development', in Michelle Achilli and Mohamed Khaldi (eds), *The Role of Arab Development Funds in the World Economy*. London: Croom Helm, pp. 59–66.

Hunter, Shireen (1984) *OPEC and the Third World*. London: Croom Helm.

Ibrahim, Barbara Lethem and Sherif, Dina H. (eds) (2009) *From Charity to Social Change: Trends in Arab Philanthropy*. Cairo: American University in Cairo Press.

ICG (2001) *Bin Laden and the Balkans*, ICG Balkans Report 119. Brussels and Sarajevo: International Crisis Group.

ICG (2003) *Islamic Social Welfare Activism in the Occupied Palestinian Territories*. Brussels and Ramallah: International Crisis Group.

ISN (2009a) *Qatar Steps in the Breach*. Zurich: Swiss Federal Institute of Technology, International Relations and Security Network.

ISN (2009b) *Understanding Bosnia, Part Four*. Zurich: Swiss Federal Institute of Technology, International Relations and Security Network.

Lawton, John (1979) 'Arab aid: who gives it', *Saudi Aramco World*, 30(6).

Meenais, S. A. (1989) *The Islamic Development Bank – A Case Study of Islamic Co-operation*. London: Kegan Paul.

Melissen, Jan (2005) *The New Public Diplomacy: Soft Power in International Relations*. London: Palgrave Macmillan.

Mertz, Pamela and Mertz, Robert (1983) *Arab Aid to Sub-Saharan Africa*. Boulder, CO: Westview Press.

Ministry of Foreign Affairs of Japan (2002) *Outline and Evaluation of the International Conference on Reconstruction Assistance to Afghanistan*. Tokyo: MoFA.

Neumayer, Eric (2003a) 'What factors determine the allocation of aid by Arab countries and multilateral agencies', *Journal of Development Studies*, 39(4): 134–47.

Neumayer, Eric (2003b) *The Pattern of Aid Giving: The Impact of Good Governance on Development Assistance*. London: Routledge.

Neumayer, Eric (2004) 'Arab-related bilateral and multilateral sources of development finance: issues, trends, and the way forward', *World Economy*, 27(2): 281–300.

Nonneman, Gerd (1988) *Development Administration and Aid in the Middle East*. London: Routledge.

OECD (2008) *Report on the Use of Country Systems in Public Financial Management*. Paris:

Organisation for Economic Cooperation and Development.

OECD (2009) Query Wizard for International Development Statistics, at: http://stats.oecd.org/qwids/ (accessed 11 August 2011).

Pascual, Carlos and Indyk, Martin (2006) 'In Lebanon, even peace is a battle', *New York Times*, 22 August.

Peuraca, Branka (2003) *Can Faith-Based NGOs Advance Interfaith Reconciliation? The Case of Bosnia and Herzegovina*. Washington, DC: United States Institute of Peace.

Porter, R. S. (1986) 'Arab economic aid', *Development Policy Review*, 4(1): 44–69.

Putz, Ulrike (2007) 'Envy, conspiracy and a Lebanese motor city', *Spiegel Online*, 3 September, at: http://www.spiegel.de (accessed 11 August 2011).

Schiavo-Campo, Salvatore (2003) *Financing and Aid Management Arrangements in Post-Conflict Situations*, Conflict Prevention and Reconstruction Unit Working Paper No. 6. Washington, DC: World Bank.

Schwartz, Stephen (2000) 'Islamic fundamentalism in the Balkans', *Partisan Review*, 117(3).

Shihata, Ibrahim (1982) *The Other Face of OPEC: Financial Assistance to the Third World*. London: Longman.

Simmons, Andre (1981) *Arab Foreign Aid*. London: Associated University Press.

UNESCWA (2007) *Economic Trends and Impacts: Foreign Aid and Development in the Arab Region, Issue No. 4*. Beirut: United Nations Economic and Social Commission for West Asia.

UNOCHA (2002) 'Donors pledge $4.5 billion in Tokyo', ReliefWeb, at: http://www.reliefweb.int (accessed 11 August 2011).

UNOCHA (2009) Financial Tracking Services, at: http://fts.unocha.org (accessed 11 August 2011).

UNRWA (2009) *Arab Donors' Unit Update, August–September 2009*. Amman: United Nations Relief and Worlds Agency, External Relations Department.

UNRWA (2010) *Arab Donors' Unit Update, October 2009–February 2010*. Amman: United Nations Relief and Worlds Agency, External Relations Department.

Van den Boogaerde, P. (1991) *Financial Assistance from Arab Countries and Arab Regional Institutions*. Washington, DC: International Monetary Fund.

Villanger, Espen (2007) *Arab Foreign Aid: Disbursement Patterns Aid Policies and Motives*. Bergen: Chr. Michelsen Institute.

WANA Forum (2009) *Report of the WANA-Led Reconstruction and Recovery Expert Consultation*. Amman: West Asia-North Africa (WANA) Forum.

Weiss, Holger (ed.) (2002) *Social Welfare in Muslim Societies in Africa*. Stockholm: Elanders Gotab.

Whitmore, Brian (2002) 'Saudi "charity" troubling to Bosnian Muslims', *Boston Globe*, 28 January.

Wilson, Rodney (2009) *The Development of Islamic Finance in the GCC*. London: Centre for the Study of Global Governance, London School of Economics.

16

GULF–PACIFIC ASIA LINKAGES IN THE TWENTY-FIRST CENTURY

A marriage of convenience?

Christopher M. Davidson

Introduction

A plethora of economic, diplomatic, cultural and other highly pragmatic linkages are finally making the long-predicted 'Asianisation' of Asia a reality.[1] As this chapter will demonstrate, the powerful and multidimensional connections that are being forged by the very eastern and western extremities of the continent are poised to become a central pillar of this process. Given time, this will finally lead to the emergence of meaningful bilateral ties between non-Western poles of the international system involving states that up until recently had been considered peripheral to the global economy and dependent on the advanced capitalist countries for their trade and investment (Ehteshami 2004: 133–4). Most notably, an important new relationship is developing between the six monarchies of the Gulf – Saudi Arabia, the United Arab Emirates (UAE), Kuwait, Qatar, Bahrain and Oman – and the three most advanced economies of Pacific Asia – Japan, China and South Korea. With little shared modern economic history, with enormous political and socio-economic disparities and separated by great geographical distances, the rapidly tightening economic interdependence between the two regions is a recent phenomenon that deserves considerable attention. What began as a simple, late twentieth-century marriage of convenience based on hydrocarbon imports and exports has now evolved into a comprehensive, long-term mutual commitment that will not only continue to capitalise on the Gulf's rich energy resources and Pacific Asia's massive energy needs, but will also seek to develop strong non-hydrocarbon bilateral trade, will facilitate sizeable sovereign wealth investments in both directions and will provide lucrative opportunities for experienced Pacific Asia construction companies, their technologies, and – in China's case – its vast labour force.

Although this increasingly extensive relationship does not yet encompass the Persian Gulf's military security arrangements – which remain exclusively with the United States, Britain and France – and although few serious attempts have been made by either side to replace or balance these with new Pacific Asia alliances, this may change soon. Meanwhile, there is compelling evidence that the two regions are seeking to strengthen their other non-economic ties. An abundance of state-level visits, often at much higher levels than with Western powers, and a considerable number of cooperative agreements, gifts, loans and other incentives, are undoubtedly binding these great trade partners ever closer. Moreover, with a number of future collaborations including 'hydrocarbon safekeeping', renewable energy projects, civilian nuclear power plants and the building of a twenty-first century 'Silk Road', the trajectory of interdependence will continue to accelerate. And with a growing realization that the Pacific Asia economies, particularly China, may recover more quickly from the global credit crunch than the Western economies thus signifying a global shift in economic weight from the West to the East – the eastwards reorientation of the Persian Gulf monarchies can only intensify.

Following a brief historical background of relations between the Gulf and Pacific Asia, an examination of contemporary hydrocarbon and non-hydro-carbon trade links will then be made before turning to the sizeable interlinking investments between the nine states involved and to the several examples of major construction and labour contracts in the Gulf that have already been awarded to Pacific Asia companies. Finally, the efforts to boost diplomatic and other relations will be considered, followed by an analysis of the many recent efforts to explore innovative future avenues of economic and technical co-operation.

Historical background

The Gulf's oil trade with the Pacific Asia economies began in the early 1950s, when Japanese oil companies were scouring the globe for resources to fuel Japan's rapid postwar industrialisation programme. Most of the Gulf sheikh-doms were off-limits to Japan, as they remained part of Britain's 'Trucial System' – a series of nineteenth-century peace treaties between London and the various sheikhs that guaranteed British protection in exchange for exclusive political and economic relations (Onley 2007). Saudi Arabia, however, was the key exception, with Britain having formally recognised King Abdul-Aziz bin Saud's independence in 1932 and being unable to prevent Standard Oil of California from beginning exploration the following year. In 1953 Japan was able to dispatch freely an economic delegation to Saudi Arabia, and the following year formal diplomatic relations began. By 1956 Japan's Arabian Oil Company had secured a 43-year concession to explore and extract Saudi oil,[2] and in 1960 production commenced. The lucrative relationship was then quickly strength-ened by the Saudi ruling family, with its first minister for defence visiting Tokyo in 1960 and its third king visiting in 1971.

In parallel, non-hydrocarbon trade between the Persian Gulf and Japan was also beginning to flourish, although its origins were rather more circuitous.

Dubai, as one of the Trucial States, had long been exploring inventive ways of circumventing Britain's tight economic controls (Davidson 2008: 19), and in the 1950s and 1960s the sheikhdom managed to position itself as the primary re-export hub for goods destined for India. Following the latter's independence and the attempts of its first prime minister, Jawaharlal Nehru, to replicate the Soviet miracle by using the state to plan and protect the economy, a number of restrictive practices were introduced that effectively prevented India-based merchants from meeting domestic demand for their products, especially fabrics. In particular, cotton from Japan was in great demand. Dubai played the role of an intermediary, its merchants carefully ordering the necessary materials well in advance so as to overcome the lengthy five-month shipping time from Japan (Buxani 2003: 109–10, 118; Davidson 2008: 70). By the late 1970s Dubai's trade with Japan had expanded to include electrical goods, with the re-exporting of millions of Hitachi personal stereos to the subcontinent (Davidson 2008: 313), and by 1982 thousands of Japanese television sets were being distributed across India and the Gulf (Buxani 2003: 117–19, 121; Davidson 2008: 71).

With Britain's granting of independence to Kuwait in 1961, and with its withdrawal from the Trucial States in 1971, Japan's opportunities for further oil concessions and more formal non-hydrocarbon trade expanded to include all the Gulf monarchies. Formal diplomatic relations were established with Kuwait in 1961, and in late 1971 Japan was one of the first countries to recognise the newly formed UAE federation. The following year relations were also established with Qatar, Bahrain and Oman. The Arabian Oil Company – by this stage 80 per cent owned by Japan and 20 per cent owned by Saudi Arabia and Kuwait – duly signed concessions in Kuwait in 1961 (CIA 2009), and the Japanese Oil Development Company (JODCO) took a stake in an international consortium to exploit UAE offshore oil in late 1972 (Abu Dhabi Marine Operating Company 2009).

Although China was also involved in some of the re-export trade in the Gulf in the 1950s and 1960s, the volume was much lower than that with Japan, and most of the activity took place in Qatar and Kuwait rather than Dubai (China, Ministry of Foreign Affairs 2009). With sizeable domestic hydrocarbon reserves and less momentum behind its industrialisation programme, China's interest in an oil trade with the Gulf was also much lower than Japan's. Moreover, during this period China's open support for anti-imperialist, revolutionary movements stymied most opportunities for closer ties with the Gulf's ruling families (Yetiv and Lu 2007: 201), most of which were political beneficiaries of the Trucial System (Davidson 2005: 29–31).[3] Nonetheless, with an eye to the future, the ruler of Kuwait visited China in 1965, and diplomatic relations were established in 1971. By 1978 circumstances were already beginning to change, as the initiation of a series of Chinese economic and political reforms – the 'Four Modernizations' – that aimed to stimulate economic growth and support modernization (Evans 1995)[4] effectively led to the downgrading of Marxist ideologies in China's external relations (Yetiv and Lu 2007: 201). The door having been opened, Oman immediately established diplomatic relations, while the UAE followed suit in 1984, and the following year Saudi Arabia held its first official meeting with China on Omani territory. Just days after the 1981 formation of the Gulf Cooperation Council – the loose organisation that was to represent the joint interests of the Gulf monarchies – China had granted it recognition (Yetiv and Lu 2007: 202). Significantly, in 1983 China began to import crude oil from Oman as a temporary measure in order to alleviate the problem of transporting its own oil from its northern provinces to refineries on the Yangtze River. By 1988, as Chinese demand for oil was accelerating rapidly in tandem with its increasing population and intensifying industrialisation, the Omani arrangement was made permanent (Ghafour 2009: 87, 89). By 1990 China's presence had extended to all the Gulf monarchies, embassies being set up in Qatar in 1988, in Bahrain in 1989 and in Saudi Arabia in 1990 (China, Ministry of Foreign Affairs 2009).

Although far less proactive than Japan and China during this period, with its major oil companies not being established until the late 1970s and with most of its other trade links to the Gulf also developing more recently, South Korea was nonetheless during the 1960s and 1970s carefully building the foundations of its present strong relationship. For the most part, it established diplomatic relations in the wake of Japan but ahead of China, embassies being set up in Saudi Arabia in 1961, in Oman in 1974, in Qatar in 1974, in Bahrain in 1976, in Kuwait in 1979 and finally in the UAE in 1980 (South Korea, Ministry of Foreign Affairs 2009).

The hydrocarbon trade

The hydrocarbon trade undoubtedly remains the central pillar in the contemporary relationship between the Gulf and Pacific Asia, and could now be worth as much as US$192 billion per year. At present, the former produces a combined total of about 16.6 million barrels of crude oil per day, which is about 19 per cent of the global total. The bulk of production takes place in Saudi Arabia, the UAE and Kuwait. The region also produces about 232 billion cubic metres of natural gas per year, which is about 8 per cent of the global total. The bulk of production takes place in Qatar, Saudi Arabia and the UAE. But, more importantly perhaps, the Gulf monarchies account for 37 per cent of all known crude oil reserves and 25 per cent of all known natural gas reserves (CIA 2009: 2007 and 2008 estimates, author's calculations for totals). Saudi Arabia alone accounts for 25 per cent of global oil reserves (BP 2008) and Qatar 15 per cent of global gas reserves (US Government 2009).

At the other extreme, Japan's current hydrocarbon consumption is 5 million barrels of oil per day, all of which it has to import, and 100.3 billion cubic metres of gas per year, 95 per cent of which it has to import. China's current consumption is 7.9 million barrels of oil per day, 58 per cent of which it has to import, and 70.5 billion cubic metres of gas per year, 5 per cent of which it has to import. South Korea's current consumption is 2.1 million barrels of oil per day, all of which it has to import, and 37 billion cubic metres of gas per year, 93 per cent of which it has to import. Respectively, Japan and China have the fourth- and third-greatest oil consumption needs in the world, while South Korea has now also entered the top ten. Japan has the fifth-greatest gas consumption needs in the world, while China and South Korea have now moved into the top twenty (CIA 2009: 2006–8 estimates, author's calculations for totals), and are likely to catch Japan in the near future. Certainly, according to the Organization of Petroleum Exporting Countries (OPEC), although Japan's demand for oil is likely to fall by 15 per cent by 2030, China, South Korea and other Pacific Asia economies are likely to make up 80 per cent of net oil demand growth over the same period (*The National* 5 August 2009).

Specifically, Japan currently imports about 1.3 million barrels of oil per day from Saudi Arabia, which is over 31 per cent of its total oil imports and worth close to $33 billion per year for Saudi Arabia (Japan, Ministry of Foreign Affairs 2009). This now makes Saudi Arabia Japan's fifth largest trading partner, and Japan Saudi Arabia's second-largest trading partner (*Saudi Gazette*, 22 July 2009). In close second place, the UAE now exports 800,000 barrels of oil per day to Japan (*The National*, 26 June 2009), with total oil and gas exports from Abu Dhabi – the most resource-rich of the UAE's seven constituent emirates – now worth over $47 billion (Japan, Ministry of Foreign Affairs 2009). Japan's hydrocarbon trade with the other Gulf monarchies is much less, but still noteworthy, its annual imports from Qatar – most of which is gas – totalling $17 billion, its imports from Kuwait – most of which is oil – totalling $15 billion, and its imports from Oman and Bahrain being $2.6 billion and $0.4 billion respectively (Japan, Ministry of Foreign Affairs 2009).

China's total hydrocarbon trade with the Gulf monarchies is substantially less than Japan's, mainly due to its domestic gas reserves; nonetheless, its oil imports have been rising sharply, with $1.5 billion of imports in 1991, $20 billion in 2004 and nearly $33.8 billion in 2005 (Ghafour 2009: 83–4). Unsurprisingly, during the latter part of this period, China's Tenth Five-Year Plan (2001–5) contained its government's first public acknowledgment that overseas oil supplies needed to be secured if China were to enjoy continued economic growth and modernisation (Yetiv and Lu 2007: 199). In the next few years China's imports are likely to double again, with one Chinese official recently stating that 'we need to find oil fast' (*International Herald Tribune*, 2 October 2006) and another commentator explaining that 'with the huge oil and gas imports predicted for the next decade and beyond, China is compelled to turn to the Persian Gulf' (Ghafour 2009: 82–3). Certainly, the International Energy Agency (IEA) predicts that China's imports will grow to over 11 million barrels per day by 2030, more than half of which will have to be sourced from the Gulf (Ghafour 2009: 82).

As with Japan, Saudi Arabia is currently China's greatest supplier of oil, with about 500,000 barrels of oil per day – or 30 per cent of China's total oil imports (Ghafour 2009: 83) – being shipped by Aramco to the China Petroleum and

Chemical Corporation (Sinopec). In second place with its hydrocarbon exports has again been the UAE's Abu Dhabi, with annual oil exports to China having risen from $3.5 billion to $4.5 billion over the past five years. Oman, courtesy of its aforementioned 25-year history of oil exports to China, still remains a significant supplier, its oil trade with Sinopec having risen from $1.5 billion in 2002 to $4.4 billion in recent years. Kuwait, Qatar and Bahrain's hydrocarbon trade with China has been more modest, but again the trajectory is impressive, Kuwait's supply of 200,000 barrels per day – currently worth $700 million – being likely to double in the next few years, and Qatar's gas exports to China having risen in value from under $100 million in 1999 to nearly $1 billion today (China, Ministry of Foreign Affairs 2009).

For South Korea the import pattern is much the same as with its larger neighbours, although, much like Japan, it requires from the Gulf substantial imports of both oil and gas, given its lack of domestic gas reserves. Saudi Arabia is its largest trade partner, supplying about 770,000 barrels of oil per day as part of an annual hydrocarbon trade worth $21 billion. The UAE is the second-largest trade partner, supplying about 430,000 barrels of oil per day as part of an annual hydrocarbon trade worth $13 billion (South Korea, Ministry of Foreign Affairs 2009). This makes South Korea the second-largest importer of Abu Dhabi's oil after Japan (*The National*, 5 August 2009). Kuwait's total oil and gas exports to South Korea are also sizeable – worth $8.1 billion, while Qatar's are worth $7 billion – almost exclusively gas exports – Oman's are worth $5.1 billion and Bahrain's $0.3 billion (South Korea, Ministry of Foreign Affairs 2009).

The non-hydrocarbon trade

Non-hydrocarbon trade between the Gulf monarchies and Pacific Asia is on a much smaller scale than oil and gas. Nonetheless, as demonstrated, there has been a historical precedent for the importing of certain goods from Pacific Asia into the Persian Gulf, especially textiles and electrical goods, and as the latter region's per capita wealth accelerated during the oil era, the demand for such imports has continued to increase, along with new demands for cars, machinery, building materials and many other products associated with the region's oil and construction booms. In total, such imports from Japan, China and South Korea could be worth as much as $32 billion per year.[5] Importantly, there is no longer a complete imbalance of non-hydrocarbon trade between the two regions, as some of the export-oriented industries that have been established in the Gulf – mostly in an attempt to diversify oil-dependent economies – are now among the world's leading producers of metals and plastics. Their export capacity continues to increase, with most of their future surpluses being earmarked for their Pacific Asia customers.

Japan's greatest non-hydrocarbon trade partner in the Persian Gulf is the UAE, as a function of historic ties to Dubai's entrepôt trade, Abu Dhabi's commitment to building up heavy, non-hydrocarbon-related industries (Davidson 2008: 70–1, 2009: 72–3), and the UAE's high per capita wealth which is now in excess of $40,000 (CIA 2009: 2008 estimate). Their total non-hydrocarbon trade is now over $11 billion per year (Japan, Ministry of Foreign Affairs 2009). Japan's second-largest non-hydrocarbon trade partner in the region is Saudi Arabia, the two countries having begun to sign economic and technical cooperation agreements as early as 1975. Presently, their non-hydrocarbon trade has mushroomed and stands at over $5 billion, most of which is made up of Saudi imports of Japanese cars, machinery and consumer durables, but consisting also of Japanese imports of Saudi metals (Japan, Ministry of Foreign Affairs 2009). Japan's non-hydrocarbon trade with Kuwait, Qatar and Oman is presently about $2 billion, $1.8 billion and $1.7 billion respectively, most of which, again, is made up of Japanese exports of cars, machinery and consumer durables. Although Bahrain remains Japan's least significant trading partner in the Gulf, it is noteworthy that their non-hydrocarbon trade has increased dramatically, from $700 million in 2007 (Japan, Ministry of Foreign Affairs 2009) to nearly $1.3 billion today, and is expected to increase by a further 20 per cent over the following year. Overall, Japanese non-hydrocarbon trade with the Gulf is set to increase even further as negotiations over a free trade agreement (FTA) between Japan and the six monarchies are currently taking place, having commenced in 2006.

China's greatest non-hydrocarbon trade partner in the Gulf has for many years been Saudi Arabia, a memorandum of understanding on bilateral trade having been signed in 1988 – as described, two years before China had even granted diplomatic recognition to Saudi Arabia. In 1992 a bilateral trade conference was staged and in 1996, under the auspices of a GCC–China consultative mechanism, annual trade meetings began between the two countries, held alternately in Riyadh and Beijing (Yetiv and Lu 2007: 202). Today, it is estimated that their total annual non-hydrocarbon trade is worth $1.7 billion, mostly made up of Saudi imports of Chinese textiles and machinery (China, Ministry of Foreign Affairs 2009), making Saudi Arabia China's tenth-largest international export destination (Ghafour 2009: 87). The UAE is presently China's second-largest non-hydrocarbon trade partner in the Gulf, total trade being estimated at $500 million, again primarily made up of imports of Chinese textiles and machinery (China, Ministry of Foreign Affairs 2009). In the near future it is likely that China's trade with the UAE will increase massively, and perhaps will soon overtake Japan's non-hydrocarbon trade with that state. Most of this growth is expected to be as a result of Dubai's strengthening relationship with China, Dubai Ports World stating in 2008 that China was already Dubai's second-largest trade partner after Iran (*Arabian Business*, 31 March 2009). China's non-hydrocarbon trade with the other Gulf monarchies is also growing, annual trade with Kuwait, Oman, Bahrain and Qatar being worth $260 million, $60 million, $60 million and $50 million respectively. These relationships have been facilitated by several agreements similar to those made by China with Saudi

Arabia and the UAE.

As with Japan, China intends to increase its non-hydrocarbon trade with the Gulf even further by achieving an FTA with all six of the monarchies in the near future. These FTA negotiations began in 2004 following a visit by a GCC delegation to China (Yetiv and Lu 2007: 206). Subsequent FTA negotiations were held in 2005 and 2006, by which stage agreements had been reached on tariff reductions. Although the talks have since stalled due to China's unwillingness to lift certain import restrictions on a number of non-hydrocarbon goods from the Gulf, in early 2009 the concept of an FTA was reinvigorated by the president of China, and in summer 2009 the GCC reciprocated China's sentiments by publishing a White Paper entitled *Economic Relations between GCC Member States and the People's Republic of China*, which similarly urged the swift conclusion of FTA negotiations (*China Daily*, 30 January 2004; *People's Daily*, 12 February 2009; Gulf Cooperation Council Secretariat 2009).

South Korea's non-hydrocarbon trade with the Persian Gulf is more modest, although as with Japan and China its relationship is strengthening, the Gulf monarchies having collectively become South Korea's second-largest export destination after China (*Zawya Dow Jones*, 8 March 2009), most of the trade being made up of cars, rubber parts and textiles. Individually, South Korea's non-hydrocarbon trade with Saudi Arabia is about $3 billion, the UAE $2.9 billion, Qatar $800 million, Kuwait $700 million, Oman $300 million and Bahrain $100 million. South Korea has not yet advanced as far as Japan and China with a Gulf FTA; however, negotiations did begin in summer 2008, a second round being held in spring 2009. Thus far, tariff-related incentives have been discussed, and the South Korean minister for commerce has predicted that the FTA could be finalised by the beginning of 2011 (*Kuwait Times*, 8 March 2009).

Investments and joint ventures

Alongside the booming hydrocarbon and non-hydrocarbon trades, the relationship between the Gulf monarchies and Pacific Asia is being greatly enhanced by a substantial flow of investments between the two regions. Significantly, these investments are being made in both directions and at all levels, and they include massive sovereign wealth investments. Although the majority are still connected to the oil and gas sectors, there is strong evidence that an increasingly diverse range of non-hydrocarbon joint ventures is also being established. In the short term these opportunities are providing the Gulf monarchies with a realistic alternative to the mature Western economies for their overseas investments. Such an alternative was viewed as being particularly necessary following the 11 September 2001 attacks, after which many Western governments and companies did little to disguise their distrust of Gulf sovereign wealth funds, many arguing that the funds were not merely commercial and that power politics could be involved (*Arab News*, 7 May 2009).

Japan is presently the largest foreign investor in Saudi Arabia, with over $11 billion of active investments being distributed among 24 different projects, including 16 industrial projects and eight service-sector projects (*Saudi Gazette*, 22 July 2009). In the other direction, Saudi Arabia's Aramco now holds a 15 per cent stake in Japan's fifth-largest oil company, Showa Shell Sekiyu. In summer 2009 the two countries entered into a $1 billion joint venture, when the Saudi Basic Industries Corporation (SABIC) and Japan's Mitsubishi Rayon agreed to build an acrylics factory in Saudi Arabia, with Mitsubishi holding the majority stake. In the UAE, Abu Dhabi's third-largest sovereign wealth fund, the International Petroleum Investment Company (IPIC), has recently sought a $5 billion package from Japan's Mitsubishi UFJ Financial Group and the Sumitomo Mitsui Banking Corporation. This in turn will allow these Japanese banks to have an interest in some of IPIC's overseas investments (Associated Press, 2 August 2009). In the other direction IPIC has now taken a 20 per cent stake in Japan's Cosmo Oil Company, which continues to hold a major Abu Dhabi offshore oil concession, thus strengthening further Japan–UAE interdependence.

In early 2005 the Chinese Ministry for Commerce revealed that Chinese investments in the Gulf monarchies had already reached $5 billion, while Gulf investments in China totalled $700 million (Ghafour 2009: 87). With a flurry of further investments and joint ventures since that announcement, these figures have since mushroomed, and will soon overtake even Japan's interests in the region. In particular, China has sought investments to help build up its oil-refining industries, in which the Gulf economies have sought to have a dominant presence (Yetiv and Lu 2007: 205). At present China's greatest investment partner from the Gulf is Kuwait, in a relationship which strengthened greatly following the setting up of a $9 billion joint venture between the Kuwait Petroleum Corporation and Sinopec in 2005 (Associated Press, 26 June 2009). In 2006 this deal was followed up by the Kuwait Investment Authority (KIA) buying over $700 million in shares in the Industrial and Commercial Bank of China, thereby making Kuwait one of the biggest investors in one of China's first major public offerings. In the other direction, China may soon become heavily involved in Kuwaiti projects, Sinopec currently having a sizeable stake in an international consortium that is bidding for an $8 billion infrastructural programme (Ghafour 2009: 89). But the most innovative aspect of the investments between the two countries has been the establishment of the Kuwait–China Investment Company (KCIC) in 2005. Set up by the Kuwait government, the KCIC is 15 per cent owned by KIA and has a capital base of about $350 million, about half of which is held in cash (*Financial Times*, 10 July 2009).

As well as Kuwait, China is also heavily involved with Saudi Arabia, Aramco having taken a 25 per cent stake in a major joint venture with Sinopec in 2001. In the near future another joint venture between the two companies may take place, but this time with Aramco taking the majority stake. This could lead to the building of the largest oil refinery in China, and may require as much as $6 billion to complete. Similarly, SABIC has already helped to initiate three petrochemicals projects in China as part of its 'China Plan', which aims to facilitate mutual investments between the two countries, support China's economic development and satisfy its increasing demand as one of its premier suppliers (Yetiv and Lu 2007: 207–8). In the other direction Sinopec has recently embarked on yet another joint venture with Aramco, taking an 80 per cent, $300 million stake in a new oil and gas exploration company in Saudi Arabia (Ghafour 2009: 87–8). Elsewhere in the Gulf, Qatar has recently followed Kuwait's lead and has signalled its intent to purchase $200 million in shares in the Industrial and Commercial Bank of China (Ghafour 2009: 87). Further, in summer 2009 it was announced that Qatar Petroleum would enter into a joint venture with PetroChina worth $12 billion. The UAE, and more specifically Dubai, is also investing in China, with its government-owned Dubai Ports World parastatal now operating seven terminals in China, three of them in Hong Kong.

Construction and labour contracts

For some years, construction and labour companies in the Pacific Asia countries have been winning contracts in the Gulf, the China National Petroleum Company (CNPC) having supplied labourers for projects in Kuwait as early as 1983 (Ghafour 2009: 87–9; Yetiv and Lu 2007: 203), and a number of other Chinese companies having supplied labourers for tourism and real-estate projects in Dubai for about six years. However, very recently a large number of major contracts have been awarded to Japanese, Chinese and South Korean companies both to build and supply labour for multi-billion dollar projects in the Gulf. Significantly, in many cases these companies have competed success-fully against Arab and Western companies that have had a much longer history of winning contracts in the region and have usually sourced their labour from South Asia. Undoubtedly these new contracts serve to solidify further the economic interdependence between the two regions while also taking advantage of the Pacific Asia companies' experience, technologies and access to abundant labour.

Of the three principal Pacific Asia countries, it has been South Korea that has made the greatest inroads into the Persian Gulf's construction sector. In the UAE, three out of five new gas facilities in Abu Dhabi's Habshan region, to be operated by Abu Dhabi Gas Industries (GASCO), will be constructed by South Korean companies. Hyundai Engineering and Construction, GS Engineering and Hyundai Heavy Industries won their contracts in 2009, totalling $4.9 billion. Remarkably, Hyundai Engineering and Construction is already be-lieved to be working on nine other projects in the UAE and has recently completed the construction of new gas processing facilities in Saudi Arabia's Khurais field. Elsewhere in Saudi Arabia, the company won a $1.9 billion contract in late 2008 to build further gas processing facilities in the Karan field, on behalf of Aramco. Three other major South Korean companies have won a combined $2.8 billion contract to build a new refinery and petrochemicals plant in Saudi Arabia (*Korea Herald*, 17 July 2009).

Diplomacy and security

Surprisingly, for many observers, there is still no obvious security dimension to the increasingly interdependent relationship between the Gulf monarchies and Pacific Asia. All the former are widely considered to be vulnerable, given their rich energy resources, small national populations and close proximity to major zones of conflict and other potential threats. Moreover, their reliance on a Western security umbrella is undoubtedly problematic, given the strained relations between the Arab world and the US, not least over the Arab–Israeli conflict, but also following the 2001 invasion of Afghanistan and the 2003 invasion of Iraq. Equally it would seem to make sense for the Pacific Asia countries to seek a more active role in the security arrangements and defensive shields of their primary energy suppliers.

Part of the explanation is that the Gulf monarchies do not yet see a reliable alternative to the West, as, for all its shortcomings it was a Western-led alliance that liberated Kuwait in 1991 and it is the Western presence that has been credited with safeguarding the Gulf from Iraqi or Iranian belligerence in the past. As such, with a few exceptions, notably a modest arms trade with China (Nuclear Threat Initiative 2007), almost all the Gulf monarchies' arms imports have been sourced from western manufacturers. Moreover, although there has been an appreciable increase in China's naval presence in the region – in part due to anti-pirate operations in the Gulf of Aden – there is little projection of Pacific Asia military power in the Gulf itself. Instead there remain a number of well-entrenched US military bases in Kuwait, Bahrain and Qatar, a British base in Oman and a new French base was even opened in Abu Dhabi in spring 2009. Some commentators have argued that the same lack of enthusiasm for a security relationship between the two regions applies in reverse: although it is not ideal that the US dominates the Gulf, the Pacific Asia countries nonetheless see little alternative to Western-provided security, given that the thousands of miles of shipping lanes between themselves and their hydrocarbon suppliers would be difficult and expensive to protect. Thus far, it has remained more practical and cost-effective to rely on experienced Western navies, which have already invested in a multi-billion dollar capability for this purpose and enjoy access to a network of maritime bases in allied states (Yetiv and Lu 2007: 200–1).

Another component of the explanation is simply lingering distrust, despite all the aforementioned economic linkages and converging histories. This is not so much related to Japan or South Korea, which are effectively neutral military powers, but rather to China, which has repeatedly created difficulties for a stronger security relationship. For many of the older generation of Omanis, including their present ruler, it is still difficult to forget that China helped to sponsor the rebellion in Oman's Dhofar province in the 1960s and 1970s, while

Britain played a key role in suppressing the rebels (Calabrese 1990: 867; Ghafour 2009: 89, 91). In the mid-1980s it appeared that China's role in the region would increase, as Saudi Arabia began to buy Chinese CSS-2 East Wind missiles. However, Saudi Arabia was unwilling to go further and purchase Chinese intercontinental ballistic missiles, preferring to keep sourcing its ordinance from the US. Most seriously, in 1990 China was unwilling to condemn openly Iraq's invasion of Kuwait, and following Kuwait's purchase of nearly $300 million of Chinese howitzers in the mid-1990s a Kuwaiti official later claimed that his government had been pressured into the deal as China was threatening to withdraw its support for future UN sanctions against Iraq (Ghafour 2009: 88–9, 91; Yetiv and Lu 2007: 211). Tellingly, China's Ministry of Foreign Affairs is currently attempting to rewrite this troubled period of history with Kuwait and its neighbours by stating:

> During the Gulf crisis in 1990, China resolutely opposed Iraq's invasion and occupation of Kuwait and demanded that Iraq should withdraw its troops from Kuwait and restore and respect the independence, sovereignty and territorial integrity of Kuwait . . . both countries share identical or similar views on many major international and regional issues, constantly rendering sympathy and support to each other.
>
> *(China, Ministry of Foreign Affairs 2009)*

Regardless of the various explanations, the present reality is that the Gulf monarchies and their great Pacific Asia trade and investment partners do not yet have a meaningful security relationship. However, this is in no way jeopardising their current and future closeness, with both clusters of countries now going to considerable lengths to improve other, non-economic aspects of their interdependency. Indeed, there now appears to be a tacit understanding from both parties that their relationship simply need not contain a military security component, at least for the time being. High-level diplomatic visits have, in particular, become central to the strategies of both regions. While economic and trade matters are certainly discussed at these events, they are nonetheless also perceived as valuable opportunities for heads of state and their ministers to meet their counterparts and consider a range of other matters. Often substantial gifts or interest-free loans are granted during these meetings, clearly in an effort to build more sturdy political and cultural understandings, and they undoubtedly generate further goodwill. In recent years the frequency of these visits has greatly intensified, and the seniority of the visitors – especially from the Gulf travelling to Pacific Asia – is significantly high, and likely now to be higher on average than the seniority of visitors dispatched to Western capitals.

Future initiatives and collaborations

With the noted exception of military security arrangements, the relationship between the Gulf monarchies and the three principal Pacific Asia economies will continue to strengthen and broaden for the foreseeable future, provided that the former remain able to balance their existing relationships with the Western powers and Pacific Asia, especially China (Moran and Russell 2008). Thus far, such geopolitical competition would seem to have been avoided, given the primary emphasis on bilateral economic linkages, which for the most part have had little direct impact on the Gulf's dealings with the West. Indeed, as this chapter has demonstrated, the hydrocarbon and non-hydrocarbon trade between the two regions has been rapidly rising in volume and value, and is projected to continue to do so. Similarly, it has been shown that the flow of bilateral investments between the two regions continues to rise, and a substantial number of construction and labour contracts are being signed with ever greater frequency. These trajectories are all being enhanced by improving non-economic ties, especially at the diplomatic level, and, as discussed, it is likely that these linkages will grow even tighter in the near future. Furthermore, the relationship will also be enhanced by several new initiatives and collaborations between the two regions, all of which augment existing economic bonds, while some have implications for future non-military security arrangements and others are highly symbolic of this twenty-first-century partnership.

In spring 2009 the UAE's ADNOC began discussions over establishing an Abu Dhabi crude oil reserve on Japanese territory in cooperation with Nippon Oil. It is intended that ADNOC begin such storage in 2010 by using one of Nippon's existing reserve bases in Kagoshima in southern Japan. This agreement will provide the UAE with an alternative outlet for its crude oil sales, not only to Japan and its neighbours, but the entire east Asia region. Such an outlet would prove vital if the Strait of Hormuz – the entrance to the Persian Gulf – was closed in the event of an emergency. From Japan's perspective the agreement is equally beneficial, as it would provide Japan with direct access and a pre-emptive right to purchase crude oil in such an emergency. Tellingly, ADNOC's spokesperson stated that the arrangement would 'contribute to enhancing Abu Dhabi's relationship with Asian markets generally and Japan particularly, and guarantee the flow of crude oil supplies to these markets in emergencies' (*The National*, 26 June 2009).

The future energy sector is another likely area of collaboration, with countries from both regions actively seeking to set up solar and nuclear joint ventures. In spring 2009 Japan's Showa Shell Sekiyu announced that it was considering operating solar power plants in Saudi Arabia in cooperation with Aramco, which, as described, is now one of its principal shareholders. Showa intends to build small pilot plants in Saudi Arabia to test its technologies, and should these prove successful then a joint venture with Aramco may be set up (Associated Press, 25 June 2009). With the UAE committed to a path of diversifying its energy sources and building up a civilian nuclear programme based on imported technologies from the US, its government has repeatedly turned to Japan and South Korea for advice and assistance. In early 2009, the UAE signed a nuclear cooperation memorandum of understanding with Japan, and in summer 2009 the UAE signed a similar agreement with South Korea. A 20-strong UAE delegation was promptly sent to South Korea – at the invitation of the Korea Electric Power Corporation (KEPCO) – to survey its nuclear facilities, and in late 2009 a KEPCO-led consortium outbid two other international consortia to win a $20 billion contract to construct the UAE's first three nuclear plants.

Perhaps most emblematic of the many new developments that will strengthen the link between Pacific Asia and the Gulf in the near future is China's attempt to reconstruct the old Karakoram Highway. This will effectively connect China to the Persian Gulf by a land route that follows the same path as the ancient Silk Road. To do so, China will build the world's highest altitude motorway in cooperation with the Pakistani government, which will not only involve a massive investment and working in difficult terrain, but will even require the pacifying of local tribes in remote areas beyond the control of the Beijing and Islamabad governments (*The National*, 6 August 2009). On completion, this new highway will connect with deep-water ports in Pakistan, most notably the port at Gwadar, in Baluchistan, which has direct access to the Gulf of Oman and lies just 250 miles from the entrance to the Gulf. China has already invested $200 million in Gwadar, the port having first opened in 2005 with three berths; China intends it to expand soon to ten berths with a new bulk-cargo terminal (Ghafour 2009: 83).

Conclusion

By the end of the twentieth century, with rapidly accelerating demand from increasingly resource-scarce China and South Korea and sustained demand from Japan, the Pacific Asia economies had all become heavily dependent on oil and gas imports, with most being sourced from the Gulf monarchies. Now, more than ever, this massive and lucrative hydrocarbon trade represents the central pillar in the strengthening relationship between the two regions and, as demonstrated, is presently worth hundreds of billions of dollars per annum. In the near future it is likely this trade will amount to trillions of dollars per annum. Significantly, few efforts are being made by either side to disguise their increasing dependency on the other, with the bulk of future Gulf hydrocarbon exporting capacity being earmarked for Pacific Asia buyers. This contrasts markedly with other hydrocarbon importing economies, especially in the West, where most often an emphasis is placed on diversifying supplies wherever possible. Although on a much smaller scale than the oil and gas trade, it is also important to note how rapidly the non-hydrocarbon trade between the two regions is also growing. In something of a twenty-first century reincarnation of the ancient Silk Road, the Gulf monarchies are importing ever-increasing quantities of textiles, machinery, automobiles and electrical products from the Pacific Asia economies, while in the other direction the Gulf states have augmented their hydrocarbon exports by selling increasing volumes of metals, plastics and petrochemicals. And with a host of new initiatives from all of the governments and business communities concerned, together with considerable relaxations on visa requirements and other erstwhile restrictions, it is becoming much easier than before for merchants from both regions to travel and take their business from one side of Asia to the other.

In parallel to these intensifying trade links, the relationship between the Gulf monarchies and the Pacific Asia economies is being strengthened even further by a massive flow of investments. These investments are in both directions and at all levels, with most being managed by giant government-backed sovereign wealth funds. Although the bulk of these investments are still associated with the hydrocarbon industry, there are, however, strong signs that an increasingly diverse range of non-hydrocarbon joint ventures are also being pursued. Such opportunities are finally providing the Persian Gulf monarchies with a realistic and more hospitable alternative to the more mature Western economies for their overseas investments and interests.

Although Pacific Asia construction companies have been winning contracts in the Gulf for some time, it is significant that over the last few years there has been a marked increase in their success. Many of the most recent contracts have been to both build and supply the labour for multi-billion dollar developments and, significantly, in many cases the successful Japanese, Chinese and South Korean companies have had to compete against Arab and Western companies. Even though Chinese and other Pacific Asia labour often comes at a slightly higher cost than labour from India, Pakistan or Bangladesh, it is increasingly viewed as less problematic by the governments in the Persian Gulf monarchies, as the presence of thousands of non-Muslim and non-Arabic speaking Pacific Asia labourers is not thought to pose a significant security threat to these states.

Despite these intensifying connections between the two regions, a meaningful security arrangement has yet to develop, despite the obvious advantages to both the Gulf monarchies – which have to balance their reliance on Western support with often contradictory domestic sentiments – and the Pacific Asia economies – which need to secure their energy supply routes. If anything, the Western powers have increased their military presence in the Persian Gulf in recent years, with new bases being established and ever-increasing sales of sophisticated weaponry to their most demanding customers. In part this has been due to a history of distrust, with the Gulf monarchies preferring to seek support from the same reliable protectors that preserved their integrity during the Iran–Iraq War of the 1980s and orchestrated the liberation of Kuwait in 1991. Moreover, there is undoubtedly a feeling on both sides that their increasing economic interdependency does not yet require a security dimension as long as the Western powers continue to guarantee – and thereby subsidise – the safety of their shipping routes and supply lines. However, there are a number of recent indicators that the Pacific Asia states, especially China and to a lesser extent Japan, are beginning to assume a more active role in the broader region's security environment.

Without a strong security component to their relationship, the Gulf monarchies and the Pacific Asia economies have all gone to considerable lengths to shore up a number of other, non-economic aspects of their interdependency. In particular, there has been a strong focus on aid-giving, grants and other donations, even if only for symbolic purposes. Moreover, there has been a marked increase in the frequency and seniority of diplomatic visits. While economic and trade matters remain at the heart of these meetings, a broad range of other issues are discussed, and strong efforts are being made to generate the most effective cultural and educational linkages. Furthermore, the increasingly interdependent and multi-dimensional relationship between the two regions is also being enhanced by several new initiatives and collaborations which will take shape over the next few years. These include innovative hydrocarbon storage projects, investments in renewable energies, further improvements to pan-Asian physical trade infrastructure, and the construction and technology transfer of civilian nuclear power from Pacific Asia to the Gulf. All of these developments will augment existing economic bonds, while some may even have an impact on future security arrangements.

The intensifying connection between the two regions also has several broader implications. The lack of significant military collaboration has certainly allowed the US and other Western powers to remain in their role as the ultimate protectors of the Gulf and the guarantors of the international oil industry's most strategic shipping lanes. This has kept to a minimum any tension between the US and China, with the latter regarded by most observers as being the most militaristic of the Pacific Asia states. Given time, however, this will likely change as the Pacific Asia states gradually seek greater influence over their primary energy suppliers. Moreover, the many other linkages between the Gulf and Pacific Asia described in this chapter, including the various economic and diplomatic ties, and perhaps especially the raft of new initiatives and collaborations, will undoubtedly prompt the US and other powers to pay more attention to this new pan-Asian relationship. Such increased attention, if mishandled and too heavy-handed, may in turn reduce trust between the Gulf monarchies and their Western allies and partners, thus providing a fresh wave of opportunities for Pacific Asia governments and companies to win lucrative contracts and thus increase their influence even further.

Notes

1. See, for example, Funabashi (1993).
2. The concession duly ended in early 2000.
3. Peace treaties signed between Gulf ruling families and the British Empire in the nineteenth century effectively guaranteed the former's security from both foreign

aggression and domestic insurgency.
4. The four modernisations were in the fields of agriculture, industry, technology and defence.
5. Author's calculations based on subsequently listed country totals.

References

Abu Dhabi Marine Operating Company (2009) Historical background documents.

BP (2008) *British Petroleum Statistical Review*, June.

Buxani, R. (2003) *Taking the High Road*. Dubai: Motivate.

Calabrese, J. (1990) 'From flyswatters to silkworms: the evolution of China's role in West Asia', *Asian Survey*, 30: 865–73.

China, Ministry of Foreign Affairs (2009) Overview files on the GCC states.

CIA (2009) *The World Factbook* – people and economic overviews of Japan, China, South Korea, Saudi Arabia, the UAE, Kuwait, Qatar, Oman and Bahrain.

Davidson, C. M. (2005) *The United Arab Emirates: A Study in Survival*. Boulder, CO: Lynne Rienner.

Davidson, C. M. (2008) *Dubai: The Vulnerability of Success*. New York: Columbia University Press.

Davidson, C. M. (2009) *Abu Dhabi: Oil and Beyond*. New York: Columbia University Press.

Ehteshami, A. (2004) 'Asian geostrategic realities and their impact on Middle East–Asia relations', in Anoushivaran Ehteshami and Hannah Carter (eds), *The Middle East''s Relations with Asia and Russia*. London: Routledge.

Evans, R. (1995) *Deng Xiaoping and the Making of Modern China*. Harmondsworth: Penguin.

Funabashi, Y. (1993) 'The Asianization of Asia', *Foreign Affairs*, December, online at: http://www.foreignaffairs.com/articles/49406/yoichi-funabashi/the-asianization-of-asia (accessed 11 August 2011).

Ghafour, M. (2009) 'China's policy in the Persian Gulf', *Middle East Policy*, 16(2): 82–93.

Gulf Cooperation Council Secretariat (2009) *Economic Relations between GCC Member States and the People's Republic of China*. Riyadh: Studies and Research Department.

Japan, Ministry of Foreign Affairs (2009) Overview files on the GCC states.

Moran, D. and Russell, J. (eds) (2008) *Energy Security and Global Politics: The Militarization of Resource Management*. London: Routledge.

Mubadala Development Corporation (2009) Press release on Pearl Energy.

Nuclear Threat Initiative (2007) *China's Missile Exports and Assistance to the Middle East*. Monterey, CA: James Martin Center for Nonproliferation Studies.

Onley, J. (2007) *The Arabian Frontier of the British Raj: Merchants, Rulers, and the British in the Nineteenth-Century Gulf*. Oxford: Oxford University Press.

S-Oil (2009) Historical background documents.

Saudi Arabia Market Information Resource and Directory (2009) Historical background on SAMA Foreign Holdings.

South Korea, Ministry of Foreign Affairs (2009) Overview files on the GCC states.

Sovereign Wealth Fund Institute (2009) Overview document on largest funds by assets under management.

UAE, Ministry for Finance and Industry (2009) Overview file on trade with Japan.

US Government, Energy Information Administration (EIA) (2009) Qatar profile.

Yetiv, S. A. and Lu, C. (2007) 'China, global energy, and the Middle East', *Middle East Journal*, 61(2): 200–14.

AFTERWORD

David Held and Kristian Ulrichsen

As this book went to press a wave of popular protest was sweeping through the Middle East and North Africa (MENA). What developed into the 'Arab Spring' led to the rapid demise of the Ben Ali and Mubarak regimes in Tunisia and Egypt and intensifying mass opposition to the regimes in Libya, Syria, Bahrain and Yemen. Its size and contagious overspill distinguished the civil uprisings from other expressions of discontent and demonstrated the magnitude of the socio-economic and political challenges facing the region. They also revealed the narrow social base of support underpinning long-standing authoritarian rulers, and their reliance on the use of coercion or the threat of force. The popular mobilisation did not spare the Gulf states, although the nature and depth of protest varied widely. Nevertheless, the trajectory of protest reflected and reinforced many of the difficulties of transitioning toward sustainable post-oil political and economic structures identified in this book.

Although the protests originated in North Africa following the self-immolation of Mohamed Bouazizi in Tunisia in December 2010, his plight resonated heavily among people across the Arab world. His act of desperation tapped into powerful feelings of helplessness and a perceived lack of prospects for a better future among youthful populations lacking sufficient opportunities for employment or advancement. In addition, it exposed the elderly, authoritarian regimes' manifest failure to manage or meet the demands of this younger generation in a rapidly changing global economy. Crucially, regional economies have been falling further behind at a time of accelerating innovation and knowledge-intensive growth in other world regions. Human and social capital has further been held back by sclerotic labour markets and uncompetitive and bloated public sectors. These risk marginalising an entire generation of young people and fostering the perception that no meaningful change is possible within existing political systems.

Accelerating forces of global change played a significant role in intensifying and channelling the underlying drivers of discontent. Throughout the broader region, a faultline opened up between young populations exposed to global modernising forces through the Internet and satellite television and ossified, oppressive regimes unable to provide opportunities for or the reality of a better life. New media and advances in communications technologies have transformed the terms of the debates between rulers and ruled and rapidly eroded regimes' control over the flow of information under the pressures of globalisation. The Internet, satellite television and social networking sites opened up profound new spaces for discussions about the widening gap between social classes and the disparities in wealth and incomes between 'haves' and 'have-nots'. Blogging and the availability of encrypted communications technologies such as Skype and BlackBerry likewise enabled suppressed and marginalised voices to make themselves heard to wide audiences both locally and around the world.

New forms of communication and mobilisation impacted most strongly with the youth bulge in MENA economies. Of the regional population 65 per cent is under the age of 30 and, like young people elsewhere, are highly technology-savvy and adept at bypassing state controls to mobilise around common issues or grievances. This synthesis of new media and younger populations has eroded the system of controls and filters carefully constructed and maintained by ministries of information and official government media outlets. The danger for authoritarian regimes arose in part when young people's greater exposure to alternative pathways and points of view converged with perceptions of exclusion from economic opportunities by corruption and other barriers to meritocracy. In Egypt and Tunisia, the hyper-modernising forces of the Internet and satellite television hit the tired gerontocracies at their weakest point, and underscored the intense vulnerability of authoritarian governments to new methods of publicly holding them to account.[1]

The rapid spread of the first phase of the civil uprisings demonstrated how demands for change affect the comparatively richer GCC states as well as the less resource-rich states of North Africa. Notably, the Gulf states share many of the same conditions − bulging young populations, high youth unemployment and imbalances in labour markets that cannot absorb sufficient numbers of them, and the reluctance of authoritarian regimes to open up to meaningful political reform − that characterised the protests in Egypt and Tunisia. It was this intersection of the political and the economic that represented the transformative aspect of the demonstrations elsewhere in the Middle East and set them apart from previous outbreaks of domestic unrest. The intergenerational clash between elderly policy-makers and a younger generation more politically aware and interconnected than ever opens important new spaces for oppositional mobilisation and debate, in the Gulf as elsewhere.[2]

Large numbers of disenfranchised and disempowered Gulf nationals exist, particularly in Bahrain, Saudi Arabia and Oman, but also in the poorer northern emirates of the United Arab Emirates. Unemployment among Saudi nationals between the ages of 20 and 24 reportedly reached 38.4 per cent in 2008, with the figure rising to 72 per cent for women alone.[3] Socio-economic discontent in Bahrain and Oman quickly became fused with political demands for reform, as earlier had occurred in Tunisia and Egypt. Moreover, the largely non-violent and inclusive nature of the initial protests mimicked the demonstrations at Cairo's Tahrir Square, and contrasted sharply with the repressive use of force deployed by beleaguered regimes in response. Throughout the region, the killing of fellow citizens constituted a red line that escalated the scale of the protests and the scope of their demands. Regimes' instinctual suppression of, rather than engagement with, dissenting voices also highlighted the continuing durability of authoritarian pathologies and patterns of behaviour.

In March 2011, the Saudi-led intervention in Bahrain demonstrated how local, regional and global considerations intertwined in framing international responses to the Arab Spring. At the invitation of the Al-Khalifa ruling family, 1,000 Saudi Arabian troops and 500 police from the United Arab Emirates crossed the King Fahd Causeway into Bahrain on 14 March. This 'GCC force' ostensibly was intended to protect critical facilities such as oil and gas installations and Bahrain's Financial Harbour from the ongoing unrest. It nevertheless sent a powerful – and visible – signal that Saudi Arabia would neither tolerate nor allow the pro-democracy campaign in Bahrain to endanger the position of the ruling family. With this action the GCC reinforced a perception held by critical observers that it was a 'club of rulers' which would rally together if one of their number felt threatened by the pro-democracy protestors.[4]

Just days after the move into Bahrain, the United Nations Security Council passed Resolution 1973 authorising the adoption of measures to protect the civilian population in Libya from the Gaddafi regime. While largely Western-led, there was some cross-involvement in both interventions in Bahrain and Libya, notably through the participation in each of the United Arab Emirates. Qatar also provided high-profile Arab support to the coalition over Libya, despatching six Mirage fighters and offering logistical support and international recognition to the Libyan opposition.[5] As members of the GCC, Qatar and the United Arab Emirates simultaneously opposed dictatorial rule in Libya while supporting the continuation in power of an authoritarian political system in Bahrain. This ambidexterity revealed how the principle of intervention can mean very different things to actors with diverging motivations and objectives. Geo-strategic and realist-centred considerations of interest also influenced differing Western-led responses to the outbreak of unrest across the region, as calls for restraint and dialogue in Bahrain and Saudi Arabia contrasted with support for the expression of opposition in other areas such as Libya or Iran.[6]

Similarly fluid interpretations of universal concepts also became apparent in regional and international discourse on issues of 'stability' and 'security'. As the Editors' Introduction to this book makes clear, stability in the GCC states is closely linked to the possession of substantial reserves of hydrocarbons. These provided the ruling elites with the ability to co-opt opposition and spread wealth, but they will not last forever. In this regard, stability is fragile and transient, and the violence in Bahrain and Oman is an indication of the troubled transition to an eventual post-oil era that lies ahead. The forces of change blasting so forcefully through the region have shown how external pressures can interact with, sharpen or reconfigure internal faultlines and fissures within polities. States in transition have a heightened vulnerability to exogenous shocks, and this is magnified in the Gulf states by the historical length and institutional breadth of their reliance on hydrocarbons-based revenues.

Large-scale programmes of economic and industrial diversification are intended to pave the way toward sustainable post-oil economies. So, too, are projects of global 'branding' that portray the Gulf states as places to do business in an otherwise insecure region. The awarding of the 2022 World Cup to Qatar constitutes the most visible success of this strategy, yet the Gulf states remain vulnerable to outside perceptions that their stability is a facade resting on unsteady foundations. Outbreaks of civil resistance in any of the Gulf States provide succour to sceptics of their global rise, particularly if existing elites prove unwilling or unable to accommodate their newly-empowered citizenry. A case in point is the Bahraini government's lethal response to peaceful demonstrators, which inflicted immense damage on its international credibility and rapidly led to the cancellation of its flagship Formula 1 Grand Prix and keynote international conferences such as the Bahrain Global Forum.[7]

These were significant blows that will reverberate across the region, not least by undermining the Gulf states' aggressive self-branding as tourist- and investment-friendly destinations. Although relatively more immune to significant unrest, Qatar and Abu Dhabi have pioneered the strategy of attracting world-class sporting events and establishing themselves on the lucrative MICE (meetings, incentives, conferences, exhibitions) tourism and trade fairs circuit. These have been integral to positioning the Gulf states so firmly on the world map, and prolonged or especially violent instability in any part of the Gulf may tar by association all neighbouring states.

For all of these reasons it is instructive to note the differing pathways of protest and levels of vulnerability to regional unrest. The chapters in this book have clearly delineated aspects of the plurality of political and economic structures in the six GCC states. The first months of the Arab Spring reflect these variations as Kuwait, Qatar and parts of the United Arab Emirates such as Abu Dhabi have been far less affected by the instability than Bahrain, Oman and Saudi Arabia. Kuwait's relatively more open political system, seen for so long as a liability holding back economic and institutional reform, also functions as a safety valve for the expression of alternative and opposing points of view. Moreover, the much higher GDP per capita in all three countries, and particularly in Qatar and Abu Dhabi, provides another layer of protection from socio-economic dissent, at least in the short to medium term. Thus, although all six GCC states face the looming shift toward post-oil political economies, a comparative assessment suggests that these transitions will unfold at very different speeds and timeframes.

The 2011 Arab Spring therefore presents the Gulf States with multiple challenges. The upsurge in popular mobilisation quickly claimed the scalps of two authoritarian rulers who lacked the vision to recognise or respond to the demands for change. Other reactions included a variety of economic inducements and political concessions that largely failed to address the political concentration of power in small and relatively unaccountable elites. Deeper issues remain unresolved, such as the extent of participatory inclusion in political systems and the direction of the ongoing transitions in Tunisia and Egypt. Moreover, the intergenerational clash between elderly leaderships and younger and more empowered populations will likely intensify in the absence of measures to integrate the latter into political and economic structures. These are all cross-cutting challenges that affect the Gulf states just as much as their more populous and resource-poorer North African counterparts. How policy-makers in the GCC states respond will influence whether the processes of transformation described in this volume ultimately reinforce – or undermine – the Gulf states' emergence as significant global actors.

D.H.
K.U.

April 2011

Notes

1. Kristian Ulrichsen, David Held and Alia Brahimi (2011) 'The Arab 1989?', *Open Democracy*, 11 February.
2. Kristin Smith Diwan (2011) 'Reform or flood in the Gulf', *Foreign Policy*, 20 February.
3. Martin Baldwin-Edwards (2011) *Labour Immigration and Labour Markets in the GCC Countries: National Patterns and Trends*, LSE Kuwait Programme Working Paper 15, March, p. 20.
4. Mohammed Ayoob (2011) 'The GCC shows its true colors', *Foreign Policy*, 16 March.
5. Clifford Krauss (2011) 'For Qatar, Libyan intervention may be a turning point', *New York Times*, 3 April.
6. Mark Landler and David Sanger (2011) 'U.S. follows two paths on unrest in Iran and Bahrain', *New York Times*, 16 February.
7. Kristian Ulrichsen (2011) 'Bahrain: evolution or revolution', *Open Democracy*, 1 March.

INDEX

Added to the page references 'f' denotes a figure and 't' denotes a table.